To Save the Children of Korea

ASIAN AMERICA
A series edited by Gordon H. Chang

The increasing size and diversity of the Asian American population, its growing significance in American society and culture, and the expanded appreciation, both popular and scholarly, of the importance of Asian Americans in the country's present and past—all these developments have converged to stimulate wide interest in scholarly work on topics related to the Asian American experience. The general recognition of the pivotal role that race and ethnicity have played in American life, and in relations between the United States and other countries, has also fostered the heightened attention.

Although Asian Americans were a subject of serious inquiry in the late nineteenth and early twentieth centuries, they were subsequently ignored by the mainstream scholarly community for several decades. In recent years, however, this neglect has ended, with an increasing number of writers examining a good many aspects of Asian American life and culture. Moreover, many students of American society are recognizing that the study of issues related to Asian America speak to, and may be essential for, many current discussions on the part of the informed public and various scholarly communities.

The Stanford series on Asian America seeks to address these interests. The series will include works from the humanities and social sciences, including history, anthropology, political science, American studies, law, literary criticism, sociology and interdisciplinary and policy studies.

A full list of titles in the Asian America series can be found online at www.sup.org/asianamerica

To Save the Children of Korea

THE COLD WAR ORIGINS OF
INTERNATIONAL ADOPTION

Arissa H. Oh

STANFORD UNIVERSITY PRESS
STANFORD, CALIFORNIA

Stanford University Press
Stanford, California

© 2015 by the Board of Trustees of the Leland Stanford Junior University. All rights reserved.

This publication was made possible by a subvention by the Trustees of Boston College.

No part of this book may be reproduced or transmitted in any form or by any means, electronic or mechanical, including photocopying and recording, or in any information storage or retrieval system without the prior written permission of Stanford University Press.

Printed in the United States of America on acid-free, archival-quality paper

Library of Congress Cataloging-in-Publication Data

Oh, Arissa H., author.
  To save the children of Korea : the Cold War origins of international adoption / Arissa H. Oh.
      pages cm — (Asian America)
  Includes bibliographical references and index.
  ISBN 978-0-8047-9198-4 (cloth : alk. paper) —
  ISBN 978-0-8047-9532-6 (pbk. : alk. paper)
    1. Intercountry adoption—Korea (South)—History—20th century.
2. Intercountry adoption—United States—History—20th century.
3. Interracial adoption—United States—History—20th century.
4. United States—Armed Forces—Korea (South)—History—20th century.   5. United States—Relations—Korea (South).   6. Korea (South)—Relations—United States.   I. Title.   II. Series: Asian America.
  HV875.58.K603 2015
  362.734095195—dc23
                                                           2014042791

ISBN 978-0-8047-9533-3 (electronic)

Typeset by Newgen in 11/14 Garamond

For my parents
Jang Mibong & Oh Dong Chul

And for my *halmunee*
Kwak Eun Sun

> 높고 높은 하늘이라 말들 하지만
> 나는 나는 높은게 또하나 있지
> 낳으시고 기르시는 어머님 은혜
> 푸른 하늘 그 보다도 높은 것 같아
>
> They say the sky is so very high, but
> I know something else that is higher still—
> The grace of my mother who gave birth to me and raised me
> I think is higher than the blue sky
>
> —어머님 은혜 (A MOTHER'S GRACE)

> When we tell a story we exercise control, but in such a way as to leave a gap, an opening. It is a version, but never the final one. And perhaps we hope that the silences will be heard by someone else, and the story can continue, can be retold.
>
> —JEANETTE WINTERSON

Contents

Acknowledgments		xiii
Introduction: Legacies of War		1
ONE	CHILDREN OF EMPIRE	
1.	GIs and Missionaries in the Land of Orphans	19
2.	Solving the GI Baby Problem	48
TWO	GOD'S WORK AND SOCIAL WORK	
3.	Christian Americanism and the Adoption of GI Babies	79
4.	Making Families on a New Frontier	112
THREE	CREATING A GLOBAL ADOPTION INDUSTRY	
5.	The Contradictions of Love and Commerce	145
6.	International Adoption in the "Miracle on the Han"	176
	Conclusion: The Korean Origins of International Adoption	203
	Notes	211
	Select Bibliography	281
	Index	287

Acknowledgments

Researching and writing this book has rarely been lonely because I have been blessed to be surrounded by generous, critical scholars to challenge me, and to cheer me on. Mae Ngai, Tom Holt, and Leora Auslander all provided valuable guidance and intervention as I conceived and developed this project. I owe Mae in particular an immense debt of gratitude for her ongoing mentorship. Many compatriots offered reliably skeptical feedback and important forms of support, related and unrelated to the life of the mind: Melissa Borja, Kornel Chang, Jessica Graham, Allyson Hobbs, Moira Hinderer, Molly Hudgens, Alison Lefkovitz, Jason McGraw, Meredith Oda, Sarah Potter, David Spatz, Michael Stamm, and Ellen Wu.

Financial support came from a number of sources: the University of Chicago (the Center for East Asian Studies' Korean on Committee Studies and the Center for the Study of Race, Politics, and Culture), the Korean-American Scholarship Foundation, the Embassy of Korea in the USA, the Immigration and Ethnic History Society, the Organization of American Historians, the Association for Asian Studies, the University of Minnesota, the Doris G. Quinn Foundation, and the Department of Asian American Studies at the University of Illinois.

Thank you to the archivists and staff at the Social Welfare History Society at the University of Minnesota; the Center for Migration Studies; the Presbyterian Historical Society; the National Archives in College Park, MD, and Washington, DC; Yonsei University Library; and the National Assembly Library in Seoul. International Social Service and the

xiv   *Acknowledgments*

Presbyterian Church (USA) granted me access to their records. George Drake kindly shared his personal collection of materials related to American servicemen and Korean children. In Korea, Myoung Yong Um and Ik Bae Kim provided important help, and Hyunjoo Lee was a fantastic research assistant.

Many people directly involved in Korean adoption took the time to share their thoughts and experiences with me, and my conversations with them have been enormously helpful. Thank you to Molly Holt and Hyun Sook Han, and to the many adoptees whom I formally interviewed or casually spoke with about my project. What they shared with me provided invaluable texture and background, and I have remained mindful of my responsibility to them and their stories as I have written this book. Thank you especially to Layne Fostervold and Katherine Kim, who helped a stranger crowdsource personal photos.

At Boston College I have received invaluable mentorship from Lynn Johnson and Kevin Kenny. My colleagues in the history department have been supportive and welcoming since day one, especially Jim Cronin, Devin Pendas, and Martin Summers—and Julian Bourg, who always manages to make things more legible. I thank the senior women in particular for being such tremendous role models of scholarship and collegiality: Robin Fleming, Lynn Johnson, Deborah Levenson, Lynn Lyerly, Karen Miller, Rebecca Nedostup, Ginny Reinburg, Heather Richardson, Sarah Ross, Dana Sajdi, Sylvia Sellers-Garcia, and Franziska Seraphim. I am grateful to Julian Bourg, Lynn Johnson, Kevin Kenny, Tina Klein, Lynn Lyerly, and Sylvia Sellers-Garcia for engaging with my work, and for the camaraderie of Julie AhnAllen, Biz Bracher, Katie Dalton, Régine Jean-Charles, Ramsey Liem, Pat DeLeeuw, and Min Song. There was nothing I asked for that superlibrarian Elliot Brandow and the interlibrary loan staff could not provide. A faculty fellowship and a week at the Intersections faculty writing retreat gave me the time and solitude I needed to complete the manuscript, and a research expenses grant helped me get this book across the finish line.

Beyond BC, many people have taken the time to talk with me about various aspects of this project over the years. Thank you to Karen Balcom, Carl Bon Tempo, Laura Briggs, Ariane Chernock, Kathy Conzen, Bruce Cumings, Sarah Park Dahlen, Kori Graves, Ellen Herman, Madeline Hsu, Taejin Hwang, Deann Borshay Liem, Steve Porter, Gina Miranda Samuels, Naoko Shibusawa, Allison Varzally, Judy Wu, and Tara Zahra. I presented parts of this book at the Massachusetts Historical Society's Boston Immigration and Urban History Seminar, the Society for Historians of American Foreign Relations, the Organization of American Historians, the Association of Asian American Studies, the Society for History of Childhood and Youth, the Berkshire Conference on the History of Women, and Brown University. I thank the audience and panelists at these meetings, especially Chris Cappozzola, Ellen Herman, Paul Kramer, Barbara Yngvesson, and Susan Zeiger, whose comments helped me develop my thinking in important ways. Eleana Kim most generously did an eleventh-hour reading and gave crucial feedback, and the anonymous reviewers for Stanford University Press also provided very helpful critique.

At Stanford University Press, I thank Eric Brandt, Gordon Chang, Friederike Sundaram, and Stacy Wagner for their enthusiasm about this book, their professionalism, and for patiently answering all my rookie questions.

I could not have completed a fraction of my work without Jeanne Lothrop or the amazing teachers at Boston College Children's Center, not to mention the many babysitters who have helped me over the years.

My family in Canada are far away but always close in spirit. I am beyond privileged to have Esther and Eric as siblings. Daniel Bornstein, Heather Finn, Jeehoon Jang, and Katie and Dave Yoon—and all the kids: Bruce Finn, Nellie, Xander, Xavier, Hyeri, and Henna—fill visits home with comfort and joy. I miss our Christmases in Williamsford with Young and Aeran Jang. I wish I didn't live so far from my friends and relatives in Korea, who have always opened wide their hearts and homes to me. Youngsup Koh, Suin Cho, Jae Soh, and Linda Lee made me wish I could go back every year. Thanks to Chris and Nancy Dreher for providing shelter in mouse and heat emergencies.

My grandmother and my parents insisted that I speak Korean and learn my history, and their own life stories have informed this project in many ways. My grandmother was just twenty-two years old when the Korean War began. Although her husband was in the north, she fled southward from Seoul with my year-old mother and infant uncle. They never saw my grandfather again, becoming just one of the millions of Korean families who became permanently separated by the 38th parallel. My mother grew up in a time and place when a woman was educated for the sake of finding a good husband, but she has herself been the ultimate liberal feminist in encouraging her own children to pursue their loftiest ambitions, regardless of their sex. My father grew up in a thatched-roof farmer's shack in the Korean countryside but managed to graduate from Seoul National University. He passed away before I finished high school, let alone contemplated academia, but I don't think he'd be surprised to see this book. His belief in me, and his faith in the value and virtue of discipline and hard work, has been with me every step of the way.

Dave has been my rock. A true partner in every sense of the word, he has provided boundless support (and the right touch of humor) and his diligence and integrity inspire me daily. I could not do any of this without him. My girls have enriched my life in ways I could never have imagined. Frannie provided company in the darkest days of writing (whether I wanted it or not), and Ellie kept me motivated by producing a book a day at preschool (sometimes more). Their gift to me—motherhood—has, I hope, made me a more compassionate teacher and scholar. I am deeply privileged to see them bloom and grow.

To Save the Children of Korea

Introduction

Legacies of War

Days after the devastating January 2010 earthquake in Haiti, Americans overwhelmed international adoption agencies with inquiries about adopting Haitian children. Missionaries, nongovernmental organizations, and private citizens rushed to the scene to rescue children, and the Obama administration temporarily lifted visa requirements to enable airlifts of about 1,150 children to adoptive homes in the United States.[1] This impulse to respond to tragedy with offers to adopt the children of that tragedy is by no means new in American history. It also arose after the 2011 typhoon in the Philippines, the 2004 tsunami in the Indian Ocean, and the fall of the Ceausescu regime in Romania in 1989. Adoption agencies now routinely field offers from Americans interested in adopting children virtually each time a natural disaster or manmade crisis occurs. And the crisis does not have to be immediate: the most recent incarnation of what has become a very American pattern comes in the form of the 2013 North Korean Child Welfare Act, aimed at facilitating the intercountry adoption of North Korean children residing in China.[2]

In each instance, the American media and sympathetic observers advance a narrative that positions the particular details of the tragedy alongside archetypal, universal images of women and children in obvious need—what has been called "the visual iconography of rescue."[3] The narrative labels these children orphans—even though many are not—and describes them in terms that resonate with profound cultural understandings of orphanhood, homelessness, and vulnerability. Their lives are bleak and their futures grim. If there are parents, they are doing their desperate best but are powerless in the face of greater forces, and it is clear that they would sacrifice everything for the sake of their children—even the children themselves. In every instance, this narrative makes it plain that the only hope for these children lies in being rescued by loving, generous, wealthy Americans.

Adoption is, in fact, an age-old practice, in normal times and in times of upheaval. But international adoption—the adoption of children from abroad—is not as old as some might think. After World War II, Americans adopted children from various European countries and Japan, but it was not until after the Korean War (1950–1953) that international adoption became a significant phenomenon in the United States. Between the Korean War and the end of the century, Americans adopted approximately two-thirds of the 150,000 children that Korea sent overseas for adoption.[4] Korean children account for the vast majority of American international adoptions: Korea was the number-one sending country of children to the United States until 1995, when it fell to third, behind China and Russia (see Figures INT.1 and INT.2).[5] More than sixty years of continuous Korean adoption has created a diaspora of more than two hundred thousand Koreans who have grown up in adoptive families overseas.

Although the rate of international adoption (and Korean adoption) in the United States has fallen dramatically in the twenty-first century, the families that it has created, the children who have been its subjects and objects, and the political and moral questions surrounding it hold tremendous cultural and political significance in both sending and receiving countries.[6] Intercountry, interracial adoption has deeply affected American ideas about race, family, and kinship, but we know little about how it began and why and how it has become so much a part of what we understand adoption to mean today. This book shows that, although Korea was not the first country from which international adoption took place, it was the place where organized, systematic international adoption began. From an ad hoc evacuation in the aftermath of a devastating war it transformed into a lucrative and culturally powerful practice that has touched many Americans, directly and indirectly. Like the GI babies who were its first intended beneficiaries, international adoption was born of the particular dynamics of the US-Korea relationship during and after the Korean War. In that sense, it is an

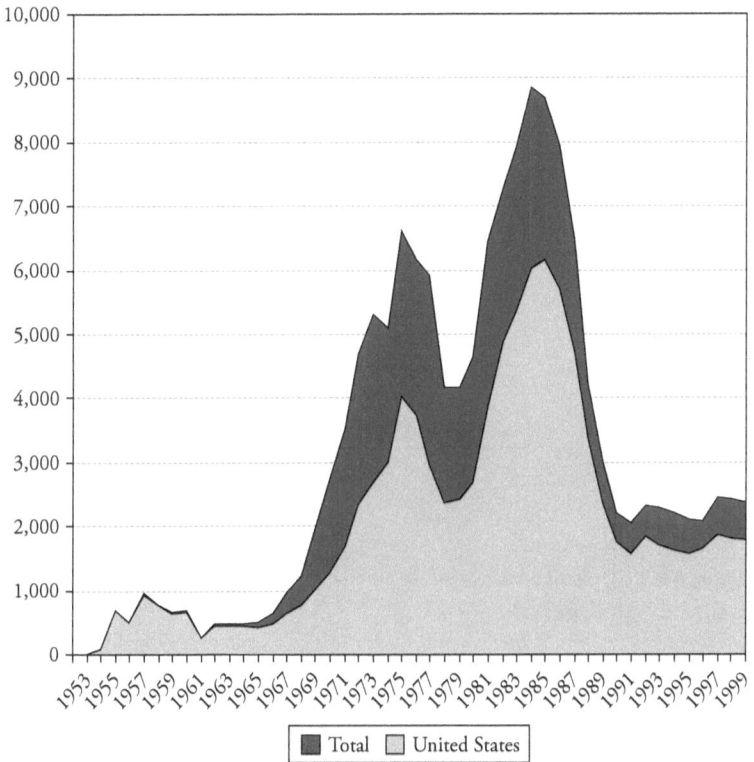

FIGURE INT.1 Korean children sent to the United States as a percentage of total Korean children sent abroad, 1953–2000
SOURCE: Based on figures by Tobias Hubinette.

overlooked legacy of a war that is commonly billed as forgotten but whose ripples have yet to reach shore.

. . .

Modern adoption, defined by the severing of the legal relationship between a child and his or her parents, and the transferring of the child's custody to another parent or set of parents, became formalized in the United States in the first decades of the twentieth century. Stranger adoption—the adoption of an unrelated person—also emerged during this period, along with the sentimentalization of childhood that dictated that children, and therefore adoption, could serve only emotional purposes, not labor needs. As adoption

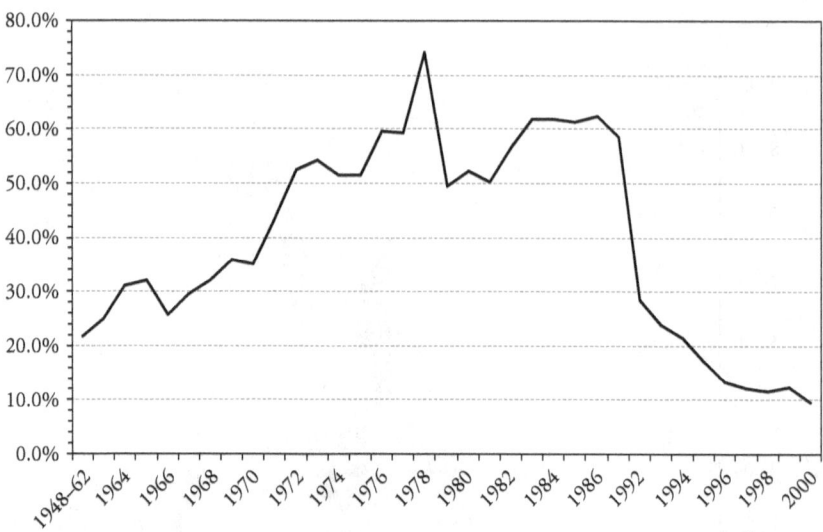

FIGURE INT.2 Korean adoption as a percentage of total international adoptions in the United States, 1948–2000
SOURCE: Based on information from Howard Altstein and Rita J. Simon, *Intercountry Adoption: A Multinational Perspective* (New York: Praeger, 1990), 14–16; Richard H. Weil, "International Adoptions: The Quiet Migration" *International Migration Review* 18, no. 2 (Summer 1984): 286–287; Evan B. Donaldson Adoption Institute (http://www.adoptioninstitute.org/FactOverview/international.htm).

evolved, states passed laws to regulate it, and increasingly professionalized social workers sought to organize the field with universal standards and procedures that aligned with the reigning scientific management principles of the time. Adoption increased dramatically in the decades after World War II, in the midst of the baby boom. The demand for healthy white infants—the children adopters most wanted—had exceeded the number available since the 1920s. It was "nearly insatiable" by the mid-1940s.[7]

Formal international adoption did not begin until after World War II, but the search for healthy white babies propelled Americans across borders before the 1940s. These somewhat clandestine adoptions occurred beyond the scrutiny of social workers or the state. Americans acquired children from Canada and Mexico through "gray" markets—networks of doctors, lawyers, midwives, and clergy who connected adopters and birth mothers—or "black" markets, in which babies could be bought for a price.[8] Although Ireland had no law facilitating international adoption until 1952, thousands of Irish children, mainly the illegitimate children of unwed mothers, were quietly adopted and taken out of the country from the 1940s to the mid-1960s, many by wealthy American Catholics.[9]

During World War II, some Americans living abroad while serving in the military or government developed attachments to local women and children but were unable to bring them home with them. The highly restrictive immigration regime of the United States contained no provisions for the entry of adopted foreign children, fiancées, or spouses, leaving them subject to the country-specific quotas and race-based exclusion instituted by the 1924 Immigration Act. However, the nation's new international role and developing Cold War and humanitarian imperatives spurred revisions to immigration law.[10] Temporary refugee and special legislation facilitated the first international adoptions, including the placement of around 1,600 European orphans with American families under onetime arrangements. The Displaced Persons Act of 1948 made large-scale adoption of European refugee children possible for the first time. The majority of those children came from Greece, Germany, Italy, and Poland.[11]

Many of these post–World War II international adoptions did not draw the attention that Korean adoptions did primarily because they were invisible. Americans tended to adopt children from their own national or cultural background. For example, Greek Americans adopted most of the Greek children, which aligned with the Greek government's preference for ethnic Greek adopters of Orthodox faith. Even when adoptions were interethnic, the perception of racial similarity—of whiteness—tended to override national or ethnic differences between parents and children. The involvement of religious organizations in these adoptions meant that most were intrareligious, which further reinforced their invisibility. Chinese Americans and Filipino Americans also adopted intraethnically.[12]

International adoption across racial lines was intimately connected to the prolonged presence of US occupation troops and shaped by military policy. Germany and Japan, where American troops have been stationed since World War II, were among the top five sending countries for Americans adopting internationally until 1974 and 1972, respectively. The majority of these adoptions were done by Americans stationed in those countries with their families.[13] In Germany and Japan (and later in Korea), sex between American servicemen and local women produced Japanese-white, Japanese-black, and German-black GI babies.[14] Although some of these children were born from consensual romantic relationships, the military actively discouraged interracial marriage, in part because it was not a foregone conclusion that the men would be able to bring their wives back with them: black-white couples would be subject to antimiscegenation laws in several US states, and anti-Asian immigration laws until 1952 prevented the entry of Japanese wives. Commanding officers refused to give their men permission to marry, and even went so far as to separate a couple by transferring the man elsewhere. Without a legal marriage recognized by immigration law, servicemen could not bring their foreign wives and children home with them. As a result, an unknown number of women in countries around the world were left unmarried and with a mixed-race child.[15]

Regarded as the living "legacies of the occupation," these children powerfully symbolized for Germany and Japan their humiliation and defeat in World War II. Furthermore, neither countries' notions of race and nation permitted the inclusion of these visibly mixed-race children. Both the German and Japanese governments saw repatriation as the solution to their GI baby problem and sought to inspire Americans to come forward and adopt "their own kind."[16] German and African American efforts to find American adoptive homes for half-black "brown babies" met with limited success. The so-called one-drop rule made these children black in the American context, and the social work principle of race matching dictated their placement with black families. African American families did express interest in adopting these children but at midcentury social work standards often shut out black adopters, in domestic and foreign adoptions alike. In total, up to five hundred brown babies were adopted during the early 1950s, mostly by black military families stationed in Germany; by 1968 Americans had adopted an estimated seven thousand German black children.[17]

Other factors hampered German intercountry adoption plans. Birth mothers resisted relinquishing their children (less than 13 percent were willing), and some American officials refused to contribute to existing race problems in the United States by facilitating the adoption of part-black children from abroad. German nationalism also played a role. Negative press claiming that the country was "selling" children to the "highest bidder" inflamed worries that white German children were being sent overseas when they were wanted at home and prompted the government to order an end to their "wholesale export." Finally, improving material conditions and a national effort to racially rehabilitate post-Hitler Germany—particularly in opposition to Jim Crow America—encouraged a recasting of half-black children as "our German children," and the German government by the mid-1950s began to discourage their emigration and adoption. Although Germany's acceptance of these children was incomplete and ambivalent, repatriation was no longer considered the proper solution for them.[18]

Parallel racisms in the United States and Japan supported proposals to send Japanese-white and Japanese-black "occupation babies" to the United States for adoption, but this movement of children remained a trickle rather than a flood. Despite the many similarities between the situations of Japanese and Korean GI babies, international adoption from Korea took off in a way that it did not from Japan. The specific local conditions in Korea, the particular individuals and organizations involved, and the nature of the US-Korea relationship partially answer the question of why this was so, but further research into the Japanese story is needed. The available scholarship suggests that Americans adopted about 1,500 mixed-race Japanese children between the end of World War II and the 1980s (and continue to, in very small numbers), with the vast majority adopted in-country by Americans living there because of military or government service. The Japanese government did not seem to demonstrate the same desire to be rid of GI babies that the Korean government did. In fact, it issued official antidiscrimination policies recognizing these children, and mixed-race children and their mothers received better social and financial governmental and nongovernmental support in Japan than in Korea. Although mixed-race people in the two countries endured similar social, economic, and legal marginalization, it seems that those in Japan fared slightly better.[19]

Korean GI babies shared many similarities with their counterparts in Germany and Japan. Born in analogous geopolitical circumstances, GI babies in all three countries became visible during closely overlapping periods in the 1940s and 1950s, and confronted legal and social exclusion based on their race, assumed illegitimacy, and the low status of their mothers. Korean GI babies were stigmatized as the children of prostitutes, and their racial mixture threatened Korea's nationalistic ideas of racial purity. Under Korean law, citizenship passed from father to child; as illegitimate children without Korean fathers, GI babies were stateless nonpersons who would never find legal or social acceptance.

As in Germany and Japan, adoption from Korea began as an effort to evacuate mixed-race GI babies, but it soon set off along a sharply different trajectory. A partial answer to the question of why Korean adoption took off while other forms of international adoption did not is because only Korean adoption had a leader like Harry Holt, a lumberman and farmer from Oregon. Although the Korean government wished to remove GI babies, and Americans wanted to adopt them, it was not until Holt established an adoption program in 1956 that these complementary desires clicked into alignment and significant numbers of overseas placements occurred. The Korean government supported Holt's efforts by revising adoption and emigration laws and creating a child-placement agency. The Holt Adoption Program quickly dominated Korean adoption, and it is now the leading international adoption agency in the world.

In a sense, Holt was the father of what became the international adoption industry. He made Korean adoption available to the masses through two innovations: proxy adoption, which obviated the need for adoptive parents to travel to Korea; and "baby lifts," which brought large groups of children at a time to the United States on chartered flights. More important, he became the inadvertent figurehead of what I call Christian Americanism. A powerful religious and patriotic ideology, Christian Americanism took on the adoption of Korean GI babies as a kind of missionary work, a way for Americans to participate in their country's Cold War project of proving its racial liberalism and winning the allegiance of newly independent countries around the world. The Christian Americanist movement lasted only a few years, long enough to drive the changes to US immigration laws that opened the way for large-scale emigration and adoption of Korean children. In response to Christian Americanist efforts, Congress amended US immigration law in 1961 to make international adoption permanently possible. That change has allowed the practice to flourish and helped a global industry to rise.

Harry Holt has been much mythologized as the founder of Korean and international adoption—perhaps overly so. It is true that systematic adoption from Korea required a catalyzing force like him, but it also required certain preexisting conditions. Americans in Korea—servicemen, missionaries, and voluntary agency workers—played a critical role in laying the foundation for the system of Korean adoption. They helped establish the orphanages and child sponsorship programs upon which intercountry adoption was built. At the same time, through the media and through their letters and visits home, they cultivated in Americans feelings of kinship with and responsibility for Koreans—bridges of imagination and sentiment that were equally vital to the creation and growth of Korean adoption.

In the 1960s, Korean adoption changed in two major ways. First, mixed-race children began to constitute a declining proportion of the children being sent abroad for adoption. Profound economic and political instability in Korea made international adoption an attractive and viable solution to the interlocking problems of overpopulation, poverty, and child abandonment. The system that had been created to remove mixed-race children became a convenient method through which to ease these problems by sending "full" Korean children abroad. The second change occurred in the late 1960s and marked Korean adoption's transformation into international adoption. As the practice of transnational adoption began to spread to other sending and receiving countries, Korean adoption provided a template of sorts. Adoption agencies expanded their operations to other countries by replicating or adapting the methods they had devised in Korea. On an imaginative level, the pioneering Americans who adopted Korean children helped enlarge the categories of family, race, and nation in the United States to include racially mixed adoptive families. Ongoing international adoption and Americans' growing acceptance of the families it created were mutually reinforcing and helped perpetuate and expand transnational adoption. The languages of humanitarianism, rescue, and colorblind love first deployed in the service of Korean adoption have persisted, and they continue to shape conversations and politics around the practice of international adoption today.

. . .

This exploration of international adoption stands at the intersection of multiple fields of historical inquiry, especially the history of Cold War domestic politics, the history of the family, and the history of race and race relations. It also contributes to our understanding of the US-Korea relationship between the 1950s and 1980s, and the impact of intercountry adoption on South Korea's economic and social development during those years.

The Christian Americanist movement to adopt Korean children illustrates the complex interplay between domestic and international Cold War politics in the 1950s, particularly within the realm of the family. Scholars have demonstrated how domestic American race relations and international Cold War politics were inseparable in the decades after World War II. Korean adoption embodied a kind of "Cold War civil rights" for Asians, a practice motivated in part by the Cold War imperative of winning friends in Asia. Ordinary Americans participated in national politics through their engagement with Asia as it was presented through mainstream media, imagining a new relationship with Asia through the trope of adoption. By adopting Korean children, thousands of American families made this imagined family relationship concrete.[20]

Using the language of Christian Americanism, American politicians and journalists who supported Korean adoption infused the practice with political and religious meaning, thereby reconstituting adoption and family-making, perceived as intensely private acts, as public and political. Potential adoptive parents likewise positioned Korean adoption as supporting a national Cold War agenda, an argument that provided added power to their appeals to Congress for adoption-friendly immigration laws. The way adoptive families used national concerns to garner support for Korean adoption challenges the notion of an insular, protected domestic sphere in postwar America and complicates Cold War ideology about separate "public" and "private" spheres. Instead, the back-and-forth flow of influence between political concerns and the private interests of families demonstrates the deep mutual imbrication of the public and private in the opening decades of the Cold War. The story of Korean adoption illuminates how international Cold War politics became domestic in the most profound way possible—not just within the borders of the nation but also within the boundaries of home and family.[21]

This study of the origins of international adoption therefore contributes to the literature on the history of the family by examining the changing ways Americans envisioned and constructed their families in the second half of the twentieth century.[22] Americans adopting from Korea—most of whom were white—overturned biological ideas of kinship, discarding social work's gold standard of the "as if begotten" family in favor of nonnormative families that could not and did not hide the fact of adoption. As such, the ostensibly private domain of the family became a public, political site for contesting the doctrine of matching, which had traditionally governed how adoptive families were made. American social workers, who had struggled to gain legitimacy since before World War II, sought to establish their expertise in intercountry adoption by helping to shape adoption and immigration policy and law at the state and national levels. Ordinary Americans, who had long resisted the incursions of the social work establishment into the space of their homes and families, saw social workers' efforts to police international adoption as just another attempt to unduly extend state surveillance into private life.

Yet American adoptive parents could not wholly detach themselves from governmental power, since they needed state cooperation to adopt from Korea. Adoptive families needed federal immigration law to permit the entry of adopted Korean children and local governments to recognize the legality of adoptive family ties. The relationship between American families and the state was one of constant, sometimes fraught, negotiation. Americans tried to maintain a boundary around their families in the face of some state actors—especially state welfare departments—even as they looked to elected officials to help defend their right to construct their families in any way they chose, without state intervention. These interactions show that the American family was a social institution and object of public policy, not simply a natural organism created through blood ties.

Nor could American adopters fully separate themselves from the commercialism that haunted modern adoption, domestic and international. Adoption commodifies children, in rhetoric and reality. As international adoption spread beginning in the late 1960s, a consumeristic attitude toward parenthood, though not new, became more pronounced. Americans' belief that they had a right to parenthood through all available means both drove and was driven by this expansion of international adoption: American parents who faced a shortage of children to adopt domestically went abroad in search of them, aided by a developing international adoption industry. Meanwhile, narratives of rescue provided the rhetorical justification for what some saw as the imperialistic, consumeristic importing of children from poorer countries. As international adoption became a global industry that included dozens of sending and receiving countries and moved children almost exclusively from the developing to the developed world, debate intensified about whether it served the best interests of poor children or those of wealthy parents, as well as about the ethics of transnational and transracial placements themselves.[23]

This book's third contribution is to our understanding of changing ideas about race in the Cold War United States. It was nothing short of revolutionary for mostly white American families to adopt mixed-race and full-Korean children during the years before the passage of federal civil rights legislation, when the United States remained a deeply segregated country.

The arrival of these children in American families and communities both reflected and caused shifts in American racial thinking and race-based ideas about kinship. Broad changes in American racial thought at midcentury and the imperatives of Cold War racial liberalism provided opportunities for Asian Americans to establish a new position in the shifting racial terrain.[24] A refiguring of Asianness, begun during World War II, continued after the war as the US government and Asian American communities themselves worked to transform formerly alien unassimilable Chinese and Japanese into "model" citizens—or, at the very least, not black.[25] Korean adoptees were part of this reformulation of Asianness—as malleable children who could be raised to be good Americans, they not only refuted arguments about unassimilable Asians but also were recast as the most desirable of immigrants.

Korean adoption simultaneously destabilized and reinscribed the black-white binary that has so dominated American racial thought. At first glance, American acceptance of Korean children as sons and daughters suggests a shift from this black-white binary to a paradigm of triangulation that explicitly made room for Asians, constructing them as an intermediate group relative to blacks and whites.[26] This geometry had been more salient than the black-white dyad in certain regions of the country and at certain moments before the mid-twentieth century. At first glance, Korean adoption might look like an example of racial triangulation, in which Korean-white and full-Korean children became racially acceptable despite not being white. But in actuality, their acceptability hinged on them being imagined as whitened in one of two ways: biologically—through blood, in the case of GI babies—or culturally, in their recategorization, along with other Asians, as not black. In other words, by racializing these children in ways that insisted on their proximity to whiteness, advocates of Korean adoption did not disrupt the black-white binary, but carefully heeded it.

Orientalist constructions that emphasized Korean children's racial difference in nonthreatening ways helped make them not just acceptable, but desirable. As waifs from a backward, war-torn, poverty-stricken country, Korean children's need for rescue heightened their appeal. Additionally, they represented a digestible diversity that Americans prized in the midst of a new emphasis on multiculturalism and colorblindness after the civil rights movement. Although these representations underscored the racial difference of Korean children, they also emphasized their "not-blackness."

The popularity of adopting not-black Korean children—and, eventually, not-black Vietnamese and Guatemalan children—and the hardening of American preference during the 1970s for a nonwhite foreign child over a nonwhite American child indicates a shift from binary racial thinking to racial triangulation. But the acceptance of internationally adopted nonwhite children because they were considered not-black also suggests a redrawing of the black-white color line.

Finally, this book contributes to our understanding of modern Korean history, and of US-Korea relations since the Korean War. Korean adoption was mutually beneficial to the United States and Korea. It removed children from a poor, war-torn country to eager parents in the United States, and it served the American Cold War containment agenda by solidifying the US-Korea friendship. But although these adoptions could be deployed as evidence to contradict images of racist Americans, the importing of children from a developing nation also provided ammunition to those who saw the United States as a new imperial power in the postwar world order. This was—and is—a powerful critique. The United States only formally occupied Korea for three years (1945–1948), but few would dispute that it has maintained a neocolonial relationship with South Korea since, as indicated by its unavoidable military presence, and enormous political, cultural, and economic influence. As such, the migration to the United States of more than 150,000 adoptees and roughly 100,000 military brides since the Korean War has to be understood as movement within the informal empire of the United States and in the context of scholarship on the way colonial intimacies reshape the "interior frontiers" of the nation.[27]

As South Korea underwent military rule and rapid but uneven industrialization in the 1960s and 1970s, international adoption changed from a Cold War institution to a kind of pressure valve for surplus Korean children. The Korean government's use of international adoption as a supplement to (some would say a substitute for) its weak social and child welfare policies had profound consequences that are only beginning to manifest today. Considering the origins of Korean adoption thus sheds light on South Korea's modernization, the emergence of the Korean social work profession, and the establishment and evolution of Korean social welfare policy.

This book proceeds in three parts. Part 1 uncovers the prehistory of Korean adoption, showing how Americans and Koreans established its practical and imaginative preconditions. Chapter 1 discusses American GIs' child-rescue efforts during and after the Korean War, and their role in familiarizing Americans with Korea and the plight of Korean children. The practice of keeping mascots—Korean boys "adopted" by military units—led to some of the first adoptions from Korea. American servicemen, voluntary agency workers, and missionaries helped nurture the affective ties between the United States and Korea that were crucial to the popularization and development of Korean adoption. Chapter 2 explores how and why mixed-race GI babies were branded a problem in postwar Korea. When it became clear that there were Americans eager to adopt these children, the Korean government and assorted voluntary agencies sought ways to create an intercountry adoption system. In the process, they laid the foundations for Korean adoption to take off: orphanages, sponsorship programs, and the perpetuation of congruent racial thought that both confirmed the unacceptability of these children in Korea and made them (just barely) acceptable in the United States.

Part 2 shows how systematic Korean adoption began and developed, both ideologically and practically. In Chapter 3, I introduce the concept of Christian Americanism, which functioned as the ideology and vernacular of the Korean adoption movement. Harry Holt was central to this movement, and not just symbolically. His practical innovations made Korean adoption faster, cheaper, and more readily available to ordinary Americans, at least those who conformed to his idea of Christianity. These innovations also alarmed professional social workers, who campaigned assiduously against Holt's unorthodox methods. Chapter 4 examines the impact of Korean adoption on the social work profession in the United States and Korea. It explains the mechanics of intercountry adoption and how social workers turned children into orphans, and orphans into adoptees. It also discusses how American social workers and prospective adoptive parents negotiated concepts of race, matching, and adoptability, and how adoption that crossed boundaries of race and nation challenged US social workers' ideas about the best way to construct families.

Part 3 examines how Korean adoption became international adoption beginning in the late 1960s, from both the perspective of the United States (Chapter 5) and South Korea (Chapter 6). In the United States, the Korean orphan underwent a profound legal and cultural transformation, from a waif who entered the country under refugee laws to a family member who entered under immigration laws. Changing ideas about race and multiculturalism during the 1960s and 1970s both fed and were fed by the practice of international adoption. Korean children's racial flexibility, their supposed need, and their availability through a highly organized adoption industry made them desirable for Americans confronting a shortage of "adoptable" children at home. In Korea, meanwhile, the transnational adoption system originally erected to remove the problem of mixed-race children became a conduit for other problematic children: the children of the poor and those of single mothers. International adoption, and the imbricated gender and nationalist ideologies that drove it, became an important but unacknowledged part of the so-called miracle on the Han River, the modernization project that propelled Korea from dire poverty to dazzling wealth in the space of a generation.

A Note on Language

Mixed-race Korean children have been labeled in a variety of ways, depending on context. The terms *GI babies* and *UN babies* underscore their non-Korean paternity and the fact that they were born as a result of foreign troop presence. *Half-breed, half-caste, mixed-breed,* and *mixed-blood* highlight their racial mixture and reflect the belief that these children are neither fully Korean nor fully American. I have used the terms *GI baby* and *mixed-race* somewhat interchangeably throughout the book, although *GI baby* was used less frequently toward the end of the 1950s.

Korean children of full-Korean parentage were commonly called *full Korean*. I initially resisted using the term, preferring to use *full-blooded* in recognition of the fact that people who are not biologically fully Korean can nonetheless be culturally fully Korean. However, *full-blooded* carries strongly racialized associations with ideas such as blood quantum. Recognizing that neither term is satisfactory, I have chosen to use the term *full Korean*.

While I use *intercountry, international,* and *transnational* adoption interchangeably, the first term is the one that appears most commonly in my archival materials, whereas the latter two are of more contemporary usage. These terms are inadequate for describing the phenomenon of white Americans adopting from Asia, since none highlights both the cross-border and interracial nature of the adoptions I discuss. They also obscure the unequal power relations and imperialist histories between sending and receiving countries, I have used these descriptors while remaining cognizant that they fail to capture these dynamics. *Korean adoption* is shorthand for "adoption from Korea," and *Korea* refers to South Korea.

Since the 1970s, adoptee and birth-parent advocacy groups have worked to promote openness in adoption, including adult adoptees' rights to their birth records. As awareness about adoption has grown, the language used to talk about it has become more politicized. When Korean adoption began, people spoke of "natural" mothers who "gave up" or "surrendered" their children to be adopted and adopters who loved their adopted children as much as they loved their "own" children. I have rejected ideas of birth mothers (not natural mothers) giving up, surrendering, or (in Korean) throwing away their children in favor of *relinquish*, because it is a slightly more neutral term. I speak of adoptive parents as heterosexual couples because for most of the period discussed in this book, this was the profile of the vast majority of adopters. I refer to birth mothers as *unwed mothers* because that is the term that organized birth mothers in Korea choose to apply to themselves.

I have romanized Korean terms following the McCune-Reischauer system and written Korean names in the Western style, with the family name last. The only exceptions are Park Chung Hee (family name Park), Chun Doo Hwan (family name Chun), and Kang Koo Ri (family name Kang), who are better known by their Korean-style names. All names of adoptees are pseudonyms. I have used initials instead of proper surnames when referring to potential adoptive parents and adoptive parents mentioned in the International Social Service's confidential adoption case records.

In Korean adoption, as in adoption in general, adoptive parents preferred girls until very recently, so I use *she* in my discussion.

PART ONE

Children of Empire

ONE

GIs and Missionaries in the Land of Orphans

> The American soldiers' love for Korean children was very impressive. They did everything to take care of us. You were like a father to us.
>
> —Yang Yun-hak, *evacuated from Seoul to Chejudo in 1950 by American forces*[1]

The Korean War (1950–1953) devastated and divided a country that was in the initial stages of recovering from thirty-five years of brutal Japanese colonial occupation and the destruction of World War II. The children of that war—orphans who lost their parents and the newly created mixed-race "GI babies"—could find little assistance from any quarter. The government of the new Republic of Korea (ROK) had neither the money nor the resources to assist any of its citizens, young or old. In the absence of government welfare, American servicemen and missionaries, along with a host of international nongovernmental organizations (NGOs), provided what little social welfare was available. Together, these groups built and supported orphanages and stimulated massive donations of food, clothing, and money from Americans at home by raising awareness of the plight of Korean children. Additionally, servicemen cared for Korean boys under a semiformal "mascot" system.

Child sponsorship programs such as Foster Parents' Plan, Christian Children's Fund, and World Vision provided a way for Americans to virtually "adopt" Korean children. Those virtual adoptions quickly became real: as servicemen began returning to the United States with their adopted Korean children, such adoptions entered the realm of possibility for ordinary Americans. This chapter surveys the Korean orphan problem and some of the ways that American servicemen and missionaries cared for Korea's children. It also examines how these servicemen and missionaries created the institutional and imaginative preconditions for the establishment of Korean adoption in the second half of the 1950s.

War Orphans and GI Babies

At eighty-five thousand square miles, the Korean Peninsula is roughly the same size as Utah. Unified as one kingdom since the seventh century, Korea's isolationism and hostility to outsiders had earned it the nickname "Hermit Kingdom." It remained fiercely independent until Japanese annexation in 1910, which ended with Japan's defeat at the end of World War II. Following Japan's withdrawal, returned Korean exiles, landlords, collaborators, and freedom fighters struggled to gain control of their newly liberated country. Instead, Korea was divided at the 38th parallel. The Soviet Union took stewardship of North Korea while the United States established a military government in the south. This division prompted an influx of refugees from the north, foreshadowing the enormous population movements that would occur during the Korean War. South Korea experienced economic, political, and social disorder: increased crime, political and labor violence, leftist uprisings, and retaliatory rightist purges. This chaos resulted in part in "heavy dependence" on the United States, which would have important consequences for Korea's future development. As a result of developing Cold War politics and a US-Soviet deadlock, separate governments were established on the peninsula in 1948. In the south, the Republic of Korea was declared, with US-educated Syngman Rhee as its president; in the north, Kim Il Sung proclaimed authority over the new Democratic People's Republic of Korea. The United States withdrew its forces by mid-1949, leaving behind about 2,500 personnel, including five hundred soldiers to train the ROK Army.[2]

On 25 June 1950, the Korean War started when North Korean forces launched a surprise invasion of the south. They quickly pushed southward, overwhelming unprepared ROK troops, and by early August had gained control of at least 90 percent of the peninsula. The next month, American and ROK troops, led by General Douglas MacArthur, made their celebrated amphibious landing at Inch'ŏn, dramatically reversing the course of the war. By late November UN, Korean, and American forces had advanced almost to the Yalu River that formed most of the North Korean border, and they talked of being home for Christmas. Those hopes were thwarted by China's entry into the war; its troops joined with the North Koreans and, in another dramatic reversal, drove UN forces back south of Seoul. By March 1951, the two sides found themselves facing off at the 38th parallel—essentially the same point at which they had begun—marking the start of a two-year period of stalemate during which truce negotiations dragged on against a backdrop of limited ground and air wars. In July 1953, North and South Korea signed an armistice that remains in effect today.[3]

Fleeing the fighting, approximately 5.8 million Koreans (one out of every five) became a refugee. The port city of Pusan, on the southeast tip of the Korean Peninsula, was never taken by North Korean forces. Consequently, it and the area around it—the thinly held defensive line known as the Pusan perimeter—became the de facto seat of the South Korean government. Pusan also housed hundreds of thousands of refugees, who built shelters from the discarded materials of warfare—corrugated metal sheets, flattened tin cans, and US Army C-ration boxes—and did what they could to stay alive. Huddled there, they endured hunger, disease, pestilence, power outages, fires, and water shortages for the duration of the war and long after it ended.[4]

It is difficult to overstate the deprivation, poverty, and destruction wrought by the Korean War. Regarded by the rest of the world as a geographically limited civil war—a UN "police action"—it was a total war for Koreans. At its close in 1953, the peninsula "was a smoldering ruin." North and South Korea each reported roughly US$2 billion in property damage, the equivalent of South Korea's gross national product in 1949. South Korea's capital city, Seoul, which had changed hands four times in less than a year, saw the majority of its office space, homes, and industrial capacity destroyed. North Korea's capital, Pyongyang, was similarly shattered. By the July 1953 armistice, "most of South Korea was a wasteland of burned villages, bombed out towns and cities, roadsides littered with the rusted hulks of trucks and tanks, bridges down, rail lines severed, factories and schools flattened." In this land of farmers and fishermen, half of the livestock and all of the fishing fleet had been wiped out. Measured in terms of "human lives lost," the Korean War was the third "most costly war of the twentieth century." Yet the civilian death toll has never been accurately assessed, partly because the North Korean government has never released official casualty statistics. Most sources agree that the war left between three and four million Koreans dead, missing and wounded—North and South, civilian and military—amounting to roughly 10 percent of the prewar population. Another ten million Koreans saw their families permanently divided. Troop deaths were just as appalling: 33,600 US troops were killed, 103,200 wounded, and more than 7,000 taken prisoner by North Korean and Chinese forces. Of the ROK troops, 70,000 were killed, 150,000 wounded, and 80,000 captured, of which the majority died from malnutrition or mistreatment. In addition, 3,063 non-US, non-Korean UN forces were also killed.[5]

Korean orphans captured the American imagination from the moment the Korean War erupted. Photographs and articles in mass-market magazines like *Life*, *Collier's*, and *Look* roused sympathy and loosed a flood of donations from Americans. In particular, *Life*—the most widely read general magazine of the 1945–1960 period—was deeply influential in structuring Americans' understanding of the world around them, including the war in Korea.[6] In magazines and newspapers, on newsreels and radio programs, Americans saw, heard, and read descriptions of a ruined Korea. The media painted a vivid portrait of a land of suffering and poverty. Smoke rose from deserted villages, ancient city gates towered over smashed buildings, and lines of laden refugees wove their way through driving snow. Feature stories offered a montage of heartbreaking sketches: widows, lepers, a family sleeping on a single straw mat, bodies sprawled on the side of a road, an open-air school tucked away in the hills, a farmer whose entire family and only ox had died digging his fields by hand.[7] Juxtaposed to the devastation were the faces of orphaned Korean children. Crying babies sat next to the bodies of their dead mothers. Gangs of children roamed the streets, foraging for food and sleeping in the rubble. Little girls with their baby brothers or sisters tied to their backs walked from Seoul to Pusan and back again. In almost every human-interest story about the Korean War, these "waifs," "urchins," and "moppets" figured prominently. Korea was, one mission group intoned, "a land of orphans."[8]

Nobody knows for sure how many children were orphaned during the war, but one hundred thousand was the figure most frequently cited. This orphan population comprised two groups: children of full-Korean parentage and mixed-race GI babies. "Full-Korean" children were children of Korean parentage who had become lost, abandoned, or orphaned during the war and its aftermath. Many found their way to institutions, whereas others became street urchins, running in gangs and finding food through pickpocketing, begging, shining shoes, or pimping. Still others lived on American military bases as houseboys and mascots, a phenomenon addressed later in this chapter. Far more troubling to the war-strained social fabric of the country were the mixed-race GI babies, an unwelcome novelty in a country that prided itself on its racial purity. Although Americans did not father all of these children, Koreans and Americans alike persisted in calling them GI babies, which reflected both the dominance of Americans in the Korean imagination and the fact that Americans were the majority of the foreign troop presence in Korea. These GI babies constituted a tiny portion of the postwar orphan population—of an estimated 100,000 orphans, approximately 1,500 were of mixed race—but they suffered a disproportionate amount of hostility and abuse on the basis of their illegitimacy, racial mixture, and assumptions that their mothers were prostitutes.[9]

GI Humanitarianism

Even before the war was over, observers reported an explosion in the number of homeless Korean and mixed-race orphans throughout the country. These children touched the hearts of American servicemen, who cared for them in a multitude of formal and informal ways.[10] The US military funded child-rescue activities through official programs such as the Korean Civil Assistance Command (KCAC) and Armed Forces Assistance to Korea.[11] Their work included establishing and supporting orphanages, and they coordinated with missionaries and voluntary agencies to distribute clothing, food, and medicine. It was no exaggeration to say, as one observer did, "There is hardly a military unit in Korea that has not adopted a hospital, orphanage or participated in some social welfare project."[12]

The situation of homeless Korean children—malnourished, alone, wearing inadequate shoes and clothes—provoked a profound emotional response in American servicemen. A marine reported from Korea that "the most pathetic victims are children—the almond-eyed, pickaback babies; the toddlers with hunger-defined, radiatorlike ribs; and the swarms of grinning, half-starved 'shoeshine boys' always on the prowl for a job, a C-ration, or a stick of gum." A soldier wrote to his parents, "At night time you can walk down any alley and find kids [age seven] and younger sleeping in big pipes and in holes in the sides of hills. All they get to eat is what they can steal or bum." Long after they left Korea, veterans remembered the children. A US Navy Seabee recalled, "A lot of times you would see 20 or 30 abandoned children, all looking for something to eat and crying." American GIs demonstrated an inclination to "give the little dudes most anything they wanted."[13]

Koreans of all ages foraged through the garbage dumps around military encampments, and homeless children clustered around US military bases and posts, knowing that they would be rich sources for handouts. "Children in Chunchon were living like animals under trains and in box cars," said a sergeant with the Fourth Fighter Interceptor Wing. "I'd shine my flashlight at the fence and regardless if it was hot or cold outside, there would be about 10 kids waiting there. I would take them candy bars, cheese, popcorn, whatever I had." The military newspaper *Stars and Stripes* reported, "It's seldom that hard-bitten, dirty-faced soldiers pass the kids on the road without digging through a pocket and coming up with a bite to eat." Korean children quickly learned the English they needed to wheedle gifts from American GIs, shouting "Hello!," "chewing gum," and "chocolate" as they passed.[14]

It seemed as if every serviceman who encountered a homeless child felt moved to action. There are countless stories about how servicemen encountered starving children in terrible conditions and banded together with voluntary agency workers and missionaries to provide food and shelter.[15] Colonel Russell L. Blaisdell, an air force chaplain, arrived in Seoul in August 1950 to find the streets "full of babies and children shivering from the cold." With the help of both Korean and American volunteers—health-care workers, military men, and civilians—Blaisdell began moving the children into shelters. "We'd go out at dawn and pick up these tiny bodies, limp as sacks of rice, and pile them in an old flat bed truck, 10 or 20 at a time.... [T]hey were sick and weak and seemed to have cried themselves out.... We brought them in, scrubbed them up, and dropped them off at the local orphanage. Then we'd go back out and do it again."[16]

During the war, American forces participated in dramatic actions to evacuate children out of harm's way. Operation Kiddy Car, Operation KidLift, and Operation Orphan Annie were just three of these undertakings.[17] In Operation Kiddy Car, which was organized by US Air Force colonel and minister Dean Hess, the US Fifth Air Force airlifted thousands of Korean orphans to Cheju Island, out of the way of an impending invasion by North Korean forces. This dramatic accomplishment became memorialized as the

1957 Hollywood film *Battle Cry*, starring Rock Hudson and twenty-five Korean orphans who were specially flown to the United States for filming. In Operation Orphan Annie, the Air Force Cargo Command moved 964 orphans from Inch'ŏn to Cheju Island in a mass airlift. The next year, they returned with gifts: "lollypops, rice bowls, and Christmas trees," as well as notebooks, toothbrushes, and sewing machines.[18]

A Christian Children's Fund employee remembered fleeing to Pusan in June 1950, in the first days of the Korean War. There, he noticed "more than 2,000 homeless children" who were living on a mountain slope outside the city:

> These tiny innocents had their own special benefactors—grimy, dog-tired American soldiers. Using their entrenching tools, the GIs had dug foxholes on the mountainside for these homeless Korean kids. At night the little ones would slide into foxholes—each big enough for just one child—and cover themselves with a piece of cardboard made from a U.S. Army C-Ration carton.
>
> As long as I live, I shall never forget mornings on that Pusan mountainside when those of us caring for the children would call to them to wake up. As we passed each covered foxhole, up would pop the cardboard lid and then the dirty but smiling face of one of the Korean children to begin another day. Those little faces popping up from the child-sized foxholes made me think what it's going to be like on Resurrection Morning.

In the midst of the fighting, however, GIs could not always stop to help the children. A veteran remembered "seeing little kids laying in ditches, starving. We'd be on trucks moving through. Nobody stopping. Kids laying in ditches with mud all over them and dirt. Nothing but bones. It was tough . . . tough."[19]

Servicemen actively educated Americans back home on the situation in Korea in the letters they wrote to solicit food, clothing, medical supplies, and money. After two months in Korea, nineteen-year-old Private Victor Leaf sent his hometown newspaper an appeal that is typical in its earnestness, its description of the children's plight, and its request for even the most modest donation. Of the fifty-four children living in an orphanage near his company, Leaf wrote:

> The kids are really badly off and need a lot of clothes and various items that this war has denied or taken away from them. We at the company try

to help, but we can't do enough. I am hoping that if anyone at home has a few loose ends lying around the house, he will gather them up and ship them over here. Anything at all will help—an old coat, shoes, even a toy.

It's going to be a hard cold winter for those children.

If anything is sent, just address it to me and I'll see that it reaches the kids. I know it will be greatly appreciated. It wasn't God's will that these children should suffer so.

Appeals from GIs like this one were particularly effective in arousing generous responses. Servicemen's letters often sparked larger collection efforts at home. When one airman wrote to his father asking for help to throw a Christmas party for an orphanage housing eighty children, his letter prompted a statewide drive, resulting in the arrival of more than one thousand packages. Some GIs launched letter-writing campaigns. George Drake, who was in the same company as Private Leaf, distributed to the other men three hundred copies of a form letter he had written and asked them to send them to their hometown newspapers. This letter, or portions of it, appeared in papers from Minneapolis to Schenectady to Philadelphia. The Pusan Replacement Depot, 8069 Army Unit, undertook a letter-writing campaign called Operation Santa Claus that received nationwide publicity in the United States. When a radio personality read one of their letters on his show, 1,320 packages, averaging fifteen pounds each, poured in from across the country, and from Hawaii, Canada, and Japan.[20]

American troops gave millions of dollars of their own pay.[21] To put those donations in perspective, *Stars and Stripes* reported that one dollar could buy "shoes for two Korean orphans, school supplies for three months including a school bag, or 18 tiles to repair an orphanage roof." On paydays, the men might set out a helmet for donations or take a collection at Sunday worship services. *Stars and Stripes* regularly reported on the amount of money and goods raised by the men in a unit and the number of orphanages they built and supported. Headlines like "Tankers Give $1,561 for Korean Amputees" and "187th Troopers Donate $5,000 for Orphanage" broadcast the generosity to fellow soldiers and contributed to an atmosphere in which giving to Korean relief was commonplace and expected. And GI interest in Korean children did not end when the men returned home—some units left trust funds for the orphanages they supported, and others continued to support individual children.[22]

Servicemen also spent their off-hours at orphanages. Besides throwing parties and bringing presents on US holidays like Thanksgiving and Christmas, servicemen visited regularly to play. Christian Children's Fund noted that, "at every orphanage, a little Kim Sung Hi or Lee Myung Hung knew a 'Mac' or a 'Mike' or a Chaplain Somebody" and that these men "usually came loaded down with good things from the PX [post exchange], or boxes of clothing and food from home." A missionary described a typical meeting of hearts and minds, which occurred when three groups of engineers gave Christmas parties for five orphanages: "The men and children fell in love with each other on that day and there has been a never ceasing stream of interest, love, and giving. It is impossible to even mention the ways in which little children have been helped by these men. And I am sure that the days in Korea have seemed less dreary to the men who have visited our orphans and loved them." Soldiers from other countries also participated in child welfare efforts in Korea, such as the Ethiopian soldiers who established and funded the Bowha Orphanage, which housed 60 to 70 children, and the Turkish forces who did the same for the Ankara Orphanage, which housed 160 children. ROK soldiers also established and supported at least one orphanage for thirty-five years, before turning it over to a Catholic order of nuns.[23] Nonetheless, American troops' efforts dwarfed those of other countries, no doubt because of their greater numbers and comparative wealth.

Koreans responded to servicemen's child-care activities with gratitude. Robert Mosier, a marine sergeant, wrote in *National Geographic*, "The Koreans I'd met had been really surprised at the kindness our troops showed toward their kids. Not that they don't like their own children, but their sympathy tends to dwindle at the limit of the family circle." Molly Holt, whose family would play a key role in Korean adoption, recalls that when she and her father mourned the death of a baby, Koreans asked why they were expending so much emotion over "just an orphan." An American perception of "Asian disregard for human life" permeated news accounts. Koreans' stoicism and apparent indifference to the suffering of their children seemed consistent with Orientalist belief that "life is cheap" to Asians.[24]

GIs understood their humanitarianism in crudely political terms—usually contrasting American generosity with communist brutality—but most of their child welfare activities were less about politics than they were about simple decency: a fundamentally human desire on the part of young, homesick American men to do something in the face of the suffering that surrounded them. A sense that they were representing their nation was also discernible, however, as Mosier indicated in *National Geographic*. Reflecting on how GIs in every branch of service had undertaken child rescue efforts, he wrote, "I guess they weren't doing anything that GIs haven't done in any country they've fought in; but, all the same, it made me feel pretty good to be an American." No doubt Mosier's wish to redeem the American presence in Korea resonated with other servicemen who like him wondered, "Will the Korean people . . . remember the GIs whose job it was to break and smash and burn things, but who tried to mend what they could and to blot the tears off at least a few grimy cheeks?" Even before the end of World War II, depictions of relationships between American servicemen and local people abroad represented the US military as wanting not to "dominate other nations but rather to cooperate with them in making the world a better place."[25]

GI humanitarianism directed at children was a crucial ingredient in US efforts to shape its international image during the Cold War, a distinctly post–World War II concern born of the country's new position as a superpower. GIs looked like benevolent fathers or big brothers, but at the same time their interactions with children reinforced and naturalized the hierarchical relationships that the United States was building with countries like South Korea. Stories and images that depicted American servicemen with foreign children "appealed to the idea of international family ties" with servicemen the "paternal representatives of America's compassionate internationalism" (see Figure 1.1).[26] Christian Children's Fund Field Director William Asbury proudly noted that it was "impossible to measure the international good will that is generated by men who love children and who go out of their way to help them. Foreign relations between nation and nation might very well be influenced by such soldier-child relationships." Asbury emphasized the mythic stature of the American soldier overseas: "The American G.I., as he tramped into one battered city after another, whether it was Munich or Singapore, Naples or Tokyo or Seoul, always had a chocolate bar or a stick of chewing gum for the ragged children. . . . Then when occupations began, or truces were signed the chocolate bars were replaced by dollars and buildings, and everything from vitamin capsules to bicycles."[27]

The military's child welfare activities helped the United States positively frame its role in Korea specifically, a country Americans knew little about.

GIs and Missionaries in the Land of Orphans   29

FIGURE 1.1 Images of GI humanitarianism toward Korean children were important in shaping Americans' attitudes about US involvement in Korea as well as influencing America's image abroad during the Cold War.
SOURCE: The LIFE Picture Collection/Getty Images.

Stars and Stripes was central to celebrating this effort. It ran a continuous stream of articles and photos with headlines like "Eighth Chief Sends Cookies to Orphans," "728th MPs Plan Fete for 260 Korean Kids," and "Yanks Befriend Korean Orphan." As the American-Korean Foundation (AKF) noted, "Almost every issue of the Korean edition of *Stars and Stripes* carries a story of G.I.'s providing scholarships for a houseboy, equipment for an institution, or assistance to widows, orphans and hospitals." *Stars and Stripes* had a clear agenda: to advance a narrative about servicemen in

Korea, in which decent American boys applied their can-do spirit to help children. Negative stories about American servicemen raping and killing Korean civilians—or fathering GI babies—did not appear. Mainstream news outlets like *Life* and the *New York Times* mimicked this resolutely positive approach, broadcasting heartwarming stories of GI humanitarianism to their American readers.[28]

The interracial friendship between American servicemen and Korean children coexisted with racism—not just within the newly integrated ranks of the US Army but also the racism of members of the military toward Koreans. If "the average G.I. arrived in Korea with the barest knowledge of where he was, who he was fighting, and why," he also "came from an American society where people of color were subjugated and segregated." Many of these men no doubt imbibed and contributed to the "ubiquitous racism" that saw Koreans as less than human. An American visitor to Korea during the 1945–1948 US occupation was "shocked by the ignorance and cruelty of U.S. military personnel," who called Koreans "dirty and treacherous." Little had changed by the time of the Korean War. A *New York Times* reporter noted that US troops "alienated the local population from the outset" by contemptuously labeling all Koreans "gook" regardless of whether they were "enemy or allied, soldier or civilian." Servicemen drove civilians off the roads for fun—killing those who did not escape in time—committed murder and rape, and destroyed and stole property. They also disparaged the men of the Korean Augmentation to the US Army (KATUSAs), who, they complained, were dirty, lazy, and incompetent; these Korean troops were often given menial tasks and suffered "yellow nigger" treatment.[29]

Both sides committed atrocities during the Korean War, but racial difference—the dehumanization of Koreans as nothing more than "a bunch of gooks"—facilitated US violence against Koreans. Servicemen deliberately or accidentally killed civilians in individual incidents. The military also killed civilians as a matter of policy, such as when aircraft strafed roads to clear them of refugees. At the same time, the lack of racial difference between friend (South Koreans) and foe (North Koreans) resulted in US Army and Air Force units killing sometimes indiscriminately out of fear that enemy soldiers disguised as refugees would infiltrate US positions. The inability to make distinctions among civilians resulted in tragedies like the massacre at No Gun Ri, in which US forces killed hundreds of refugees (the exact figure is unknown) as they sheltered under a railroad bridge. That incident, however, is far from the only example of the US military's general devaluing of Korean lives.[30]

Constrained by military censorship and Cold War political considerations, the American media glossed over the racism and brutality that was the ugly underside side of the US military's benevolence in Korea. American journalists reportedly "saw lines of bullet-riddled refugee bodies along roadsides in South Korea, but little more than hints of what was happening ever got to American newspaper readers." Furthermore, American disregard for Korean life was not confined to the military but also manifested among many of the war correspondents, a fact that they probably would not have wanted to advertise.[31]

Houseboys and Mascots

The use of boys and men as "houseboys" to do domestic work has a long history. It was common in colonial Africa and Asia, where houseboys embodied hierarchies of racialized masculinity. In the American context, houseboys were most prominent in the slave South; the colonial Philippines; and on the West Coast. In the US military, only officers had historically employed houseboys, but during the US occupation of Japan, servicemen's wealth relative to the local population allowed them to hire a local boy or man to do chores such as cleaning, polishing shoes, gathering firewood, and washing and ironing clothes. US servicemen continued to employ houseboys in Korea (see Figure 1.2); some literally imported the practice by bringing their houseboys with them from Japan.[32] Houseboys also served as diplomats and brokers between troops and the local civilian population, providing translation or procuring goods and services.

Military mascots also have a long history. American, British, and French military units used a variety of animals as mascots, from Kentucky, a pig mascot from the war of 1812, to Jacob, a goose of the Coldstream Guards. These mascots were thought to bring luck and provided companionship.[33] Drummer boys probably served as the first human mascots; in the United States, the military began using them as mascots during the Civil War.[34] During World War I and II, armies across Europe continued this tradition, housing their mascots and "lavishing" them with clothing, food, and candy. American soldiers in Korea continued to use animal mascots, perhaps

FIGURE 1.2   Bobby Griffin and his houseboy, Butch, in 1953
SOURCE: Courtesy of Bobby Griffin.

most famously Reckless, a horse that performed so well in battle that she was made a sergeant and profiled in the *Saturday Evening Post*. They also took in local boys as mascots, a habit that other UN forces copied as they arrived on the scene.[35]

In Korea, servicemen and the media used the terms *mascot* and *houseboy* interchangeably, but the two categories could be quite distinct. A mascot did the domestic labor of a houseboy, but his role was more symbolic and complex. Servicemen fed, clothed, and even educated mascots, integrating them into their units, into military culture, and into American culture.[36] Pint-sized Sergeant Yo-Yo had "a bed, footlocker, and clothing rack" and stood "inspections with the other members of his unit."[37] Although Koreans used cast-off military items for everything, from clothing to cooking implements, mascots' wearing of child-size army and marine uniforms marked their symbolic importance and their association with the rich and powerful Americans. Men could receive permission to have mascots live in the barracks with them.[38] Robert Mosier, the marine who wrote about mascots for *National Geographic*, had a typical arrangement with his mascot, Kim, saying he "policed our quarters, washed my clothes, and guarded my belongings" in return for "tent space and part of my rations and whatever odd bits of clothing and gear I could scrounge."[39] Kim, like some other mascots, was not an orphan, but he was nonetheless "adopted" by Mosier in the same way that other Korean children with living parents would come to be adopted by Americans. Indeed, Mosier's use of the adoption trope to describe his relationship with Kim is typical of how many men described their relationships with their mascots: "I adopted Kim. Or perhaps it was the other way around. At any rate, we took care of each other."[40]

Off the base, mascots' knowledge of the countryside sometimes had military value. Eleven-year-old Butch Chango saved two Marines' lives when he warned them that enemy soldiers were nearby. When they asked how he knew, he responded, "Because the crickets have stopped chirping over there in the rice field." At that, reported *Stars and Stripes*, "The Marines turned a machinegun on the rice paddy and smoked out a squad of Red Koreans." Former mascot Joseph Anthony's ability to translate from Korean to pidgin English saved lives. Anthony was riding with his company towards a bridge when a Korean man warned them that the communists had wired it with explosives. Anthony interpreted—"Capi-tan, we go back, hubba hubba! This boom!"—quickly enough to save the lives of several men.[41]

Mascots came to their units in a variety of ways. The First Cavalry Division received their seven-year-old mascot as a gift. "A bunch of us guys were sitting around the fire one night when some South Korean walked up with Henry hand in hand and said, 'Presento,'" recalled a corporal. "He just gave him to us." Other servicemen made mascots of children they found on the streets or hanging around the base. Link S. White, a mascot who was adopted by an air force sergeant and emigrated to the United States in 1955, progressed from houseboy to mascot to adopted son in the space of four years. One day, without checking with anyone first, he began sweeping up the mess tent at a nearby base. He returned and worked the next day, and on the third day, he was offered a paying job as a full-time messboy. White eventually developed the emotional bonds with the men around him that allowed him to make the transition—arguably, the promotion—to mascot.

Stars and Stripes was not wrong when it wryly observed that a Korean boy could become a mascot simply by smiling the right way.[42]

Servicemen were buddies or big brothers to their mascots, but the men also acted in a parental capacity. The Nineteenth Quartermaster Company in Taegu made sure that its mascot, eight-year-old Bonzo, "was in bed by 9 p.m. and took regular showers." *Stars and Stripes* published images and carried stories of servicemen doing fatherly things like giving a mascot a bath, teaching him to manage his money, and administering spankings. Two bachelor "dads" even went to a parent-teacher association meeting at a local school to represent their "adopted" son, Mike. Mascots also received punishment within the military structure: Bonzo was demoted from the rank of honorary master sergeant to corporal when he missed reveille.[43] Whether the American GIs assumed the role of big brother or father, these relationships, with their huge differentials of wealth, status, and power, enacted the geopolitical relationship between the two countries the GI and the mascot represented.

The press unfailingly depicted mascots as spunky, pint-sized Horatio Algers—"amiable Oriental orphan[s]" who did not trouble their American benefactors by betraying any traces of the ordeals they might have experienced.[44] They were, in short, the living embodiments of plucky orphan Short Round, the child sidekick in the hit 1951 Korean War film *The Steel Helmet*.[45] They impressed servicemen with their cheekiness and endeared themselves through their hard work, their earnest imitations of their caretakers, and their dogged loyalty to "their" servicemen. When his marines pulled out without him, Butch, the eleven-year-old mascot of the First Marine Band, walked nearly twenty-five miles from Seoul to Inch'ŏn. There, he found an army unit that was moving out by ship and convinced them to take him along. Dressed in a cut-down army uniform, Butch then hopped a train and rode almost one hundred miles through guerrilla country until he found his marines. Servicemen likewise showed dedication to their mascots, but they nonetheless left mascots behind or took them to an orphanage when a unit pulled out or when superiors ordered it. Mascots often ran away from orphanages—one reason social workers frowned on the practice of keeping mascots—and either found a new unit to move in with or returned to life on the streets.[46]

As the distinctly un-Korean name Bonzo suggests, mascots were sometimes thought of as toys or pets. A serviceman explained, "You can re-name these kids without any trouble or money because they don't have birth records." Sambo Pribbenow's would-be adoptive father bragged about the boy's ability to "sketch portraits, juggle, sew, [and] sing." Mascots also entertained GIs by putting on boxing matches. These features of the mascot-serviceman relationship suggest another function of the mascot: emotional object. The mascot provided an object of affection for the servicemen around him. As a toy or pet to be teased, played with, and cared for, he offered a semblance of family and everydayness for servicemen who were far from home, weary, and often miserable. Speculating on the reasons for keeping mascots, *Stars and Stripes* wrote, "Perhaps they serve as symbols of the clean and decent things homesick soldiers have left behind. Perhaps to see these tattered, hungry, sick in heart and body, war waifs regain the healthy, happy radiance which is childhood's birthright, compensates to some extent the soldiers' daily contact with war's senseless waste and drudgery and suffering."[47]

Mascots understood their role as emotional outlets for servicemen. Former Washington State senator Paull H. Shin, who was a mascot from the time he was fifteen until his adoption and emigration to the United States at age eighteen, was frank about the practical and emotional jobs he performed. In addition to his domestic work, he helped servicemen "find some comfort in what was an otherwise difficult situation." When he was still a houseboy, Link White learned about being a mascot from another Korean boy, who informed an astonished White that a mascot "plays and has fun with the G.I.s." White outfitted himself in pint-sized khakis and cap, and set out to practice his new trade. He found that being a mascot was as "fun and easy" as his mascot teacher had described it: "I did a lot of horseplaying with the unit's G.I.s. . . . We wrestled, teased, and even cussed at each other, just for the fun of it." Despite his new position as mascot, and the opportunity to earn money by doing errands for the GIs, White felt insecure, as he did not have a paying job. In this sense, being a mascot was a more tenuous and unstable position than being a houseboy, with the latter's clearly defined tasks, rules, and rewards. By entering into unwritten, uncertain contracts with servicemen, and providing emotional and physical services in exchange for material and other care, mascots operated in the same kind of economy as prostitutes.[48]

The bonds of affection that developed between servicemen and their mascots led to some of the first intercountry adoptions from Korea. Grinning servicemen and their adopted—or soon-to-be-adopted—Korean sons appeared regularly in *Stars and Stripes*. Sergeant Bernard L. Cook began adoption proceedings soon after six-year-old mascot Wild Bill joined the 724th Ordnance Battalion, telling *Stars and Stripes* in 1954 that he would not go home "until I can take Billy with me." These stories described the determination of the adopters and their patience and persistence in navigating the military and immigration bureaucracies.[49] As pioneers, the servicemen had little guidance for how to adopt so they wrote letters to any authority they could think of—the US Immigration and Naturalization Service; the US embassy; their ministers, priests, or members of Congress—for information and advice, which they shared with one another.

Stars and Stripes presented mascot adoptions in ways that foregrounded the boys' metamorphosis from orphans to Americans, an approach picked up by mainstream magazines like *Life*. In the pages of these publications, the children being adopted by servicemen transformed from dirty, hungry, homeless waifs into cheerful, natty fellows—little Americans through and through. Even before their adoptions, mascots appeared in *Stars and Stripes* in ways that underscored how they fit with a distinctive kind of masculine Americanness, signaled by their behavior and dress—almost always a cut-down military uniform or cowboy outfit. *Stars and Stripes* showed So Yong Chong, a six-year-old who was being adopted by Sergeant Raymond L. Hill, taking his turn at the plate during a game of baseball. This photo of a Korean boy, clad in fatigues, suspenders, and a cap, and flanked by similarly dressed white GIs juxtaposed a classic American pastime to a distinctively foreign background. By demonstrating how a mascot like So Yong could cross from one world into another, the image emphasized his suitability for adoption and potential for assimilation into American society.[50]

The description of the actual journey from Korea to the United States served as an analogy for how a mascot made the journey from Korean orphan to American son. Adopted mascots usually traveled on military transport and in military style. Roger set off for his new home in Henderson, Nevada, wearing a T-shirt and jeans, and carrying a duffel bag that matched the one toted by his escort, Corporal Stanley Kaufman. Seven-year-old Ernie Joe, who had been adopted by Sergeant Ravil B. Branham and his wife, Dorothy, was photographed in his traveling clothes: a cut-down army uniform, with *JOE* stenciled over the left side of his chest and his hat cocked over his right eye. *Stars and Stripes* reported that Ernie Joe would be dressed in fatigues from Seoul to Tokyo and then "switch to khakis for the flight to the States." While the new father and son were in Tokyo for processing, Branham had "plans to see Ernie Joe eat some fancy preparations of his favorite American foods—Navy beans, fried eggs and ice cream." Once in the United States, Ernie was slated for a visit to the zoo before starting school.[51]

Media coverage took pains to show how seamlessly these Korean boys traveled from Korea to their new American homes, not just physically but culturally: in their interests, enthusiasms, and easy adaptation to all things American. Five-year-old Jimmy Raynor was described as being "intrigued by coin-operated vending machines" and "an avid reader and swapper of comic books." A photo in *Stars and Stripes* showed Jimmy with Mrs. Raynor in the kitchen of his new South Dakota home, with milk, cookies, and baking supplies spread out on the counter before them. Profoundly domestic scenes like these emphasized the distance that these Korean boys traveled from the poverty and devastation of war-torn Korea to the cleanliness, safety, and modernity of the United States.[52]

Chief Boatswain's Mate Vincent J. Paladino's adoption of Kyung Soo Lee received a considerable amount of attention from both *Stars and Stripes* and mainstream media outlets. Renamed Lee James Paladino, the four-and-a-half-year-old came "home" to New Rochelle, New York, in 1953 (see Figure 1.3). *Stars and Stripes* described Lee as "a first grader, proud possessor of a new bike, and avid follower of television western serials, and the pride and joy of Paladino's parents, grandparents and about 30 uncles, aunts and cousins." Accompanying the article were photographs of a beaming Lee standing on a swing, riding a bicycle with streamers fluttering from the handlebars, and striding down a sidewalk jauntily swinging his schoolbooks. The *New York Times* heralded Lee's arrival with the caption "Future Citizen Arrives," indicating the country's embrace of him and other Korean mascots like him.[53]

Although the children being adopted were presented in highly conventional ways, many of these mascot adoptions were in fact quite unconventional. First, people who were ordinarily not allowed to adopt under American social work criteria—single people and older couples—were adopting. Lee Paladino and Jimmy Raynor were adopted by bachelors and Ernie Joe's adoptive parents were forty-three. Additionally, some servicemen arranged for others in their families to adopt mascots rather than adopting themselves. The Beauchamps adopted Kim, who had been their son's stretcher

FIGURE 1.3 Vincent Paladino's adoption of mascot Kyung Soo Lee (renamed Lee Paladino) received coverage in local and national media.
SOURCE: Corbis Images.

bearer in Korea. When their son died of his injuries, his parents fulfilled his "last wish," that they "bring Kim to the States and give him a home." Lieutenant Robert W. Field's parents adopted ten-year-old Rocky, his company's mascot, and another soldier asked his parents to adopt a seven-year-old mascot who, he said, was like a brother to him.[54]

Problems of Mascot Adoption

Mascots lived with servicemen in a hypermasculine environment, and not all of the young men around them assumed the role of parent or big brother. One GI criticized his fellow servicemen for failing to curb their obscene language around a mascot. Former mascot Link White thought that most American men "were a bunch of sex hounds" and noted that many of the English words he learned had to do with sex. As a result, social workers regarded mascots as having been corrupted by their contact with the military. One described mascots as spoiled by soldiers and "domineering, bullying, boastful and recalcitrant." They had difficulty adjusting to nonmilitary life in the orphanages and "almost without exception gave trouble." He concluded, "From this number came a large part of the juvenile delinquents." Social workers were cautious about placing mascots for adoption, especially the older boys. A social worker with International Social Service (ISS) explained that it was difficult to predict whether a mascot could adjust to "ordinary family life . . . to respond to a 'mother-person,' to attend school and to behave as any American child of that age." She also stated that past placements of mascots had not been encouraging and that the adjustment would only be more difficult in cases of interracial adoption.[55]

The irony for some mascots, then, was that while contact with the US Army presented opportunities for them to be adopted, that very contact made them seem unsuitable for adoption.[56] At the same time, a mascot's long exposure to Americans also made social workers wonder if he might be better off in the United States. Ruefully evaluating one mascot adoption that went wrong, an ISS worker wrote, "It was always felt that there was so little for him in Korea since he had no . . . friends or family there, and had been partly Americanized by his long association with the U.S. Army."[57]

The Americanization that made mascots such strong candidates for assimilation in the United States was also seen as threatening the prospects of those who remained. An observer speculated of one mascot that he "would find his re-assimilation among his own folk difficult."[58] Indeed, the potential negative effects of Americanization complicated the heartwarming nature of mascot stories. An ISS social worker remarked on how seven or eight years of living with American soldiers had Americanized one mascot, as evidenced by his discomfort in a Korean environment, his proficiency in English, and his preference for Western clothing.[59] This boy would be adopted and leave Korea, so his Americanization was to his benefit, but for other mascots, their liminal cultural position suggested problems to come. Six months into the Korean War, a Canadian journalist met a two-and-a-half-year-old mascot—fattened up on army rations, dressed in a corporal's uniform—whom he described as unable to speak intelligibly in either Korean or English. The journalist noted, "Nobody seems to have figured out what's to become of him when the US Army moves out . . . but that's a detail."⁶⁰ His dismissive (or perhaps ironic) attitude about what might happen to a child like this highlighted the uncertainties of mascot life. Mascots might eat and live well while they were associated with the US military, but it was unclear what would happen to them after the military left, when they had neither the protection of their American benefactors nor the support of a Korean family network.

While mascots were presented by the media as sunny Horatio Alger types, they could fall under a darker shadow of suspicion when it came time to examine them as candidates for adoption and emigration. While investigating a nine-year-old mascot, a Korean social worker uncovered some details that he found unsavory. He described the boy as lazy, vain, and using adoption as a means to enter the United States.⁶¹ This attitude was much more widespread among officials when it came to marriages between Korean women and American servicemen, and it is striking that the social worker would describe this child in terms that made him sound more like a prostitute than a little boy. Although only boys became mascots, little girls who were thought to have spent too much time around US servicemen were described in the same language of decay and corruption used to describe their male counterparts.⁶² One three-and-a-half-year-old Korean girl who lived on a military post with her mother was described as having different speech and mannerisms from having been around Americans so much. Pointing to the child's flirtatious behavior, an American social worker said it was obvious that the girl had been spoiled by a large group of men.

Lee Paladino, whose adoption received so much press, briefly served as the mascot of the AKF's national fund-raising campaign in 1954. Less publicized, however, was the failure of his adoption. Five years after his arrival in the United States, Lee was no longer living with his adoptive father but had gone to live with his adoptive grandparents—following an eleven-month stay in foster care—after friction developed between him and his adoptive father's new wife and children. While the reasons for the Paladinos' problems were quite clear, social workers tended to attribute troubled mascot adoptions to the harmful effects of army life on the boys. A mascot adoption that went so far awry as to be described as a "*serious* breakdown" resulted in the adoptive parents putting their Korean son into a children's home after his resentful, withdrawn behavior flared into violence. The boy told an ISS worker that he was unable to "take" the demands of family living. In one extreme case, a twelve-year-old former mascot was shuttled around the United States after his adoptive parents decided they could not accept him. In the end, the boy was returned to Korea, where he was reported to be living in another army camp.[63]

Breakdowns like these confirmed the fears of those who worried that intercountry and mascot adoptions were too risky to allow on a regular basis. Social workers in Korea and the United States tended to discourage them, suggesting alternatives like sponsorship. As early as 1951, soldiers received warnings from the military authorities against becoming too fond of their mascots since US immigration law would prevent the entry of even legally adopted Korean children. By the mid-1950s, when mascot adoptions no longer dominated adoptions from Korea, it seemed as though they would cease altogether, since the US military was moving toward prohibiting the practice of keeping mascots at all.[64]

Besides mascots, servicemen also adopted full-Korean girls and GI babies of both sexes. Adoptions in which a serviceman selected and adopted a child while he was stationed overseas were quite popular for reasons having to do with the nature of military life. Military couples did not stay in one American home for long enough to go through the long process of adopting, and in any case, all prospective adoptive parents faced the same shortage of children domestically. Servicemen sometimes went to Korea charged with the task of finding a child to adopt—for their own families, and sometimes for their relatives and friends.[65] Army policy discouraged wives from accompanying their husbands to Korea, so finding a child to adopt was usually the man's job. Men wrote to their wives from Korea and proposed a certain child, usually enclosing a snapshot or two.[66] Since servicemen were physically in Korea, it was fairly easy for them to gain custody of the child they wanted to adopt and then bring him or her to the United States.[67] The displacement of a traditionally female job on to the most masculine of men—a man in the service—altered the conventional gender dynamics around adoption, which usually figures the procedure as one initiated by a woman and processed by a female social worker.[68]

ISS tried to discourage these "split home" adoptions, raising concerns about the fact that the adoptive mothers had not met these children. Often, however, their efforts proved to be moot, since in the midst of arranging for home studies and other paperwork, they would receive word that the adoption had been completed. The information that servicemen shared with one another about intercountry adoption procedures sometimes made them more knowledgeable than the social agencies and therefore more adept at getting their adoptions processed. In such cases, ISS and the state welfare departments could do nothing more but impotently offer assistance after the fact.

Missionaries and NGOs

American missionaries and churches were vital to the development of intercountry adoption. Having played an important role in Korea's development since their arrival in the late nineteenth century, they had long functioned as "producers of knowledge" about Korea for ordinary Americans and government officials alike.[69] In the context of the Cold War, missionary internationalism that emphasized intimate, person-to-person contact served broader US interests too, by promoting American values in geopolitically important countries like South Korea. Thus, missionaries functioned as two-way conduits for the material goods, cultural knowledge, and sentimental ties that helped create the imaginative bridges linking Americans and Koreans, which in turn allowed for an expanded definition of family that included Korean children.

Christian missionary groups cooperated with international relief organizations to provide aid after the Korean War. With so many families torn apart by the war, Koreans could no longer rely on their extended families, which had historically provided what amounted to social welfare. Nor could the South Korean government offer any help, for it was itself heavily dependent on foreign aid throughout the 1950s.[70] The US military, missionaries, and NGOs cooperated to gather and channel relief supplies and money to various needy groups: widows, wounded veterans, amputees, lepers, the destitute elderly, and, of course, children. The missionary groups most active in child welfare included the Seventh-Day Adventists, Catholic War Relief Services, and Church World Service, which represented the major Protestant denominations. Besides missionaries, a vast and complicated network of NGOs assisted Korean orphans as part of their broader rehabilitation and relief efforts. These organizations included various organs of the United Nations, as well as CARE, American Relief for Korea, and the elite AKF.[71] Umbrella organizations such as the Korea Association of Voluntary Agencies and the Joint ROK/KCAC/UNKRA Committee for Child Welfare added to the alphabet soup.

Child relief activities did not necessarily mean participation in intercountry adoption. The Mennonite Central Committee in Korea operated vocational schools and orphanages, Church World Service provided food and material aid to childcare institutions, and the Methodist Committee for Overseas Relief's Korea mission operated a number of orphanages around Korea—but none of these organizations arranged adoptions. The Presbyterian mission stopped operating orphanages soon after the Korean War but continued to support several dozen that identified as Presbyterian, and most Presbyterian missionaries in Korea were involved with local orphanages as part of their day-to-day activities. As the two largest denominations in Korea, both the Presbyterian and Methodist churches were also influential in the establishment and development of Korean adoption in more indirect—but no less important—ways: the medical and educational training they had provided throughout the twentieth century prepared Korean doctors, nurses, social workers, clergy, and others active in child welfare and social work.[72]

Nonsectarian Christian organizations such as World Vision, Save the Children Federation, Foster Parents' Plan, and Christian Children's Fund established sponsorship programs through which Americans could "adopt" Korean orphans. Their advertisements featured photographs or line drawings of emaciated Korean children and carried ominous headlines like, "*You could have saved this little girl!*" These organizations put the onus to help directly on American Christians: "For these children there is only the hope that kindly Americans will send aid to them." A sponsor took on the financial responsibility of a child for several dollars a month. The child corresponded with his or her sponsor, and the latter received photos and reports on the child from the director of the orphanage.[73] The American-Asian family created by this sponsorship was an important site for establishing affective ties, which were critical to the US government's garnering public support for its anticommunist activity in Asia.[74]

Missionaries in Asia—especially missionary women—functioned as "cultural bridges" between American Christians and the rest of the world, putting "a human face on foreign peoples and cultures." Through Korea missionaries, ordinary Americans became acquainted with Korea and the idea of adopting from Korea. Their vivid, pathos-filled accounts of how God transformed the lives of hungry orphans and hopeless widows appeared in letters to their friends and family, in their reports to their denominational or organizational offices, in pamphlets that churchgoers or Sunday-school groups could buy for a dollar or two, or in their denominational newsletters or magazines. Korea missionaries also educated Americans about Korea through radio broadcasts. The Nobel Prize–winning novelist Pearl S. Buck, a child of China missionaries, moved beyond church boundaries to write for the general public. Through her fiction, nonfiction, and advocacy, she sought to nurture cross-cultural understanding, and she was widely regarded as an authoritative interpreter of Asia for Americans. Buck also championed the cause of mixed-race children in Asia and established an adoption agency of her own.[75]

Missionary women, and quasi missionaries like Buck, functioned especially effectively as "conduits of information about women and children." All Korea missionaries, male and female, came in contact with widows and orphans, but caring for them was still considered woman's work. This belief dovetailed with mainline churches' view of mission work as "the preeminent 'woman's cause.'" Churchwomen in the United States embraced this view, and they worked for their cause by collecting money and relief goods, as well as participating in traditionally domestic undertakings such as knitting afghans and mittens to send to Korea.[76]

Missionaries also created Korea for Americans through their trips home, when they visited their home churches and other churches around the United States. In their presentations, they made their mission fields come alive in the imaginations of ordinary American churchgoers:

> No churchgoer born before 1960 can forget the childhood thrill of hearing a missionary speak in church. The missionary arrived in native dress to thank the congregation for its support and . . . showed slides in the church hall. The audience sat transfixed, imagining what it might be like to eat termites in Africa, or beg on the streets in India, or study the Bible in a refugee camp. The usually mundane Sunday service became exotic and exciting, as the world beyond the United States suddenly seemed real. In an age before round-the-clock television news, and the immigration of Asians and Latin Americans even to small towns in the Midwest, the missionary on furlough was a major link between the world of North American Christians and the rest of the globe.[77]

After a missionary's visit, a church might follow up by collecting donations or by deciding to support an orphanage. Members of the congregation also sponsored individual children, which created important psychological and material connections. The letters and photos that passed between the Korean child and his or her "parents" in America created a deeply felt emotional bond; once these relationships had been established, adoption was a short step. If they did not adopt a child they already sponsored, a couple might ask their church's missionary to find a child for them to adopt. In other cases, individual missionaries would seek adoptive parents for specific children they knew.[78]

For their part, Korean Christians had long been aware of their connections to American Christians, and they appealed to their common bonds of religion and love of liberty to gain American support for causes ranging from Korean independence from Japanese occupation to post–Korean War reconstruction.[79] During a 1953 visit to Korea, an American member of the Presbyterian Church's Division of Foreign Ministries had a particularly moving encounter with a Korean Christian. "He began by expressing appreciation for the Christian missionaries. He asked me to carry back Korea's gratitude to the Christians in America. He urged me to tell you what it meant to have Christian missionaries share Korea's suffering."[80] The ROK government newspaper, *Korean Republic*, tirelessly showcased South Korea's Christianity alongside its anticommunism and pro-Americanism. Both the ROK government and Koreans—in Korea and overseas—conscientiously referred to their President's devout Christian faith.

Organized Christianity was central to shaping the connections between Korean emigrants and Americans. Because of restrictions imposed by the Japanese colonial government and US immigration law, Koreans emigrated in limited numbers during the early twentieth century. With the aid and encouragement of American missionaries, roughly 7,500 Koreans left to work on Hawaiian sugar plantations between 1903 and 1905; some remigrated from Hawaii to the mainland United States. One thousand Korean women entered the United States as picture brides until they were stopped by the anti-Asian provisions of the 1924 Johnson-Reed Immigration Act. Finally, two thousand students and intellectuals sought refuge in the United States as political exiles during the period of Japanese occupation.[81] Because of American missionaries' role in facilitating emigration, the Koreans who migrated to the United States were disproportionately Christian (mainly Protestant), and a small but significant number were educated and from the upper classes.[82] Thus, the few Koreans that Americans encountered in the United States were likely to be Christian and quite educated, even if economic and social conditions forced them to work as unskilled laborers. After the Korean War, the hundreds of Korean students who studied in the United States each year often did so with the support of a church or church-related organization. At Christmastime in 1953, the *Korean Republic* featured a front-page photo of a Korean family receiving a sewing machine, sent by the women of a church in Louisville, Kentucky, after they learned of the family's need from their daughter, a student at University of Louisville.[83] With hundreds of students going abroad each year, mainly to the United States, these kinds of person-to-person interactions offered opportunities to strengthen the connections between Koreans and Americans, particularly within church circles.[84]

Conclusion

Many people believe that Korean adoption began when Harry and Bertha Holt, a farming couple from Oregon, launched the Holt Adoption Program in 1956, but the practice originated earlier, in the efforts of American missionaries and GIs to rescue the children of Korea during the Korean War. The servicemen who adopted mascots pioneered intercountry adoption, paving the way for the thousands of adoptions that would occur in the years to come. These early adoptions were crucial to the development of Korean adoption on two levels. Practically speaking, as social workers and government agencies learned to regulate and process these early adoptions, they lay the procedural groundwork for the systematization of intercountry adoption from Korea. Because US immigration law still barred most Asians, members of Congress often had to pass private bills allowing the entry of these children. Lawmakers' familiarity with Korean adoption would prove useful to Congress' efforts to craft permanent orphan legislation throughout the 1950s.

At the ideological level, GIs' child welfare efforts served an important political function for the US military and the country it represented, which sought to justify, mitigate, and positively project its role in Korea and in the new world of the Cold War. GI humanitarianism wordlessly refuted charges of US imperialism while modeling for Americans at home the ways in which individuals could participate in fostering international goodwill. Missionaries, who had promoted US-Korean friendship and understanding throughout the twentieth century, were instrumental in cultivating in Americans a sense of responsibility for the people of Korea, especially its children. Americans' sense of responsibility for Korea, Koreans, and particularly for mixed-race Korean GI babies would be a key component of the Christian Americanist adoption movement that emerged in the mid-1950s, which would in its turn be a force in the development and institutionalization of Korean adoption.

TWO

Solving the GI Baby Problem

> I do not know a more piteous sight than to see a half-American child wandering the streets of Asia, orphaned because no one wants him, because no one knows what to do with him.... More than half of them die before they are five years old, for only the strong and intelligent can survive the cruel circumstances of their life. But those who survive are superb. I appeal to you, America! These are the children of our sons.
>
> —Pearl S. Buck[1]

From the moment that Koreans and Americans perceived a GI baby problem, virtually all proposed solutions entailed removing the children from Korea. Once it became clear that Americans were eager to take these children, the Korean government focused almost exclusively on building an intercountry adoption program.[2] At the same time, the US Congress passed the 1953 Refugee Relief Act, which provided a vital, unprecedented opening for the immigration of adopted Korean children.

Together with its allies in the US government and various missionaries and voluntary agencies in Korea, Syngman Rhee's government sought to surmount the enormous bureaucratic obstacles that stood in the way of Americans who wanted to adopt Korean GI babies. The intergovernmental cooperation between Korea and the United States reveals that the endeavor to send GI babies overseas for adoption was not just a manifestation of American people-to-people humanitarianism but a state project too. Critics of intercountry adoption, then and now, claimed that the practice constituted virtually the whole of the Korean government's child welfare policy; at the beginning at least, intercountry adoption was meant to be an extraordinary, temporary measure to cope with an emergency.

"Even If We Have to Drop Them in the Pacific"

Historians have noted the correspondence between foreign troop presence and a rise in prostitution and the birth of illegitimate children.[3] This has been a major feature of the US presence in Korea since the end of World War II. During the period of US occupation (1945–1948) camptowns, or *kijich'on*, quickly sprang up around American military bases throughout South Korea. The system of US-oriented prostitution was built on the foundations established by the Japanese colonial government (1910–1945). Although prostitution was officially outlawed, the US military government accepted it, and the Korean government saw the sex and entertainment industries of the camptowns as a way to maintain good US-Korea relations and earn foreign currency. As in US-occupied Japan, camptowns were meant to serve as a buffer between American servicemen and decent Korean women. In fact, Madame Rhee claimed that the government had had to establish camptowns because the foreign military men kept "taking" any woman they wanted. Rape of local women by UN forces was largely undocumented but widespread enough to prompt complaints from South Korean officials.[4]

A convergence of conditions "mass-produced" prostitutes: the poverty, desperation, and relative lack of gainful employment for young Korean women in the years after the war; the decimation of the male breadwinning population; the lucrative nature of sex work relative to other forms of employment; and the wealth of virtually any American in comparison to the average Korean. Women gravitated to US military installations hoping to find a respectable job working in the kitchens, dining facilities, post exchanges, or offices. However, the job seekers far outnumbered the jobs available, and obtaining them required language skills or personal connections. Many women had few options other than questionable employment in tearooms, restaurants, and bars, where a thin line separated the hostess and the sex worker. Other women were seduced through false promises, or raped. Widows often resorted to sex work to support their children. In 1952, the US State Department reported that 2,658 "UN Aunties"—one of many terms used to describe prostitutes who served foreigners—had been arrested in a five-month period in Seoul alone; of this number, half were widows.[5]

Meanwhile, US military policy ensured a continuous customer base for prostitution. Because of the ongoing technical state of war with North Korea—the July 1953 armistice did not actually end the Korean War—South Korea was designated a battle zone. Rotations were short, lasting about a year, and considered "hardship tours." The military sent young single men there and discouraged those who did have wives and dependents from bringing them. Approximately six million American soldiers served in Korea between 1950 and 1971, and up to one million Korean women provided sex for them in the camptowns.[6]

Ambiguities within the Korean system of prostitution complicated how Korean women and foreign servicemen understood their relationships. Prostitution could entail anything from a brief transaction to a long-term living arrangement, in which a man financially supported a woman in exchange for monogamous service for the duration of his stay in Korea.[7] The latter scenario blurred the line between prostitution and a romantic relationship, since the couple often referred to each other as boyfriend or girlfriend, or even husband and wife. In these situations, children could be born to parents who held different understandings of what the birth represented and what expectations and obligations would result.

Women who became pregnant and kept their babies did so for a number of reasons. Both Koreans and Americans assumed that women who bore mixed-race children, especially those known to be prostitutes, did so to use them "as a lever" to press the naive fathers into marriage. A Presbyterian missionary expressed a common skepticism about military brides: "There are very few American service men marrying Korean women who are not prostitutes."[8] However, many women claimed they had kept their pregnancies because the birth fathers had promised marriage; there is no way to know how many of these cases there were. Not all of the mixed-race children were the product of sex work or rape. Stories of tragic love affairs and thwarted marriages also abounded. Sometimes couples were separated by commanding officers, who acted out of their own prejudices or in line with US military policy that discouraged such marriages. Sometimes a couple was married in the Korean tradition, but the marriage was not recognized by US law and could not be considered a basis for the woman's emigration. Other times, a man divorced his Korean wife after he returned to the United States; sometimes women were not notified of the divorce and were left waiting with their children, unable to remarry or move on with their lives. Other times the men left, promising to return for their girlfriends and children, and were simply never heard from again.[9]

GI babies bore the heavy burden of a triple stigma: they were mixed race, they were fatherless, and Koreans and Americans alike assumed that their mothers were prostitutes. Without a father, a GI baby could not be entered into a *hojuk* (family register), which was the Korean equivalent of a birth certificate. A family register identified a male as the head of the family, with all other members listed in relationship to him. Although an illegitimate child of full-Korean parentage could be secretly added to a family register, obvious physical differences made this impossible for GI babies. Unregistered, a GI baby did not have Korean citizenship. Unrecognized by her father, she did not have US citizenship. Legally stateless, she was socially a nonperson who would find it extremely difficult to attend school, find work, or get married.[10]

Koreans labeled GI babies as *t'wigi* (an extremely offensive term meaning "hybrid" but used derogatorily to mean "half-breed" or "half-blood") or the more neutral *honhyŏl* (mixed blood), and considered them completely alien. A long-standing emphasis on racial purity justified open discrimination against GI babies, whose distinctive physical appearance made them stand out. The United Presbyterian Mission of Korea noted that "Korean society massively rejects the mixed-blood" and that they faced "*a radically impossible situation.*" Virtually every observer of the orphan situation echoed this dramatic assessment. Children and adults alike stoned, chased, beat, and otherwise persecuted mixed-race children. President Rhee acknowledged the ostracism awaiting these children, stating that they "will never have any real place in Korean society."[11]

Mothers hid GI babies for as long as possible. The international social work agency International Social Service (ISS) reported that mothers "made pathetic attempts to disguise the identity of their children by dyeing their hair and eyelashes black, or keeping the hair always covered up." Despite the hardship of concealment, a mother often kept her child with her in the hope that the father would marry her and take them both to the United States. Only when all hope was gone would she abandon the child. GI babies were found in every place conceivable—at missions, churches, and orphanages, "in train stations, shops . . . public toilets, the market place, [and] on doorsteps." In the most desperate cases, the babies were left to die in garbage dumps or on mountainsides, or worse: "some little blonde-haired babies were washed up on the seashore."[12]

Estimates of the number of Korean GI babies ranged widely, although their symbolic importance far outweighed their actual numbers. ISS noted various figures between 300 and 5,000 while the US Embassy felt "confident that there are 1,500 of them." The Korean Ministry of Health and Social Affairs (MHSA) estimated in 1954 that there were more than four hundred mixed-race Korean children, with approximately three hundred more born each year—a figure far lower than the eighty per week reported to the Navy Chaplain Corps. Even five years after the end of the war, the MHSA stated that it had "no reliable figure on legitimate births much less illegitimate births." As the widely varying estimates of the GI baby population suggest, the fear that Korea might be overrun with "half-caste" or "half-breed" children loomed large. "Missionaries who work up near the 38th Parallel where there are stationed many foreign servicemen describe the woods as being full of girls with such children," reported an ISS worker. President Rhee was said to be "under the impression that the orphanages are full to overflowing with these mixed-blood children."[13]

The "GI baby problem" actually comprised two tightly interlinked issues. GI babies' racial mixture made them a problem for a country ideologically invested in an image of itself as racially pure. At the same time, the GI baby suffered discrimination and hardship because of her racial mixture, illegitimacy, and low status. The "GI baby problem," then, referred to the problem the GI baby posed for Korea, and the problems in store for her if she remained in a country that did not want her. Supporters of adoption and emigration often spoke to the latter dimension of the problem, framing their arguments in terms of sparing these children the difficulties they would face in Korea. However, the record reflects that these advocates, and the Korean government itself, were far more interested in the first dimension of the problem: the challenge the GI baby posed to a Korea that imagined itself as racially homogeneous.

The solution to the problem seemed obvious to many Koreans and Americans: remove the children from Korea. A well-informed American observer confirmed the interest in such a plan, stating that "well educated, thoughtful, influential Koreans"—including President Rhee and his wife—considered it a top priority to send as many mixed-race children to the United States as possible.[14] The only question was how. A partial answer came from Congress in the form of the 1953 Refugee Relief Act (RRA), which provided four thousand visas for refugee orphans adopted by US citizens, and therefore put into place a key component of an imagined Korea-US adoption system.

Americans amply demonstrated their desire to adopt Korean children, sending requests for orphans to media outlets, members of Congress, President and Mrs. Eisenhower, President Rhee, the Child Welfare League of America, the US Children's Bureau, the Christian Children's Fund, and adoption agencies like Welcome House, which the writer Pearl S. Buck had established to serve mixed-race Asian children. In July 1953 US radio reports about aid for Korea led to approximately one hundred requests from Americans interested in adopting Korean children. That December, media coverage of George and Grace Rue's Seoul Sanitarium and Hospital Orphanage, a Seventh-Day Adventist institution, noted that the Rues were seeking homes for fifty "Korean-American war babies." In response, the Rues received 608 requests from would-be parents.[15]

The Rues had in fact facilitated the first nonmilitary adoption from Korea, when Irene Robson, the director of nurses at the hospital, adopted Patricia Lea, a Korean-white girl whom Robson had cared for from the time the child was five days old. Robson brought Patricia Lea back to the United States in July 1953, the same month the Korean War ended. As director of the Seoul Sanitarium orphanage, Grace Rue helped to process Patricia Lea's adoption, and would go on to arrange overseas adoptions for many more children in the hospital. However, she made it clear that she did not intend to operate an adoption agency, and she became involved in the adoption work of other organizations in Korea only because they requested her help. Rue's adoption activities would always be a matter of expediency, and remained secondary to the work running the hospital.[16]

Koreans and Americans alike argued for the removal of GI babies on the assumption that their racial mixture and physical difference would make it impossible for them to fit into Korean society, which conceived of itself as racially homogeneous. Korean ethnic nationalism based on a belief in a common prehistoric origin and bloodline had existed since before the Korean War. This understanding of Koreanness conflated the categories of race, ethnicity, and nation; even when they were treated as separate, they were self-reinforcing: the Korean term *minjok*, for example, means "nation," but can also be used for "ethnicity" and "race." As the first president of the newly liberated Republic of Korea, Syngman Rhee promoted *ilmin juui* (one peopleism) as state policy. This form of nationalism conceived of Korea as a natural entity "characterized by shared bloodline and ancestry." Rhee, who was rabidly anticommunist and pro-reunification, appealed to *ilmin juui* primarily to argue in favor of a "unitary Korean nation . . . that should be occupied by one united people." His successor, Park Chung Hee, used the same racially rooted nationalist language, proclaiming that, despite the division of the country, "We are one entity with a common destiny, bound by one language, and by one history and by the same racial origin."[17]

This brand of nationalism had clear implications for GI babies: they had no place in the homogeneous Korean nation. Rhee's government expressed its desire to send GI babies abroad in benevolent language, stating, "We . . . want to help in any way we can." In private, however, Rhee was less compassionate. ISS social worker Margaret Valk reported, "There is anxiety to get the children out of the country by any means and the President . . . is said to have stated at a Cabinet Meeting that he did not care what happened so long as the children were got out of the country—and quickly. [Mrs. Rhee], an Austrian by birth, is apparently of like mind." Pearl Buck quoted President Rhee as saying that he "wanted the Korean-white children removed 'even if we have to drop them in the Pacific Ocean.'" The Korean public too seems to have welcomed the adoption of mixed-race children by Americans. Since GI babies were not accepted as part of the Korean population, the "general feeling" was that the "children should be given a chance elsewhere" and that Koreans were "pleased to have their beggar and unwanted children adopted."[18]

Korea's ambassador to the United Nations framed these adoptions in terms of US-Korean friendship, stating that they "would constitute a fine humanitarian gesture by the American people towards Korea and would further enhance the already deep friendship which the Korean people felt toward the United States." The Catholic Committee for Refugees and ISS were more candid when they described the adoptions as being "entirely consistent" with Korea's "welfare and reconstruction." Since most of the children being sent overseas would no longer need to receive institutional care and assistance, their emigration would benefit the Korean economy.[19]

The Rhee government tried to streamline adoption and emigration procedures in anticipation of a possible intercountry adoption program. Even before the Korean War ended, the MHSA began working with the UN Korea Reconstruction Agency (UNKRA) to establish procedures for the release, adoption, and emigration of Korean children, and the government set out to craft new law that would permit intercountry adoption.[20] It drafted the Special Orphan Adoption Act to permit foreign adoptions and tried to bring it before the National Assembly seven times in six years. However, interparty conflict prevented the bill from ever being seriously discussed, let alone signed into law.[21] Instability, factionalism, and corruption within Rhee's own Liberal Party also hampered the process of legislating any real change in postwar Korea. Rhee was so preoccupied with the goal of reunifying North and South Korea that reconstruction and development received little attention. Needless to say, the question of what to do about mixed-race GI babies remained mostly unaddressed.[22]

Unable to pass a law permitting intercountry adoption, the Rhee government facilitated the adoption of GI babies and war orphans through administrative means. Intercountry adoption was so novel a concept that the government and Supreme Court had to reach back to laws promulgated in 1898 and 1912 as a starting point for addressing the question of whether foreigners could adopt Korean children. By 1954, the Korean courts established an "official interpretation" that "aliens . . . can legally adopt Korean nationals," and had approved many adoptions.[23] In addition, the Korean government implemented a "Basic Policy for Endorcement [sic] of Emmigration [sic] to the United States."[24]

For its part, the US government's representatives in Korea cooperated as fully as possible with the Rhee government to facilitate intercountry adoption. The US embassy stated that it attached "importance to the GI baby problem for political reasons, and is attempting to get as many of them as possible removed from Korea." The coordinator for the State Department's Far East Refugee Relief Program pledged to broadly interpret the RRA to ensure that applicants from the area would receive a "reasonable proportion of visas." US embassy staff cooperated with adoption agencies to file paperwork ahead of application deadlines. In December 1955, the embassy hired an ISS social worker to help in the effort to match children with adoptive parents as quickly as possible and to process the maximum number of Korean children for entry to the United States.[25]

The Korean government's most important move in support of intercountry adoption was its creation of a quasi-governmental adoption agency, Child Placement Service (CPS), in 1954. CPS was financed by the American-Korean Foundation, which partly supervised the new agency along with all of the major agencies in Korea that were involved in intercountry adoption. The MHSA provided a token grant of about US$60 in 1955 and $400 in 1956, and the Church World Service and National Catholic Welfare Conference contributed $500 each. The new agency operated on a shoestring budget out of two "cold and draughty" offices at the MHSA, where the telephones were so unreliable that the staff went to an office two blocks away to place important calls. Lacking even the funds to pay for postage for correspondence with potential adoptive parents in the United States, CPS's staff of four did virtually everything to operate Korea's nascent intercountry adoption program.[26] They interviewed birth mothers and children, made arrangements for the children's care, prepared the necessary Korean and US government documents, checked on the children at the orphanages, and escorted children to the hospital for their medical examinations.

The director of CPS was Oak Soon Hong (see Figure 2.1), a nurse who had trained at Severance Hospital, the well-known Methodist institution in Seoul. Despite her medical training, she had no social work qualifications or experience. Nonetheless, Hong proved invaluable to launching Korean adoption: she was an extremely hard worker, quick to learn the practical aspects of running an adoption program, and gentle and loving toward the children and their birth mothers. Harry Holt called her an "angel." Hong was so dedicated that she often took orphaned children to her own home—where she had five children of her own—when it was more expedient than taking them to an orphanage.[27] She was also one of only two CPS staffers who spoke English.

Although CPS's establishment was widely understood as a positive step forward, ISS worker Margaret Valk expressed cynicism, feeling that it was a temporary fix for a problem that required more substantive attention. A meeting with the MHSA reinforced her sense that the Korean government did not plan to look further than intercountry adoption in its search for solutions for GI babies, an impression seconded by representatives from US governmental and nongovernmental agencies alike. Valk felt that the MHSA was "relying upon international aid to solve this particular problem."[28]

Solving the GI Baby Problem 57

FIGURE 2.1 An early flight of children (possibly 1954) adopted through Child Placement Service. Oak Soon Hong, CPS's first director, is in the back row, second from left.
SOURCE: Courtesy of Social Welfare Society.

Orphans and Orphanages

Just as the number of GI babies was hard to pin down, the size of the overall population of institutionalized and homeless children was similarly difficult to accurately gauge. UNKRA estimated that approximately 317 facilities housed 38,700 children when the Korean War ended in 1953, and the MHSA believed that a total of 50,000 children needed "help of some kind very badly," even if not all of them were actually orphans.[29] Orphanages mushroomed after the Korean War. By 1955, an estimated five hundred orphanages housed approximately fifty-three thousand children, more than double the comparable figures when the war began; the number of orphanages would remain above five hundred until well into the 1970s.[30] Foreign missionaries had historically built and operated orphanages in Korea. They and voluntary agencies continued to finance and support these institutions after the war. Indigenous orphanages also became established during the war: a Korean minister or layperson would shelter and feed a small group of homeless children, sometimes in his or her own house. This small operation would eventually become a formal child-care institution, linked to the network of aid and mission groups and sponsorship agencies that kept these orphanages going. Many indigenous orphanages bore the imprint of foreign influence: the building might have been constructed by American servicemen or the orphanage director educated in mission schools. For example, the Choong Hyun Babies' Home in Seoul was owned and managed by a Korean director and staffed by Koreans, but donations

FIGURE 2.2 Korean orphanages were a key source of aid for families and children after the Korean War. Servicemen regularly visited orphanages to play with the children and distribute relief goods. This photo was taken by Colonel Alexander J. MacNab while he was serving in Korea.
SOURCE: From collection of Col. Alexander J. MacNab.

from American servicemen had funded the building, and CCF supported the orphanage.[31]

The sheer number of orphanages made an indelible impression on American visitors, and the conditions they found in them elicited unanimously horrified reactions. Many housed several hundred children and were staffed by workers who were inadequate in both numbers and training.[32] Even those with extensive experience in Asia were shocked, lamenting the apathetic, malnourished children and the "dirty and unsanitary[,] . . . dark, cold and cheerless" conditions.[33] After a weeklong trip to Korea in March 1953, Howard Rusk of the American-Korean Foundation remarked on the deprivation of the orphanages: "It is doubtful if 50 . . . are giving a quality of care that would be comparable to the lowest standards tolerated in the United States."[34] At an orphanage in Kunsan, CCF's field supervisor William Asbury counted "120 children . . . jammed into two rooms with a total floor space of not more than 400 square feet."[35] The situation was not much better three years later, when ISS worker Margaret Valk characterized the typical Korean orphanage as crowded and lacking adequate heat and water:

> [The orphanage consists] of a number of small rooms in each of which a large number of children sleep, sit, eat and play. There are often no beds, no tables, no chairs, the children sleep close for warmth. Their diet is rice and vegetables . . . twice a day or three times if lucky, supplemented by powdered milk distributed by the foreign relief agencies. A room full of small children may be supervised by a ten or twelve year old girl, a room full of babies in wooden boxes by an untrained woman or teenager.

She concluded, "Children come and go; they die."[36]

These woeful institutions comprised the sum total of Korean child welfare. An orphanage could look to the Korean government for only a ration of rice for each child. For the rest, it relied on what it could produce itself, voluntary support from US Army units, US government agencies, and voluntary agencies. This degree of dependence made observers like Valk worry "what on earth will happen when all foreign aid is withdrawn." The task of overseeing the overcrowded and underequipped orphanages fell to the MHSA, which was itself described as "a pitiful handful of mostly untrained people . . . trying to run a national organization." Then again, the sheer scale of the social welfare problems under the ministry's mandate would have overwhelmed even the most sophisticated government body: "The size and complexity of the Ministry's problems," reported CCF's Asbury, were "almost beyond description." Three years after the war had ended, the ministry had not made much headway: "there is no general child welfare program and [its] budget . . . is totally inadequate for coping with all its many other problems such as tuberculosis treatment and control, venereal disease and leprosy."[37]

It is true that the Korean government was constrained by the massive economic, political, and social challenges of postwar reconstruction, but it is also true that it did not consider social welfare a high priority. There was a sense within the Korean government and population that social work was the domain of "western Christians or millionaires" and that social problems—such as the family breakdown that created orphans—could not be corrected through policy.[38] Most of the government budget went to the military, with only a small portion allocated to other areas, including health and welfare.[39] CCF's Asbury saw this inattention to social welfare as historically rooted and systemic: "the Korean government has no history of child welfare, no adequate legislation and an insufficient understanding of social responsibility."[40] Having witnessed the outpouring of relief aid during and after the Korean War, the Rhee administration continued to rely on foreign agencies and individuals to take care of the country's social welfare needs.[41] From 1953 to 1956, foreign relief aid constituted the entirety of the Korean government's spending on social welfare, and the majority of social welfare spending for the rest of the decade.[42]

Given the relatively large sums of money that were available from voluntary organizations and missionaries, it is unsurprising that some orphanage directors sought to turn their institutions into profit-making businesses. Aid programs that provided a certain amount of money or goods per child inadvertently presented incentives for orphanages to keep a maximum number of children on the rolls. Directors padded their figures with so-called ghost children who lived nearby and could be summoned for head counts. Sometimes they refused to release children for adoption. In one case, ISS Korea stated, "We had a devil of a time prying this child away from the orphanage. . . . The director wanted to continue to receive a check from World Vision and a bribe from ISS so that he would not try to block the adoption." The relative lack of policing of how relief supplies were used allowed some orphanage directors to profit from corrupt practices such as pocketing funds meant for their institutions, selling donated food and clothing on the black market, and hiring children out for domestic work.⁴³

The more crooked orphanage directors specifically targeted American servicemen for donations. A Presbyterian missionary described how directors sought to "brazenly" exploit GIs by posting "innumerable big signs and arrows pointing out orphanages" along roads that they often used.⁴⁴ The GIs proved to be easy marks:

> [Orphanage directors] discovered that American soldiers, hardened fighting men, trained to kill . . . were moved to tears at the sight of orphans. They would give five and ten dollar bills to anyone claiming to be a Presbyterian minister, who had a group of pitiful, ragged, under-nourished, dirty, scabby little children—the dirtier, raggeder, hungrier, scabbier the better, for the purposes of obtaining bank notes. Once this discovery was made, it was only a question of how many different American Army Chaplains or units could be contacted.⁴⁵

A social worker condemned the spectacle that some orphanages made of children, especially those of mixed race: "it is a crime the way that orphanage superintendents in Korea want mixed blood children in their orphanages, then push them to the front for sightseers to see, and feel sorry for."⁴⁶

Missionaries also criticized the orphanage directors who targeted generous Christians in the United States. Although they praised CCF and World Vision for making "a systematic and honest effort to see that a genuine Christian life is maintained" in the orphanages they sponsored, other orphanages and their directors were not so upstanding. Unscrupulous sponsorship agencies and orphanages falsely claimed to be Christians, or members of specific Christian denominations, in the course of their fund-raising efforts. A Presbyterian missionary described these appeals with a jaundiced eye:

> The most completely unreliable orphanages are those which write begging letters directly to donors in the United States. These all run a common pattern, in charmingly ungrammatical English they (1) thank God in most pious language, for kind-hearted people in the United States; (2) describe the pain and humiliation they feel in writing a letter like this; (3) resolutely ignoring this pain, they make an expert touch for money; (4) pictures are usually included.⁴⁷

Some of these institutions, it turned out, "existed only on paper."⁴⁸

By 1959, oversight of orphanages had increased, as indicated by reports that a number of orphanage directors had been sentenced to jail for misdeeds such as forgery and selling relief supplies. That fall, the Korea Church World Service and other agencies refused to provide material aid to a number of orphanages in Korea that did not meet minimum standards and were found to be exploiting children. At the same time, an investigation by the US Army chief of chaplains into the orphanages at the demilitarized zone resulted in the closure of some and orders to improve for the others.[49] Still, as the number of orphanages continued to grow, questionable practices persisted.

Parents in dire straits in the United States and elsewhere have historically used orphanages as temporary or long-term child-care facilities. During and after the war, Korean parents temporarily placed their children in orphanages so they could receive food and shelter. Although parents would describe the child as available for placement to gain her admission, they would sometimes return for her when adoption became imminent. For some parents, of course, placing their children in an orphanage was effectively a permanent act. Many of the roughly half a million war widows entrusted their children to orphanages knowing that they would probably never be able to retrieve them. In keeping with Confucian tradition, widows in Korea did not remarry, and single mothers without extended family support were unlikely to achieve the financial stability that would enable them to keep their children with them.[50]

The growth of child sponsorship programs gave Korean parents even more reason to board their children in orphanages, since living at home would disqualify the children. This practice further complicated the process of determining the orphan status of a child. In one case, a boy living in an orphanage was being considered for adoption, but his father, who could not provide for him, would not give his consent. Some felt that this was a fraudulent use of well-meant programs like CCF and that CCF should know of these families who were "not carrying any of the responsibility, and yet choosing to keep the child from anything else." In other words, this father's strategic use of the orphanage was exploitive of both the orphanage and the sponsorship program, because his son lived in an orphanage but was not available for adoption. Looked at in another way, however, the father was making a rational choice given the options available to him. Recognizing that directing resources to institutions encouraged this kind of activity, some sponsorship programs began in the 1960s to shift their emphasis to helping children in their own homes. Nonetheless, aid to children continued to flow primarily through institutions well into the 1990s.[51]

The term *orphan* was subject to manipulation because of its vagueness and capaciousness. Orphanages wanted a maximum number of children in their facilities so as to maximize their access to relief goods and money, so directors represented the children as orphans, even those who had living parents. Birth parents had to present their children as orphans so they could benefit from the relative wealth of orphanages—so they simply made their children into orphans by abandoning them. These mutually reinforcing motivations ensured that orphanages would remain full of children and continue to thrive as an industry long after the Korean War had ended. These institutions, and the manipulation of orphan status that they encouraged, were essential preconditions to the systematization of intercountry adoption.

Roads Not Taken

Despite the hundreds of requests pouring in from Americans wanting to adopt, some observers did not perceive a demand for Korean children in the United States. The US embassy stated that a lack of potential adoptive parents was "the big stumbling block in getting any considerable number of children going." It proposed that if CCF found adoptive parents, embassy staff would "do the rest": completing all necessary paperwork and "deliver[ing] the child to the 'parent' at his or her home in America." This confusion over whether there was a surplus or shortage of potential adopters raises the question of how market forces operated in early Korean adoption. Did the newly discovered supply of Korean children meet a pent-up demand on the part of Americans who had been seeking to adopt? Or did supply create demand? In a 1954 meeting about intercountry adoption, Father Laurent Youn of the League of Korean Social Workers asserted that it was Americans who were driving efforts to facilitate adoptions from Korea. Youn emphasized, "Koreans not only fully accept the responsibility for caring for their own children but are anxious to do so, and . . . only the unsolicited interest of people outside of Korea in Korean children has led to the activity of Korean agencies and individuals in considering placement of their children abroad." But Youn's was a minority position. Most observers in Korea were unanimous in believing intercountry adoption was the best solution.⁵²

Little dissent came from inside the Korean government. Some did question the wisdom of promoting emigration, fearing that Korea might export the talented, "right-minded and able-bodied" people it needed for national rebuilding. However, the Rhee administration "wholeheartedly supported" the RRA's orphan program, underscoring its belief that GI babies were not truly Korean. Their emigration would not undermine the strength of the Korean nation but in fact enhance it by removing an impure element. An intercountry adoption system would provide what was later described as the "racial cleansing mechanism and outlet" that Koreans believed their country needed to "purge" itself of what did not belong.⁵³

Americans were somewhat more critical about the prospect of intercountry adoption, although their opposition was quite muted. ISS, UNKRA, and the American-Korean Foundation (AKF) in particular expressed reluctance. Since they worked closely together, their common stance on this issue likely resulted from interagency conversations. ISS did not consider it possible to provide US-Korea adoption services for administrative reasons: because of a lack of personnel in the United States, as well as the absence of a qualified person or agency to work with in Korea. ISS also expressed concern over how well Korean children would be accepted in the United States. Although it was willing to endorse the adoptions of European children, the "additional unknowns when an Asiatic child is concerned" gave the organization pause.⁵⁴

Those skeptical of intercountry adoption questioned whether international placement served a Korean child's best interests. A staff member at UNKRA thought overseas placement would be "hazardous" for Korean children, who would migrate primarily to Western countries and face "a particularly difficult physical, racial and social adjustment." A colleague agreed, predicting the children would find themselves to be "'fish out of water,' lonely, far from home with all the consequent emotional difficulties on both sides." The Association for the Aid of Crippled Children (AACC) echoed ISS's concern about uprooting a child from her birth country and culture: "International adoptions have revealed many problems in connection with the separation of a child from his own relatives and associates not to mention his country and his removal to a completely different setting.

This is a far graver decision to make than in the case of a child placed with his own cultural group."⁵⁵

A small minority resisted the almost unanimous assumption that Korean society could not absorb GI babies. Canadian missionary and social worker Anne Davison asserted that "their acceptance here has not been very well tried yet." World Vision, which supported four thousand children in Korean orphanages in 1955 through its monthly sponsorship program, also believed that GI babies could be integrated. It aimed to provide care for these children in Korea, "a familiar situation where they know the language and the customs." But these protests seem not to have registered widely. A Korean social worker who helped establish intercountry adoption did not remember any organization voicing disagreement with the government's policy of sending GI babies abroad or mentioning the possibility that allowing them to stay might eventually result in acceptance.⁵⁶

Critics also expressed concern about the questionable character of the people who wanted to adopt transnationally. A UNKRA worker summarized these fears, betraying her deep suspicion of "emotionally needy" prospective adoptive parents. She noted that many applicants had turned to intercountry adoption after being rejected "for wise and good reasons" for domestic adoption in their own countries. She also warned that some people used adoption as a "device to secure cheap domestic service." The AACC was similarly dubious, speculating that many of those applying to adopt from Korea were unqualified. When Oak Soon Hong reported in September 1954 that she had filed visa applications for 167 children, and had on file more than 500 applications from Americans wishing to adopt, some voluntary agencies estimated that "probably about 100 of these parents would qualify under their state adoption laws." CCF's J. Calvitt Clarke estimated that "from 50 to 75%" of adoptive applicants were poor risks.⁵⁷

The issue of transportation posed a major impediment to intercountry adoption. For most adoptive parents, travel to Korea was prohibitively expensive, but they could have their children brought to them, since immigration laws allowed the entry of children who had been adopted abroad or were coming to the United States for adoption. Agencies like ISS flew groups of several children over at a time, escorted by missionaries, expatriates, or Korean students studying abroad. Although migrants from Europe, Palestine, and Hong Kong received transportation assistance from the US government and international nongovernmental organizations (NGOs),

Korean orphans received no such aid. The cost of transportation from Korea, which was $253 per child in 1956, was high enough that ISS and the Catholic Committee for Refugees estimated in early 1956 that they would need to find funding to subsidize transportation for approximately 200 cases that they were processing: "There is a serious danger that unless the costs of ocean transportation are defrayed, many of these children will not have the possibility of immigration to the United States." Skeptics speculated on the wisdom of paying the high costs of moving children overseas at all, arguing that "the potential cost of transportation would be more than adequate to provide care for an individual child in Korea until he reaches adult life."[58]

Indeed, looming over the whole Korean adoption enterprise was the question of whether channeling funds, expertise, and energy into an intercountry adoption program was the best use of resources. Processing a child for emigration and adoption required staff, time, money, and the close cooperation of multiple agencies and government offices, all of which might "be better spent in aiding indigenous child welfare programs and agencies, in the training of personnel, and in the development of home finding, boarding and foster home and adoption programs in Korea." Critics of international adoption preferred sponsorship programs that would keep Korean children with their families, or at least in their own country: "I think we would agree that in most cases neither Korean children nor 'UN' babies should be removed from Korea for adoption if their mothers are living and are anxious to keep them."[59]

For all of these reasons, groups like UNKRA, AKF, and ISS believed that international adoption could not "be regarded as one of the main solutions of the child welfare problems of Korea." Although Rhee had hoped that AKF would help with intercountry adoption from Korea, he was disappointed. AKF's president Howard Rusk explained that his organization agreed with the skeptics, stating, "I, personally, do not . . . think that we can, or should, anticipate any substantial number of the children of Korean mothers and UN soldiers being brought to the United States." The opposition, however, was mostly limp. Rather than actively resisting the practice, those skeptical of the practice simply did not cooperate in the creation of an intercountry adoption system.[60]

Despite its qualms, ISS ultimately did participate in Korean adoption, probably because it recognized that intercountry adoption was an acceptable short-term solution to the GI baby problem, even if it was not sound long-term government policy. Having processed adoptions of Japanese GI babies in Japan, ISS had experience with international adoption that would be valuable in Korea. It also probably realized that enough parties of consequence favored Korean adoption and would forge ahead with a program with or without ISS. In its capacity as international overseer of social welfare programs, ISS likely believed that it could at least uphold some social work standards by participating in Korean adoption rather than arguing against it from the sidelines.

GI Babies in Korean and American Racial Thought

American and Korean conceptions of race and nation were central to the transnational consensus that intercountry adoption was the best way to solve the Korean GI baby problem.[61] For Americans and Koreans in the early 1950s, ethno-racial and political definitions of Americanness and Koreanness were in flux, shaped by internal and external politics and recent history. At the start of the Cold War, the United States sought to prove its racial liberalism and fulfill its self-image as a nation of equality and opportunity.[62] Meanwhile, the new Republic of Korea, liberated from Japan but severed from its northern half, sought independence and self-definition. Both countries espoused views of the nation in which race was central: racial diversity and tolerance in the United States, and racial purity in Korea.

Koreans and Americans assumed that most mixed-race children had been fathered by Americans, probably since they constituted the vast majority of the non-Korean troops that fought under the UN Command during the Korean War.[63] The continuing presence of thousands of American troops after the war made the assumption of American paternity even more logical. The quick fading of the early terms *UN baby* and *UN orphan* reflects this equation of non-Koreanness with Americanness, while the use of terms like *Yank* for Caucasian-looking children indicates its pervasiveness.[64] Birth mothers shared a widely held belief that their half-American children would benefit by going to live in the United States. Beyond the improvement in their material conditions and future prospects, GI babies would be living among "their" people.

This widespread feeling that whiteness or blackness rendered a half-Korean child wholly American reflected a peculiarly Korean iteration of the so-called one-drop rule.⁶⁵ One drop of black blood made a person black in the United States, but in Korea a drop of white or black blood made a child American. At midcentury, when many Koreans and Americans still used *American* and *white* interchangeably, Korean racial thinking classified both Korean-white and Korean-black children as equally American—at a minimum, they were decidedly not Korean. American social workers who called Korean-black children *Negro* in their correspondence and records may have omitted the *Korean* tag since it was obvious they were talking about Korean children. In contrast, they might have been indicating compliance with the American one-drop rule.

At the heart of the dilemma of what to do about GI babies was the question of their racial and national identities: were they Koreans who should remain in Korea or were they Americans who should live in the United States? To most Koreans the answer was clear. The GI baby had no legal or social standing in Korea—and therefore no place. She belonged to America and was America's problem. Americans accepted responsibility for the children of their "boys" overseas but still puzzled over the racial identity of GI babies. Their Korean "blood" made them foreign, yet the distinctly "Western" appearance of many of the children—blonde hair, skin coloring, "round" eyes—prompted a powerful, visceral sense of identification in white and black Americans. In fact, some thought GI babies' "Caucasian or Negro characteristics" were so predominant that they could easily pass in the United States. Then again, others noted how the children's racial appearance depended on context, explaining how they "looked American . . . in Korea, but once they went to the US, they looked Korean."⁶⁶

Americans and Koreans struggled to classify these children using a variety of terms, most commonly *half-breed*, *mixed-breed*, *mixed-blood*, and *half-caste*. Koreans described GI babies as American while Americans called them Korean, Korean American, or half-American—where *American* meant "white." The African American press labeled children fathered by black men as "Korean brown babies" or "half-Negro." In the files of social workers, the language was more pseudoscientific. Children were labeled *Korean-Caucasian*, *Korean-Negro*, or *Korean-Other*. This last label was applied in cases where the father's identity was neither white nor black, and included children whose fathers were, for example, Filipino or Puerto Rican.

The term *Korean-Oriental* also appeared occasionally, presumably to denote children whose fathers were Asian but not Korean.

Biology and ideas of essential Koreanness or Americanness shaped not just the language used to describe GI babies but also the logic behind the proposals about what to do with them. The minority of Koreans and Americans who believed that these children should remain in Korea used seemingly nonbiological logic, arguing that Koreans could come to accept the children, and that the children should not be uprooted from their birth culture. However, by prioritizing the Korean "half" of the children, their reasoning was just as biological as those who argued that the American "half" of the children dictated their emigration. In fact, their arguments almost relied more on biology, by assuming that Korean culture was somehow innate to a biologically half-Korean child or that a half-Korean child living abroad would be unable to adjust to her new environment because of some biologically encoded Korean essence.[67]

Just as important as the racial mixture of these children was the patriarchal Korean view of children as belonging, legally and socially, to their fathers.[68] Intercountry adoption advocates positioned sending GI babies to the United States not as an act of separating them from their mothers or country of birth but as an opportunity to return to the "land of their fathers." As such, intercountry adoption was not emigration or immigration but repatriation: children being restored to their rightful places, to enjoy the privileges that came with their American paternity. GI babies internalized the idea that they were going to their father's land, which they heard from their mothers and virtually every other Korean they encountered.[69] David Kim, who would be instrumental to the Holt Adoption Program, imagined one young mother's thought process as she prepared to tell her daughter, Soon-ja, that she was going to be adopted: "She would slowly introduce to her daughter that she was an American, as her father was an American military officer, and therefore she needed to go to the United States to be with him." Soon-ja was not in fact going to her birth father. Her mother had not heard from him, despite sending him "countless" letters, and had simply asked Kim to send her child to "the nicest family in the United States." On the day of Soon-ja's relinquishment, the child's understanding of the situation had been cemented: "I will be going to my daddy in America." This equating of the United States, the nice American family, and Soon-ja's unknown American birth father was typical among Koreans.[70]

Given the racial and national logics surrounding the question of the GI babies' belonging, it makes sense to situate the Korean GI baby problem within the scholarship on race mixing in colonial history. Although the United States only briefly experimented with formal imperialism, it erected an informal empire during the twentieth century that was particularly visible in the Pacific. South Korea occupied a submissive role in its deeply asymmetric relationship with the United States. This relationship has been characterized in terms both fraternal—big brother and little brother—and paternal, but in its heterosexual form, it became concrete at the most intimate level, between American GIs and Korean women.[71]

Fraternization between servicemen and local women is hardly unique to the United States military. Scholars have documented many analogous examples in other parts of the world, and established the importance of the sexual and intimate in colonial rule.[72] Mixed-race Eurasians in British, French, and Dutch colonies throughout East and Southeast Asia enjoyed an officially recognized identity, the right to acquire the nationality of their European fathers, and higher status than the native population. In contrast, although American men stationed overseas in military or government capacities had fathered children since the Philippine-American War (1898–1902), the US government ignored their existence and did not provide them with access to citizenship or a means to immigrate until the 1980s.[73] Examining European colonial policies in Asia reveals the "historically exceptional" nature of the US government's "lack of responsibility."[74]

Comparing French policies toward Eurasians in Indochina after World War II and American policies toward Korean GI babies less than a decade later shows how assumptions about race, nation, and gender shaped the ways these two powers approached the problem of race mixing. Before the 1930s, the French colonial government in Vietnam had viewed "abandoned Eurasian children"—children abandoned by their French fathers but not necessarily by their mothers—as "social pariahs" and legally classified them as indigenous. But by the beginning of World War II, these children had become reclassified as "white French." This reconceptualization in turn justified the colonial government's policy of actively seeking out Eurasians and separating them from their mothers—sometimes by force—to remove them from the harmful cultural influences of Vietnamese society. The colonial government's goal was to place the children in special orphanages where they could be raised as little French men and women—that is to say, civilized and whitened—and then deployed to serve in the colonial government and as "visibly white" settlers who could augment the white presence in the colony. Using these children in this way was consistent with a long tradition of employing mixed-race people as brokers and mediators. Furthermore, this faith that Eurasians could be taught to be French demonstrated the colonial government's belief that culture did not emerge from race but that race came from culture—even if that culture had to be learned.[75]

This policy illuminated a contradiction between metropolitan and colonial race thinking at the time: in France, where "scientific" theories of race had become popular, racial categories had narrowed, and Eurasians were considered "neither white nor French."[76] In contrast, the government in Indochina became more inclusive, classifying Eurasians as French. It is important to note, however, that phenotype constrained this seemingly progressive attitude: the colonial government was interested only in white-looking Eurasian children; those whom it thought could not pass for white were left where they were.

In the midst of post–World War II decolonization, the emphasis shifted away from exploiting Eurasians for colonial ends to protecting France's "imperial legacy." Fears that Eurasian children left behind in Vietnam would symbolize a failed French empire prompted the colonial government to begin evacuating them to orphanages in France in 1947. There, the state tried to assimilate Eurasians into French society: it paid to support them in foster homes or camps, and it paid for their educations. Social workers supervised the children's progress. France also amended its nationality laws to provide multiple ways for Vietnamese Eurasians to acquire French citizenship, regardless of where they lived.[77]

There are striking similarities between French colonial Indochina and American neocolonial Korea with regard to mixed-race children. In both countries, the number of these children was unknown but thought to be small. More important was their symbolic power. In European colonies, Eurasians were a problem in part because their hybridity challenged supposedly discrete categories of ruler and ruled. In the context of Korean nation building, GI babies embodied "the tension between national purity claims and the realities of US occupation," thus challenging Korea's conception of itself as independent and racially homogeneous.[78] But this tension, while of great concern to Koreans, hardly registered in the United States. Instead, the argument that resonated with Cold War Americans was that neglected GI babies might grow up to become dangerous sources of anti-American sentiment in a region that was crucial to American geopolitical interests. Europeans had believed that Eurasian children born in overseas colonies to "native" women and French fathers, and then abandoned by their fathers, were potential sources of moral and national degeneration, political subversion, and harm to European prestige. Some Americans aired similar concerns about abandoned GI babies. Pearl S. Buck, the most prominent advocate of this school of thought, promoted the view that GI babies were destined for lives of poverty, low status, crime, and prostitution. She warned that the outcast children would grow up to resent their American fathers and become enemies of their father's nation.[79] In other words, they would be highly susceptible to communist influence.

Assumptions about maternity and paternity marked other similarities and differences between the French and American approaches. Although both Eurasian children and Korean GI babies lived with their mothers, they were deemed "abandoned" because they had been deserted by their fathers. This abandonment can be seen as social death: left by their fathers, these children were banished from European (or American) society, in a place beyond patriarchal and colonial order. At the same time, Frenchness and Americanness were thought to be so powerful that they could be transmitted biologically. Both the French and Americans believed that, with the proper environment and education, this dormant civilized essence could be cultivated and the child therefore rehabilitated. Of course, the figuring of these children as potentially French or American required that their mothers be effaced as degraded and inferior, usually as prostitutes. Thus, Eurasians were labeled "abandoned" and GI babies "orphans," despite the fact that many of these children were neither. But here the American and French cases diverge. Eurasians who were not recognized by their French fathers could nonetheless acquire (after 1928) French nationality; Korean GI babies who were not legitimated by their American fathers had no such access to US citizenship but were, instead, stateless.[80]

As the French manipulation of nationality laws suggests, the main difference between the Vietnamese and Korean cases is the markedly different roles played by the French and American states. In removing Eurasian children from their mothers, colonial bureaucrats acted as surrogate fathers.[81] In contrast, neither the US government nor military in Korea became involved in searching out Korean GI babies or separating them from their mothers. While evacuating and integrating the mixed-race children of its colonies was a French state project, the US government and military turned a blind eye to the existence of GI babies, despite their having been fathered by men sent abroad to pursue national objectives. Instead, individual Americans and lawmakers addressed the GI babies' plight by advocating and implementing private solutions—intercountry adoption—to a public problem. Whereas the French state stepped into the paternal role, in the US case it was families that filled the vacuum created by state inaction and irresponsibility.

. . .

Although the call to return GI babies to their fathers' land was broadly useful at the conceptual and rhetorical levels, the situation was more complicated when it came to actually working out where they should live. A US embassy staffer thought Hawaii would be the best place to resettle GI babies, given its large population of racially mixed people, and wondered if CCF could start a home there. Because of the time pressure imposed by the imminent expiration of the RRA, CCF's Clarke offered to try to "ship all of the children up to eighteen years of age to Hawaii" if the US government would pay for transportation. Clarke thought organizations there could care for the children until they could be adopted into Hawaiian homes: "There would be no racial problems in Hawaii. For that matter, there would be none in Puerto Rico either, but Puerto Rico is already overpopulated."[82]

Clarke's suggestion of racially diverse places like Hawaii and Puerto Rico—and other agencies' mentions of Cuba and Brazil—indicated an awareness that Korean GI babies would have to be gingerly inserted into the American racial hierarchy. While their white or black blood made GI babies a problem in Korea, their Korean blood could make them a problem in the United States. Their nonwhite blood and racial mixture made them better suited for places like Hawaii, which Americans saw as a kind of racial paradise. The naming of American and European colonies, past and present, as potential (indeed preferred) homes for the mixed-race children left behind by American GIs is an irony that nobody seems to have commented on at the time. The American consul in Formosa held the opposite opinion, asserting that it would be better to "disperse" Asian children throughout the country. This model of assimilation through dispersion is one that the

US government implemented in resettling Japanese Americans after their World War II internment and in its resettlement of Southeast Asian refugees after the Vietnam War. Others looked to racial matching to guide the placement of GI babies in the United States, proposing that only Asian parents adopt "Oriental orphans."[83]

Both Americans and Koreans recognized early on that special arrangements would have to be made for Korean-black children. Although African American couples expressed interest in Korean adoption, airfare costs and agency fees posed an enormous obstacle, and as Chapter 4 shows, money was only one of the factors that deterred African Americans from adopting in general. President Rhee asked his consul in San Francisco to gather information about placing Korean-black children for adoption, and the Refugee Relief Program Coordinator for the Far East asked "the three Negro Congressmen"—Adam Clayton Powell Jr. (D-NY), Charles C. Diggs (D-MI), and William Dawson (D-IL)—to help find adoptive families for Korean-black GI babies. The US embassy also asked CCF to help enlist "the sympathy of some prominent coloured people in America who might be prepared to adopt one of these children" in the hope that they might inspire other African Americans to follow their example.[84]

Conclusion

Although it was not a completely foregone conclusion that international adoption was the appropriate way to solve the GI baby problem, and various agencies and individuals voiced reservations, the will of the Korean government to remove GI babies and the desire of Americans to adopt these children proved powerful enough to override any dissent. In the years after the Korean War, the United States and South Korea made legal and administrative changes to facilitate adoptions of Korean children. Social work, religious, and voluntary agencies were developing expertise in processing intercountry adoptions. The situation, then, was one in which all the concerned parties stood poised, ready to embark on this grand scheme of adopting Korean GI babies. (All concerned parties, it must be noted, except Korean birth mothers, who were nowhere represented in the discussion).

But Korean adoption was far from inevitable, because it was missing a crucial element: someone to facilitate and coordinate it, to bridge American demand and Korean supply. Rhee noted, "We need help from some source—an authority who will be recognized by the American authorities here—to receive the requests and deal with them expeditiously on the spot." A member of his office concurred, stating, "We need the personal interest of an American person who has some godliness in his heart to get these children to the parents who want them so much." That person would arrive in the form of a farmer from Oregon named Harry Holt.[85] He would catalyze the transformation of Korean adoption from an idea and a wish to a system that would make adoption across borders a worldwide phenomenon in just a few short decades and send thousands of Korean children abroad by the end of the century.

PART TWO

God's Work and Social Work

THREE

Christian Americanism and the Adoption of GI Babies

> The Lord started this undertaking Himself, and it is He who is carrying it through. He should have all the praise for it. . . . [F]olks think we deserve the credit. But we quote Psalms 118:23[:] "This is the Lord's doing; it is marvelous in our eyes."
>
> —Harry Holt[1]

> We, as Christian parents, simply cannot stand idly by and see these children neglected, not only physically, but spiritually. We in our hearts, know that God loves these little children just as dearly as He loves our own two children (He does not mind at all if their skin is somewhat darker than our children's), and our hearts go out in deep sympathy to those poor little unwanted ones. We do not have too much in the way of material things to offer this adopted child, but we can certainly give her much in love, a good home and a good education, both Christian and otherwise. It is very difficult to close one's eyes to the heartbreaking situation involving these little orphans—surely they do not deserve the life which they have to face in their own country.
>
> —Robert and Dora Bersagel[2]

Basic human compassion explained American relief efforts to Korea in the aftermath of the Korean War, but something more complex motivated certain families to take these efforts a step further by adopting Korean GI babies. A peculiar kind of secular religion propelled the movement to adopt these children. "There seems to be a wave of enthusiasm for a rather undefined 'religion' in America," noted *Christian Century* in 1954. That undefined religion—which I call Christian Americanism—was a fusion of vaguely Christian principles with values identified as exceptionally "American": an expansive sense of responsibility and a strong belief in the importance of family. Although it was never fully articulated as a doctrine,

American churches, the government, and the mainstream media promoted it, and it took hold in white, middle-class America—the segment that adopted the majority of the GI babies. Christian Americanism encapsulated the prevailing attitude that equated being a good Christian with being a good American.[3]

A broad array of Americans embraced the adoption of Korean GI babies as a new kind of missionary work. Generally speaking, adoptive families adopted for religious or humanitarian reasons. They were a subset of a second, much larger group: Christian Americanists, as represented by the American mass media and Congress. This second group infused the religiously motivated adoptions with nationalist meaning and celebrated them as an affirmation not only of the adoptive parents' Christian goodness but also of their Americanness. In addition, Christian Americanists used the apparent colorblindness of the Christian adoptive families to support American Cold War claims of racial democracy. Through this interplay of religious and nationalistic concerns, what began as a mainly religious adoption movement became the shared crusade of devout Christians and Christian Americanists alike.

Harry Holt was the figurehead of this Christian Americanist project. In 1955, he brought twelve Korean GI babies to the United States: he and his wife, Bertha, had adopted eight, and the other four went to three other families. The publicity around this undertaking was so great that the Holts were inundated almost immediately with inquiries from Americans who wanted to adopt.[4] Seeing the need of the orphans in Korea and the demand for them in the United States, Harry Holt began shuttling between the two countries, bringing Korean GI babies to parents in the United States while simultaneously leading the fight for adoption-friendly immigration laws. In 1956, the Holts placed 211 orphans and established the Holt Adoption Program (HAP). (That agency, now called Holt International Children's Services, operates in more than a dozen countries and continues to be a leader in intercountry adoptions.) It is important to note that Harry Holt himself was not a Christian Americanist. He saw his work as serving God, and he never articulated a connection between his Christian faith and nationalistic beliefs. Nonetheless, he became emblematic of the Christian Americanist adoption movement through media portrayals that celebrated his good works as a Christian as an affirmation of his Americanness.

Korean adoption arose from a convergence between the Korean government's desire to remove mixed-race children and the American public's demand for these children, but that convergence would not have amounted to anything more without the catalyst of Harry Holt, who provided the channel through which Korean children could emigrate to the United States in great numbers. Holt restructured the rudimentary adoption mechanisms already in place and introduced two crucial innovations that made Korean adoption possible on a large scale: proxy adoption and charter flights. His Christian Americanist allies recast Korean adoption on an imaginative level, as a new kind of missionary work for a new kind of world, and helped expand the notion of the American family to include interracial and international adoption.

The Christian Americanism that powered the early Korean adoption movement was short lived, fading away in the early 1960s. In 1961, largely as a result of Christian Americanist lobbying, Congress made provisions for international adoption a permanent part of US immigration law. With Korean adoption becoming more mainstream, its advocates were no longer outsiders in need of a movement and a language for the movement. At the same time, the racial composition of the children being adopted shifted from mainly mixed race to mainly full Korean, reducing the potency of arguments that Americans were responsible for children fathered by American GIs (see Table 3.1). Nevertheless, the Christians and Christian Americanists who launched Korean adoption as a systematic practice sparked a revolution on a number of fronts: they opened the floodgates of intercountry adoption, triggered important changes in US immigration laws, changed Americans' ideas about what families looked like and how they should be made, and overturned social work doctrine about race and adoptability.

Christian Americanism

Many scholars have shown how American domestic race relations became inextricably linked with international politics with the dawning of the Cold War. Displays of racism like segregation and lynching threatened American efforts to gain the allegiance of nonwhite nations. The United States

TABLE 3.1 Number of mixed-race and full-Korean children placed abroad for adoption, by race and agency, 1955–1961

	1955	1956	1957	1958	1959	1960	1961	**Total**
BY RACE								
Korean-Caucasian	43	467	285	396	289	184	325	1,989
Percentage of total	72.9	69.6	58.6	42.6	39.0	28.8	48.9	47.5
Korean-Negroid	9	151	128	227	92	61	36	704
Percentage of total	15.3	22.5	26.3	24.4	12.4	9.6	5.4	16.8
Full Korean	7	53	75	307	360	393	304	1,499
Percentage of total	11.9	7.9	15.4	33.0	48.6	61.6	45.7	35.8
Total	59	671	486	930	741	638	665	4,190
BY AGENCY								
Child Placement Service	34	363	83	249	170	136	65	1,100
Percentage of total	57.6	54.1	17.1	26.8	22.9	21.3	9.8	26.3
Holt Adoption Program	—	211	322	546	407	411	523	2,420
Percentage of total	—	31.4	66.3	58.7	54.9	64.4	78.6	57.8
National Catholic Welfare Conference	14	34	29	31	41	26	17	192
Percentage of total	23.7	5.1	6.0	3.3	5.5	4.1	2.6	4.6
Seventh-Day Adventists	11	63	47	42	32	18	18	231
Percentage of total	18.6	9.4	9.7	4.5	4.3	2.8	2.7	5.5
International Social Service	—	—	5	62	91	47	42	247
Percentage of total	—	—	1.0	6.7	12.3	7.4	6.3	5.9
Total	59	671	486	930	741	638	665	4,190

SOURCE: Compiled and adapted from figures from the Korean Ministry of Health and Social Affairs, "Measures for the Welfare of Mixed-Blood Children in Korea," prepared for 19th Social Work Summer School, Central Theological Seminary, 8 Aug. 1967, Seoul, Korea, 6, box 35, folder "Korea—Correspondence. Vol. I," ISS Records; Hi Taik Kim and Elaine Reid, "After a Long Journey: A Study on the Process of Initial Adjustment of the Half and Full Korean Children Adopted by American Families, and the Families' Experiences with These Children During the Transitional Period" (MA thesis, University of Minnesota, 1970).

NOTE: These figures do not include smaller adoption programs run by organizations like American Soul Clinic and Christ Is the Answer. They also double-count some adoptions, such as those that Child Placement Services and Holt Adoption Program processed together.

scrambled to correct its racist image, which Secretary of State Dean Acheson claimed was "a source of constant embarrassment" and jeopardized "the effective maintenance of our moral leadership of the free and democratic nations of the world." He called on social and cultural institutions to assist in winning public support for the government's new internationalism by creating a "global imaginary" that would make Americans feel linked to "nations and peoples around the world." One way to accomplish this was by using and promoting antiracist rhetoric.[5]

Acheson's directive partly explains why the American media represented Korea in a relatively positive way. Journalists enjoyed considerable latitude in constructing an image of the Korean people because Korea was mostly absent from the national consciousness, and actual Koreans were missing from the landscape. The several thousand Koreans who had entered the United States before the anti-Asian Immigration Act of 1924 were concentrated in Hawaii, with just a small number on the mainland. Anti-Asian racism, directed at the Chinese and the Japanese, rarely recognized Koreans as a distinct group. Alternatively, Americans grouped Koreans with the Japanese, especially after Japan colonized Korea in 1910. Once the Korean War began, the American media applied political distinctions to separate the "good" South Koreans from the "bad" North Koreans (and their Chinese allies), who were "Nazis, locusts, primitives, hordes, thieves."[6]

Some of the positive coverage of Koreans originated from the fact that they had fought together with Americans against the communist foe, but a perception that the two peoples shared a similar character and a common Christianity also strengthened Americans' affective ties to Korea. In a 1956 article for *Life*, Howard Rusk, president of the American-Korean Foundation, wrote sympathetically about how the "gallant" nation was rebuilding. He used an assortment of vignettes to illustrate "the deep personal and spiritual resources of the Korean people: their remarkable mixture of stoic courage, dignity, adaptability and humor; their thirst for education; and their deep traditions of the family as the basic social unit." Most important, Rusk portrayed Koreans as being as committed to freedom and democracy as Americans. He concluded his piece by recounting the words of one anonymous Korean, who spoke for all Koreans when he asked Rusk, "Won't you help us off our knees so we can continue to fight for the free world?" Cold War Americans could not help but respond to such a person except as a brother and friend.[7]

Koreans and Americans also shared a common Christian belief. In truth, only a small fraction of Koreans were Christian around the time of the Korean War, but American missionaries, who had nurtured bonds of sympathy between their fellow Christians and Asians since the nineteenth century, helped shape an image of the country as Christian. The widely read nondenominational Christian periodical *Christian Century* contained an editorial or feature story on the war in almost every weekly issue. These pieces documented the persistence and ingenuity of the Korean people and pleaded on their behalf for aid from American churches. In addition, the Christian press highlighted the bravery and faithfulness of Korean Christians by publishing stories about how they were the special targets of communist guerillas and describing refugee camps as overflowing with Koreans incessantly reading their Bibles, singing hymns, and holding prayer meetings.[8]

Stories about orphans emphasized their supposed Christianity by depicting them praying or singing Christian songs such as "Jesus Loves Me." Although it is possible that the children had no idea what they were singing, the song carried deep significance for the American public, and images of children receiving Christian education no doubt helped to mitigate their foreignness. In these ways, the American media presented the Korean War as a battle between Christian South Korea and communist North Korea. Against such a backdrop, the adoption of Christian South Korean babies was a deliberately anticommunist act that directly supported the Christian Americanist cause.[9]

In the early 1950s, the now-familiar Cold War rhetoric that positioned the United States as the savior of the world and the standard-bearer for democracy and freedom was still new, and the division of the world into spheres of good and evil, democracy and communism, United States and Soviet Union, provoked profound anxiety in Americans.[10] The situation in Asia only heightened that anxiety, for between Mao's China, the Korean War, Ho Chi Minh's North Vietnam, and communist insurgencies in Burma, Malaya, and the Philippines, it seemed that the United States was rapidly losing ground to Moscow. Relief efforts became a way for Americans to win "the allegiance of Asia." Ordinary Americans could take part by adopting Korean war orphans and—in yet another iteration of the white man's burden—raising them up: bringing them into their homes and inculcating them with the values of Christianity and the American way of life.[11]

The conviction that Americans had an international Americanizing and Christianizing mission permeated popular and Christian media alike. In *Life* magazine's Christianity issue, published in December 1955, the editors noted that the United States was "the world's largest and most dynamic Christian country" and located American Christianity firmly at the center of "world Christendom."[12] The issue opened with "The Testimony of a Devout President," a compilation of seven speeches given by President

Eisenhower between 1946 and 1955. Eisenhower praised the righteousness of the American people, emphasizing the importance of America's mission and its responsibility to the world: "Our forefathers proved that only a people strong in godliness is a people strong enough to overcome tyranny and make themselves and others free. Today it is ours to prove that our own faith, perpetually renewed, is equal to the challenge of today's tyrants." Because their country held a special position in the world and in the eyes of God, Eisenhower exhorted Americans to "ask that Almighty God will set and keep his protecting hand over us." Almighty God would answer the American prayer, was the underlying message, for in a world divided between good and evil, God was on America's side.[13]

Gauged by any metric—for example, church or synagogue membership, professions of faith to pollsters, or religious themes and content in popular culture—it seems evident that the 1950s witnessed a nationwide religious revival. Contemporary theologians expressed unease and suspicion about the superficiality of much of this religious activity, but whatever its character or depth, there is no question that it was pervasive. The fact that the words "under God" were added to the Pledge of Allegiance, "In God We Trust" added to the money, and the National Day of Prayer inaugurated during this decade neatly illustrates the pious mood of the country.[14]

Criticism of the conflation of American values with Christianity came not from popular magazines like *Life* but from the Christian press. In a *Christian Century* article condemning "the new look in American piety," religion scholar A. Roy Eckardt expressed concern at the zeitgeist of the times, which seemed to be that "it is un-American to be unreligious." He called American Cold War culture a "cult of 'we' versus 'they'" and denounced as perverse America's smug conclusion that its cause was God's cause.[15] *Christianity and Crisis*'s resident satirist, Saint Hereticus, took the matter even further, claiming that American Christians had abandoned Christianity altogether in favor of something he called "Americanity," which had as its doctrine, "'extra American nulla salus est' (outside America there is no salvation)."[16] Cold War religion was "a religion not only of the American Way of Life but of America itself."[17]

What many Americans called Christianity in the 1950s was actually a watered-down collection of selected Christian values. It contained little of the practice and belief of doctrinal Christianity, retaining instead vague principles about kindness and doing unto others, and it became general enough that Americans of all religious denominations could use a common rhetoric. In fact, it became so emptied of any specific Christian meaning that Oregon Senator Richard Neuberger, a Jew, came to regularly employ the language of Christian Americanism on the Senate floor to appeal to his colleagues' religious and nationalistic sentiments during debates about orphan-friendly immigration legislation. After reminding them of the words of Emma Lazarus that were engraved in the pedestal of the Statue of Liberty, he drew a direct line from Jesus Christ to Thomas Jefferson: "Somehow, I feel that the author of the Sermon on the Mount and the writer of the Declaration of Independence would approve of granting sanctuary in America to abandoned orphans and other persons who are wracked by sickness and misery."[18]

In Christian Americanism, this religiosity intersected with American exceptionalism in two specific areas: in its sense of responsibility and its belief in the importance of families. With regard to the Korean situation, Americans believed they had a three-pronged responsibility: to the world, to Korea, and to the GI babies of Korea. The United States had a general charge to fulfill its new roles as world power, protector of democracy, defender of freedom, and bulwark against communism. These were some of the duties that the powerful publisher Henry Luce had famously outlined almost a decade before the Korean War began in his proclamation of "The American Century."[19] To support their country in these roles, it was important that patriotic American citizens take seriously their moral and civic obligations as leaders of the free world. If they failed to shoulder "the responsibilities of freedom" they would be victims and slaves.[20] As President Eisenhower asserted, religious faith was essential to American success in this task: "religion nurtures men of faith, men of hope, men of love; such men are needed in the building of a new world reflecting the glory of God."[21] The United States, as the most powerful country on earth and the nation most loved by God, had a special responsibility to build a new, Christian, American world order.

Americans' second responsibility was to South Korea, where war had wreaked such havoc and produced such extraordinary numbers of refugees, orphans, and civilian dead. In the absence of a clear-cut victory against communist North Korea, the United States could salvage an ideological win by caring for Korea's people and helping with reconstruction.[22] The American media was particularly adept at showing that it was Korea's children who were the true victims of communist aggression, the "real" reason their nation was involved in the war on that little-known, faraway peninsula.[23] Their grimy little faces were oddly photogenic, filling article upon article about the Korean War. Such images were often accompanied by detailed descriptions of how orphans lived—where they slept, how they found food to eat and clothes to keep warm. A description of nine-year-old Tae in *Collier's* was typical of the stories that showed how orphans teetered on a razor's edge between life and death:

> During [the nearly three years that he'd been orphaned], the only food Tae had eaten was what he could steal or beg or buy with the few pennies he earned. His only home was the closest shelter he could find—a dry corner in some bombed-out building, a pile of boards in an alley.... But then Tae got sick. One of the worst things that can happen to a war orphan is to get sick. When you're sick, you can't work to get food and there's nobody to look after you. You may die for lack of treatment or you may starve to death because you can't help yourself.[24]

Stories in this vein made it clear that Americans could win the ideological battle with North Korea and its allies by helping these orphans. Even before the war had ended, popular magazines like *Life* and *Collier's* carried articles and photographs showcasing how GIs cared for Korean waifs: cuddling them, sewing handkerchiefs and overcoats and dolls for them from rags, feeding them, and distributing Christmas gifts. American military units built or supported orphanages and hospitals and gathered contributions of food, clothing, and money from friends and family back home. The story about the sick orphan Tae was representative not only because it described a Korean orphan's miserable life, but also because it included the stock character of a good Samaritan American GI: Tae met an American sergeant, who took him to a hospital for treatment. As in many other similar stories, it was the American who brought a ray of happiness and hope to a wretched orphan's life.

The third form of American responsibility—responsibility for children fathered by US troops—was the most specific and the most potent. Extensive media coverage alerted Americans to the ostracism and persecution that GI babies suffered, and although condemnation of the men who fathered the children was limited in the mainstream press, Americans betrayed a sterner attitude in their private correspondence. Pressing for the legislation that would allow them to adopt, prospective parents expressed a profound sense of national and personal responsibility towards the GI babies. "There is not only the moral obligation we Americans feel toward all uncared for children, but the more definite obligation, knowing our Armed Forces were responsible for these little Korean outcasts," wrote one couple. Another couple expressed a more prescriptive, though equally widespread, sentiment: "We feel it to be the duty of the United States Government to take over the care of these unfortunate children, for the United States Government sent the fathers of these children into the foreign countries and is therefore responsible for their conduct." A letter sent to Oregon Senator Wayne Morse and signed by more than thirty people stated: "We feel that since so many American boys have proved themselves delinquent fathers, that other American families who feel so inclined should be given the opportunity of taking these children who so badly need a home." These writers believed that private American citizens like them could act as proxies for their government and demonstrate their patriotism by "taking over the care" of these orphans themselves.[25]

The imperatives of anticommunism demanded that the country address the problem of the mixed-race children that American GIs had left behind all throughout Asia, for it would hardly do for the leader of the free world "to have half-American children running about as beggars and potential criminals in the streets of Asian cities." In announcing her own intention to adopt a Japanese-black GI baby in 1958, the novelist Pearl S. Buck reminded readers, "It is important from a political as well as a humanitarian view, to concern ourselves with the futures of those who will remain in Asia." Given the difficulty they would face in obtaining education and jobs, she warned, these children would be "the natural dissidents in coming years and prey to the worst Communist propaganda."[26]

One way Americans responded to the new world of the Cold War was by turning inward: getting married, having babies, and moving to the suburbs. In an age of profound danger and uncertainty in the public political arena, Americans embraced private life, clinging to their homes and families for a sense of safety and reassurance. For such a society, the thousands of dispossessed Korean waifs in the midst of their devastated country were a stark reminder of the tenuousness of the American image of the home and family as a "secure, private nest removed from the dangers of the outside world." Seeing the plight of Korean orphans was like seeing their own nightmares made real. The utter aloneness of these children, the simple fact that they had neither the comforts of home nor the love of their families struck at the very heart of the values that were important to white, middle-class Americans and offended their vision of how the world should be.[27]

Journalists writing about the orphans increased the emotional power of their articles by hooking into Americans' obsession with domesticity. Like many other pieces of the time, a *Time* story contained the standard description of the privations of an orphan's life—"they sleep in doorways, each noon go to the Pyongyang Noodle Shop, where the proprietor fills their pails with slops from the tables. Neither of them has a pair of shoes"—but the story was made all the more poignant because it included one orphan's memories of his vanished home and family: "at first I used to dream of my mother holding out her arms to me. When it rains I still remember how it was on the warm floor at home. But I don't think so much about my mother now."[28] Similarly, *Life*'s story about five-year-old Kang Koo Ri—whom the magazine dubbed "the little boy who wouldn't smile"—gained force through the author's description of Kang's homey little village, the few precious toys that his father had lovingly crafted for him, and the rhythm of his family's daily life before the communist invasion. Having painted this idyllic background, the author related how American GIs found Kang in his deserted house, which reeked with the odor of decay: the naked little boy was sitting next to the decomposing body of his mother.[29]

These stories and images provoked strong responses from American adoptive parents. Many took a child virtually sight unseen, with only a picture and a brief description of him or her. Americans sent newspaper and magazine clippings to various government offices and child welfare organizations, asking to adopt specific children pictured or mentioned. In fact, after *Life* featured the story of "the little boy who wouldn't smile," he was adopted by a reader who "got down on [her] knees and prayed and was told to adopt him." Although dramatic, this adoption was typical of how the thousands of other Korean orphans were adopted. A few pictures, some prayers, and—notwithstanding some red tape—the adoption was complete.[30]

A Mission from God

Harry Holt was the public face of Korean adoption. A successful lumberman and farmer, he and his wife, Bertha, had six children between the ages of nine and twenty-one, and they lived comfortable, devoutly Christian lives in the small town of Creswell, Oregon. In 1955, when they were both in their fifties, the Holts adopted eight Korean GI babies. The attention that surrounded the adoption, and the media presentation of their story, made them into model Americans, model Christians, and the poster family of the Christian Americanist movement. Bertha Holt made a major contribution to this discourse in 1956 with her book *The Seed from the East*, an account of the Holt family's adventures in 1955: their decision to adopt, Harry Holt's experiences in Korea, their allies' efforts in Congress to pass a bill allowing the adoption, Harry Holt's return to the United States with eight new sons and daughters, and the children's initial adjustment to their new home. Although Bertha Holt wrote the book to raise money for Korean orphan relief, she also shaped public perception of the family and HAP through it.[31]

The Holt story begins with a moment of epiphany that has, in the continual retelling, acquired a mythic flavor reminiscent of Paul's experience on the road to Damascus. In the fall of 1954, the Holts attended a World Vision meeting led by its founder, Bob Pierce, who was recruiting for his child sponsorship program.[32] Pierce showed two documentaries at the meeting, of which one, *Other Sheep*, focused on the war widows and orphans of Korea. It featured amputees, lepers, and children who had been left blind, deaf, or dumb by the trauma of war. Although the entire film affected the Holts deeply, the scenes that Bertha Holt says "shattered their hearts" were those that depicted the "tragic plight" of the unwanted GI babies. The Holts, who had been unaware of the situation in Korea, were thunderstruck. The entire family soon signed on to sponsor thirteen Korean orphans. But sponsorship did not ease the guilt the Holts felt about enjoying prosperous lives when orphaned children were starving to death in Korea. By the spring of 1955, the Holts had decided to adopt eight GI babies. They would continue to sponsor full-blooded Korean children through World Vision, but it was the GI babies who were most in need, and the Holts felt that the only solution for them was evacuation.

In May 1955, Harry Holt left for Korea. Fittingly, he entered the country as a missionary, since only they and statesmen were permitted entry. As Bertha Holt wrote, "Harry was only a farmer . . . but he had a definite mission."[33] Although he was not affiliated with any particular religious organization, Harry Holt was indeed a missionary, for he had been called by God. In fact, a key component in the founding myth of the Holt agency is how Harry Holt received his "marching orders."³⁴ Plagued with self-doubt on his way to Korea that May, he had prayed for a sign that God was with him. As he later recounted to his family in a letter:

> I shook my Bible open and put my thumb on part of the page and turned on the light. Out of all the wonderful Word of God, I had my thumb pointing to these words, in Isaiah 43:5, 6 and 7: "Fear not for I am with thee: I will bring *thy seed from the east*, and gather thee from the west; I will say to the *north*, Give up; and to the *south*, Keep not back: bring my sons from afar, and my daughters from the ends of the earth. Even every one that is called by my name: for I have created him for my glory, I have formed him; yea, I have made him."³⁵

Once back in Oregon with their new brood, the Holts again studied this crucial passage from Isaiah and realized that God was directing them to establish an adoption program. Bertha Holt explained:

> [W]e had considered "I will bring thy seed from the east," and the later verse, "Bring my sons from afar," the same command. . . . Now with hundreds of people begging to adopt children, we discovered those two sentences were not the same. "I will bring" is a promise: God said He would bring our eight children. The other sentence is a command: "Bring."³⁶

Thus, a trip that had been intended originally to bring back eight new Holt children also came to mark the beginning of the project that would consume Harry Holt for the remaining nine years of his life. It was a mission that the Holts had been waiting for ever since Harry Holt had suffered a heart attack in 1950. The near-death experience caused the already-religious Holts to become even more devout. They prayed that "God would give us a job" they could perform in thanks for sparing Harry Holt's life.³⁷ Between 1955 and 1964, when he died of a heart attack, Harry Holt worked tirelessly to find homes in the United States for Korean GI babies. He carried out his work despite persistent and serious health problems. His family supported him fully in this endeavor, and they continued the work after his death. The Holts poured their personal savings into the project while also continuing to support World Vision. By 1956, they were sponsoring thirty-six children.³⁸

Harry Holt had gone to Korea in May 1955 without visas for the eight new sons and daughters he planned to bring back. This was because the

Refugee Relief Act of 1953, the immigration law that temporarily allowed the adoption of foreign orphans, limited the number of orphans that Americans could adopt from abroad to two. The Holts would need Congress to pass a special bill that allowed them to adopt eight children. Before leaving for Korea, Harry Holt had asked his senator, Richard Neuberger, for his help in passing such a bill.[39] Wayne Morse, the other senator from Oregon, enthusiastically signed on as a joint sponsor, and Representative Edith Green guided the bill through the House. Although Neuberger originally warned that the "Holt Bill" would likely not pass until early 1956, Bertha Holt was confident: "Don't worry. This is the Lord's work. We can pray and have faith that the Lord will do his part." Indeed, Congress "miraculously" passed the bill that very summer rather than in the several months that a private bill normally required.[40]

Holt remained in Korea from May to October 1955. With the help of World Vision, he found the eight children he would adopt—as well as four others for three other families—and nursed them so that they would pass their physical exams for entry to the United States. In addition, he met missionaries and social workers and toured orphanages and leprosariums. Realizing that GI babies were being abandoned or hidden rather than put in orphanages, he worked with World Vision to establish a reception center to collect mixed-race children and prepare them to be placed in families abroad. Meanwhile, the publicity around him began to build.

Beginning with the local newspaper and radio station, the press came calling at the Holts' farm; soon after, *Time* and *Life* sent photographers to see Harry Holt in Seoul. At the same time, Bertha Holt began fielding occasional inquiries from people interested in adopting a Korean baby. By the time Harry Holt left for the United States with twelve GI babies, media attention was so great that he was greeted at stopovers in Tokyo and Honolulu by sizable press contingents. When he finally landed in Oregon with his new brood—Betty, Helen, Mary, Christine, Robert, Paul, Nathaniel, and Joseph—he was met at the airport by his family, friends, and more than fifty reporters and photographers. Another sixteen photographers awaited him at his home.[41]

The publicity around the Holts and their eight new children turned the trickle of inquiries about adopting Korean babies into an avalanche, with calls from across the country coming in the very morning after Harry Holt's return. The following week, six hundred letters arrived, the vast ma-

FIGURE 3.1 Harry Holt in Korea
SOURCE: Courtesy of Holt International Children's Services.

jority from people who wanted to adopt. But that interest was by no means limited to the first week after Harry Holt's return: by 1956, an average of twenty-five letters from prospective parents streamed into the Holt home each week. Continuing publicity helped to sustain American interest in GI babies; for example, a Thanksgiving Day story about the Holts by a Portland newspaper prompted another avalanche of mail. By the end of the year, letters had come in from forty-six states, Hawaii, and Canada, and more than five hundred couples had requested information about adoption. In addition, hundreds of prospective parents visited the Holt farm each week to see the eight tiny celebrities.[42]

The press attention to Harry Holt's return to the United States in October 1955 was just the first indication of the role that the media would play in the Holts' life from then on. Over the following months and years, the

Holt family would be featured in both local and national newspapers, in major magazines like *Life* and *Look*, and on television and radio. Each new planeload of orphans that the Holts brought to the United States was met by more reporters and photographers than the one before, and each new wave of publicity ushered in a flood of inquiries from American couples interested in adopting GI babies. As Congress continued to grapple with the problem of crafting permanent orphan-friendly immigration legislation in the late 1950s, proponents of intercountry adoption—such as the Holts' allies, Oregon Senators Neuberger and Morse—repeatedly mentioned Harry Holt and his noble efforts to save the Korean GI babies.

In Harry Holt, the American media had found a modern-day saint. This humble, plainspoken man, whom his wife described as "a fifty-year-old farmer with a big scar on his heart," was depicted by the press in biblical terms. They called what he was doing a "mission" and a "crusade," and endowed him with the power of a creator, saying: "he has virtually given life to hundreds of children." In Congress, Senator Neuberger declared: "Harry Holt . . . has symbolized to me the Biblical Good Samaritan." Indeed, *American Mercury* published a piece about him titled "Good Samaritan of Korea." Korean President Syngman Rhee—himself a devout Christian—also used Christian language when he called Harry Holt an "apostle of international understanding and good will." Just as his Lord had been more than a carpenter, Harry Holt was much more than simply a farmer.[43] And just as Christ's disciples left their nets to become fishers of men, Harry Holt "left his plow and began the enormous task of shepherding [hundreds of orphans] across the North Pacific." Senator Neuberger invoked a theme of atonement on the Senate floor, stating, "In view of the shabby legacy left by American GI's who fathered these infants . . . Holt's work stands out like a beacon of light. We may hope that the Korean people judge America just a little bit by his standards."[44]

His wife was described in equally glowing terms. "Bertha Holt is typical of women who have worked hard to make America a sanctuary for family life," wrote World Vision's Bob Pierce. With her old-fashioned braids wound around her head, unrouged face, plain dresses, and sensible shoes, she embodied the "utopian vision" of post–World War II domestic life, which "included 'replenished' families with male providers 'secure in stable careers' and female housewives 'in comfortable homes' who would 'raise perfect children.'" Bertha Holt was not just an ideal wife but also an ideal mother, as evidenced by her six biological children, who were all religious, hardworking, and family oriented—in other words, "perfect children." Moreover, they participated fully in the Holt "family business," whether by taking care of their new eight new brothers and sisters, working on the farm in Oregon, in the orphanage in Korea, or as missionaries in other parts of the world. For his part, Harry Holt had been a success as a lumberman and farmer before embarking on his second career as a missionary and crusader. The Holts, in short, were a model American family.[45]

HAP and the Restructuring of Korean Adoption

Harry Holt established HAP in February 1956 with only one goal: to place as many GI babies in US adoptive homes as possible before the RRA expired on December 31 of that year. Since HAP was meant to be temporary, its procedures were as streamlined as possible.[46] Holt's first innovation was to make intercountry adoption faster, cheaper, and more accessible to thousands of Americans by using proxy adoption. In this kind of adoption, American adoptive parents assigned power of attorney to Holt—or some other proxy—who completed adoption procedures in Korean courts according to Korean law. The child then entered the United States on a non-quota visa, as the legal son or daughter of the American couple. US law permitted this method of adoption, and it was used in many adoptions from Japan and Greece. The Korean government also preferred it, since the child was legally adopted before she emigrated. In addition to obviating the need for adoptive parents to make the expensive and time-consuming trip to Korea, proxy adoption was much faster, taking as little as three months, compared to the one or two years that an adoption through channels of mainstream social work could require. This time frame was shorter because parents who adopted by proxy did not have to undergo a home study by a licensed social welfare agency, a process that could take several months. The social work establishment was extremely alarmed by proxy adoption, arguing that it placed children in families who had not been properly or thoroughly assessed. HAP's stubborn use of this adoption method in the face of vigorous opposition from mainstream social workers exemplifies the expedience and practicality that characterized Holt's approach to Korean adoption.[47]

Potential adoptive parents applied by completing a form that was enclosed with HAP's "Dear Friends" newsletters. This form, which was half a page long, asked for the father's name, age, race, occupation, and address and the mother's name, age, and race. Applicants provided the names and ages of any children they had, as well as the names and addresses of two references. Because of RRA restrictions, adoptive parents could request only two children. They could specify the preferred sex, age, and color of the children they wished to adopt, or they could provide the names of children they already knew of, perhaps through a friend or church contact. Finally, the form asked, "If you are Christians, please give brief statement of personal faith on back of card." This statement was described in the "Dear Friends" letters as a "most vital matter." HAP preferred "a consciously Christian home, preferably with a record of active church participation and loyalty" and considered even "social drinking" to be "an adverse indication."[48]

Harry Holt hoped to fulfill "a three-fold purpose: to save lives, to get these children into homes, and to get them into Christian homes." Moreover, he sought out a certain kind of Christian home for his charges. Pearl S. Buck, a fellow advocate for mixed-race children in Asia, remembered her shock at her first contact with Harry Holt and his brand of Christianity:

> [It was] in the form of a questionnaire, which, it seems, he sent to all prospective parents. To me it was an astonishing document. Very few of the questions related in a material sense to the adoptive family. They pertained to religion and, to my thinking, rather a primitive kind of religion. I had grown up in a missionary environment and had seen and known all kinds of Christians. The questionnaire was distinctly what is called Fundamentalist.... The point was that Harry Holt was giving children to couples who believed in Christian dogma, and not to others who might be far more worthy of parenthood but who did not so believe.

In defense of her father, one of the Holt daughters explained to Buck, "It is the quickest way he knows of finding out whether people are good.... He realizes that it is an inadequate method, but... in his experience the people who believe in a simple practical Christianity are usually good people and will be good to the child."[49] Holt's paramount goal was to place children in "the homes of born again believers."[50] He justified rejecting people of certain sects—for example, Mormons, Jehovah's Witnesses, and Christian Scientists—since he considered these religions "cults" that were "founded and established by Satan himself." Holt directed people belonging to these sects to apply to another agency. He also referred Jews and Catholics elsewhere, but he eventually changed his attitude toward the latter.[51]

HAP's placement practices relied more on God's guidance than on social work principles. As Holt explained it, children were "carefully and prayerfully chosen for a home by an assigner who has undertaken this very important work for our Lord." Bertha Holt defended this strategy by referring to cases in which the child and family turned out to be so well matched that they resembled each other: "I've had some miraculous letters saying 'he looks just like his father's baby picture' . . . and his father never went to Korea and left anybody."[52] The task of matching children with parents fell at first to Oak Soon Hong at Child Placement Services but eventually became distributed among an unspecified number of people in Korea, including HAP's representatives there and at least one American missionary. In Oregon, matching was done by HAP office staff, as well as by those workers whom HAP called "social workers," even though, as Bertha Holt later conceded, they "weren't always trained in that."[53] Professional social workers, who placed enormous importance on matching, were troubled by the participation of all of these untrained people in such a crucial step in the adoption process.

Holt applied a few other criteria to potential adoptive parents. He gave preference to childless couples and those with only one child, and he tried not to place children where there had been a divorce. A shortage of girls meant that HAP could place only one in a home. Adoptive applicants could select the age and sex of their child, and Holt assured them, "You are never given one with a deformity unless you specifically ask for it." If applicants knew of a specific child they wanted to adopt, HAP would try to accommodate them. Couples wishing to adopt children fathered by their own sons or relatives while they were in service in Korea were out of luck. Although ISS and other agencies did not indicate any philosophical opposition to helping in such a situation, Holt believed that it was better for a child born out of wedlock to be adopted by a complete stranger: "Being half Oriental is a big problem for a child to face, but being an illegitimate of someone close by adds to the discrimination and disgrace." Finally, Holt was clear on one race-based consideration, stating, "Colored children go only to colored homes."[54] Then there were the restrictions imposed by the US government, which would not issue a visa for a child being adopted by a single parent, including widows, widowers, and unmarried people. A family wanting to adopt more than two children had to appeal to their congressional representative to pass a special bill on their behalf. For its part, the Korean government preferred that older couples with a better financial profile take older children.

Holt did not apply any financial requirements, but he did note the costs of adopting from Korea in his "Dear Friends" letters. In late 1955 and early 1956, plane fare from Korea to the West Coast cost $253 per child. A $50 adoption fee to be paid to Child Placement Service in Korea covered the cost of the child's Korean paperwork and passport as well as the physical exams that were needed for visa purposes. For those who found a lump-sum payment burdensome, HAP offered a monthly payment plan. Bertha Holt remembered turning away adoptive parents who failed to make necessary financial preparations: "If they didn't have money, lots of them would just order a baby and [wouldn't] have any money at all. For years we ran in a hole because they cost lots and lots of money, and then we had to make up the difference, our family money."[55] She added that children who had been "ordered" but not paid for were kept at the Holt family home in Oregon. If the adopters did not pay, HAP placed the child with another family.

HAP also charged a $10 home-study fee, which it refunded if the home was not approved. Although the social work establishment claimed that HAP did not require home studies—a central reason proxy adoption, and HAP, were dangerous—the agency did in fact screen potential adoptive parents through the American Service Bureau (ASB), a national trade association that produced credit reports, mainly for life insurance companies.[56] Of course, the ASB screening hardly approached what the social work establishment considered an adequate study because it was not conducted by trained social workers and did not conform to social work norms.

Besides proxy adoption, Holt introduced a second innovation that facilitated Korean adoption: the use of charter flights. As indicated in Chapter 2, the question of how to transport Korean children to the United States was a serious problem that had stymied early efforts to construct an intercountry adoption program. Children processed by the smaller adoption programs flew, usually five at a time, with an escort on Northwest Airlines.[57] HAP, however, ferried large numbers of children to the United States at a time, a practice that originated in the agency's attempt to get the maximum number of children to the United States before the RRA's expiration in December 1956. After the first six such flights, Holt began regularly chartering planes to transport children to the United States in groups ranging from fifty to well more than a hundred, escorted by American missionaries, Koreans going to the United States to study, HAP staff, and members of the Holt family. Twenty-six charter flights brought almost two thousand children to the United States between December 1956 and December 1961. The last HAP charter airplane left for the United States on 16 December 1961, after Congress banned proxy adoptions.[58]

These flights were long and tedious. After leaving Korea, they stopped over in Guam, Hawaii, or the Aleutian Islands, then proceeded to destinations on the West Coast: Seattle, Portland, San Francisco, or Los Angeles. The planes would return with equipment and supplies for HAP's Korean facilities, the escorts, and sometimes new volunteers or visitors. The Holts paid for the early charter flights in the same way they paid for facilities and supplies in Korea, by selling their stocks and property in the United States. The airplanes were outfitted especially for the purpose of ferrying children by removing the seats and replacing them with large bassinets that held two or three children each or heavy white cardboard boxes that held one child each (see Figure 3.2). Although Korean National Airlines offered the best prices and conditions of use, the planes themselves were not optimal. Because the cabins of the Korean National Airlines planes were unpressurized, they could not fly higher than nine thousand feet. When the planes flew higher than nine thousand feet, the ride grew smoother but the passengers had difficulty breathing and the children's lips turned blue. Below nine thousand feet, the turbulence resulted in a planeload of nauseated children and escorts.[59]

The conditions on the flight were also less than ideal. A Korean pediatrician who was on the March 1958 Holt flight reported on her "ghastly experience" to ISS.[60] Besides her, only four or five other attendants—all teenage girls—were on hand to help with more than ninety children, most of whom were less than a year old.[61] According to this witness, one child died of typhoid en route, and "a quarter of the children were tubercular"— in general, she reported that "the condition of the children was such that they should have had better medical care immediately prior to plans for their departure."[62] Yet the conditions this pediatrician described were not extraordinary. Given the inadequate health care in Korea in even the most modern facilities, as well as the widespread nature of diseases like tuberculosis, children were not always in optimal condition to make the long,

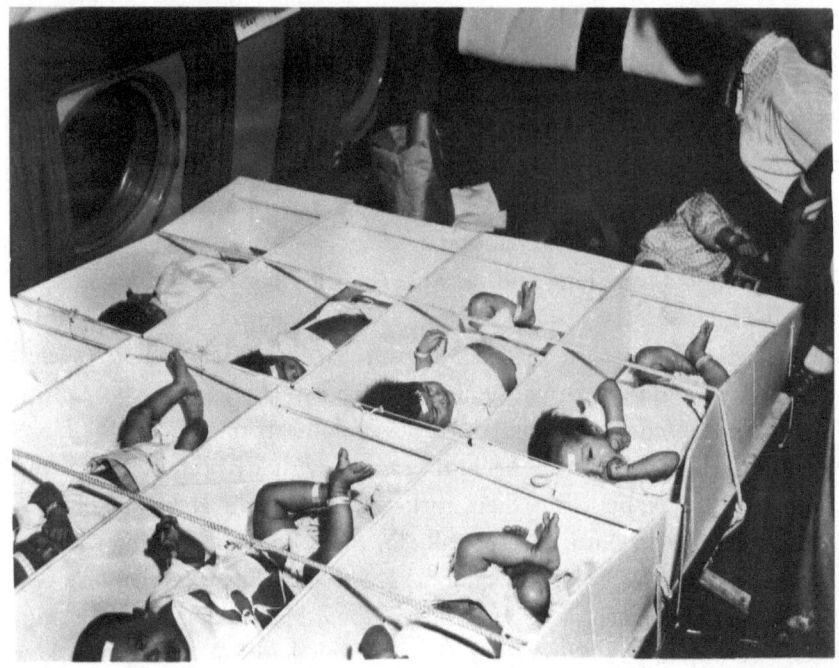

FIGURE 3.2 On the flights operated by Holt Adoption Program, some of the airplanes' seats were removed to make room for bassinets.
SOURCE: Courtesy of Holt International Children's Services.

difficult trip to the United States, and some died en route.[63] The number and qualifications of the escorts were also bound to be deficient at times, given the limited number of people who were willing and available to escort children to the United States under such trying conditions. David Kim of HAP's Korean operations remembered a March 1957 flight of eighty-seven children as hours of deafening crying, earaches, nausea, vomiting, diarrhea, and soiled clothing.[64]

The Holt "babylifts," as they were sometimes called, received publicity in both the national and local press. Portland's *Oregonian* was particularly interested in the activities of its longtime state resident, and local papers across the country carried photos and stories featuring the newest members of their communities. The flights were also covered by national mainstream and African American newspapers. Although it is unclear whether HAP orchestrated press coverage of the flights, ISS did ask parents their permission

Christian Americanism and the Adoption of GI Babies   101

to have reporters present when flights landed, particularly if the publicity could help stimulate more applications for hard-to-place Korean-black children.⁶⁵

Media coverage of the arrival of flights carrying newly adopted Korean children was an important ingredient in the popularization of Korean adoption on both sides of the Pacific (see Figure 3.3). Some of the first Holt flights to depart Korea received a joyful send-off by representatives of the Korean government and others, who cheered as the planes took off. After the first charter flight departed Seoul on 16 December 1956, David Kim of HAP Korea remarked, "There seemed to be more reporters than children, Holt staff, and volunteers combined." Kim explained, "This was a big postwar human-interest story in Korea," and "the warm humanitarian cause was refreshing to everyone after the hardship of the war." Korean newspapers and radio extensively covered the early flights and circulated stories from the United States about the arrival of Korean orphans there.⁶⁶

FIGURE 3.3   Arrival of a Holt baby lift in San Francisco, 17 December 1956
SOURCE: AP Photo/Ernest K. Bennett.

In the United States, newspaper photos showing beaming parents cuddling adorable—if bewildered—Korean children helped Americans become accustomed to the sight and idea of families made up of parents and children of different races. Often the coverage amounted to no more than an untitled photo with a caption that emphasized the celebratory nature of the day: "From No Homes to New Homes," "Gets Home for Christmas" and "An Orphan No Longer," for example.[67] The fact that these stories multiplied around the holidays contributed to their feel-good nature.

Adoptive parents came from all over the country to meet the flights. Reporters and photographers joined them, as did Koreans residing in the United States and other curious onlookers.[68] After the children disembarked from the plane, they went into the airport's immigration office, where public health doctors examined them and volunteers bathed and fed them while the adoptive parents waited outside. Sometimes children were changed into new clothing provided by their new parents. When a child was ready to be released, a HAP worker would call out the adoptive parents' names. They then went into a small office where they met their child for the first time and completed any remaining legal paperwork. After that, the adoptive parents were free to take their new son or daughter home.

Although the arrival of a Holt flight was almost universally treated as a festive occasion, Arnold Lyslo offered a less celebratory point of view. A child welfare worker who headed the US government's Indian Adoption Project, Lyslo was present when the *Flying Tiger* arrived in Portland on 27 December 1958, carrying Harry Holt and 107 Korean children ranging in age from a few months to ten years old. Rather than seeing the event as the media did—a day of joy, when loving parents were finally united with the needy Korean waifs they had adopted—Lyslo underlined his doubts about the adoptive parents, criticizing their appearance and behavior. His alignment with ISS—which essentially dictated an anti-HAP stance by 1958—no doubt colored his perspective. Lyslo described the adoptive couples as largely lower to middle class, and he found "startling" the modest appearance of most of the women: "without makeup and extremely plain dress—almost drab." Lyslo assumed that the appearance of these women indicated that the families were "of a strict religious sect," which was probably a safe conclusion in light of HAP's screening criteria. The African American adoptive parents, he reported, were "the most strikingly dressed and groomed of the group."[69]

After meeting their children, adoptive parents displayed a range of reactions, almost all of which met with Lyslo's disapproval. He condemned some adoptive parents for not responding to the arrival of their children with enough emotion, whereas other parents were so thrilled to receive their children that they covered them with hugs and kisses while crying tears of happiness. Cameras were everywhere as families posed for strangers, friends, and extended family. Onlookers "pawed" and "aggressively examined" the children, who were "utterly bewildered by all this posing and the flickering of flashbulbs."[70]

The irony of Lyslo's criticizing the parents who did not whisk their children away but remained at the airport and contributed to the public spectacle of the plane's arrival is that this spectacle is precisely what he had gone to the airport to witness. The parents' anticipation, the flight's arrival, and the drama of parents and children meeting for the first time were the central rituals of this critical day in the adoption process (so important that it came to be known to some as Gotcha Day). The joyous, moving images that the American media used to report on these arrivals helped popularize and normalize adoption nationally, advancing a positive narrative that could override any objections based on the children's racial difference or foreign birth. After all, what was more natural and beautiful than the love between parent and child? In arrival scenes, adoption, believed to be a highly private act, became an extremely public site where newly expanded American ideas about race and family became embodied and celebrated (see Figure 3.4).

In the midst of delighted parents, onlookers, and reporters, the children surely suffered some trauma. Lyslo noted that some of the older children stiffened and trembled when touched by their new parents. Adult adoptees who were old enough to remember their arrival in the United States recall fear and confusion. A Travelers Aid Society worker described the harrowing scene that occurred when a five-year-old Korean-white boy arrived at a Midwestern airport:

> [He] cried almost constantly after he arrived. He wanted to return to the escort on the plane, and it was necessary to carry him. He screamed and kicked and cried as though his heart would break. He resisted any overtures to comfort him. It was difficult to witness this child's reaction and passengers tried to offer treats, candy, gum. Each gesture brought forth louder wails and it was necessary to explain to them, his situation and remove him to private office.

FIGURE 3.4 Yung Hee Kim arriving, 29 August 1974
SOURCE: Courtesy of Yung Hee Kim.

His adoptive mother was "very tender and understanding," so that by the time their connecting flight was ready to depart, the child had "calmed down, sobbing only slightly and walked himself to airplane with his new mother."[71]

Christian Americanism, Race, and Colorblindness

Antiracism may have been the official language of the Cold War, but at ground level, below the high-minded media and government spheres, the United States was still intensely racist and deeply segregated. Bringing a foreign, mixed-race child from a third-world country into their homes, schools, churches, and communities was an extraordinarily progressive act for any American, and even more so given the profile of most of the early adopters: very religious, politically conservative, middle-aged, middle-class, white Protestants with a high school education and living in small towns or rural areas. They often had one or two biological children, and most adopted more than one Korean child.[72] Adoptive parents claimed that love, a missionary mind-set—or both—enabled them to transcend questions of race. As one typical adoptive couple declared: "Our girls are our mission field, this brings us great pride. We never see a nationality difference." Bertha Holt wrote, "Most of the letters indicate the people don't care whether the children look oriental or not," and noted, "One woman wrote, 'Send me an ugly baby, or a retarded one that nobody wants. I'll transform that little life with love and tender care.'"[73]

It was the Holts' opponents who made the race of the GI babies an issue. People occasionally called or wrote to protest bringing diseased, "slant-eyed Orientals" into the country, the offspring of Korean women and American men of questionable morals. In 1956, Bertha Holt reported, "One crank wrote . . . that he was saving his money for a gun and bus fare to come and shoot Harry for 'bringing in those slant-eyed monsters.' Harry replied that he would pay for the gun." Bertha Holt was equally dismissive of these threats, pointing out that the children were simply "returning to their fathers' land." Like their religious activist predecessors in the abolitionist movement and their contemporaries in the civil rights movement, the Holts demonstrated a progressive attitude toward race that almost seemed incompatible with their media image as a traditional American family. Interestingly, the Holts did not acknowledge a relationship between their efforts and the civil rights movement. In fact, Bertha Holt grew frustrated at Congress's inability to consider an orphan bill because of the volume of civil rights legislation before it: "Congress wouldn't quit squabbling about civil rights long enough to save orphans' lives."[74]

A more formidable opponent of the Holts was the American social work establishment, represented by International Social Service and its network of cooperating state and private welfare agencies. The Oregon Department of Welfare had declined to assist the Holts in the adoption of their own eight children for a number of reasons: the Holts wanted eight children, which far exceeded the limit of two set by the RRA; Harry and Bertha Holt's ages; the fact that they already had six biological children; their "reluctance to send their own children to school beyond the compulsory school age"; and their motives for adopting, which the department of welfare deemed "unrealistic." Already aggrieved by this rejection, Harry Holt's animus toward social workers grew further when ISS and state welfare departments later refused to cooperate with HAP in placing Korean children for adoption.[75]

HAP's use of proxy adoption was the flash point between it and professional social workers. ISS and its cooperating agencies believed that properly executed adoptions overseen by trained social workers was the best way to protect "the best interests of the child"—the standard for modern child welfare practice. In contrast, Holt and others who supported proxy adoption—including many aid workers and missionaries in Korea—believed that protection meant removing children from Korea as quickly as possible. In the precarious conditions of Korean orphanages, a child could get sick and die during the long months or even years it took for an ISS-approved adoption to be completed. Proxy adoption practitioners—including Holt—expressed some ambivalence about the practice, acknowledging that the emphasis on speed forced them to "cut corners at times," but they maintained, "When one must choose between social work standards and the life of a child, we choose the life of the child."[76] The fight over proxy adoption lasted until 1961, when Congress banned it at the same time it made provisions for international adoption a permanent part of immigration law (see Chapter 5).

The Holts believed that mainstream social workers resisted HAP not just because it used proxy adoption but also because they opposed intercountry adoption in general. According to social work orthodoxy, the Holts explained to their constituents, adoptions could be successful only if they were concealed, by carefully matching children and parents with similar hair and eye color, as well as similar personalities. Clearly, Asian or even mixed-race Asian children could not be placed in white American homes under these guidelines. Consequently, Bertha Holt noted that "in three years they had adopted only seven children overseas."[77] The Holts also faulted the social work establishment for prioritizing social work doctrine over children's lives. By not moving quickly enough, they were endangering children.

But the truth was more complicated than this. Although it is true that professional social workers expressed reservations about intercountry adoption for GI babies, their opposition was not rooted solely in an unyielding belief in race matching. Instead, social workers were more willing than others to explore alternative solutions for GI babies, including the possibility of them remaining in Korea. Their hesitation while others rushed to evacuate the children from Korea could be read by opponents as a general reluctance to participate in a project that was widely seen as unquestionably noble.

At the same time, the importance that social workers placed on race matching made it easy for their critics to blame social workers' hesitation on racism. ISS, the main representative of the social work establishment, categorically denied accusations of racial prejudice. It attributed such accusations to criticism of social workers' close questioning of prospective adoptive parents, which was meant to explore and test adopters' feelings about racially mixed children.[78] As Chapter 4 shows, many professional social workers actually wrestled sensitively with the implications that international, interracial adoption would have for US race relations and the future happiness of adopted children. It is true that some social workers did try to steer applicants interested in Korean GI babies toward children in the United States who needed adoptive homes, which could be perceived as the social work establishment's rejection of Korean adoption. Some American social workers had difficulty truly understanding the plight of Korean GI babies. They were, ISS observed, "often apt to feel as great a concern for the children in their communities in institutions who need adoptive homes, especially the Negro children."[79] ISS tried to address this problem by educating American social workers about conditions in Korea so that they could understand mixed-race children's genuine need for intercountry adoption.

Although Harry Holt's colorblindness stemmed from his belief that race did not matter in the face of Christian love, others who rejected race matching deployed a different version of colorblindness. This line of reasoning claimed race did not matter—but it also paradoxically celebrated the potential of race mixing to increase racial tolerance and end racism.[80] Some of the most visible international, interracial adoptions were the province of celebrities like Josephine Baker, who assembled a "rainbow tribe" of twelve children from around the world in the 1950s and 1960s.[81] Pearl S. Buck not only founded an adoption agency that specialized in placing mixed-race Asian children and wrote extensively about the promise of racial mixture but also was an adoptive mother herself, adopting a German-black daughter in 1953 and a Japanese-black daughter in 1958, in addition to the five white children she had adopted in the 1920s and 1930s.[82] Ordinary Americans also assembled large, multiracial "rainbow families" through adoption. Two notable examples were the Doss family, with their "One-Family UN" of twelve children created through domestic transracial adoption, and the DeBolts, who added to their six biological children fourteen adopted children, most from East and Southeast Asia, most with disabilities. These families received national press coverage, both matriarchs published memoirs, and the DeBolts' story inspired an Academy Award–winning documentary.[83] These motley assemblages symbolized the promise of diversity and harmony that mixed-race individuals and interracial families represented.

Adoptive parents and the public at large responded to the Christian Americanism that became associated with Harry Holt, and Christian Americanist discourse became the language of the Korean adoption movement. Although humanitarian impulses and desire for a child remained the prime motivator of the adoptive parents, Christian Americanist logic seems to have penetrated with them too. Many adoptive parents regarded adopting Korean GI babies as a way to bear witness to their Christian faith and meet their missionary obligation, which was often a Christian Americanist one as much as it was a Christian one. The causes of Christianizing and Americanizing—each with its own unique logic of rescue—were so closely interwoven in Cold War America that Christian and nationalistic purposes were uttered in the same sentence: "this is a wonderful missionary opportunity to bring these children into American Christian homes and raise them to be American citizens."[84] Both Christianity and Christian Americanism contributed, in varying proportions, to the decision to adopt.[85]

Even when adoptive parents stated they wanted to adopt for religious reasons, nationalist impulses were not far behind. One couple explained that their Christian faith was a primary motivation in their decision to adopt: "We all had a strong feeling that to live as professing Christians, we had to do something to help relieve the misery of malnutrition and death for at least one person . . . not just sending monies. . . . Korea seemed like a logical place at that time." At the same time, these parents indicated that a feeling of responsibility for the GI babies also influenced them: "we felt these illegitimate children, abandoned by our brother Americans, was our area of service."[86] Other parents baldly declared both religious and nationalistic reasons for wanting to adopt. In a letter to Senator Morse, a couple wrote: "we would like to urge you to do all you can to pass [this] bill so children of our American soldiers can be brought to the States to be brought up as good citizens in a Christian nation." Another couple who also wrote to Morse contrasted their desire to do something positive with the irresponsibility of the children's fathers: "as these poor little babies were fathered by our American soldiers—don't you think it is justifiable that we as true, honest Americans should do our level best to give them a chance in this country of ours, where they will have a good education, a wonderful time growing up in the peaceful surroundings, and the heritage that will be their due—as citizens of a free nation?"[87]

Market forces played a much larger role in early Korean adoption than Christian and Christian Americanist adopters might have been willing to admit. Demand for children to adopt in the United States exceeded supply through most of the twentieth century; in the 1950s, demand was thought to be nine times the supply.[88] Would-be adoptive parents recounted their fruitless efforts to adopt through standard channels: "Also have our name on four different doctor's lists but to no avail. It seems impossible to adopt a child."[89] Other couples were rejected by agencies because they were too old, did not meet income requirements, already had biological children, or for various other reasons. It is likely that an unknown number of these couples turned to Korean adoption because they simply had no access to children in the United States. It made sense for these prospective adopters to use the language of Christian Americanism to add weight to their appeals, to emphasize that although adopting from Korea would fulfill their personal desire for children, it would also serve altruistic purposes too, by giving foreign orphans "a Christian home," and "an opportunity to live normal lives."[90] Parents who strategically deployed Christian Americanist language in this way were not necessarily being dishonest about their true reasons for adopting; and in any case it is impossible to know what adopters' true motivations were. What matters is that they understood that they had to use a certain Christian Americanist vocabulary to get what they wanted.

With its rhetoric of helping America and the world, Christian Americanism provided power and legitimacy to adoptive parents' entreaties to lawmakers to help them adopt from Korea. Arguments based only on a profound wish for a child, a shortage of adoptable babies in the United States, or on religious motivation alone would not have gained the traction achieved by the intertwined religious and patriotic languages of Christian Americanism. Furthermore, Christian Americanism provided a language of love through which Americans could counteract the imperialistic, colonialist echoes in the practice of white Americans adopting nonwhite children from Korea.

Conclusion

Commenting on the 1958 memoir *White Mother*, written by a black woman who had been raised by a white woman in the American South, Pearl S. Buck praised what she saw as the book's solution to racial conflict: "I am not saying too much when I declare that were we all to follow in the footsteps of this one white mother, we would need not ask how to achieve peace on earth. Peace would be here." For Buck, and for Christian Americanists like her, international adoption, like the domestic interracial adoption of *White Mother*, was not just a personal act. It was also a profoundly political act available to any concerned American. By ending racial conflict, these adoptions could ultimately end the problem of communism, for a United States that showed such love to nonwhite children could be assured of winning Asia's allegiance as well as the loyalty of the entire free world.[91] The adoptions of Korean GI babies offered Christians and Christian Americanists alike a means by which to enact their beliefs. For devout Christians like Harry Holt, adopting a GI baby was missionary work through which they could bear witness to their faith and serve God. For Christian Americanists, these adoptions were a way for patriotic Cold War Americans to participate in their country's international Christianizing and Americanizing mission.

The American social work establishment stood conspicuously outside this arrangement, for whereas both Christians and Christian Americanists claimed to be unconcerned with race, social workers were far more preoccupied with it. Perhaps their attentiveness to race reflects a candor about the subject that is absent from the more simplified perspectives espoused by Christians and Christian Americanists, who somewhat naively—or perhaps disingenuously—believed that "the deliberate nonrecognition of race" would end racial conflict. The hope of ultimately eradicating racism may not have been their primary motivation for adopting, but both groups clearly believed in the power of colorblindness and the idea that simple Christian and parental love could conquer all.[92]

Yet colorblindness is itself a racial ideology, and colorblind interracial adoption insists on racial difference at the same time it disavows it. On the one hand, the adoptive parents of a GI baby demonstrated a willingness and ability to rise above race; but on the other hand, they acted out a central allegory of imperial discourse, in which the coupling of the white parent and nonwhite child justified and naturalized hierarchical power relations between white and nonwhite races. It may be that social workers were the only ones to acknowledge fully that conscious colorblindness might not make race—or racism—disappear. Race would continue to do work in interracial or intercountry adoptions, whether or not the people involved denied its existence.[93]

The US government used the idea of love to counteract what looked like imperialistic activity in Asia throughout the Cold War. In a sense, it was Christians like Harry Holt and the other adoptive parents of GI babies who provided this tool, by demonstrating that a family's love could "transcend the boundaries of race and nationality." For Christian Americanists, the American nation was the family that lovingly transcended boundaries and spread the Christian and American values that would help to end racism and communism everywhere.[94]

FOUR

Making Families on a New Frontier

> I, the above described, had losen all of my family by the broke out of Korean War in 1950 and been suffering from a severe material hardness without any income till I had been acqainted with an American soldier and shared bed with him several months. When I had conceived for two months he had moved to the front line unrecognizingly that I had conceived. . . . On [date] I gave birth to a child. . . . It has been a big burden for me to bring her up without any regular income and I am very regretful . . . to hand her over to anybody else, but I accepted to let her be adopted to an American family. . . . I swear to the followings: a. I accept the adoption of [child] by the [adoptive family] . . . b. I will abandon the parental authority . . . and will never manifest any right as a mother.
>
> —A birth mother[1]

> She knelt down and kissed me, inside my torn jacket she hid 2 pictures, one of herself, and one of my birth father. . . . She wrote information on the back, so we would always be connected, then she said find your father in America. I could see my mother through the plane window, she was crying, and so was I. I still don't remember crying as hard as I did again. The whole plane of children were crying, that was the last time I ever saw my mother again. I vomited all the way to America.
>
> —An adoptee[2]

By 1956 intercountry adoption had become a critical component of Korean welfare. The Korean government, from President Rhee down, openly stated that its "number one welfare project" was to send as many GI babies as possible to the United States by 31 December 1956, the expiration date of the Refugee Relief Act (RRA).[3] But Korean reliance on international adoption did not end in December 1956. Instead, repeated renewals of the RRA's orphan provisions, together with the ongoing efforts of foreign missionaries, adoption agencies, and social workers to refine the emerging Korean adoption system, ensured that the practice would not only continue but also grow.

American social workers—who had struggled to gain legitimacy since before World War II—sought to establish their expertise in intercountry adoption by shaping policy and law at the state and national levels. But the geographic and conceptual broadening of adoption to include children from Korea sparked new questions about the relevance of social work practice. For decades, many adoptive parents had bypassed social workers in favor of independent adoptions. Already resistant to the social work establishment's intrusions into the sacred space of their homes and families, seeking quick adoptions, or impatient with the social work profession's rules and procedures, many adopters saw social workers' efforts to police international adoption as another attempt to unduly extend state surveillance into private life.

In Korea, international adoption helped spur the development of the social work profession. Korean social workers supported the developing international adoption industry, which in turn required and stimulated the production of more social workers. Even so, the number of professional social workers remained low and the quality of their training dubious.[4] The fact that Korean adoption remained largely in the hands of amateurs until well into the 1980s contributed to its haphazardness, even as it was being systematized. The inconsistent and questionable methods applied to turn children into orphans, assess adoptive parents, and construct families were products of people trying to find their way in the brave new world of international adoption.

The Rationalization of Modern Adoption

Birth mothers and adoptive parents have historically driven modern adoption practice in the United States, with policy makers and social workers following in their wake. "Stranger" adoption—adoption by nonrelatives—began in significant numbers in the opening decades of the twentieth century, replacing earlier forms of private and institutional childcare. At first, child welfare workers opposed placing children in permanent adoptive homes.[5] Concerned with the preservation of the family and the primacy of blood ties, and doubtful that parents could truly love an adopted child, these workers preferred "placing out" dependent children in paid foster homes. Yet Americans wanted to adopt—and they did, finding children through networks of friends, relatives, lawyers, doctors, nurses, midwives, civic leaders, and members of the clergy.[6] Couples also adopted through private agencies and commercial maternity homes. In a variety of ways, unmarried mothers and adoptive parents made arrangements without government involvement.

In the 1920s, professional social workers, who had replaced Progressive Era child welfare reformers, claimed adoption as part of their domain and sought to manage it through professional protocols, expert supervision, and psychoanalytic theory. The US Children's Bureau (established in 1912) became actively involved in shaping the "expert consensus" about adoption practice and standards. The Children's Bureau's private counterpart was the Child Welfare League of America (CWLA), an association of private child welfare agencies that had been established in 1915. Under the leadership of these two organizations, social welfare professionals began to modernize and systematize—to rationalize—adoption. This rationalization transformed what was thought of and defended as a profoundly private act into one that was unmistakably public. The CWLA believed adoption affected "at least four groups—the natural parents, the child, the adoptive parents and society as a whole." As such, it was something "with which society as a whole has a right to be concerned." Modern adoption thus "forcefully moved childhood and kinship into the public sphere."[7]

Although social workers held increasing authority over adoption after World War II, they were never able to fully establish their expertise. Instead, their role continued to be "one of negotiated power" in which they wielded influence but not authority. In the mid-1940s, for example, they were involved in only half of all stranger adoptions. Meanwhile, independent brokers placed children with little oversight, both domestically and—like Harry Holt—internationally. But for Americans adopting from abroad, state power was obvious and unavoidable. Prospective adopters had to negotiate federal refugee and immigration laws, which were in a state of flux in the 1950s. Adoption law and policy varied across states but the postwar increase in domestic and international adoption and concerns about baby trafficking prompted individual states to strengthen their adoption laws.[8]

International Social Service (ISS) embodied the self-conscious professionalization of social workers in the early twentieth century. An international social welfare organization headquartered in Geneva, ISS had been founded as International Migration Service in 1924 to coordinate social welfare efforts across national boundaries (it changed its name in 1946). To its detractors, ISS workers were self-styled experts who wielded degrees in a field that required nothing more than common sense, good judgment, and a well-tuned "maternal instinct." ISS had become familiar with the problem of GI babies in Japan, where mixed-race "occupation babies" suffered the same prejudice and hostility as in Korea. Although ISS opened its first Korean adoption case files in 1953, it did not promote intercountry adoption as a way to solve the problem of mixed-race children. Instead, as it had in Japan, ISS implemented a dual approach in Korea: it placed some GI babies abroad but at the same time emphasized the need to develop local solutions. ISS hoped that attitudes toward these children could be changed so that they could stay in Korea. It was not until the Holts founded the Holt Adoption Program (HAP) in 1956 and popularized the practice of proxy adoption that ISS began to actively participate in Korean adoption.[9]

The kind of intercountry adoption that ISS approved of mapped the time-consuming domestic adoption process across borders. ISS did not process adoptions but instead coordinated the work of a local US adoption agency or state department of public welfare with that of a Korean agency, usually Child Placement Service (CPS). (The National Catholic Welfare Conference operated in a similar fashion.) If there was no local agency for adoptive parents to work with—and several state departments of social welfare provided no intercountry adoption service at all—the only way they could adopt from Korea was by using a proxy.

Social workers approached both domestic and intercountry adoption with extreme caution, seeking to manage its risks by thoroughly screening both child and adoptive parents. The first step in an intercountry adoption was a preliminary interview of the prospective adopters by an agency in the United States. If it deemed the couple eligible, it scheduled a home study, which could take months to complete and often did not begin until months after the preliminary interview had taken place. The home study was meant to probe the motivations for adopting and the fitness of the applicants. Working with a vision of the ideal home and family that was strictly defined by race, class, and gender, social workers assessed everything from the applicants' marital relationship and conformity to gender roles, to the physical environment of the home.[10] Although the principles of home studies were becoming standardized, the studies themselves were not uniform. They varied in length and quality according to agency and worker; some contained a great deal of detail and analysis of multiple visits, whereas others were purely descriptive, ending with a brief recommendation.

Social workers accepted a variety of motivations for intercountry adoption, which were usually similar to those behind domestic adoptions: infertility, for example, or a desire to address a gender imbalance in the family. Couples who were rejected for a domestic adoption—whether because they already had biological children, were too old, or did not meet income requirements—had an easier time qualifying for an intercountry placement. Professional social workers tended to look askance at applicants who seemed overly zealous about their altruistic or religious reasons for adopting from Korea. Among the acceptable reasons for wanting to adopt was what one social worker recorded: "It is part of their religious belief that all races are equal and they feel that this is the best way to demonstrate their belief." In contrast, another social worker's observation that a couple was motivated "by a religious fervor rather than for the good of the child" disqualified them from further consideration.[11]

Because conditions in Korea precluded the kind of thorough child assessment available in domestic adoptions—such as medical histories and exams, or intelligence and psychological tests—social workers were particularly careful to caution potential adoptive parents about the health of the children. The Korean agency provided a child study, which included as much information as possible about the child's general health, development, and family background. This document was often perfunctory, written in broken English, and not always completed by a professional worker. The only thing the agencies could promise potential adopters was that the child's medical examination in Korea—required before she could receive a visa to enter the United States—guaranteed that she had passed the requirements of US immigration law, meaning that she was neither tubercular nor mentally deficient. Beyond that, an ISS worker stated, families adopting from Korea had to "realise that they are willy-nilly fully responsible for bringing the little child to their home and for accepting him as their own." Even into the 1970s, many children immigrated to the United States "more on hope than assurance that they would develop normally."[12]

In addition to meeting the standards of the social work agencies, prospective adoptive parents had to satisfy the requirements of the Immigration and Naturalization Service (INS). Once a local adoption agency approved the home, ISS would endorse the adopters' promise that their adopted child would not become a public charge, which the State Department verified. At the same time, parents provided copies of their marriage certificate, a bank statement, and proof of employment. The Korean adoption agency then applied to the Korean Ministry of Foreign Affairs for the child's passport, and once the child passed the immigration medical exam, she received a visa from the US consulate. After the child arrived in the United States, ISS still had legal custody of her for a six- to twelve-month supervisory period, during which a local child welfare agency regularly visited the adoptive family. If the agency was satisfied with the child's and family's adjustment to each other, it recommended the placement to ISS, which endorsed it. Parents could then finalize the adoption in a US court, thus concluding a process that may have taken years to complete.

Making Paper Orphans

With the advent of international adoption, Korean bureaucrats, orphanage directors, and social workers—together with their American allies—scrambled to facilitate an unprecedented procedure. They improvised almost everything as they went along: from identifying and collecting "adoptable" children, to processing and preparing them for adoption abroad, to matching them to families when racial matching was largely impossible. Stranger adoption was truly strange to Koreans, who traditionally adopted only males from the paternal line, and only in the interest of maintaining the family name. Like American social workers earlier in the century, Koreans expressed doubt about a parent's ability to truly love an adopted child.

The Korean social work profession and the adoption system emerged in parallel, and by mimicking American methods and standards. Hyun Sook Han's early career corresponded with both. Han, who began work at ISS in the early 1960s, had graduated from one of the very first social work programs in Korea, but she did not think her degree was worth much. Korean social work programs provided students with only theoretical knowledge, not practical experience. Few agencies had the time or resources to properly train new social workers, and adoption and foster-care standards did not yet exist. Han learned through on-the-job experience, and she herself trained the social workers who came after her.[13] Although she felt ill equipped for her job, she was better prepared than those of her colleagues who had graduated from Yonsei, a top university. Yonsei did not have a social work department, so the workers were drawn from the English department. Presumably, agencies believed that the students' English-language skills would compensate for the lack of social work education.

As discussed in Chapter 2, the category of "orphan" was a capacious one in postwar Korea, and orphanhood could not be presumed only on the basis of the fact that a child lived at an orphanage.[14] In the highly fluid postwar milieu, it was not always clear whether a child without her parents had been lost or abandoned. Rather than simply documenting the existing fact of orphanhood, then, orphanages and adoption agencies had to make children into orphans through administrative means. Under the Korean *hojuk* system, a child did not receive an individual birth certificate but was registered as part of a family. A *hojuk* listed the male head of the house, his wife, and dependents. Families carefully named their children with help from fortune-tellers, and naming conventions not only embedded the child in the patrilineal line (through her father's surname) but also linked her to her extended family, past and present. A child's inclusion in the *hojuk* thus signaled her social and legal Korean citizenship in the fullest sense—membership in a patriarchal family lineage, and membership in her nation. To make a "paper orphan," city or district officials created a new *hojuk* for the child that listed her as the head of her household, with parents listed as unknown. This document, containing one lonely name (often made up), was a literal representation of the child, stripped of her family, history, and nation.[15] It produced an orphan, ostensibly free of family ties, who was available for overseas adoption.

Children who seemed to have been deliberately abandoned were classified as foundlings, and required no relinquishment papers. An infant might be left on the doorstep of a hospital, orphanage, or church with her name and birthdate written on a piece of paper pinned to the blanket. Sometimes there was a note asking that the child be adopted abroad. Alternatively, a child was left in a crowded place like a market where an adult was bound to find her and take her to a police station. From there, she would go to an orphanage or reception center, where parents could find her if she had been lost and not abandoned. Older children sometimes had a clear picture of their families but did not know their parents' names and addresses, making it impossible to return them to their homes.[16] At any rate, most child welfare institutions were too overburdened to expend any resources searching for birth parents. Relinquishment was not always absolute, however. Even after they relinquished their children, birth parents or relatives sometimes appeared at orphanages and took their children away, usually with few formalities.[17]

Birth mothers or relatives also brought children in for formal relinquishment. Koreans used a *dojang*, a wooden stamp, to place their seal in red ink on official documents, but birth mothers also stamped relinquishment papers with a thumbprint, using lipstick for ink, which produced an especially poignant memento for some adoptees. In some cases, birth mothers provided written statements describing the hardship they had suffered and the reasons behind their decision to send their child abroad for adoption.[18] Some birth mothers boarded their children with older women while they worked elsewhere; these caregivers brought in children when they could no longer care for them, or if the mother failed to keep up with payments. Sometimes, these relinquishments occurred without the mother's knowledge or consent.

Agencies actively searched for GI babies to place abroad. ISS workers visited areas where there were many such children, usually in the vicinity of military bases. A social worker would spot a mixed-race child, locate her mother, and speak with her about her plans for the child. During this first visit, the birth mother and the social worker exchanged information, and the latter planted a seed in the mother's mind. If the woman was living in poor circumstances, the social worker might promise to bring her some flour, coal, or other supplies. Sometimes, birth mothers were quickly persuaded and decided to relinquish their children in time for the social worker to return to Seoul with the child after the second or third visit. Molly Holt, one of Harry and Bertha Holt's biological children, remembers riding around in HAP's distinctive red and white Chevrolet station wagon collecting babies. According to her, birth mothers told one another, "When the red car comes the next time we have to give up our children." HAP workers also plucked mixed-race children from orphanages. Although they had no procedures for determining a child's racial makeup, they were not troubled about it and felt that a few full-Korean children slipping through was an acceptable risk.[19] As international adoption increased in the late 1950s, agencies tried to gather mixed-race children in one place so as to make it easier to locate and prepare them for emigration. A structure quickly arose that funneled mixed-race children scattered about the country in local orphanages to a few institutions in Seoul. World Vision used various facilities as reception centers for these children until it established its own Child Center in February 1956.[20] HAP created a separate orphanage soon after, in Hyochang Park, and ISS housed the children it was processing in a special wing of the Choon Hyung Babies Home.

HAP solicited GI babies with newspaper advertisements and through tracts that it distributed around country. The tracts "urged relatives of mixed race children not to delay; otherwise this opportunity might not be available after the law expired at the end of the year [1956]." The flip side contained "a gospel message, urging mothers to change their lifestyles and become Christians." As news of HAP's activities spread, people with mixed-race children to relinquish would call the agency to "come get the baby." David Kim, Holt's right-hand man in Korea, carefully managed the public perception of intercountry adoption by easing the fears of those who regarded it as mysterious and possibly sinister. Rumors circulated that children were being adopted to work as domestic servants, to be trained as acrobats, or so that their organs could be harvested. Like many other Koreans, Kim had initially been skeptical of Americans' desire to adopt mixed-race children, but he became a believer when he traveled to the United States and saw the children thriving in their homes and communities. He shared these observations with women who were considering relinquishment, as well as those who came to ask for news of the children who had left for the United States. Kim cultivated relationships with the Korean government and media that paid off, with positive media coverage of intercountry adoption and special treatment for HAP—for example, government offices processed its paperwork more quickly than that of other agencies. The Korean Ministry of Health and Social Affairs (MHSA) did its part to publicize intercountry adoption by distributing letters that encouraged mothers to relinquish their mixed-race children.[21] In 1957 it awarded Harry Holt a medal in recognition of his humanitarian efforts.

Whether they were well meaning or punitive, social workers and others pressured birth mothers to relinquish their mixed-race children for adoption. Korean social worker Hyun Sook Han, who was responsible for an area that included the US Air Force town of Osan, placed hundreds of children in American adoptive homes during a twelve- to eighteen-month period in the early 1960s. "I had the highest numbers among the ISS social workers at the time," she remembers, and being "young and new to the work, I thought this was a good thing." Years later, she learned that her visits to the town were preceded by panic as women warned each other to hide their children. Han writes, "All that time, I did not know that the mothers were afraid of me, afraid that I was going to make them agree that their children should be placed for adoption." Like her colleagues, Han persuaded birth mothers by contrasting the child's grim prospects in Korea with the bright future that awaited in the United States. She asked, "'What is your plan for your baby? What do you think the baby's future will be in Korea? Koreans will not accept your child. How can your children live?'" Han reminded birth mothers of the ridicule and rejection that life in Korea would hold for their mixed-race children. HAP workers employed a similar strategy: "Of course we don't urge them to give them to us, but they know the children will never fit into Korean society."[22]

Looking back on her early years as a social worker as well as the early years of Korean adoption, Han expressed regret about her zealous approach. "I really believed, in my youth and naïveté, that I was doing the best I could for these children. I was giving them a better chance. That was how social work agencies were in Korea back then." She explains, "I misunderstood my job and thought I was supposed to make the birth mothers relinquish their children; I pushed those mothers to sign the papers." Oak Soon Hong of CPS evidently shared Han's philosophy. In a meeting with several foreign voluntary agencies, she indicated that mothers were reluctant to relinquish their children for adoption (see Figure 4.1). Although most of those in attendance believed that children should remain with their mothers in these cases, Hong seemed unconvinced. In fact, she was described as being "impelled by one consideration: that any Korean orphan is better off with any family in the U.S."[23]

Some birth mothers were outright coerced into relinquishing their children. ISS accused HAP of using the police to help force mothers to release their mixed-race children, and a Korean pediatrician claimed to have witnessed birth mothers being physically compelled to relinquish their children to HAP staff on three different occasions. One woman, who changed her mind after relinquishing her child to HAP, was assaulted when she

FIGURE 4.1 Diane Shigley (born Jung Soon Joo) and her Korean mother (Mi Sun Joo), May 1961
SOURCE: Courtesy of Diane Shigley.

asked for her baby back. Harry Holt's daughter, Barbara, and her boyfriend, admitted to striking the woman but claimed it was to stop her hysterics. Holt asserted that HAP's official policy was to meet a birth mother's demands: "I always return the children to their mothers," he stated. "We are not kidnaping [sic] anyone's child." The woman who was struck, however, was not able to retrieve her child, as she had already been sent overseas.[24]

Even if birth mothers did not feel forced to relinquish their children, certain realities loomed over them. US laws facilitating international adoption changed constantly throughout the 1950s, so it was unclear how long it would remain possible. US immigration law set the upper age limit for immigrant orphans at ten (later raised to fourteen), but in reality it was very difficult to place children who were older than five. Birth mothers usually delayed deciding about relinquishment until the child experienced some kind of blatant discrimination. This usually occurred once the child began attending school. If they were even admitted, mixed-race children usually encountered teasing, bullying, and worse, from teachers and fellow students alike. The beginning of school, and the first real taste of the ostracism that awaited the child, coincided with the end of the period when a child was considered most adoptable. A birth mother who was unsure about relinquishing her child had a narrow window of time in which to act.[25]

As the positive publicity spread about adoption for mixed-race children, it became less difficult to locate them—at least for HAP. Its facility became the first place that birth mothers, police officers, military personnel, and missionaries took mixed-race children. HAP was so dominant that from 1956 to 1960, when it transported dozens of children at a time to the United States on chartered flights, its recently emptied orphanage immediately filled up again with more children to be sent abroad. In contrast, despite being one of the agencies recommended by the State Department to do intercountry adoptions, ISS was never a major conduit for Korean children. Between 1955 and 1963, its most active years, it placed at most 13.7 percent of the Korean children who were adopted overseas.[26]

By the late 1950s, HAP had secured a virtual monopoly over the supply of mixed-race Korean children available for adoption. In contrast, ISS Korea's workers spent at least two to three days a week fruitlessly seeking them out. It blamed the government and missionaries for failing to support its adherence to social work standards. From ISS's point of view, only it and its cooperating agencies were qualified to place children, whereas agencies like HAP were dangerous renegades. Not only did HAP place children by proxy; ISS believed that HAP collected mixed-race children without providing counseling to their mothers or securing appropriate relinquishment documents—claims that have some basis in truth. But from the standpoint of HAP and its allies, ISS simply moved too slowly in the face of an emergency; its emphasis on social work standards over speedy placement put the lives of children at risk.[27]

Korean adoption supposedly offered a second chance to every member of the adoption triad. A childless American couple could construct a family; a child could be rescued from the poverty and shame of illegitimacy and racial mixture; and a birth mother could put her past behind her and reenter respectable society. The geographical distance of intercountry adoption also offered a unique finality that domestic adoption did not: birth mothers had the assurance that their children would not reappear in the future and complicate their lives, and adoptive parents could feel confident that the birth mother would not return one day to reclaim her child.[28]

Whether birth mothers had been sex workers, raped, or unlucky in love, Korean social workers represented them as "victims of the war." They described birth mothers in ways that ranged from neutral to positive, with the most common narrative being that of the decent girl or widow who resorted to sex work as a result of desperate circumstances. These stories, told by the birth mothers to social workers, were recorded by the latter for the consumption of their colleagues and sometimes the adoptive parents. Initially, Korean social workers matter-of-factly described birth mothers who were prostitutes as prostitutes, but after adoptive parents began to complain, they used euphemisms like "entertainer" or simply stated that the birth mother had lived with an American soldier. Some social workers—Korean and American—pathologized prostitutes, who they believed chose their professions because of personality defects. However, this kind of condemnation does not appear in ISS files. It is less clear how an explicitly religious agency like HAP or the Seventh-Day Adventist operation might have treated this issue, but evidence suggests that these organizations, like ISS, focused more on the wrong done to Korean women than on the sins of the women themselves.[29]

Birth fathers, however, could be dealt with much more harshly. When the paternal grandparents of a mixed-race girl pleaded with Harry Holt to send their grandchild to them instead of the family he had already selected for her, he responded with contempt, writing, "Frankly, I personally have no sympathy whatsoever for the fathers of these children or [their] . . . relatives. A family who has raised a son who has ruined the lives of two women [he had married and divorced twice since returning from Korea] would not be considered as an adoptive family by our agency." ISS saw these statements as "very typical of his attitudes" toward American birth fathers. Indeed, Holt's anger at the irresponsible men who had left children behind to suffer and die was palpable from his first trip to Korea when he wrote to his wife, "I think these children's natural fathers are probably back home in the U.S. living comfortably with their family. However, God who knows their sins will cast judgment upon them."[30]

Social workers and the Korean public interpreted relinquishment as the ultimate expression of maternal love and sacrifice. Many birth mothers were single women who were socially ostracized and lacked the economic means to support a family, a situation exacerbated by the existence of illegitimate, mixed-race children. The reigning consensus that these children's lives would be better in the wealthy, powerful United States intensified the pressure to relinquish.[31] Social workers praised the courageous and selfless mothers who "realized" that "foreign adoption . . . will give more opportunity to the child, than anything she can give." Rather than lacking in maternal instinct, these women were heroes. Having been "victimized by . . . war, poverty, and injustice," and then by "racial bias, national pride and . . . the moralism of Korean society," these women nonetheless found the strength to fulfill their "parental duty" by releasing their children to find better lives abroad.[32]

In contrast, social workers and others criticized birth mothers who attempted to keep their children as doing so to have some security and fulfillment in their otherwise empty lives. Social workers believed that birth mothers who kept their children were hoping to use them for "blackmail purposes" or were entertaining a fantasy: that the birth father would come back, marry the mother of his child, and take his family to the United States Although many of these men left Korea vowing to return, most did not. Korean social worker Hyun Sook Han attributed birth mothers' frustrated dreams to naïveté and cultural differences. Coming from a society in which people did not typically express feelings of love verbally, Korean women were eager to believe their American lovers' declarations: "'I love you, I want to marry you, I want to raise our baby.' Waiting for these words is why many birth mothers raised their children on their own as long as they could," Han explained.[33]

Once it became apparent that marriage and emigration were unlikely, mothers tried to send their children to their birth fathers or paternal relatives in the United States. But many had trouble locating the fathers of their children.[34] Others brought the children to the gates of military installations hoping to find their birth fathers; when they could not, some women simply left their children there. When Korean women and American servicemen parted ways, they often knew little about each other, including surnames, addresses, and other basic identifying information. ISS adoption records are full of instances in which a birth mother could say little about the father of her child besides a vague description—tall, strong, cheerful—and one or two equally unhelpful details, like rank.

For Koreans, one of the most foreign elements of the deeply foreign concept of international, interracial, stranger adoption was its finality, the notion that a parent permanently severed ties with his or her child. Harry Holt described a birth mother who "almost had hysterics in the office. She thought she could keep track of her baby after he had gone to America. I had to tell her it is a clean break and forever. Poor girl, her baby wasn't weaned yet and she cried and cried."[35] Some mothers failed to grasp the irrevocability of relinquishment or refused to accept it, as reflected in stories about birth mothers who discovered their children's whereabouts in the United States and established contact with them.

Even as they relinquished their children, birth mothers attempted to exercise some control over the adoption process. Speed was important. Once they had decided on relinquishment they wanted quick action, a reason so many preferred to have their children adopted by proxy through HAP. Others released their children to more than one agency at a time in the hope of placing them as quickly as possible.[36] Birth mothers also tried to wield power in other ways, manipulating identities and stories to shape outcomes. One birth mother, for example, tried to have a friend's child placed with the same family that had adopted her own child.[37] As agencies competed to amass a supply of desirable children for adoption abroad, some birth mothers saw an opportunity for financial gain. ISS reported that mothers and foster mothers were demanding money in exchange for children, claiming that other agencies were paying. ISS had no evidence to support these rumors but was aware of cases in which a serviceman who became interested in a child's welfare would pay the child's mother to release the child for adoption. As a result, ISS believed "many children are being held with this prospect in view."[38] Some foster mothers were owed money by the women whose children they were caring for and expected someone to compensate them for services rendered. In cases when they demanded payment before turning over a child, they could be seen as not selling children but collecting what was owed them.[39]

It is important to recognize that despite what could be extreme powerlessness, birth parents did exercise some agency. Birth mothers came from a range of backgrounds: they could be sex workers with mixed-race children or women with multiple children who had been separated from their husbands and extended families during the war. By the mid-1960s, most children leaving Korea for adoption were full-Korean children, relinquished not because of their racial mixture but because of other social or financial pressures. Birth parents might be a respectably married couple with too many girls in a society that valued boys or simply unable to take care of another child. Koreans were well acquainted with the United States' material abundance, thanks to years of American military presence, and many birth parents wanted their children to have a better life in the wealthiest country in the world. Many thought of international adoption as an opportunity, perhaps the only way for a child from a poor family to receive an education.

It is true that in some cases birth parents were tricked, coerced, or even had their children stolen from them. But for many others, relinquishing a child was an anguished decision but not an irrational one—it was birth parents trying to select the best from a few very bad options.[40]

Race, Color, and Adoptability

Complementary Korean and American racial thinking facilitated Korean adoption. In Korea, GI babies' unacceptable racial mixture made them available for international adoption. On the US side, that same racial mixture made them palatable to white American parents who may not have been able to accept full-Korean children, or the Native American or African American children who were available to be adopted domestically. But that racial mixture also made GI babies a problem under US social work orthodoxy, which classified nonwhite and mixed-race children—along with older children, those with health problems, and the mentally or physically disabled—as "unadoptable." Social workers initially regarded full-Korean children as difficult to place, mainly because of American anti-Asian attitudes—including those of the adopters themselves. A social worker recommended that a Korean-white child rather than a full-Korean child would be a better fit for the family she was studying, since the potential adoptive mother felt negatively about "particularly dark skin. . . . [T]he children from Korea that she has seen and admired have been light-skinned children."[41]

The presence of white blood eased the "otherness" of Korean-white children. Whereas one drop of black blood made a person black according to American racial thought, one drop of Asian blood did not render a person irretrievably Asian. Instead, in a reversal of the one-drop rule, Korean-white children were whitened—redeemed—by the presence of white blood. A kind of geneticism rendered Korean-white GI babies "our" babies in American eyes; a belief in the power of nurture suggested that their racial mixture could be overcome with the proper environment and upbringing. Although still "other," they were tolerably so. In fact, the sight of blond-haired or blue-eyed Korean children provoked particularly visceral responses from the Americans in Korea who first publicized the plight of GI babies. What an ISS worker called "a certain family and community identification with these children as half-American" helped mobilize American support for GI baby adoption.⁴² These feelings of sympathy for, and identification with, mixed-race children were akin to those that American abolitionists stirred a century earlier, when they circulated images of very white-looking slave children to gain support for their cause. Americans' acceptance of mixed-race Korean children also paved the way for the later adoption of full-Korean children. The logic of racial triangulation drastically altered the fate of Korean-white (and later, full-Korean) children. Once labeled "unadoptable" because they were not white, they became "adoptable" because they were not black.

Because white Americans adopted the majority of Korean children, race matching was impossible in most cases.⁴³ Social workers thought matching was important because it made the adoption invisible, which would spare the adopted child the stigma of illegitimacy and save her parents from being exposed as infertile or otherwise deficient.⁴⁴ But while social workers fretted over how to create ideal families without matching as a tool, Americans who adopted Korean children demonstrated an adoption truism: that adopters were often more willing than agencies to cross racial and religious lines to create families.⁴⁵ When it became clear that Americans were far less interested in racial matching than social workers were, this consideration fell by the wayside, though social workers, psychologists, and others did continue to worry about the outcome of these placements that were at once international and interracial.

Although adoption agencies became accustomed to placing Korean-white, and then full-Korean, children in white homes, they toed the black-white color line. There are few documented cases of white families adopting Korean-black children. In one case, HAP re-placed a full-Korean child whom it had accidentally placed with a black family.⁴⁶ Although Bertha Holt claimed that HAP solved the persistent problem of finding homes for Korean-black children by placing them in white homes, there is no evidence to support this.⁴⁷ When Korean adoption began, anti-miscegenation statutes—many of which prohibited Asian-white intermarriage—still existed in many states. Korean adoption's simultaneous transgressing of the Asian-white divide on the one hand, and careful policing of the black-white color line on the other, shows the continuing power of the black-white divide.

The racial ambiguity of some GI babies inflamed fears of the "specter of white children placed with African American adopters." In 1958 alarm bells rang at ISS when it learned of a family in New Jersey who had adopted through HAP a dark-skinned girl who was supposedly Korean and Native American. ISS's informant saw the girl and reported, "I lived in Florida for many years where we have Seminole Indians and Negroes and I believe that I can tell them apart. . . . [T]his child . . . was definitely of Negro blood and had been placed . . . in a white home situated in a white neighborhood." She subsequently learned that the family was planning to sell their home and move because the community would not accept their daughter. ISS regarded this inappropriate placement as an example of the dangers of proxy adoption.[48]

Social workers labored to accurately classify mixed-race children. Some were so difficult to categorize that social workers suggested a range of acceptable adoptive families for them. ISS Korea thought that one boy could be placed with a light-skinned Negro family, a Filipino family, or a family of Latin American extraction. Photographs of children available for adoption sometimes bore the marks of ongoing, pseudoscientific attempts to identify their racial origins (see Figure 4.2). A girl at an orphanage in Pusan was labeled "Korean & Philippino (?)," another as "Mongoloid-Philip." One toddler was classified as "Mongoloid-Philippine" with *Philippine* later crossed out and *Negroid* written below it. The same adjustment was made to the card of a little girl, but an exclamation point after the word Negroid emphasized the change in racial categories: "Mongoloid-Negroid!" A slightly older boy was deemed "Mongoloid Philippino" with the handwritten notation, "or Negroid." An additional note stated: "Legs and arms are now very dark." ISS workers also investigated ways to employ scientific methods to distinguish between mixed-race and full-Korean children, such as using Mongolian spots to determine a child's racial makeup.[49] Young Korean social workers with extremely limited experience with non-Koreans or non-Asians struggled, in Hyun Sook Han's words, to "guess the race of mixed-race babies." She declared, "No one gave us any ideas or suggestions. . . . Maybe if I lived in America for many years and saw many people of all difference races and mixed, I might learn how to tell, but I live in Korea. . . . How could I know?"[50]

In describing mixed-race Korean children, everyone from social workers to casual observers became self-styled experts on race. The ISS Korea director described a little girl as "a pleasing combination where the more obvious Negro features would appear to be washed out into a pleasing blend of Oriental skin tone and dark brown hair." Another ISS caseworker

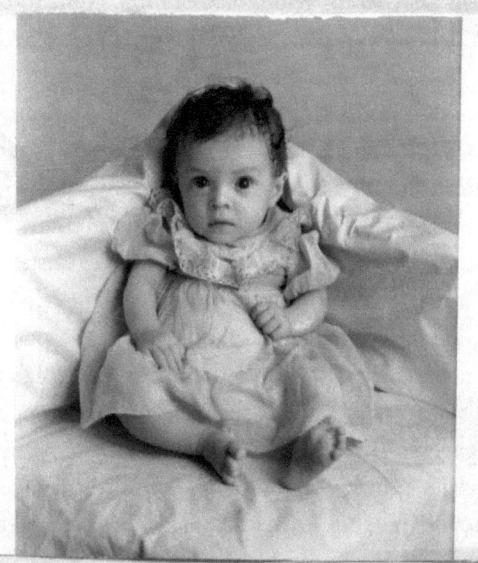

FIGURE 4.2 Two of the children whose photos fill an album held by the Center for Migration Studies. Although these two information cards are unedited, notations on others indicate the trouble that orphanage workers sometimes encountered in trying to racially classify the children.
SOURCE: Center for Migration Studies of New York.

questioned the placement of two children based on the assumption that they were Korean-black: "It would be my impression that they are part Mexican or Puerto-Rican, rather than negro. The little girl has a very brown skin, straight hair, a slender nose with an almost chiseled bridge, finely-cut lips, and big liquid dark eyes. The little boy . . . has very soft-looking yellow-brown curls, regular, fine features, and a complexion with a golden-yellow cast." In the end, the children were placed with a family of Portuguese descent. Nor was racial expertise limited to social workers: an American expatriate in Korea, seeking parents for a mixed-race child he knew, carefully described her as having "skin and facial indications most nearly representative of the Caucasian rather than of the truly Oriental race. Her skin is quite light with a trace of auburn-red hair; blue eyes and only a slight almond shape to the eye itself."[51]

Korean-black children faced a much more difficult situation than Korean-white children did. Existing Korean ideas about color hierarchy had been corroborated by the racial ideologies that accompanied Japanese imperial rule in the first half of the twentieth century. Through their intense contact with Americans after World War II, Koreans knew that blacks occupied the lowest status in American society. Korean-black children suffered from this antiblack racism. Some observers believed that these children perished at greater rates than Korean-white children, either because they were abandoned more frequently or because they were not cared for when they were discovered. All mixed-race children who were housed in integrated orphanages were at risk for victimization by the full-Korean children, and even the orphanage workers, but Korean-black children were particularly at risk for mistreatment both in and out of institutions. Some questioned whether intercountry adoption was the best solution for Korean-white children, but there was no doubt that Korean-black children had to emigrate. An ISS caseworker conveyed the urgency of the situation to a colleague, writing: "these children will simply die if we do not find something for them."[52]

All agencies working in Korean adoption had difficulty finding American homes for Korean-black orphans from the outset, although placement followed gender lines: prospective adoptive parents of Korean-black children, like other adoptive parents, preferred girls. In 1956 the Holts noted that the orphanages were filled with Korean-black boys; by 1959, they listed "homes for little Black-Korean boys" among their prayer requests. Bertha Holt noted that although some white families offered to adopt Korean-black children, she and her husband thought it would be "kinder for the children to grow up in the society of the race their fathers belonged to."[53] The US State Department cooperated with *Jet* magazine to publicize the plight of Korean-black babies and recruit black adoptive parents for them.[54] African American media outlets were accustomed to this kind of task, having played a similar role with "brown babies" in Europe (especially Germany) and Japan. Still, despite these efforts, the number of Korean-black children adopted by Americans was never large; these adoptions peaked in the late 1950s and then dwindled into the single digits by the 1970s.[55]

The perennial problem of finding homes for Korean-black children was part of the larger challenge of finding adoptive homes for black children in the United States. In April 1952 the influential African American newspaper the *Chicago Defender* ran a three-part series on its front page under the urgent headline, "PARENTS WANTED!" Three months later, *Ebony* addressed the question of "Why Negroes Don't Adopt Children" and lamented the imbalance between available children and available homes: "For every white baby offered for adoption, there are at least ten eager, prospective parents. The situation in regard to Negroes is just the reverse." *Ebony* reported that only three thousand black children were adopted each year while approximately fifty thousand more needed temporary and permanent placements. Although there were "six childless Negro couples for each Negro waif," these couples did not apply to adopt because of "misinformation concerning the adoption process, economic factors and deep-seated prejudices about taking 'other people's children.'"[56] Many adoption agencies simply would not serve black adopters or interracial couples. The National Urban League tried to promote domestic adoption among African Americans beginning in the 1950s, but the shortage of black adoptive homes persisted.[57]

The high cost of international adoption was a major deterrent to African Americans' ability to adopt from Korea. Boston Children's Service Association (BCSA), one of the few agencies cooperating with ISS to find black adoptive homes, noted that of the black families they had found who were interested in Korean adoption, almost none was able to produce the hundreds of dollars in required fees. Although all potential adopters had questions about costs, the issue was particularly acute for African American couples—to the point that BCSA believed that it prevented many from even applying. HAP, which charged less for Korean adoption than ISS and its affiliated agencies did, had an easier time finding black adopters, but it too worked hard to recruit them, with appeals on television and in its newsletter. These efforts were successful enough that one African American commentator said that blacks thought of HAP as "essentially a Negro program."[58] For its part, ISS publicized its Korean-black adoptions in the hope of generating more interest, and BCSA undertook a home-finding campaign. BCSA tried to promote Korean adoption by instituting a system of time payments. It suggested that agencies explicitly state all costs up front and tell potential adoptive parents which costs could be waived, spread over time, or funded through outside sources.[59] The need for adoptive homes for Korean-black children was so great, and the costs of adoption so daunting, that BCSA reasoned that social agencies should pay for the children's transportation rather than delaying until the parents had saved up plane fare.[60] In some cases, ISS paid for the child's transportation costs as well as special medical care in Korea.[61]

The majority of African Americans could not meet the economic and social standards that adoption agencies required of applicants. Jim Crow and other forms of racial discrimination constrained black economic success by narrowing opportunities for education, jobs, and housing. Most African Americans could not afford to conform to the extremely gendered normative family model in which men were the sole breadwinners while wives stayed home with their children. Nor could many provide the kind of physical environment or material comforts that agencies liked to see. Aware of these limitations, and aware that enforcement of unreasonable standards was a major reason behind the perpetual shortage of black adoptive parents, many agencies handling domestic adoptions became more accommodating in evaluating African American applicants. ISS urged its cooperating agencies to exercise similar flexibility in screening potential parents of Korean-black children.[62]

Most applicants felt vulnerable as they entered the adoption process, but the fear of having their privacy invaded by social workers who would judge and possibly reject them was heightened for black adopters. This was a major reason many turned to agencies like HAP, which did not require so much investigation. African Americans had adopted privately before World War II either because they did not wish to approach an agency or because agencies refused to provide them service. After World War II, as professional social work agencies became more central to adoption, African Americans were less able to avoid them. These couples had to navigate a taxing process made more fraught by the possibility of misunderstandings and prejudices that could arise in their dealings with a (usually) white social worker and a white social work establishment that often did not recognize black families as legitimate. The social workers who were most successful in placing Korean-black children were those who were able to recognize the role racial inequality played in African American family formation and domesticity.[63]

The agendas of local agencies could hinder adoptions of Korean-black children in other ways too. Social workers sometimes blocked the efforts of African American couples to adopt from Korea, preferring to encourage domestic adoptions. Between September 1956 and the end of 1957, ISS received only eighty inquiries about Korean children from African American families and did not expect "more than a handful" to be approved as adoptive homes. Among the reasons for ISS's pessimism was local agencies' unwillingness

FIGURE 4.3 The Anderson family at Thanksgiving, 1960. Noel Cross (the girl in the middle) is Korean-black, and the girl on her left is full Korean. They were adopted a month apart by two sisters and grew up as cousins in the suburbs of Boston.
SOURCE: Courtesy of Noel Cross.

to do a home study for a foreign child when so many black children in the United States were available for adoption. Indeed, one worker at a Midwestern Children's Aid Society—the only one in the area that even accepted applications from African Americans—"demonstrated considerable resistance to offering service to families desiring to adopt foreign children, particularly Negro families." When the M family approached the New Jersey Board of Child Welfare for help with a Korean adoption, the director there instead suggested that they adopt one of the many black children available for adoption locally. The Ms adopted three children this way and withdrew their application to adopt from Korea.[64]

Although race matching was impossible for most white adopters, black adopters, including couples in which one partner was black, had the possibility of creating an "as if begotten family." An ISS worker noted, "The features of the half Negro children seem to be predominantly Negroid, and they fit well into Negro families here." Some black adoptive parents took seriously the opportunity to engineer not only the overall appearance of their family by selecting their child's age and sex but also her complexion. An African American couple applied to adopt at least two Korean-black children, preferably "a gold brown in color." But color was a delicate issue within black communities, and not often discussed with outsiders. Social workers, most of whom were white, recognized that the question of complexion would be important in cases of black parents adopting Korean-black children. At the same time, they were aware that black adopters might not want to discuss color with a nonblack social worker. This hesitation to speak frankly could lead to misunderstandings. In one case, ISS matched the Ls to a Korean-black girl and started the adoption paperwork, only to have the Ls change their minds. Their caseworker explained that although the Ls had asked for a light-skinned child, "their concept of a light complexion differs from that of Korea. After they had lived for a while with [the child's] picture they realized that the girl was much lighter than either of them, and that physically she did not match them." In the end, the Ls adopted a different Korean-black girl. Their social worker took away a lesson about the importance of color to mutual acceptance in adoptive families: "It is understandable that all adoptive parents . . . want their children to resemble them, at least somewhat. In the case of Negro parents, still another element enters; the fear that a child much lighter than either of them might find it hard to accept them."[65]

The case of the S family shows how adopters' own ambivalences about color could complicate an adoption. The S family, who applied to adopt two children from Korea through BCSA, was a topic of much comment among the BCSA workers. They described Mr. S as so light skinned that he could pass for white and Mrs. S as light brown. Not surprisingly, the S's social worker decided that the S family would be "happiest with very light children" and matched them to a girl and a boy who were both described, in the summary sent from Korea, as "light brown."[66] After her new daughter arrived, Mrs. S admitted feeling that "Sally" was "too dark." When she saw how happy her husband was, however, "any feelings of insecurity Mrs. S had felt because she is so much darker than her husband disappeared in a moment." In fact, Mr. S was so delighted with Sally that he told the social worker that "it wouldn't matter to him if [she] got really black." Problems developed, however, when the S's second child, Arthur, arrived. Despite being lighter than Sally, Arthur was "still too dark" for Mrs. S to accept: "she felt that she just could not give her husband two dark children." In Mrs. S's vision of her ideal family, color was differently important depending on sex. She felt insecure about her husband's ability to love a dark child and saw his acceptance of Sally as a reflection of his love for his wife. But when it came to a son, Mrs. S saw coloring as nonnegotiable—she had wanted Arthur to be lighter skinned so she could come "as close to possible to giving her husband a son who looked like him." Although Mr. S mentioned only that he had expected Arthur to be lighter, and Mrs. S admitted that her husband would "outwardly" accept any child, the caseworker nonetheless felt that he would prefer a son "whose coloring resembles his."[67]

Within a day of Arthur's arrival, the BCSA began to hunt for a new home for him and was able to re-place him with the Ys, who had filed an application to adopt with BCSA several months before. With obvious relief, the agency described the Ys as being "completely accepting of their own race" regardless of color. Mrs. Y was "light brown," their biological daughter was "medium brown," and Mr. Y was "dark brown," which, the BCSA noted, was the same color as Arthur. The BCSA worker saw the Ys embrace of Arthur as a sign of sound mental health: "Secure in themselves, they could be content with a child of any shading, from nearly white to completely dark." In contrast, social workers interpreted Mrs. S's inability to accept Arthur, despite her guilt and the censure of her friends, as a pathology, "a problem which goes quite deep and which we believe we should leave alone."[68]

The low level of photographic technology available to social workers in Korea limited how well they could communicate with their American counterparts about color and complexion. This was especially problematic in the case of Korean-black children, whose coloring was so important to their placement. ISS asked ISS Korea if it could send both color and black-and-white photos of Korean-black children, as "this would give the families and local agency here a much better idea of the child's skin coloring and help them in the matching process." In one instance, a social worker used objects to help describe a Korean-black girl as accurately as possible, sending light-brown paper and a nylon stocking that matched the child's face. She also sent a crayon sample and a dark-brown sample (of what is unclear) that matched the girl's stomach and thighs, though she explained that, with regard to the dark sample, the girl "is this dark but may be a bit more on the browner side, and not quite so chocolate coloured." Cultural and language differences between Korean and American social workers could also complicate how a mixed-race child was described. A social worker in the United States asked her counterpart in Korea to clarify what she meant by calling a child black: did she mean "'black' as suggestive of being Negro or is it the color?" A Korean social worker replied, "We daresay 'black' means being negro, not the color. As a matter of fact there are no black children who are under our care."[69]

Measures of Acceptance

In general, social workers and experts in adoption-related fields were pessimistic about how Americans would respond to adopted Korean children and worried about the possible negative impact of racism on a child's well-being. An anthropologist fretted about adopted children's future marriage prospects: "interracial marriage, though on the increase, is still a real problem in this country. . . . [E]ven if the child learns to compensate for his foreign background and physical distinction by competitive striving—what about intermarriage?" Concerns about marriage might seem irrelevant in discussions about infants and small children, but a potent argument for racial segregation historically has been fears that social contact and equality will lead to interracial sex, and precisely the kind of racial mixture that Korean GI babies represented.[70] Furthermore, Korean adoption began at a time of upheaval for American race relations, soon after the 1954 *Brown v.*

Board of Education decision and as the civil rights movement was gaining national attention.

ISS was realistic about the fact that Korean adoptees would probably confront racism. As an international leader in social work practice, it sought to guide cooperating agencies and other social work professionals on the subject. ISS's Margaret Valk, who wrote about these issues for social work publications, noted that it was important to help prepare white American adoptive parents: "It is very helpful . . . to be able to show them that it will be no help to the child if they simply try to close *their* minds to the painful fact of discrimination and cannot recognise it. It will be real for the child and they must meet it with him and understand what it may mean to him."[71] While social workers worried over how the child and his adoptive parents might handle racism, they failed to note the irony of why they were considering relocating him to the United States in the first place: because he was already experiencing racism in Korea.

ISS was sometimes more thoughtful about race and racism than willfully colorblind adoptive parents or local workers were. It tried to educate local agencies on subjects related to intercountry and interracial adoption, but it is not clear how effective this was. During a follow-up visit to the home of an adoptive family, the parents reported that some children had laughed at their new Korean daughters and called them "China girls." The parents and caseworker agreed that, since the girls did not understand English yet, they were not hurt by such incidents. The worker concluded that "Orientals" were well accepted in the area and that the only prejudice the girls were likely to experience was having people stare at them—"but this would not be mean." Situations like this showed how white privilege could be more powerful than good intentions, as well as how ill-equipped local social workers might be to help adoptive parents talk with their children about topics related to race. In describing their adoptive parents' handling of racial difference, adult adoptees often recount similar alienating occurrences, in which their white adoptive parents dismissed staring, inappropriate questions, and language bordering on epithets as well-meaning curiosity.[72] Before it began hiring professional social workers in the 1960s, HAP was much more concerned with faith than open-mindedness; there is little evidence that it looked closely at adopters' racial views.

ISS instructed local agencies to carefully probe both a family's and community's racial attitudes when it conducted home studies. It recommended that social workers consider how the adoptive parents might respond to the discrimination and prejudice that the child would inevitably face: "Would she find strength and security in them on this score? Would they be able to face with her the questions which could arise—especially beginning in adolescence over dating and friendships with boys?" ISS advised local agencies to speak not only with the adoptive family's acquaintances but "ordinary people" in the area—"the man at the drug store, the grocery store, the bank, other mothers"—to find out what they thought "about bringing a little Korean or half-Korean orphan into the community. . . . Are there other such children there and are they accepted?" In assessing community openness to a Korean or half-Korean child, workers used whatever indicators they could. A worker investigating a home in a mostly white Midwestern city noted that there were very few Asians in the community but that a few children adopted from Greece had been well accepted. On the basis of these observations, the home study stated, "The Worker does not feel that an oriental child would be especially discriminated against in the community. The orientals are so few in the community that the Worker does not feel that there would be a great deal of prejudice against them." An adoptive mother told her social worker that acceptance would not be a problem for her son, given the acceptance of the Hawaiian family at her church.[73]

Community opposition to an adoption could be strong enough to disqualify a family from consideration. A local child welfare official concluded that the potential adoption of a mixed-race Korean boy by a family in the Midwest could not proceed. The correspondent explained that previous attempts to place mixed-race children in the state had been unsuccessful and that "it has been quite rare that we have found a family or community in which such a child is accepted." Further exploration confirmed these suspicions. A school board member stated, "I am not in favor of bringing a boy of unknown quality to this region since my children will have to associate directly with him. There is the possibility of close union ties in the future, of which I am firmly against." A farmer agreed, stating, "Our community would never accept the boy. Not only would he be ostracized but probably the [other children in the family] as well."[74]

Adoptive parents employed their own methods to handle racial issues within both the family and the larger community. One particularly proactive couple who was purchasing their first home at the time they applied to adopt looked in racially diverse neighborhoods, "specifically Mexican and Oriental, and Caucasian," where mixed-race children also lived. In her follow-up report about Lorraine, a Korean-black girl, a caseworker described some of the ways that her adoptive parents, the Bs, tried to help her develop an understanding of her racial identity. The worker described Lorraine as "quite interested in her Negro blood. She had always considered herself as Korean and believes that now she is an American. She had to fight to protect herself from a boy at school who called her 'nigger.'" Mrs. B, who was black and white and Mr. B, who was half Mexican, spoke with her about prejudice and racial mixing, and took her to see a production of Uncle Tom's Cabin, which Lorraine reportedly "loved." Many adopters were sanguine in the face of actual and possible discrimination. Mr. T's relatives opposed his family's adoption of a Korean-white boy, but he and his wife felt certain that they would love Steven when they met him. With regard to the future, the Ts "do not plan to overlook or obscure his Oriental background. They rather hope that he learns to accept it as they do. They will suggest the University of Hawaii to him.... Although they realize that local conditions and attitudes may change considerably before Steven is of college age."[75]

Other parents betrayed discomfort with the racial mixture of their adopted children. Mrs. H, who adopted the child her son had fathered in Korea admitted to her caseworker that because the boy looked very white, she sometimes wanted to simply let him pass. Indeed, the possibility of passing lurked when children were thought to have a strongly non-Asian appearance. When ISS asked the adoptive parents of a Korean-black boy if it could use their family picture as part of its publicity efforts to recruit African American adoptive parents, the adoptive mother expressed reservations about calling attention to her Korean son. "He has enough of a handicap being part Negro, she felt, without adding to it by calling attention to his Korean ancestry."[76]

Conclusion

The advent of Korean adoption complicated American social workers' efforts to exert influence over adoption in the post–World War II United States. Children now crossed not just state lines but national and racial boundaries too. Social workers were able to transpose some elements of established domestic adoption practice, such as home studies, but not others, like race matching. Instead, they had to rethink how they evaluated children, adoptive parents, and communities. If the goal were no longer to create an as-if-begotten family, what principles could guide them in designing families? Meanwhile, in Korea, young social workers in a newly created profession struggled to implement an alien practice with few models and little guidance.

Together, social workers on both sides of the Pacific improvised a practical and ideological framework for international adoption that normalized what was at once highly natural and highly artificial. On the one hand, it seemed perfectly natural to find homes for homeless children; but on the other hand, it was unnatural to sometimes purposely separate a child from her parent or family and send her overseas to live with completely unknown, unrelated people. Americans and Koreans alike had swiftly reached the conclusion that GI babies could not possibly remain in Korea. The only thing left to do was to make it reasonable to send a child overseas for adoption. To meet the requirements of Korean and American law, children were given names, birthdates, and *hojuks* that showed them to be orphans and available for adoption—whether or not they were. These bureaucratic moves turned children into orphans and justified, legitimized, and necessitated their adoptions.

The ideologies that supported the removal of children who were not necessarily orphans were rooted in old assumptions about gender and class, and newer ones about geopolitical power: the assumption that single women were morally unfit to raise their children but could redeem themselves by giving their child the opportunity to be part of a superior household; that the best way for poor parents to be good parents was by giving their children a chance to grow up in the United States; and that Americans with their material abundance and liberal, democratic society could provide for a child—physically, emotionally, psychologically—in a way that nobody else could, not even her birth parents. These ideas and beliefs traveled with international adoption as it spread, and they continue to be embedded in the way we still talk about the practice today.

PART THREE

Creating a Global Adoption Industry

FIVE

The Contradictions of Love and Commerce

> Adoption abroad is one of those situations where everybody wins. Western families who want a child can have their dream fulfilled. Instead of becoming a miserable social misfit, the child finds a new life overseas and gets a real chance for happiness and success. The orphanage is left with one less mouth to feed and is thus hopefully one step nearer to shutting its doors forever.
>
> —Harry C. Stickler, *Asia Magazine*[1]

The thousands of mixed-race GI babies and full-Korean children adopted by American families starting in the 1950s are absent from histories of war orphans. Nor do they appear in histories of refugee law and policy, which usually begin after World War II, focus primarily on Europeans and Cubans, and then shift to influxes from Southeast Asia after the Vietnam War.[2] This historiographical disappearance reveals how these Korean refugee orphans have been reimagined as little immigrants. Indeed, the fact that Korean orphans are typically described—if they appear at all—as an early group of immigrants in Asian American and immigration histories shows how thoroughly their refugee roots have been erased.

From the 1950s to the 1980s, the Korean child traveled a legal and cultural trajectory from refugee and orphan to immigrant and family member. American understandings of Korean children as potential family members drove the Korean orphan's legal transformation from refugee to immigrant between 1953 and 1961. Within each adoptive family and nationally, the constant narration and renarration of the journey from wretched Korean waif to beloved American son or daughter undergirded and enabled the growth of Korean adoption by positioning it to resonate first with Christian Americanist Cold War imperatives, and then with a more generalized humanitarianism.[3]

Against a backdrop of fraught negotiations over whether and how to liberalize other areas of immigration law, orphan statutes became permanent with little comment or opposition. Barred from entry under race-based immigration quotas, Korean children became admissible by virtue of their orphanhood and adoption by US citizens. In fact, the Korean child came to represent a particularly exemplary immigrant due to her youth and perceived malleability. Constructed as an orphan regardless of whether or not she had living relatives, and imagined to have no prior history, she could be raised to be a good American, and thus allow Americans to fulfill the liberal promise of the nation of immigrants: a nation forged through kinships based on choice rather than on blood. She was the quintessential immigrant, whose biography began the day she landed in the US, becoming "American in a very old sense."[4]

The Korean child altered intertwined American understandings of race, nation, and family, but in ways that reaffirmed existing definitions. The adoption of the visibly different Korean child demonstrated the racial liberalism of white Americans while at the same time reinscribing boundaries of race, gender, and sexuality. Americans' acceptance of Korean children as family members and legitimate citizens helped to erode some of the anti-Asian racial thought behind the national origins quota system, which was under assault throughout the 1950s and finally abolished by the 1965 Hart-Celler Act.

As systematic international adoption spread from Korea to other sending countries in the 1970s, the rise of a global international adoption industry exposed the complicated tensions between humanitarianism and consumerism, between narratives of saving children and accusations of buying them. Modern adoption presumably placed the "best interest of the child" as paramount. This child-centered approach stood in contrast to earlier practices in various countries, where children were adopted for inheritance, religious, or labor purposes—in short, to serve the interests of adults. But the development and proliferation of international adoption, and the many allegations and cases of fraud, baby stealing, and corruption that accompanied it, suggested that it remained oriented toward the best interests of adults—specifically, privileged, white adults in first-world countries.

Refugees and Immigrants in US Law

Korean adoption took root at an unlikely moment in US history, in spite of a restrictive immigration regime and as an unintended consequence of refugee laws. Throughout the 1950s, liberal politicians and scholars tried unsuccessfully to liberalize American immigration laws in two key ways. The first was to abolish the national origins quota system, put in place by the 1924 Johnson-Reed Act and maintained in the 1952 McCarran-Walter Act (also called the Immigration and Nationality Act, or INA); they would not achieve this goal until 1965. Second, liberals agitated for more humane refugee legislation befitting the country's new role as a world power.[5]

Despite restrictionist attitudes and fears about communist infiltration, refugee policy did emerge, albeit in an extremely ad hoc fashion. Because orphan laws were enacted as part of refugee laws they were similarly makeshift. The post–World War II refugee crisis in Europe produced a huge backlog of applications for US visas, with all national quotas heavily oversubscribed. President Harry Truman admitted 1,387 European orphans through a presidential directive, but immigration laws did not provide for intercountry adoption until 1948, when the Displaced Persons (DP) Act made 5,000 visas available to European children. While the law was in effect (1948 to 1952), only 4,065 visas were used, making the orphan visa allocation the only one that was not exhausted. Of this total, 1,246 children were born in Greece, 1,154 in Germany, and 568 in Italy. Adoption from Europe was hampered by structural problems such as slow financial appropriations, insufficient staff, and lack of transportation. After the DP Act expired, the Act of 29 July 1953, provided 500 additional visas for children adopted by Americans serving the US military or government overseas. Because it did not specify nationality requirements for eligible orphans, it opened the door to Japanese children, who received 287 of the 466 visas issued.[6]

A second reason for the relative failure of the DP Act was that there were simply not enough of the right *type* of European child to meet American demand. Although the media circulated photos of very young children, many DP children were adolescents. This was especially true of Jewish children, since the Nazis had killed those who were too young to work. Americans wrote to apply for the little blonde girls they saw in the newspapers, but they were often disappointed that there were few to be had. Most of the available children were Jewish, and Jewish agencies claimed authority over them, seeking to keep them in Europe or resettle them in Palestine. Postwar pronatalism across Europe drove vigorous efforts by national governments to reclaim their DP children, and some countries prohibited adoption by parents of a different nationality. A substantial number of European children adopted by Americans came from seven countries, but primarily Germany,

Greece, and Italy. Italy and Greece had the most available orphans, whereas the assumption that "innumerable orphans" would be available in Germany and Austria proved incorrect. Americans' demand for children of these nationalities considerably exceeded the number available.[7]

The Refugee Relief Act of 1953 (RRA) provided the first crucial opening for what would develop into large-scale, systematic adoption from Korea. Steeped in Cold War politics from its formulation to its administration, the RRA was intended to address problems in Europe, and it "cemented in the law and in political discourse the association between refugees and European opponents and victims of communism." This equivalence between "refugee" and "European" was powerful, despite the significant numbers of refugees in Asia and the Middle East. Buttressing the Eurocentrism of the RRA was the general bias in American immigration affairs against giving visas to nonwhites and non-Europeans.[8]

Although the RRA named its intended beneficiaries by nationality, specifying the distinct but overlapping categories of "refugee," "national," "escapee," and "expellee," the "orphan" category contained no such delineation, thereby constructing the orphan as an exceptional, apolitical category that superseded both nationality and race. Additionally, orphans were not required to meet the definition of refugee, although if they failed to qualify for a visa as orphans, they could claim refugee status on the grounds that they had been moved by military operations. Congress added the orphan program to the RRA at the last minute, in response to the hundreds of private bills that had been introduced by prospective American adoptive parents.[9]

Originally conceived to assist European refugees, the RRA proved extremely useful for Americans adopting Asian children. In fact, more than half of its four thousand orphan visas went to children born in Asia. The RRA provided a critical "back door around the hated immigration system" for Korean children, who would otherwise be subject to their country's miniscule annual quota of one hundred.[10] Although only 460 (12.2 percent) of the RRA's orphan visas were issued to Korean children, that small number was unprecedented in the history of Korean immigration. And that initial trickle quickly grew: Korean children received the largest share of visas issued under subsequent temporary orphan laws. By 1961, when orphan laws became permanently incorporated into the INA, Korean children had received one-quarter of all orphan visas issued since 1953.

The RRA's orphan provisions were so popular that the four thousand orphan visas it provided were exhausted by September 1956, three months before it was due to expire. Congress passed no further laws to facilitate intercountry adoption for nine months, creating near panic among adopters.[11] Although Americans adopted from a variety of countries, it was those adopting from Korea and their allies who led the fight for new orphan laws.[12] Harry Holt, whose Holt Adoption Program (HAP) was the main conduit for Korean children at this time, placed children through proxy adoption, a controversial method that allowed parents to remain in the United States and legally adopt their children through a representative in Korea. Professional social workers decried this practice, but it received broad support from parents and agencies involved in Korean adoption, and it was widely used in Greek-US adoptions. Holt urged his supporters to ask their members of Congress to extend orphan laws and to allow proxy adoption to continue, and he provided a rough template for their letters: "Explain briefly but pointedly how badly you want a child for your home and how impossible it is to get one in America. Explain that if adoption by proxy is stopped you will not be able to get a child."[13] Letters conforming to this advice poured into Congress, the vast majority from Americans adopting from Korea. Potential adoptive parents also pressured Congress to pass new orphan laws by submitting private bills.[14] The senators from Holt's state of Oregon, Richard Neuberger and Wayne Morse, were vocal champions of Korean adoption. They helped press Congress for new orphan laws throughout the 1956 to 1961 period, as temporary laws continually expired and adopters faced uncertainty over whether and how they would be able to bring their Korean children to the United States.[15]

This assiduous campaign helped produce a series of temporary laws that allowed Korean adoption to continue. The first was the Act of 11 September 1957. Introduced by Senator John F. Kennedy and supported by other pro-adoption members of Congress, the law was mainly concerned with new refugees created by the unsuccessful 1956 anticommunist uprising in Hungary.[16] But for Korean adoption advocates, the 1957 act was cause for celebration. Section 4 not only extended the RRA's orphan provisions but also expanded them by authorizing entry for an unlimited number of alien orphans for two years and by raising the maximum age for an "eligible orphan" from ten to fourteen years.[17] After the 1957 act expired on 30 June 1959, Congress extended orphan laws for one year at a time, in 1959 and again in 1960 (the latter extension was part of the Fair Share Refugee Act).[18] Although it was becoming clear that intercountry adoption would be a permanent part of US immigration law, Congress made only temporary extensions to provide time to assess the existing program and investigate concerns over possible abuses.

The act of 26 September 1961, was momentous in the development of intercountry adoption. By amending the INA to make non-quota visas permanently available for foreign-born adopted children, it institutionalized the practice of intercountry adoption, legitimized American demand for foreign children, ensured the continuation and growth of the nascent intercountry adoption industry in Korea, and encouraged the spread of the practice to other countries.[19] The law also validated the social work establishment's concerns about proxy adoption by eliminating it as a basis for visa issuance. In other words, Americans adopting internationally could no longer adopt by proxy. Instead, as of 1961, a child could be adopted abroad only if her adoptive parents had seen her in person before or during the adoption proceeding. If the child was to be adopted after arrival in the United States, a licensed agency had to complete the placement. Although proxy adoption advocates like Holt were initially angered and discouraged by the ban on the practice, Joseph Swing, Immigration and Naturalization Service (INS) commissioner, soon opened an important loophole for them. He interpreted the law so that Americans could still adopt a child from abroad without seeing her first as long as they proved to a licensed adoption agency that they intended to readopt her in the United States.[20] Consequently, proxy adoption effectively continued—but with the involvement of the social work establishment.

The 1961 act definitively marked the Korean child's legal transformation from refugee to immigrant by elevating foreign-born adopted children from the legal status of "eligible orphan" to the more privileged category of "immediate relative." The 1957 act had required that a child first apply for admission through the quota system. If the quota for the child's country of origin was oversubscribed, she could then receive a special non-quota immigrant visa based on her status as an "eligible orphan." As of 1961, Korean children bypassed the quota system altogether. As family members who entered the United States with the status of "immediate relatives," they benefited from the immigration system's emphasis on family reunification, even when it conflicted with race-based exclusion.[21] Between 1955 and 1961,

4,190 mixed-race and full-Korean children entered the United States in numbers that far exceeded the annual quota of 100 allocated to Koreans by the McCarran-Walter Act; they constituted a significant proportion of the 7,025 Koreans who immigrated during the 1950s.[22]

The orphan program became permanent quietly and seemingly with little dissent.[23] In fact, there was no discernible opposition either to the creation or extension of temporary orphan laws after World War II or to making them permanent in 1961, even as the battle over general immigration reform continued. Oregon Senator Maurine Neuberger did note there was "some opposition to the admission of foreign orphan children, as well as other immigrants," and the Holts received a few threatening letters and phone calls objecting to their Korean adoption activities.[24] A few doctors expressed fears that Korean children were bringing tuberculosis into the country. Overall, however, there is no evidence of organized protest against either intercountry or Korean adoption, most likely because vexed conversations about thousands of potentially subversive adult refugees overshadowed the comparatively small number of intercountry adoptions.[25] In addition, would-be opponents of Korean adoption were no doubt silenced by reminders of US obligations to the GI babies, given their presumed American paternity.[26] Ultimately, the image of innocent, imperiled children was so powerful, and the imperative to save them so self-evident, that no politician saw any incentive to campaign against the interests of, in the words of one senator, "the crying orphans on the other side of the water" or the "weeping mothers" in America who longed to adopt them.[27]

Redefinitions of Family, Nation, and Race

As Korean adoption became systematized between the legal bookends of the 1953 RRA and the 1961 amendments to the INA, Americans tried to work out what the Korean child represented. The Korean child, as children often are, was a bearer of great social and cultural weight. A protean and powerful symbol, she simultaneously occupied multiple legal, social, racial, and political categories: "immigrant," "refugee," "orphan," "Asian." And the answer to the question of what the Korean child represented held important implications for American redefinitions of race, nation and citizenship, and family.[28]

The Korean child's legal status was straightforward: she was an "eligible orphan" who had been adopted by US citizens.[29] Broadly speaking, an eligible orphan was an orphan because of the death or disappearance of her parents or because she had been released for adoption by a living parent. Bureaucratic labor severed the child from her birth family and nation to produce an "eligible orphan," who was "free" for adoption. Legally and rhetorically made into an orphan, she was then "'reunited' with 'immediate family' in the U.S."[30]

Media coverage reinforced the transformation from orphan—the dirty, hungry, homeless waif—to adoptee: the well-dressed, beloved son or daughter grinning in the midst of domestic plenty (see Figure 5.1). Adoptive parents used the language of transfiguration to describe how their children had flourished in American homes: from "undernourished waif" and "frightened, hopeless, little things," to "happy, healthy, well-adjusted," and a "roly-poly sunbeam." Many parents continued to campaign for new orphan laws even after they had completed their own adoptions. The letters they sent to members of Congress included snapshots of their thriving adopted children and reports that they "fit into our family circle perfectly" and were doing well in school.[31]

While these narratives framed the American family as a site of transformation, the Korean child also reaffirmed the family's power as "normalizing institution." Her adoption was revolutionary, for her obvious racial difference disrupted ideas of the monoracial (white) family, upended conceptions of kinship rooted in blood and biology, and challenged the dominant social work doctrine of using careful matching to create "as-if begotten" adoptive families. But Korean adoption was also deeply conservative, for the Korean child shored up "an idealized notion of kinship": the Cold War heterosexual nuclear family. She verified her adoptive parents' worthiness for inclusion in the nation at a time when status as a parent was equated with citizenship. This reinforcing of hierarchies of heteronormativity and race, and the containment of the Korean child's otherness within conventional family forms suggest why some conservative evangelical Americans embraced the seemingly radical cause of Korean adoption.[32]

International adoption highlighted the ambivalent relationship of many Americans with the state even as it exposed the falseness of the distinction between private and public spheres. Adoptive parents often resisted the incursions of social workers into their homes and families, insisting that the

FIGURE 5.1 The Shigley family in San Francisco, 1968. Diane (right) was adopted by an army colonel and his wife in 1965 while they were stationed in Korea. She later discovered her biological father was an American GI.
SOURCE: Courtesy of Diane Shigley.

state had no business in their intimate matters. Yet they could not and did not completely sever themselves from state power, since they needed orphan laws to admit their adopted children. They appealed to lawmakers to enact adoption-friendly laws, presenting their desire to adopt as furthering national Cold War objectives.[33] In doing so, they sought to protect their vision of family as "personally chosen private freedoms" while at the same time leveraging the institution's symbolic importance as "public emblem of the nation."[34] The way that adoptive families used national concerns to gain support for Korean adoption demonstrates the deep mutual imbrication of the public and private spheres.

Indeed, the adopted Korean child embodied the inextricable linkages between the private and the public. Simultaneously selected to be a member of both a nuclear family and the national family, her adoption resonated with old and enduring ways of thinking of the family as a microcosm of the nation, and the hope that social and racial unity within the family could lead to the same in the community and the nation.[35] One prominent supporter thought even more grandly than this, arguing that intercountry adoption would "prove a solid contribution to the culture and strength of our Nation and to the welfare of mankind as a whole."[36] Proponents of Korean adoption celebrated the ways that having a Korean child in their midst broadened their horizons.[37] An adoptive father declared that his Korean daughter had "helped to remove prejudice, and fear, and increased the understanding and vision of the people," which were "vital to our nations future [sic]."[38]

Adoption transformed the Korean child from "needy object" to "treasured subject," from a "pathetic" child to "our precious" child.[39] Whether object or subject, the Korean child was nonetheless a child—without agency, but powerful as a cultural, social, ideological, and political symbol.[40] Imagined as an orphan, she was a *tabula rasa*, allowing politicians, adoptive parents, journalists, and social workers to project a multitude of ideals and burdens onto her: victim of communism, herald of multiracial harmony, and ideal citizen.

Asian American and Korean American histories typically overlook intercountry adoption and adoptees, but adopted Korean children were instrumental to the larger refiguring of Asianness that occurred during the Cold War. This process began during World War II, when Congress repealed the Chinese exclusion laws and offered token quotas to Filipinos and East

Indians. Postwar, both the US government and Asian-American communities worked to transform the image of unassimilable Chinese and Japanese into "model" Asian American citizens—from definitively not white to definitively not black. Against the shifting racial terrain produced by global war, Cold War racial liberalism, and a nascent civil rights movement, Asian Americans positioned themselves as a model minority: hardworking, family and education oriented, capitalist, and therefore superlatively equipped to be good American citizens.[41]

These domestic reconfigurations mirrored geopolitical developments, in which US relations with Asian countries were presented in gendered, familial terms that emphasized relationships of love and care. Older images of the coolie or the hypermasculine Yellow Peril were replaced with more appealing war brides and orphans, who affirmed colonial and Orientalist tropes of Asians as childlike and feminine.[42] It is true that the war bride was not a wholly unproblematic figure, for she presented the specter of miscegenation and raised questions about whether she was actually a cunning prostitute using marriage to gain access to America. Children, however, were beyond such suspicions.

Enduring anti-Asian sentiment delayed the liberalization of US immigration law affecting Asians. The 1952 INA had established an Asia-Pacific triangle and imposed immigration quotas of one hundred per year on each country within it, with an overall limit of two thousand for the entire region. Liberals condemned this as "racist policy" that hurt America's image in Asia. But eliminating it was not considered an option by conservatives like the powerful congressman Francis Walter, who was openly hostile toward Asian immigration. In 1961, the same year that provisions for international adoption became a permanent part of the INA, he "flatly declared his commitment to preventing a horde of Asiatics from overrunning the United States."[43]

Yet mixed-race and full "Asiatic" babies and children, otherwise inadmissible under race-based quotas, not only were acceptable but also idealized in conversations about immigration and refugee policy. The State Department declared that "orphans make the best possible immigrants from the standpoint of their youth, flexibility, and lack of ties to any other cultures." Adoptive parents presented their children as being proud of their special status as US citizens. The mother of a three-year-old Korean-white girl described her as saying "I'm a 'cinzen'" and reciting the Pledge of Allegiance.

A father in California pronounced his two Korean daughters "the most enthusiastic loyal Americans I have ever met" and claimed that they and other Korean children would "become wonderful citizens of our country." As lucky recipients of American citizenship—"the greatest gift to be given them!"—these children would one day give back to the nation, and eventually the world.[44]

For Americans, the healthy white infant was the ideal adoptive child. Demand for these children had exceeded their numbers since the 1930s, but by the 1970s Americans confronted an acute "white baby famine." Applicants waited years to even join agency waiting lists, which were themselves months long; by 1975, the wait for a white baby was three to seven years.[45] The "baby drought" was widely attributed to four factors: the declining birthrate, the legalization of abortion in 1973, increasing use of contraceptives, and the lessening stigma against single motherhood that resulted in more women keeping their babies. It was compounded by the bureaucracy that adopters had long complained about: agencies continued to insist on proper protocol, but most were understaffed (especially the public agencies), which resulted in long processing times.

As an alternative to agencies, couples tried to find a baby on their own, through the "gray" or "black" markets. Most Americans had historically adopted this way, and after World War II, half of all adoptions continued to be done independently, despite the professionalization of social work and proliferation of agencies. Gray-market adopters made arrangements through personal networks or paid attorneys and doctors to locate a child for them. Black-market brokers were more unscrupulous, selling babies to the highest bidders, charging exorbitant fees, and exploiting vulnerable birth mothers. Although Congress had investigated the black market for babies in the 1950s, concern that the shortage of white babies would lead to the reemergence of baby trafficking prompted new congressional hearings in 1975 and again in 1977. Witnesses at the hearings described a "seller's market" in which babies were traded across state and international lines, and desperate couples paid anywhere from $8,000 to $25,000 for a white infant (a newborn for the very lucky).[46]

Those adopting through agencies had to broaden their vision to include so-called hard-to-place or unadoptable children: older, mentally or physically disabled, part of a sibling group—and nonwhite. White adoptions of black children had never been very popular in the United States, with the number peaking in 1970–1971 at around 2,500 (just 1.4 percent of all adoptions). In 1972, the National Association of Black Social Workers (NABSW) issued a much-quoted statement that condemned the practice as "cultural genocide," arguing that white adoptive parents could not properly equip black children to cope in a racist society. In the wake of the civil rights and Black Power movements of the 1960s, and in the context of the identity politics of the 1970s, these arguments carried great force. The NABSW statement did not end the practice of black-white adoption, as some have claimed. But many agencies did respond by enacting policies against it, including the Child Welfare League of America, which revised its adoption standards in 1973 to emphasize that same-race placements were preferable for black children. The NABSW's statement validated the child welfare establishment's skepticism about black-white placements. More important, it vastly heightened the political stakes surrounding them, making international adoption more attractive to mainly white parents who did not want to have to tackle the social and political issues that would accompany raising a black child.[47]

American preference for a foreign nonwhite child over a domestic black child became firmly established during the 1970s. Unable to obtain a white child, and unwilling or unable to adopt a black child, Americans turned to Korean children: a "racial middle ground" that did not require white parents to cross the highly charged black-white divide. Korean children also seemed more worthy of rescue. The demonization of black families as "pathological" and caricatures of single black mothers as drug-abusing welfare cheats shaped a view of their children as damaged. This devaluing of black children increased the desirability of foreign children who, while seen as unhealthy and coming from backward places, were not associated with "delinquency or violence" and needed only to be rescued by a modern American family. In fact, the lack of homes for African American children has led to the United States' peculiar status as both a receiving and sending country—it has sent hundreds of black children to Europe and Canada each year for adoption.[48]

Americans also adopted Native American children, in small but politically significant numbers. The federal Indian Adoption Project (IAP), which lasted from 1958 to 1967, placed 395 Native American children with mainly white families, mostly on the East Coast. The IAP was sponsored by the Bureau of Indian Affairs and operated with the help of the Child

Welfare League of America (CWLA). In 1968 the CWLA merged the IAP with a new program, the Adoption Resource Exchange of North America, which placed "several hundred more" Indian children in non-Indian families over the following decade. In addition, state welfare systems placed hundreds, perhaps thousands, of Indian children in non-Indian homes during the 1960s and 1970s. These state and federal programs were part of a long history of culturally destructive assimilationist policies that involved child removal.[49]

Like Korean adoption, Indian adoption exposed the strength and shape of racial preference among white adoptive parents. Many adopters of Native American children admitted that they would not have chosen a black child, although most claimed they would accept an Asian child. In fact, the populations of couples willing to adopt Asian and Native American children overlapped considerably. Both groups of adopters indicated a desire to rescue children (even if it was not their primary motivation) and saw the "racial characteristics" of Asians and Native Americans as similar. Culture and sentiment were also important to both groups of adopters. Adopters of Native American children indicated a desire to reconnect with a lost native heritage, access Native American culture, or make amends for wrongs done to Native Americans.[50]

Indian adoption shared a key similarity with black adoption: both slowed substantially as a result of resistance from their respective communities. In language similar to the NABSW's, Native American activists and their allies denounced Indian adoption as genocide and brought about the 1978 passage of the Indian Child Welfare Act, which placed adoption and custody cases under tribal sovereignty and made it very difficult for whites to adopt Native American children.[51]

Compared to the controversy over adopting black and Native American children, Korean children appeared free of cultural and political baggage. Aside from the occasional burst of criticism from North Korea, Korean adoption was largely uncontested, and the South Korean state did everything possible to support it. Korean children were also seen as free in another important sense: abandoned or relinquished by faraway birth parents who would not return for their child. Korean adoption thus offered adoptive parents a "clean break." This was an important consideration at a time when adoptees and birth parents began organizing to advocate for adoption reform, including open adoption and access to birth records. The perception of foreign adoption as a "closed transaction" was a popular reason for adopting internationally.[52]

In addition to the racial triangulation vis-à-vis black children that increased Korean children's desirability, Americans thought of Korean children as possessing a certain racial flexibility, a "benign . . . racial difference" that promised both easy assimilability and manageable exoticism. Media stories highlighted the accomplishments of Korean children who in the span of several years had transformed from waifs into Harvard graduates, beauty pageant winners, and Naval Academy midshipmen. By the 1970s, HAP newsletters carried a column called "Grandma's Brag Book" that featured successful Korean adoptees—with success denoted by academic achievements and religious faith. These representations of Korean children showcased not just their assimilability but also their superiority. More than one Korean adoption proponent argued that Korean adoptees were the cream of the crop, because they had the strength and intelligence to survive long enough to reach the United States.[53]

Whereas social workers had previously advised adoptive parents to Americanize their children as quickly as possible, the 1970s brought a new emphasis on culture, reflecting the wider attention to ethnic identity in the United States. Adopters focused increasingly on the importance of nurturing the adopted child's racial and cultural identity, and they sought ways to expose themselves and their children to Korean culture, such as through classes in cooking, dancing, music, and language; later adoptees and their families took advantage of culture camps (beginning in the late 1970s) and motherland tours (which began in the early 1990s). When they could, they turned to local Koreans as a resource. Most parents completely renamed their children, but as attentiveness to ethnic identity increased, it became more common to integrate elements of a child's Korean name into her new name.[54]

Ignorance of Asian cultures, or an Orientalist view of them as monolithic, increased Korean children's racial flexibility. An adoptive mother voiced a common attitude when she explained, "We decided on an Oriental child because we admire Oriental people and their culture." Advice for Americans adopting from Asia sometimes replicated Orientalist stereotypes. In 1968 Jan De Hartog, a well-known writer and adoptive father, conflated Korean, Vietnamese, and "Asian" children in his manual for other adoptive parents. Asian children, he wrote, were appealing, respectful, and smarter than average, though also obstinate, from "the Stone Age," and in need of proper civilization. They reacted to stress with "the frozen face of the inscrutable East" and would try to please their new parents by behaving like an obsequious "little Mr. Chinatown" or "miniature Doctor Fu Manchu." In a similar vein, Marjorie Margolies, a journalist and adoptive mother, marveled in her memoir at her Korean daughter's ability to win over a difficult great-grandmother—"Was it the wisdom born of centuries of Oriental respect for elders?"—and extolling her "Korean values": discipline, orderliness, and determination to succeed.[55]

Racialized gender stereotypes increased Asian children's desirability as adoptees. Korean adoption was dominated by girls, who were far less threatening than black boys could ever be. Depicting them as dolls further defused their racial threat, although it did not negate their being inscribed with sexualized racial characteristics. During a visit to a Korean orphanage, a social worker asked Margolies what kind of child she sought. She remembered that her "first reaction was to say, "someone exotic and beautiful like the girl in *Flower Drum Song*"—a film about Chinese Americans—even though she claimed, in the same train of thought, to understand the negative effects of linking sexuality and exoticism. Nonetheless, her description of her Korean daughter includes unrelenting attention to her doll-like beauty and seemingly pan-Asian physical features: "almond-slit eyes," "classic Mandarin face," and "delicate, fragile structure of an Oriental dancer." De Hartog's view of Asian children was similarly gendered, as demonstrated in his situating the charms of his two Korean daughters within his understanding of Confucian Korean society: "Maybe because they are considered inferior by the men, they have developed over the centuries a demure mischievousness, an elusive twinkle of quicksilver mirth that I, for one, find utterly irresistible." His description of how his daughters wrapped him around their little fingers conjured stereotypes of Oriental femme fatales: "Many fathers of little girls may be similarly enslaved, but I suspect that little Korean girls are experts at this form of lion-taming. Like all women from countries where the male rules the roost, they have the magic power of making our breeches drop at the crest of our strutting self-confidence."[56]

Koreans in the United States, particularly those in the adoption field, acted as native informants, offering insights into Korean culture and tradition to help adoptive parents to understand their children. Their advice sometimes reinforced Orientalist attitudes. One writer validated Orientalist perceptions of Asians as passive, emotionally distant, authoritarian, and sharing a common mind-set. She explained virtually every aspect of a Korean child's adjustment to her American family in terms of the vast differences between Korean Confucianism and American individualism, without much consideration of noncultural factors like the trauma of separation from living parents and families or the experience of institutionalization. Even advice manuals that provided information about Korean culture without casting Koreans as Oriental others could feed a tendency to see the children as irrevocably foreign at a time when some still saw culture as biologically rooted.[57] This kind of well-meant advice had the potential to advance a damaging cultural essentialism that believed that Korean culture (conceived of as ancient and unchanging) could explain much (if not everything) about adopted Korean children, even those adopted as infants.

Stories about adopted Korean children conformed to a heartwarming narrative of seamless integration—with a few comical but harmless hiccups along the way. Adoptive parents reported that their children quickly learned English and fell in love with quintessentially American foods like pizza, chocolate-chip cookies, and peanut butter. Parents also joked about how Korean children's assimilation could be gauged by their becoming as impossible as any American child. Two Korean girls "were quiet and respectful" when they arrived, "the very model of the Oriental child," but within months they were as resistant at bedtime as their five nonadopted siblings. Even physical differences seemed to melt away. An adoptive mother wrote of her Korean daughter that when she first saw her, "her eyes and tiny features certainly looked even more oriental than I expected. By the second day my eyes were starting to look odd to me." An adoptive father insisted of his Korean-white son, "I can't imagine that there will ever be any kind of problem for him because of race. In fact, I think my eyes are slantier than his. And his skin color really is beautiful."[58]

By the 1970s, a body of expert knowledge promoted a largely positive view of Korean adoption.[59] Studies in fields like social work, pediatric medicine, and psychology found that Korean adoptees adjusted very well—at about the same rates as children who were adopted domestically and intraracially, and just as well as their nonadopted siblings.[60] These studies reassured adoptive parents that loving homes could help adopted children overcome the physical and emotional deprivations they might have suffered in infancy or early childhood. This knowledge about Korean adoption

FIGURE 5.2 Kim Hanson with his adoptive family in 1976, during his father's sabbatical in Nottingham, England
SOURCE: Courtesy of Kim Hanson.

became increasingly relevant as international adoption became popularized, because later adopters often relied on the experience of those who had adopted Korean children, and research touting the success of Korean adoption became an important part of policy making.[61]

Although these studies were a boon to advocates of international adoption, they were flawed in several respects. They only looked at parents' perspectives or relied heavily to exclusively on parents' reports of their children's behavior and feelings. Many studies occurred quite soon after the adoption had been completed, when adoptees were still adjusting. Others collected data on adoptees who had not yet entered adolescence, when many issues surface, and many did not follow up with adoptees after they were grown. Then there is the question of how the studies defined and measured success.

Nonetheless, the consensus about the "success" of transnational adoption stood largely unchallenged until the 1990s.[62]

As Korean adoptees grew up, they were able to articulate their own experiences, providing a forceful counternarrative to the celebratory tone that dominated discussions about Korean adoption. In addition to the psychological issues that can accompany any adoption, Korean children had to navigate the complexities of race. Many adoptees, especially those adopted in the 1950s and 1960s, were extremely isolated, one of the few people of color in overwhelmingly white communities. But even those who were adopted later, or who lived in more multiracial settings, were acutely aware of how their physical differences marked them, complicating their daily lives and identities. One seventeen-year-old summed up a common experience of dissonance when she told a reporter, "I think of myself as totally American. Sometimes it's easy to forget, but people make you remember." Some endured outright, sometimes violent, racism. Teasing, stares, and a range of both hostile and well-intentioned treatment constantly reminded them that they were foreign, however they might feel inside, and made them embarrassed about their appearance.[63] American representations of Korea as backward and poor might have explained their need for rescue but also made them ashamed of where they came from. At the same time, they struggled with the high expectations placed on them as members of a so-called model minority.[64] Black social workers who doubted that white parents of adopted black children would be able to help them cope with a racialized society would not have been surprised to hear that Korean adoptees felt alone in dealing with racism. Many felt they received little guidance from their white parents, who were ill-equipped to help them or unable or unwilling to identify racism unless it was overt. Memoirs, films, and academic studies, by and about Korean adoptees, which have increased exponentially in recent years, brim with these kinds of stories.[65]

Of course, it is impossible to summarize the individual experiences of the tens of thousands of Korean children who were adopted by Americans between the 1950s and the 1980s.[66] But the work being done by some Korean adoptees to share unvarnished accounts of their lives, and to interrogate the political, economic, and social dynamics around Korean and international adoption challenges the "dominant representation" of it as "an overwhelmingly positive experience marked by familial fulfillment, generosity, and unconditional, colorblind love."⁶⁷ In short, it allows them to be subjects of their story, and not just objects—of desire or of scrutiny.

Rescuing the Priceless Child

Although proponents of Korean adoption used the term *orphan* to access deep cultural understandings and mythologies about parentless children, in truth it was a capacious and easily manipulated category.⁶⁸ A child could be—and often was—made into an orphan through a simple administrative act by an orphanage director or a social worker, or into a "social orphan" when released for adoption by a living parent. Whether genuine or not, orphanhood was an essential narrative precondition to adoption. The conflation of global politics and domestic family concerns—the "collapsing of home and world"—in sentimental narratives of rescue required that the children be figured as orphans; in the words of adoption advocate Pearl S. Buck, as "piteous lonely children whom no country claims."⁶⁹

Indeed, Korean children could be seen as a metaphor for Korea itself: deemed irrelevant to American security interests, she had been abandoned by the United States in 1948. During and after the Korean War, the US mainstream and military media showcased the many ways GIs cared for Korean children: for example, by building orphanages, throwing Christmas parties, and distributing relief goods. If GI humanitarianism offered a way for Americans to salvage a moral victory out of the stalemate of the Korean War, then adopting a Korean orphan was a way to atone for abandoning—for orphaning—the land of her birth. The relationship between American parents and Korean children mirrored geopolitics by enacting the asymmetry that has characterized the neocolonial US-Korea relationship since World War II.

Although by the 1960s and 1970s the crisis of the Korean War had passed, Korean children remained attractive because of their perceived "rescuability." Americans could rescue them from poverty and neglect, from permanent institutionalization, and from a narrow life of limited opportunities. After the explicitly religious, patriotic Christian Americanism of the early Korean adoption movement dissipated in the early 1960s, Americans explained their desire to adopt from Korea in more general terms, referring to concerns about neediness and overpopulation, and a desire to enact their belief in multiculturalism and human rights. But the logic of rescue faltered as Korea became rich and the question arose of just what it was that Americans were rescuing Korean children from.

It is too simplistic to say that Korean adoption originated as a humanitarian movement and then transformed into a market, but it does seem clear that by the 1970s, it had become an industry that had largely moved from supply-driven to demand-driven—from emphasizing "finding families for children" to "finding children for families."[70] In commercial terms, one could say that Harry Holt opened up an untapped market in Korea in the 1950s: he located a supply of adoptable children for which there was enormous demand in the United States, and he established a "vertically integrated" supply chain to meet that demand.[71] He collected children, housed them in an orphanage, delivered them via mass flights, and processed them through proxy adoption, the most efficient method available. In addition, he and his supporters created a favorable regulatory environment by lobbying Congress to change anti-Asian immigration law. Other agencies hurried to stake their own claim, and by the end of the 1960s, Korean adoption was a highly organized, competitive business.

Market thinking and practices have accompanied adoption throughout its history. In the nineteenth-century United States, it was acceptable to assign a market value to a child based on her labor power, and children transported west on orphan trains were displayed on platforms for selection—hence, "put up" for adoption.[72] But as childhood became sentimentalized in the early twentieth century, the child was sacralized as a "priceless child," who should be removed from the cash nexus. Thus, the value of a child in the twentieth century had to be set by emotional value alone, and this value was thought to be "radically incompatible" with ideas of her economic worth. But this shift had a "profoundly paradoxical and poignant consequence": the scarcity of adoptable children led to the emergence of domestic and transnational black markets in babies, ultimately resulting in "the increasing monetization and commercialization of children's lives."[73]

For decades, what one adoptive parent criticized as "snappy market analogies" pervaded the language of adoption, and media coverage of international adoption was no different.[74] Journalists wrote about how Americans living in a "baby-poor" country addressed the "lopsided distribution of babies worldwide" by going to "the baby-rich" developing world where war, poverty and "excess fertility" had produced an oversupply of children.

Newspaper articles discussed the "variety of options" available in the "adoption market," listing waiting periods, estimated costs, and other country-specific information. The *New York Times*' personal finance columnist advised readers to "shop around" for an agency and recommended questions to ask about fees and procedures.[75]

Although Korea was still by far the number-one supplier of children for adoption until the 1990s, Americans were able to choose from a widening menu of sending countries (see Table 5.1).[76] International adoption continued to spread mainly along pathways formed by neocolonial relationships, and sending countries modified their laws to facilitate it. By the late 1970s Americans could adopt fairly dependably from several Central and South American countries.[77] Colombia became a popular source of children, second only to Korea by 1976. Because most Colombian adoptions were done privately rather than through agencies, they were riskier and more expensive than Korean adoption—but often faster. Colombia also had a greater number of young infants available, and it offered adopters the possibility of a white (or white-looking) child. With an increased array of choices available to them, prospective adoptive parents engaged in what looked like consumerist behavior: comparing different countries' baby markets in search of faster processing times, flexible regulations, and healthier infants, or attempting to increase their chances by offering to take a sick, handicapped, or older child.[78]

Of the available options, South Korea's adoption system was the oldest, and considered the most transparent and easiest to navigate, and Korea had a ready supply of healthy children because of its high rate of child abandonment and low rate of domestic adoption. Furthermore, Korean adoption continued to be convenient: whereas South and Central American countries required adopters to travel there to pick up their child and complete paperwork, a process that could last weeks, those adopting from Korea could meet their child at a nearby US airport. Although the Vietnam War sparked interest among adopters, agencies and friends redirected them to Korea because of the time, cost, and difficulty of Vietnamese adoptions. Korean adoption was easier and resulted in a similar child: Asian, rescuable, and assimilable.

The Vietnamese case, in fact, suggests the profound entanglement of humanitarianism and consumerism in the growth of international adoption.[79] Americans began to adopt Vietnamese children in the late 1960s

TABLE 5.1 Top five countries sending children for adoption to the United States, 1971–1976

Year	Sending country	Number of children	Percentage of total
1971	Korea	1,174	43.1
	Canada	345	12.7
	Germany	295	10.8
	Philippines	153	5.6
	Vietnam	89	3.3
	Other	668	24.5
	Total	**2,724**	
1972	Korea	1,585	52.4
	Canada	355	11.7
	Germany	204	6.7
	Philippines	136	4.5
	Vietnam	119	3.9
	Other	624	20.6
	Total	**3,023**	
1973	Korea	2,183	54.5
	Vietnam	324	8.1
	Canada	289	7.2
	Philippines	205	5.1
	Germany	197	4.9
	Other	817	20.3
	Total	**4,015**	
1974	Korea	2,453	51.4
	Vietnam	561	11.8
	Colombia	245	5.1
	Philippines	223	4.7
	Canada	188	3.9
	Other	1,100	23.1
	Total	**4,770**	
1975	Korea	2,913	51.7
	Vietnam	655	11.6
	Colombia	379	6.7
	Philippines	244	4.3
	Mexico	162	2.9
	Other	1,280	22.7
	Total	**5,633**	
1976	Korea	3,859	58.9
	Colombia	554	8.5
	Vietnam	424	6.5
	Philippines	323	4.9
	Mexico	127	1.9
	Other	1,265	19.3
	Total	**6,552**	

SOURCE: Adapted from US Congress, House of Rep., Comm. on the Judiciary, *Alien Adopted Children: Hearing before the Subcommittee on Immigration, Citizenship, and International Law*, 95th Cong., 1st sess. (15 June 1977), 72–76.

NOTE: Immigration and Naturalization Service fiscal years ending 30 June.

in ways that echoed the early years of Korean adoption: privately; in very small numbers; and by individuals who were in Vietnam because of military, government, voluntary agency, or missionary work. Plans to establish mass adoption in the mold of Korean adoption, however, met substantial resistance.[80] Aid organizations declared that there were very few real orphans because extended family networks had remained strong. There was no consensus that GI babies would experience the same discrimination that they had in Korea, partly because of Vietnam's history of race mixing under French colonial rule. Although child welfare workers conceded that part-black children would probably need to emigrate, they were cautious about launching broader-scale international adoption, which would help only a handful of the country's estimated 750,000 orphans, including 15,000 to 25,000 mixed-race children. In fact, child welfare experts seemed to see Korea as a kind of cautionary tale. International Social Service (ISS) had concluded from its experience in Korea that relying on international sponsorship programs and adoption helped to fuel a cycle of child abandonment and orphanage expansion. HAP cautioned against rushing into Vietnamese adoption, underlining the need to differentiate between "whether we really want to help children and save lives or simply 'get children' for adoption." Most important, the South Vietnam government strongly opposed any large-scale program of foreign adoption for Vietnamese children. To this end, in 1969 it banned any mass child-emigration schemes.[81]

The demand for Vietnamese adoption came not from within Vietnam but from prospective adoptive parents in the United States and other Western countries.[82] In 1967, for example, HAP reported that its supporters were pressuring it to begin a Vietnamese operation, and the CWLA stated in 1975 that "thousands and thousands" of Americans had inquired about adopting Vietnamese children.[83] Reports circulated of people buying and selling children for adoption abroad. In 1972, the South Vietnam government slightly relaxed its stringent regulations, resulting in about 500 adoptions that year (397 to the United States), more than double the number in 1970 and 1971 combined.[84] In 1973 it allowed adoption agencies to begin arranging international placements. The same year, the US embassy in Saigon launched efforts to increase adoption from Vietnam in response to pressure from Congress and the American public.[85]

American demand for Vietnamese adoption can be interpreted in two ways: as a manifestation of humanitarianism or, more cynically, as an indication of a consumerist desire to have access to Vietnamese children. The pressure to bring international adoption to Vietnam suggests that the practice contains an expansionary thrust, what HAP called a "natural and obvious logic."[86] The humanitarian impulse partly explained why people saving children in Vietnam also adopted from neighboring Cambodia and Thailand, where children were suffering from similar conditions. But markets—be they for rubber or diamonds (or babies)—also need to expand. International adoption was an industry, and customers (adoptive parents) and brokers needed new sources of supply and a larger array of choices.

The hotly contested 1975 evacuation of 2,700 children from Vietnam through Operation Babylift offers a prism through which to examine humanitarianism, consumerism, and the troubled ethics of international adoption. The controversy surrounding Operation Babylift was partly rooted in suspicions that the US government was exploiting children for political purposes.[87] The ensuing custody battles between adoptive and biological parents, the attempts by biological parents to locate children they had never intended to permanently relinquish, and the class-action lawsuit filed by adoptees charging they were not orphans and had been wrongly removed from Vietnam all raised uncomfortable questions about the ethics of intercountry adoption.[88] Was it right to take children away from the only country they had ever known, where extended family might find and care for them? Was a potentially substandard home in the United States preferable to a life of poverty, probably in an orphanage, in their countries of birth? Did the exigencies of war excuse sending children abroad for adoption whose orphan status had not been sufficiently documented? Should Americans adopt children whose biological parents did not lack the desire to keep them but wanted only for material support? And perhaps most troubling of all, had these children been rescued or kidnapped? These moral and legal questions, with their tangled subtexts of race, culture, belonging, and rights, had shadowed Korean adoption, and they remained contested as intercountry adoption grew. At the same time, the narrative of rescue held such power that adoption only became more deeply embedded in conversations about relief, rehabilitation, and development in the third world.[89]

Throughout the twentieth century Americans had discussed adoption in one of two registers—rescue of waifs and purchase of babies. Although criticism of international adoption remained muted, especially compared to the more impassioned debate over domestic transracial adoption, its proponents nonetheless tried to dissociate it as much as possible from the idea that Americans were importing babies. But the fact remained that, regardless of how benevolent their motives might be, adoptive parents had to venture into the marketplace to obtain a child. This is the clash between love and commerce that produced the uncomfortable tension at the heart of international adoption. Americans had in principle declared that children cannot be assigned a market value like some ordinary commodity but in reality people engaged in what looked like market transactions: paying to obtain children priced according to race, gender, age, and country of origin.[90]

Adoptive parents responded to the consumerist aspect of adoption in various ways: they embraced it by joking about how they picked their children out of catalogs or by saying their children were "imported," or they countered it with religion, like the adoptive mother who continually told her Korean daughter that she was a "missionary project." They also deflected charges of consumerism by portraying adoption as a gift: the child was a gift from God, for example, or a sacrificing birth mother had given her child the gift of a better life in America. This gift language reframed the adoption of a poorer, nonwhite child by richer, white parents in terms of consent and choice. As such, it masked the structural inequalities and violence that underlay relinquishment and soothed any ethical qualms adopters may have felt. Another way to disavow adoption's relationship with the market was by denying that adopters paid for children. Agencies emphasized that fees were solely for administrative costs, the care of the child, and donations to the orphanage—but never for the child herself. This strategy ensured that the child remained uncommodified—priceless—even though every element around her had a price tag attached. Finally, adopters denied consumer behavior with ideas about fate. They adopted, or offered to adopt, children they had seen in a magazine, sending clippings to adoption agencies and orphanages with circles or arrows denoting the child they wanted. Others visited orphanages to select a child, employing what one social worker condemned as a "cafeteria approach." Adoptive parents invoked destiny to claim that, rather than selecting their child, their child had chosen them. But these strategies to minimize consumerist behavior only underscore how consumerism haunts international adoption.[91]

As consumers of adoption services, adopters felt it was their right to switch from one agency to another, especially in the early years, when the kind of adoptions approved by social workers were much slower than proxy adoption through agencies like HAP. Potential adoptive parents wanted to adopt quickly, cheaply, and with minimal fuss. Frustrated adopters like the Fs demanded to know what was taking so long: "This is supposed to be the legal, authorized way to adopt a child and then you wonder why people go to the black market," they complained in a letter to the president of ISS. "We know many people who have gotten children from the so-called black market. They paid less than half the price we are paying and have adopted and recieved thier [sic] children in six weeks time. . . . [W]e have been working on this for over a year." Other families simply abandoned their ISS adoptions to adopt by proxy through HAP. Like good consumers, they used the most expedient method available to get what they wanted.[92]

Whether international adoption was a rescue mission or a market, it held great potential for commodifying children. Adopters could select a country and handpick a child of the right age and sex to complete their families according to their vision. They could pick an older child if she would better fit their lifestyle, or they could decide the outer limit of the physical or mental disability they felt they could accept. One adult adoptee imagined how a friend of her mother's, believing that it was God's will for her to adopt from Korea, initiated the process: she "made a phone call to Holt International Children's Services to place an order for one female baby, no defects." Furthermore, international adoption became increasingly the province of the middle and upper classes during the 1970s and 1980s, as private agencies became the norm and costs rose into the thousands, and then tens of thousands, of dollars.[93]

A grave consequence of the commodification involved in international adoption was its erasure of birth parents and families. Adoptive parents did not necessarily wish to contemplate why children were available for adoption, and social workers did not always know or tell the truth. Parents erased birth mothers outright in comments like, "I've told my girls that while they happen to have had a Korean mother . . . they were really born to us, because we wanted and chose them." This trope of the "chosen child," common in adoption language, emphasized the adoptive parents' agency and the preciousness of the child but denied the birth mother's existence as an individual altogether. Other adoptive parents professed gratitude to the birth mothers of their children: "the awesome sacrifice of the unknown, uneducated Asian woman."[94] But sentimentalizing the birth mother in this way—as a mythic, tragic-romantic heroine—is itself a kind of erasure that collapses all birth mothers into one poor woman, strips her of agency, and ignores the myriad circumstances and decisions that led her to relinquish her child.

The adoption community widely acknowledged that the Korean child's orphanhood was mostly a fiction. Adoptive parents knew that poverty, combined with Westerners' relative wealth, made Korean adoption possible and that, beginning in the late 1960s, the majority of Korean adoptees had "living parents whom they remember but are unlikely ever to see again." Further eroding the fiction of the Korean child's orphan status was the fact that, long before open adoptions became common, some birth parents maintained contact with their children. This openness could exacerbate a child's distress, as in the case of the twelve-year-old girl who cried over pictures of her Korean family every night. Her adoptive family, she said, "couldn't figure out why I was crying. They thought I'd be happy because I had a piano and two cats." Another adoptee kept photos of his birth parents hidden in his dresser until his adoptive mother found and destroyed them. More traumatic still, some birth parents accompanied their children to the airport on the day of departure to say their farewells (see Figure 5.3). A social worker expressed unease with the practice but rationalized it by saying it refuted "the implication that these mothers are 'forced to surrender.'" Instead, she suggested, "It seemed abundant proof that they go along with this plan wholeheartedly, in spite of the anguish and heartache at the point of separation."[95]

The fiction of Korean orphanhood persisted because humanitarian rescue fantasies required it. If these were parentless children whose only future was life in an orphanage followed by a marginal existence in the depths of Korean society, adopters did not need to consider the possibility that they could help in ways that did not involve adoption—or, as a four-year-old Korean boy asked his adoptive mother: "Why don't the American moms and dads just send money to the Korean moms and dads so they can keep their children?" The emphasis on acquiring a child through adoption rather than helping families to stay together shows how adoption as a method of rescue is not always about the best interests of the child.[96]

The disingenuousness of the rescue narrative becomes more apparent when one considers that the children who truly needed rescue were not the ones who were adopted. Those considered "hard to place"—older children, those with mental and physical handicaps—remained largely unadopted,

FIGURE 5.3 Julie Young with her Korean parents and brother at the airport in 1974, on the day she left for the United States. She did not see her Korean family again for thirty years.
SOURCE: Courtesy of Julie Young.

even though they were the ones who were most likely to grow up in institutions. (It is possible that these children were not offered for adoption by agencies worried about harming Korea's image abroad.) Nonetheless, if Korean adoption had really been primarily about rescuing unwanted children, then GI babies, whose evacuation had been the original goal of intercountry adoption, should have continued to constitute a majority of adoptees. Instead, beginning in the early 1960s, they represented a declining segment of children emigrating for adoption. In 1977, more than two decades after Korean adoption had begun on their behalf, children of mixed race were still among those who needed homes the most.[97]

Conclusion

Between the end of the Korean War and into the 1980s, the Korean child was transformed from refugee to immigrant in the legal and cultural spheres. Supporters of Korean adoption drove changes in refugee laws—ultimately codified in immigration law—by advancing views of the Korean child as a racialized subject who was nonetheless wholly adaptable to Americanization. Her presumed orphanhood, her wretchedness, and the threats posed to her by communism and racial discrimination made possible her entry under refugee laws; she legally became an immigrant thanks to depictions of her as a superlative reflection of the best of American democratic values.

Korean adoption contributed to the larger redefinition of Asianness in the United States after World War II. Together with the war bride, and Asian American communities who actively participated in creating an image of themselves as a model minority, the Korean orphan offered a new image of Asians in the United States: anticommunist, assimilable, conforming to American values, and therefore contributing to a stronger nation. Of these, the Korean orphan was the best kind of immigrant. Free of the taint of the potentially subversive adult refugee or the sexual threat of the war bride, and full of the promise of childhood, she was the worthiest of immigrants, deserving of entering the "circle of care" provided by both the nuclear and the national American family.[98] She was the ideal future citizen, at once a model minority and a model immigrant.

As a political symbol, the Korean child served to "smooth out or even submerge complicated political issues under the veneer of sentiment."[99]

That veneer was central to the hegemonic narrative of Korean adoption, which claimed that love could conquer all divisions of race and nationality and that the adoption of a Korean child by an American family signified nothing more than the uncomplicated mutual completion of a homeless orphan and the parents who wanted her. The narrative erased birth mothers and ignored histories of imperialism, militarism, racism, and patriarchal sexism, as well as any suggestion of exploitation in an emerging adoption market. But as Korean adoption became international adoption beginning in the late 1960s, the romantic narratives of orphanhood and rescue that helped sustain Korean adoption became disrupted by complicated questions about the intersections of humanitarianism, racism, and consumerism—questions that we have yet to fully answer.

SIX

International Adoption in the "Miracle on the Han"

> Before South Korea became known for its low-priced cars and television sets, it was known for its orphans.
>
> —Peter Maass, *Washington Post*[1]

In 1988, modern South Korea made its debut on the world stage by hosting the summer Olympic games. The Seoul Olympics were the coming out party for the "miracle on the Han River," the label applied to Korea's astonishing metamorphosis from postwar devastation to first-world status in just thirty-five years. In the run-up to the Olympics, and during the games themselves, domestic and foreign media showcased not just the country's colorful history and traditions but also its vibrant, prosperous cities. Alongside the celebration of Korea's success, however, were stories by foreign journalists that emphasized Korean otherness and primitiveness, the tone of which one scholar has aptly summarized as "too noisy, too spicy, too proud, too nationalistic, these people." In the midst of unflattering accounts about sweatshops, prostitution, and dog eating, none were more embarrassing to Koreans than the ones that described their country as an exporter of babies. But this characterization was made more poignant, and cutting, because it was, in many ways, accurate: by the 1980s international adoption had become big business in Korea.[2]

International adoption became entrenched as a national industry and a permanent feature of Korean child welfare policy under the military dictatorship of General Park Chung Hee (1961–1979) and in parallel with the country's emergence as one of the "four tigers" of Asia. Park's unyielding growth-oriented policies both produced a supply of abandoned children and sustained the social, economic, and legal structures that encouraged their overseas adoption. Under his regime, Korean adoption, initially meant as an escape route for mixed-race children, transformed into a mechanism for sending abroad the children that Korea could not, or would not, care for: those with disabilities and the children of poor families and single mothers.

Building on the provisional measures put in place in the 1950s, the policy and practical mechanisms for Korean adoption hardened during the 1960s to support its takeoff in the 1970s and 1980s. During these decades, the number of children emigrating for adoption each year rocketed into the thousands. Indeed, some have argued that South Korea achieved its position as a first-world nation thanks in part to one of its most popular but unacknowledged exports: its children. The international adoption industry played an important role in Korea's "economic miracle" by bringing in foreign exchange, helping to nurture goodwill with powerful Western allies, functioning as a safety valve for excess population, and relieving the government of a large part of the burden of developing indigenous social welfare institutions (see Figure 6.1).

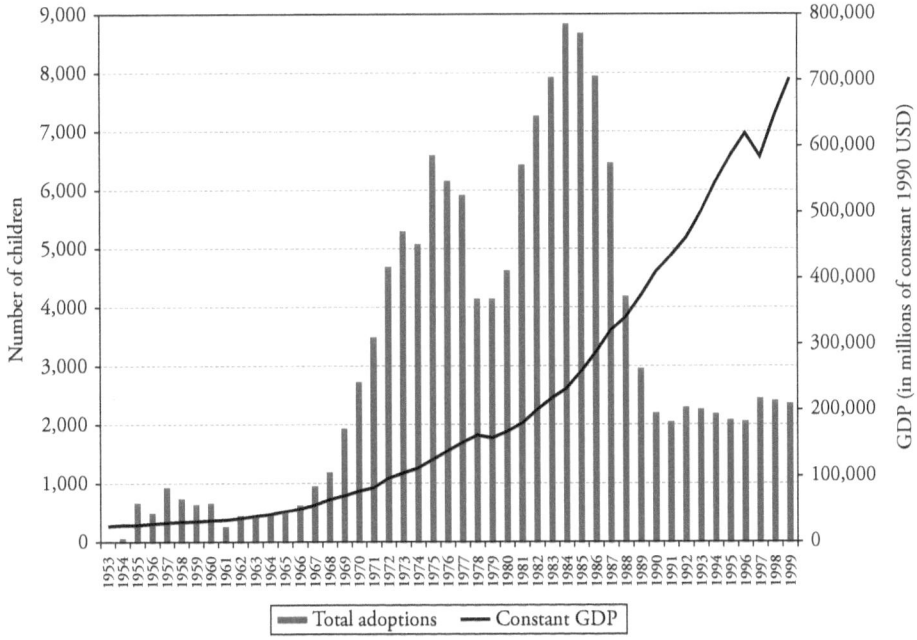

FIGURE 6.1 Number of Korean children placed abroad by year versus Korean annual gross domestic product
SOURCE: Based on data from Tobias Hubinette, the Conference Board, and Total Economy Database.

Korean adoption did not develop as an industry solely for practical reasons. It fulfilled ideological purposes too, by serving the patriarchal nationalism that drove Korean nation building and modernization. Considering international adoption as a business throws into relief the importance of Korean women's reproductive labor to the country's ascent into the developed world. The Korean state kept women trapped in a social, cultural, and legal system in which single motherhood was effectively impossible, leaving single women with babies with no other choice than to relinquish them for adoption. In supporting the industry that sent these children abroad, the patriarchal Korean state not only reaped economic benefits but also protected the normative patriarchal family and, by extension, the nation itself.

The Expansion of Korean Adoption

International adoption was an unacknowledged but important component of Korea's storied modernization, which occurred between the mid-1960s and mid-1980s but is most associated with its chief architect, General Park Chung Hee, who ruled from 1961 to 1979. For Park, economic growth and military strength were the only way to meet the communist threat from richer, better-armed North Korea. He instituted an aggressive program of state-led, export-oriented industrialization, embodied in a series of five-year development plans, combined with extreme political and social repression, to produce record growth.[3]

Foreigners deemed the emergency in Korea over even before Park came to power. Although Korea had been widely regarded as a "sinkhole of American aid," the United States began to reduce direct aid in 1958, although military assistance continued, and in fact increased. Around the same time, the United Nations phased out two of its large aid programs in Korea, the UN Korea Reconstruction Agency (UNKRA) and UN Command's Civil Relief in Korea (UNCRIK), and the Korea Church World Service and its partners at the National Council of Churches of Christ moved their programs to a nonemergency footing. The US Congress similarly signaled a shift away from emergency thinking when it abolished proxy adoption as a basis for visa issuance for immigrant orphans. Lawmakers had tolerated this controversial adoption method in the belief that it was the most expedient way to remove mixed-race Korean children from a life-threatening situation; banning it indicated that Congress believed the justification for it no longer existed.⁴

But many others considered the orphan emergency to be far from over. Even as some American politicians began to heed social workers' pleas for more caution in intercountry adoption, child welfare workers and missionaries in Korea continued to urge speedy evacuation. The overcrowded, understaffed, underequipped, and unsanitary orphanages continued to trouble many observers. Author and intercountry adoption advocate Pearl Buck publicly claimed that children were "dying like flies" as a result of their extended stays in them. In 1962, a visitor was "appalled to observe almost 200 infants laid out in long rows of little white baskets, in various stages of emaciation, with no individual attention possible from the few harassed attendants on duty"—a scene reminiscent of the Dickensian Korean orphanages of the 1950s. Conditions had improved three years later, when the same baby home had become part of the municipal hospital. Less crowding, more attendants, and better sanitary conditions had reduced the mortality rate from 80 percent to 12 percent per month. Nonetheless, the cribs still held two to three children each, and many of the children were tubercular, undernourished, and unresponsive.⁵

In the 1960s a new child welfare crisis emerged: a dramatic increase in child abandonment, spurred not by racial mixture—as in the case of the GI babies—but by poverty.⁶ Yet Korea was no more equipped to provide child welfare in the early 1960s than it had been immediately after the war. Although an estimated 60 to 70 percent of Koreans lived in poverty into the mid-1960s, the country could not provide even the basic support that would help poor families stay together. Park's "growth-first, redistribution-later" strategy devalued social welfare, and because of security concerns about North Korea the majority of the national budget, including aid from the United States, went to military expenditures.⁷

Child abandonment, particularly of girls, had been a problem since the end of the Korean War, but in the 1960s the problem became acute. According to the Korean Ministry of Health and Social Affairs (MHSA), 715 children were abandoned in 1955—surely a serious underestimation—a number that doubled the next year. From 1957 to 1960, more than 2,000 children were abandoned annually and more than 4,000 children were abandoned in 1961 and again in 1962. In 1964, the number of abandoned children peaked at 11,319. These numbers declined but were still astounding: 7,866 children were abandoned in 1965, 6,500 in 1967, and more than 6,000 in 1972. Furthermore, these figures do not capture the whole picture, because "many discarded babies and infants die from exposure or malnutrition before they have a chance to become government statistics."[8]

Two reasons lay behind the sharply escalating epidemic of child abandonment in the early 1960s. First, rapid industrialization produced profound transformations in social and economic conditions. Urbanization accelerated as the landless rural poor flocked to the cities to work in new industries. The subsequent erosion of the traditional multigenerational family led to an increase in family breakdowns and illegitimacy. Many newcomers to the cities, lacking the personal networks that could have helped them in their villages, were unable to find jobs. Families who could not provide for their children abandoned or relinquished them, beginning with the youngest and the girls. A traditional preference for boys skewed the abandonment rate, reported in 1964 to be five girls for every boy. In fact, the sex ratio depended on age: in the 1960s, forty-five male infants were abandoned for every hundred female infants, but this ratio reversed for children older than age six, when girls became economic assets (as domestic labor), whereas boys became liabilities because they had to be educated.[9]

A second and closely related reason for child abandonment was the relative wealth of the orphanages. Most were largely supported by Americans, usually through monthly sponsorship programs like Christian Children's Fund, which played a crucial role in the lives of institutionalized children: in 1965, CCF supported at least three-quarters of the sixty-eight thousand children in Korean orphanages. As discussed in Chapter 2, Korean parents used orphanages in the same way that poor parents in other countries historically have done: as makeshift child-care facilities. In 1961, a Presbyterian Church official reported that "many, if not most of those now being received, are not orphans at all," but probably "children of poor parents who are glad to have them fed and clothed and educated . . . and then get them back when they are big enough to work." A decade later the Korean government estimated that half the children in orphanages had families.[10]

Orphanage directors were happy to comply with this way of using their institutions. It relieved them of the responsibility of providing vocational training for older children and teenagers. More important, temporary residents padded the rolls, which increased access to government money and relief goods, and strengthened fund-raising appeals overseas. Consequently, orphanage directors resisted efforts to reduce the number of institutionalized children. Allegations abounded about corrupt directors who embezzled money or refused to release children for adoption for fear of losing sponsorship dollars.[11] In the early 1960s, the MHSA launched efforts to improve conditions in the country's hundreds of child-care institutions. It stiffened requirements for orphanage permits—previously available to virtually anyone—and forced the most substandard establishments to close. But these efforts proved largely ineffectual. Most orphanages were privately owned, and the superintendent-owners did not wish to lose their incomes or investments by shutting down.[12] Orphanages had become big business and were difficult to dislodge.

The relationship between orphanages and child abandonment was insidiously harmonious: donations increased to meet orphanage expansion, and as more dollars became available, orphanages expanded further. As the *Korea Times* noted in 1966, this dynamic created "a sort of perpetually expanding cornucopia." Social workers noted that the growth of orphanages created another kind of "vicious circle": "the more there are, the more inclined the parents are to abandon the children." By 1975, orphanages and intercountry adoption had become so intertwined that International Social Service (ISS) speculated that "the presence of efficient foreign adoption facilities encouraged . . . abandonment." Furthermore, because institutions required that children be parentless, parents abandoned their children rather than formally relinquishing them.[13]

Although most welfare workers had accepted international adoption as a reasonable solution to the GI baby problem, some feared that it would expand to include full-blooded children, whom they did not think required evacuation. One warned that "agencies will not be able to withstand the pressure to bring children of pure Korean blood and even to occasionally bring children whose parents are living but are destitute and willing to give them up for a price." ISS, World Vision, the Presbyterian and Methodist missions, and the Rhee government all agreed that only mixed-race children should be placed for adoption abroad. Harry Holt also initially believed it was best for full-Korean children to stay in Korea, but he changed his mind when he saw children dying. Because it was his agency that placed the majority of children from Korea, his attitude shaped the trajectory of Korean adoption.[14]

Intercountry adoption did expand in the 1960s to include full-Korean children, a development that troubled many social workers. Anne Davison, who had worked in Korean child welfare since the 1950s, reported in 1961 that "99.99% of the foundling infants are pure Korean . . . [with] legitimate parents who are still living in the community. Poverty is the only reason they felt they had . . . to abandon a child they loved." Like others who believed that full-Korean children belonged in Korea, Davison argued that social workers should focus on finding in-country solutions: "Have we not a responsibility to strengthen the few ties they have left in Korea, rather than for us to assume that a family that has never seen him on the other side of the world, is without question the right answer for him? The question of mixed racial child migration and full-Korean child migration should be kept quite clearly separate." Wholesale adoption of children—mixed race, full Korean, and those with living parents—distorted the original intent of Korean adoption, which had begun to remove mixed-race children from an emergency situation. For Davison, continuing to export children for economic reasons was a perversion of the practice.[15]

Because of a lack of adoptive families domestically, relinquishing a child for adoption in Korea effectively meant sending her abroad. The rise of a professional intercountry adoption industry, combined with ongoing poverty, encouraged a popular view of intercountry adoption as a good option for poor families. On the other side of the Pacific, American parents faced a shortage of "adoptable" children. As Korean adoption became increasingly familiar and accessible, potential adopters turned to Asia, taking advantage of the symmetry between adoptive parents' historical preference for girls and what one social worker and adoptive parent called "the Asian penchant for abandoning them."[16]

The synchronization between these Korean "push" factors and American "pull" factors was helped by adoption-friendly legislation passed by both governments. Days after international adoption became a permanent part of US immigration law, the Park government hurriedly enacted the Extraordinary Law of Adoption for the Orphan Child, which made it easier for foreigners to adopt Korean children. Thus, the Park administration continued to promote a view first established under President Rhee, which equated providing welfare for orphans with sending them abroad for adoption. The new law did offer some protection for birth families by requiring that a child be advertised as abandoned in the local newspapers at least twice within fifteen days before she could be considered available for adoption. However, this provision was ineffective because, as the head of Child Placement Service (CPS) explained, "even though [the child's relatives] know whereabout [sic] of their children, [they] do not want to have the children back due to poverty stricken life."[17]

The Park government cultivated the international adoption industry by formalizing rules and procedures across agencies. It required them to employ specific kinds of staff—for example, a psychologist, doctor, and professional social workers—and to provide certain services. Perhaps most important, it reduced the number of agencies licensed to provide intercountry adoption services to four by the early 1970s: Social Welfare Service (formerly CPS), Holt Children's Services (formerly Holt Adoption Program, or HAP), Korea Social Service (KSS), and Eastern Child Welfare Services (ECWS). KSS, Korea's first indigenous adoption agency, was established in 1964 and initially focused on placing mixed-race children abroad; ECWS was the newest agency, established in 1972. These four agencies were central to perpetuating and enlarging Korean adoption. In theory, by continuing intercountry adoption while simultaneously developing foster care, domestic adoption, and family preservation programs, these agencies should have run out of a supply of children and put themselves out of business.[18] Instead, intercountry adoption only became more widespread, and the number of children sent overseas grew.

Efforts to promote in-country adoption began in the early 1960s. The Korean government smoothed the way by changing the law in 1960 to allow adoption of unrelated children ("stranger adoption") and requiring the four intercountry adoption agencies to process domestic adoptions.[19] In addition, it authorized thirty-one other adoption agencies (including orphanages and government offices) to place children domestically. The Christian Adoption Program of Korea (CAPOK) began a domestic adoption program in 1962 that was so informal that, "many times, the babies were just given to those who asked." It was not until the late 1960s that the government and agencies themselves began to establish laws and procedures for in-country adoption. CAPOK merged with HAP in 1975 in a logic that revealed a great deal about the role of money in the developing international adoption industry: to comply with newly imposed domestic adoption quotas, HAP needed the domestic adopters that CAPOK had cultivated, and CAPOK needed HAP's resources—paid for by international adoption fees—so it could continue to recruit Korean families willing to adopt.[20]

But finding in-country placements was difficult. The Korean emphasis on patrilineal bloodlines meant that parents resisted adopting a child whose background they knew nothing about. Economic, bureaucratic, and legal obstacles dissuaded those who were willing to adopt, and laws favored birth parents if they changed their minds and tried to reclaim their child. Like Americans a decade or two before, Koreans adopted mainly to hide infertility. Prospective adoptive parents asked for newborns so they could fake a pregnancy and deceive their families, neighbors, and—in the case of women who came to agencies alone—their husbands. In fact, the secrecy around adoption was so absolute that Korea's low domestic adoption numbers might be significantly higher if they counted unrecorded adoptions. On the other side of the desk, some child welfare workers worried about the danger of exploitation in domestic adoption. In-country placements could amount to mere servitude, and there were reports of adoptive families using four- or five-year-old girls as domestic help.[21]

Hoping to reduce the number of children in institutions, the Park government promoted domestic adoption and foster care beginning in 1962 under slogans like "Let's raise one orphan per family." The program aimed to place two thousand children per year in foster families, but even when such families could be found, there was no money to pay for fostering. Difficulties monitoring the placements also led to negative outcomes, with many children winding up back in institutions or on the streets. Ultimately, insufficient funds, lack of political will, and the plan's haphazardness caused it to collapse within three and a half years, having accomplished little. Through advertising, recruitment, and public relations programs, the government and adoption agencies did manage to increase domestic adoptions fifteen-fold between 1970 and 1980, but the practice still struggled to gain wide acceptance. Although they considered international adoption a national embarrassment, and disparaged intercountry adoption agency workers as baby sellers, Koreans continued not to adopt.[22]

Baldly put, adoption agencies prioritized intercountry adoption because it was profitable. It generated high fees and donations, which agencies needed to continue operations or subsidize domestic adoption services. The irony, of course, was that agencies' focus on foreigners and their superior "purchasing power" came at the expense of service for domestic adopters and birth families. In 1974, a family adopting from abroad paid between $600 and $1,500 in fees, whereas domestic adopters contributed $25 to $50 toward the actual cost of approximately $350 (including service to the birth parents, foster care, and adoption). Agencies were unable to charge more for domestic adoptions because of concerns that high fees would cause Korean adoptive parents to turn to the black market instead. In 1966, an observer speculated that because of the country's "strong need for foreign exchange," the MHSA evaluated agencies primarily "in terms of dollars they bring into Korea. The quality of service or service rendered is only secondary."[23]

The Korean government also pressured adoption agencies to increase revenue. Beginning in 1976, it required international adoption agencies to maintain child-care institutions, which it supported; when these institutions were full, the government mandated that children be placed in foster homes, which it required the agencies to fund.[24] Of course, this meant agencies needed more money, which they could earn through foreign adoptions. Korean agencies did not place children directly in the United States but through partnerships with American agencies licensed by individual states, so increasing revenue meant increasing placements, which they could only do by creating relationships with as many US agencies as possible. Korean agencies competed for these, sometimes aggressively, as in the case of the KSS director who sought to be the "only supplier of Korean children" to certain American agencies. Korean agencies also explored other receiving countries, especially in Europe, where looser standards meant faster adoptions. In 1966, CPS signed an agreement with the Swedish National Board of Health and Welfare, kicking off a wave of agreements and network building between agencies in Korea and abroad. Over the following several years, the number of countries receiving Korean children rapidly expanded to include all of the countries in Scandinavia, several Western European countries, Australia, and Canada.[25]

Competition among agencies to maintain a supply of adoptable children—defined as healthy, attractive infants—spurred practices that placed market considerations over child welfare in three main ways. First, agencies established reciprocal relationships with orphanages: in return for financial assistance, orphanage directors not only housed children being processed for adoption but also gave paying agencies priority in selecting the most desirable children to offer prospective adopters. Using orphanages in this manner, as way stations for children being sent abroad, was a positive because it meant that children were not institutionalized for the long term. But the channeling of certain children into temporary care and then overseas for adoption checked efforts to reunite lost or abandoned children with their birth families or relatives.[26]

Second, interagency competition perpetuated the unsavory practice of "baby hunting." Agencies were dogged by constant innuendo about their baby-finding methods, such as coercing and bribing birth mothers or misrepresenting their activities and intentions. In 1968, an ISS worker was distressed to discover that ISS Korea had engaged in the same practice that it had accused other agencies of: paying bonuses to their workers for finding children. Recruiting children like this exposed the falseness of the claim that adoption was intended to find families for children and not children for families. Additionally, agencies worried that paying bonuses might leave them in the position of being responsible for children who had been relinquished but were not necessarily adoptable—liabilities rather than assets, from a business point of view.[27]

Finally, competition among agencies meant that they acted in effect as "relinquishment' services" rather than developing other functions, like domestic adoption or much-needed counseling for birth parents. An early critic noted, "For an agency involved in overseas adoption, faced with a waiting list of applicants and relying on fees for operating expenses, the appeal to develop an in-country adoption service is more than a little lacking in urgency." Another observer claimed that international adoption agencies "focused on supporting orphanages rather than other services."[28] Poor families or single mothers searching for an alternative to abandoning their children found little guidance.

Women's Work in Korean Modernization

Women's productive and reproductive labor were central to South Korean economic development, to its integration into global capitalism, and to the development of international adoption.[29] Combining Korea's Confucian culture and gender norms with masculinist and militaristic ideology, General Park mobilized the country through a patriarchal nationalism that positioned economic development as "our" collective effort.[30] Aligning the state-society relationship with other Confucian hierarchical relationships, he cast the state as the Confucian patriarch to which the nation was subordinate, like a good Confucian woman. Park was clear about women's role in modernization: as "bodies carrying wombs and labor power."[31]

Confucianism held that women's bodies belonged to their fathers, husbands, and sons. Under Park's patriarchal nationalism, they also belonged to the state. As good wives and mothers in the Confucian mold, married women were to participate in modernization from the private sphere: by supporting their husbands, efficiently managing their households, and—most important—bearing and raising good national subjects. (This ideal was a middle-class one, however; lower-class women continued to work outside the home after marriage). Demonstrating how essential control over women's bodies was to nation building, the Park regime implemented a family planning program in 1962, which used a range of tactics—sex education, promotion of various forms of contraception (such as the "patriotic" intrauterine device), sterilization, and tax incentives—to drive the average birthrate down from 6 per woman in 1960 to 2.6 in 1979.[32]

Unmarried women fulfilled their filial duties by conforming to a state-driven reconfiguration of what it meant to be a dutiful daughter. Instead of staying under her father's roof until marriage, as tradition dictated, a good daughter in modernizing Korea was expected to leave her family behind in the countryside and migrate to the city to work. From there, she sent home money for her family's living expenses or a brother's education. Hundreds of thousands of young women—many only teenagers—made this move to the cities. They took menial jobs in domestic or food service, as bus conductors, or became sex workers.

Those able to obtain a higher-status factory job joined the ranks of the factory girls (*yŏgong*), who were the emblematic female workers of industrializing Korea. They supported the nation and their families by toiling long hours in exploitative conditions for meager wages, churning out shoes, clothing, and electronics. Hailed as "industrial soldiers" and "daughters of the Korean peninsula," factory girls were depicted in ways that resonated with old Korean archetypes of "young women as dutiful daughters willingly sacrificing themselves for the good of the nation." Their portrayal as "noble filial girl," however, was complicated by another stereotype of laboring women: *kongsuni* (working girl, or a pejorative version of *factory girl*), a fallen woman who had been tainted by work—whether in a factory or brothel. Some factory girls did turn to sex work out of a desire for more money and independence (and the victims of the rampant sexual harassment in the factories often resigned themselves to sex work), but most protected and asserted their status as virtuous girls and good citizens. These young women—cheap, docile, plentiful, and temporary—were critical to Korea's growth.[33]

As in many other societies, industrialization and urbanization created space for some social and sexual freedoms, especially for young working women who were beyond the control of their fathers and brothers for the first time. But these new freedoms ran counter to traditional Confucian, patriarchal norms of female chastity, which forbid women from expressing or exploring their sexuality and kept them ignorant about it by proscribing formal sex education for unmarried women. This tension highlights the unevenness of Korea's modernization: rapid and compressed on the economic front, less so socially or culturally. Park's patriarchal nationalism essentialized all women into one of two categories: unmarried women producing for the nation or married women reproducing for the nation. Within this scheme, unwed mothers were an impossibility—and yet they were a reality. In the absence of state or social support for them or their children, intercountry adoption filled in the gap.[34]

Beginning in the 1970s, single mothers, especially factory girls and teenaged girls depicted as delinquents, became a substantial source of children for intercountry adoption. Severe social sanctions and legal obstacles made it unthinkable for a woman to raise her child alone; even divorced women and widows faced stigma. Unmarried girls and women who became pregnant had only two choices: abortion or adoption. Abortion was illegal but widespread—but it was expensive, and some women, ignorant about sex, discovered their pregnancies too late to terminate them. Adoption agencies were virtually the only source of counseling and support, and some even provided accommodation at a maternity home. By the early 1980s, adoption had become "the major social service for the unwed mother" in Korea's underdeveloped welfare system. A 1984 study counted just eighteen women's counseling services and five employment agencies in the country, compared to the twenty-eight branch offices of the four international adoption agencies. Unsurprisingly, the majority of single pregnant women relinquished their children for adoption.[35]

Estimates of how much revenue Korean adoption generated in the 1970s and 1980s range from $20 million to $40 million a year. This was at a time when the government gave special recognition to any company with annual exports of more than $1 million. This revenue, moreover, came in the form of precious foreign currency, which the government controlled tightly. This is only part of the picture, though, because a truly accurate accounting of the dollar value of the Korean adoption industry would include the various donations to and among agencies, orphanages, and hospitals, and the "cost savings" of exporting the social welfare needs of children and families. But even if financial models could show that international adoption brought not $40 million but $400 million into the Korean economy each year, that is a drop in the bucket for a country that had achieved gross domestic product of $165 billion by 1979, when Park was assassinated, or $322 billion by the 1988 Seoul Olympics. And the number of children adopted overseas, though significant, is small compared to population growth over the past fifty years. Less important than the dollar figure, or the number of children "exported," is the fact that the Korean intercountry adoption industry enacted the logic of industrialization, buttressed by the same gender ideologies, that propelled the country's economic development. As such, the consolidation of the Korean adoption industry was emblematic of Korean modernization.[36]

The use of adoptees as ambassadors between Korea and the West fit with the ways the Korean state, as the head of a nation imagined as a patriarchal family, used Korean bodies to attain national goals. The Park regime promoted both temporary and permanent emigration to control population growth and unemployment, and it selected migrants on the basis of their potential to send back remittances and valuable foreign exchange.[37] Thus, it sent tens of thousands of nurses and miners to Germany, engineers and construction workers to the Middle East, and groups of settlers to Latin America. It exchanged male bodies for an array of economic and political benefits when it deployed more than one hundred thousand civilian workers and three hundred thousand troops to assist US forces during the Vietnam War.[38] And Park's government used patriarchal nationalism to justify the use of female bodies in particular.[39] It harnessed the sexual labor of camptown prostitutes to cement the US-Korea military alliance, and of *kisaeng* sex workers—prostitutes who catered to foreign (mainly Japanese) sex tourists—to bring in foreign capital and promote tourism.[40] These women, while scorned by respectable society, were lauded by their government as "patriots" and "servants of the nation."[41]

From GI Babies to Amerasians

GI babies exposed the discrepancy between the mythology and reality of Korea's modernization and national identity. By the 1970s they had been renamed "Amerasians," a term that Pearl S. Buck had coined in the 1930s to describe mixed-race Chinese children but that came into widespread use only during the Vietnam War. Whereas in the 1950s they had represented Korea's military and economic—and sexual—subordination to the United States and threatened Koreans' view of themselves as racially pure, in the 1970s they represented an additional challenge: as living symbols of Korea's continuing, feminized economic and military dependence on the United States, they undermined Korea's masculinist story of itself as a nation that had pulled itself out of destitution through sheer force of will. The Korean state had focused from the beginning on international adoption as the solution for Amerasians. It had failed to propose or implement any substantial alternatives by 1978, when the director of the Women and Children's Welfare Bureau summed up the Park government's position: "The only true solution to the problem is for all these children to be adopted by U.S. families or allowed to emigrate to the U.S." Twenty-five years after the end of the Korean War, Korea still considered mixed-race children to be an American problem, for Americans to solve.[42]

Declining numbers of mixed-race children helped lessen the sense of urgency about them. Estimates of how many of these children lived in Korea in the 1960s ranged widely, from 1,500 to 20,000, with 500 to 600 more supposedly born each year. In the 1970s, estimates ranged from 2,000 to 6,000. Their numbers correlated with the US military presence, rising in the 1960s and declining after 1971 along with overall troop reductions. Increased use of contraceptives and abortions prevented the number of mixed-race children from growing despite the flourishing of Korea's military and civilian sex industries. Higher rates of marriage between Korean women and American servicemen also reduced the Amerasian population, because more emigrated with their married parents.[43]

Amerasians remained the concern of foreign aid groups, but they too focused mainly on emigration. Only a few organizations attempted to integrate these children into Korean society. In 1963, George Whitener, a Presbyterian missionary, joined with ISS Korea to create Eurasian Children Living as Indigenous Residents (ECLAIR), which focused on education: securing mixed-race children's entry into public schools and providing financial aid for school fees, books, uniforms and transportation. It also provided counseling to their mothers. When he left Korea in 1965, Whitener turned the program over to CPS, which administered it with some state funding. The Pearl S. Buck Foundation established a similar integrationist program in 1965 that included monthly sponsorship, scholarships, counseling, and recreation programs; by 1977 it served approximately 950 children.[44]

Evacuation through intercountry adoption did partially achieve the goal of removing mixed-race children from Korea. Studies done in the 1970s suggested that the majority of Amerasians born in the 1950s had left the country. And they constituted a diminishing proportion of the children adopted from Korea by Americans: an estimated 2,270 mixed-race children emigrated for adoption during the 1950s, and another 1,829 during the 1960s. After that, the numbers declined to 1,292 during the 1970s, and 694 during the 1980s. Between 1974 and 1991, which included the peak years of Korean adoption, only 0.5 percent of the children leaving Korea for adoption were mixed race.[45]

Amerasians disappeared from the international adoption system partly because they were not in orphanages. Instead, they tended to stay with their mothers in the quasi-American areas around the military bases, where they became a "normalized" part of the camptown milieu. This was particularly true of Korean-black children, who were at risk for maltreatment in institutions. When mothers did relinquish Amerasian children for adoption, they did not abandon them but turned them over directly to agency workers. Adoption agencies found it easier to select from children collected in institutions than to "hunt around in far villages" for Amerasians. To begin with, it was difficult to find them. They were scattered over a wide area, so agency workers had to travel great distances over unpaved roads (where roads existed) to locate them and obtain birth mothers' releases. Some social workers lacked the training, skill, and maturity to work with these women, and they did not want to be seen in camptowns or with mixed-race children for fear of damaging their reputations. Because social workers tended to approach Amerasians and their mothers as candidates and suppliers for international adoption, they sometimes tried to pry apart children and mothers who did not necessarily want to be separated rather than offering counseling or support.[46]

By the 1970s, Amerasians not only had disappeared from actual adoption practice but were being rhetorically erased too. Although a 1968 revision to Korean law allowed a woman to add a child born out of wedlock to her family register, most women did not do this. Unregistered, Amerasians were also uncounted; no governmental or nongovernmental organization maintained records of their numbers. Amerasians remained invisible on their paternal side as well, where they were unacknowledged by their fathers, ignored by the US military and government, and largely forgotten by the American public that had been so eager to rescue them just two decades earlier.[47]

Renewed attention to race mixing, this time in Southeast Asia during the Vietnam War, brought the spotlight back to Korean Amerasians. As the mainstream press began to fill with the same images of sad-eyed Amerasian children that had appeared during the Korean War, journalists "checked in" with the cohort of approximately two thousand mixed-race Koreans who had been born in the 1950s and grown up in Korea. They found them trapped in the lives of poverty and marginality that observers had predicted for them. The girls seemed destined to become prostitutes, like their mothers, and the boys for lives of criminality. Although military service was a key ingredient in male Korean citizenship, Amerasian men were excluded even if they tried to enlist, thus "preemptively placed outside the boundaries of 'normal' masculinity." Korean-black individuals continued to face the most discrimination; even the well-intentioned around them assumed "that becoming entertainers or athletes is the most they can aspire to." And the dehumanizing treatment they suffered could be extreme: a Korean-black man born in the 1950s had been "given to a traveling circus as a freak to be displayed, following the death of his grandmother who brought him up."[48]

Koreans had pathologized mixed-race children since they first appeared, and the government labeled them "handicapped" along with the blind, epileptic, and paralyzed.[49] In the 1970s, even sympathetic social workers and journalists continued to pathologize Amerasians, describing them in terms that echoed the trope of the "tragic mulatto": socially maladjusted; resentful and bitter; prone to delinquency; and alienated from even their own mothers, who they blamed for not relinquishing them for adoption. Insecure home lives, absent fathers, confusion over their identities, and feelings of rejection by both Americans and Koreans were said to have twisted their personalities. Some might have lived average, satisfactory lives—and one, the Korean-black singer Insooni, became a celebrity whose success Koreans often use to counter charges of discrimination—but those stories were overshadowed by those that conformed to the narrative of the "tragic Amerasian."[50] Like the Korean government, the US military, and many social workers, Korean Amerasians saw emigration to the United States as their only hope.

Plans to withdraw US troops from Korea in the late 1970s reinvigorated efforts to find solutions for Amerasians. This time, they produced substantial results. This was partly because the US military command in Korea became involved for the first time. More important, Congress and the American public were focused on the eighty-five thousand to hundred thousand Amerasians that US troops had left behind in Southeast Asia. Efforts to help Korean Amerasians thus converged with initiatives to establish special immigration laws for "America's children in Asia." Although Amerasians from Southeast Asia could and did enter the United States through the United Nations' Orderly Departure Program, some politicians thought their ideological and geopolitical value made them deserving of special immigration privileges. Because they were too old for adoption, their advocates championed legislation that would allow them entry on the basis of their paternity. Congress responded with the Amerasian Immigration Act of 1982 and the more effective Amerasian Homecoming Act of 1987 (amended in 1990). By 1994 more than sixty-nine thousand Amerasians—mainly from Vietnam—had settled in the United States under these programs.[51]

These Amerasian immigration laws represented the first time the US government had ever accepted responsibility for the children its soldiers had fathered abroad. The laws sectioned Korean Amerasians off from other Korean children and folded them in with other mixed-race children from across Asia as "exceptional immigrants" to be welcomed "home" to their nonimperialist fatherland. Newly positioned as repatriates, they, along with other Amerasians, became key figures in an American ideological and political project of post–Vietnam War remasculinization, reconciliation, and redemption.[52]

The End of Korean Adoption

While the term *orphan* typically conjures images of a child whose parents have died, many—perhaps the majority—of the Korean children who emigrated for adoption were social orphans, who had at least one living parent. Whereas the war orphans or abandoned GI babies of the earlier period of Korean adoption aligned more closely with conceptions of the orphan as a parentless child, the Korean "orphans" of the 1960s, 1970s, and 1980s came from a wide variety of situations, and complex and powerful economic, social, and cultural forces shaped their separation from their birth families. Children became orphans when their families became unable to feed another mouth because a breadwinner had died, deserted, lost his or her job, or become sick or injured. A family might relinquish or abandon a child who had a disease, condition, or disability they could not afford to treat, or because it was a girl when they wanted a boy. In a society where divorce was difficult and social welfare services scant, wives who were abused or suffered from their husbands' alcoholism or gambling sometimes felt they had no other option but to flee, leaving their children behind. Perhaps they hoped to return for their children, or perhaps they left without looking back, knowing that children belonged to their fathers by law. Fathers sometimes relinquished these children or the newborns their wives died giving birth to. Children born of extramarital affairs, rape, and incest might be relinquished. Or children might become orphans after a divorce, when both parents wanted to make a fresh start. Children were also relinquished without their parents' knowledge or consent, by relatives and new spouses, who had their own agendas and ideas about what was best for the child and the family. In short, without a strong extended family a child could fall through the cracks in Korean society in a multitude of ways, be classified as an orphan, and swept into the international adoption system.

By the time of the 1988 Seoul Olympics, Korea's adoption industry had become an efficient machine. A closely interconnected system of institutions positioned adoption as virtually the only solution for a woman carrying a child she did not want or could not raise. Agencies maintained a "steady supply of healthy children" by supporting or operating maternity homes, hospitals, and orphanages, and they cultivated relationships with the police and multiple hospitals, so as to be notified first when there were babies available for adoption. The agencies were "so desperate . . . to meet the demand . . . from the American side" that they sent social workers to hospitals to persuade new mothers to relinquish their children and paid the delivery and medical costs for those who did. This competition to secure enough children for their overseas clientele meant that agencies prioritized profit over welfare concerns. In 1989, the MHSA reported that the four international adoption agencies had overcharged both domestic and international clients, and—despite a written pledge not to—paid "delivery fees" and gratitude fees to welfare facilities and hospitals that provided children.[53] Two decades later, government audits found that adoption agencies continued to overcharge their clients (especially those overseas), maintained poor records, did not try hard enough to find Korean homes for children, and misreported their income.[54]

Professional social workers had been skeptical of Korean international adoption from the beginning, and in the 1960s and 1970s it was they who voiced concerns about the evolving practice. Canadian social worker Anne Davison had anticipated in 1961 that Korea's reliance on intercountry adoption would slow the development of indigenous welfare institutions. In 1974, another Canadian social worker warned that because of Korean adoption, "instead of a broad range of family welfare and community welfare services, we see the development of an 'escape system' which allows both government and private agencies, and the general public, to avoid meeting the real need" of birth parents and families. Other critics characterized the practice as "a means of efficient disposal of needy children," "exploitive," and evidence of the Korean state's "non-commitment" to child welfare.[55] Betty Jean Lifton, an adoptee and outspoken adoption-reform advocate, viewed the future of international adoption with unease: "We glimpse the specter of wealthy countries using the 'excess' children of the poor to replenish their own dwindling baby markets, rather than supporting programs to help destitute mothers keep their children."[56]

These early critics were right. The siphoning overseas of "surplus" and "unwanted" children allowed South Korea to direct most of its resources to national security and economic development. By the end of the Park regime in 1979, Korea was a "leading 'middle power,'" widely considered a "success story," with one of the fastest growing economies in the world.[57] But as the country became wealthy, welfare spending did not grow, and legal and social reform with regard to women's, children's, or family's rights did not proceed. It did not need to. Intercountry adoption relieved the Korean government of this responsibility. Midway through Park's rule, in 1967, his government allocated 2.5 percent of its national budget to social welfare (compared to 29 percent to national defense); a decade later that figure was 7 percent—more than before, but well below other countries with similar per capita incomes.[58] Social welfare expenditures remained low well into the 1990s, with mere fractions of percentages of the government budget parceled out to women's and children's welfare—and even that level of spending was the result of sustained increases during the 1980s. Despite abundant lip service and paper reform, no South Korean administration displayed a serious commitment to providing social welfare until after the 1997 financial crisis and International Monetary Fund bailout.[59]

In the mid-1960s there were some indications that Korean adoption might, in fact, end. CPS director, Youn Taek Tahk, expressed deep ambivalence about the practice and his role in it, and CPS was exploring alternatives such as support programs for unwed and poor mothers and measures to combat child abandonment. As a Korean, Tahk's opposition to continuing intercountry adoption was partly rooted in national pride. He worried that it signaled his country's failure to care for its children. Overseas Koreans told him "quite frequently . . . that they disapprove[d] of sending Korean children abroad to be adopted by foreigners." At the same time, concern with his country's reputation caused him to emphasize good "customer service," to the point where, he admitted, considerations of national pride overrode "sound adoption practices." Others also saw a possible end to Korean adoption. In 1966, an ISS representative stated that fewer Korean children were emigrating for adoption and that the government was "gradually assuming greater responsibility for planning for dependent, neglected or abandoned children." She was hopeful that, with economic improvement, fewer parents would feel forced to give up their children. The director of HAP echoed ISS's assessment of the Korean government's attitude. Believing that his agency was "at a crossroads," he had begun to put together plans for the future that did not involve international adoption. An observer with the Church World Service saw the development of new forms of child care as important "steps in the right direction," and away from overreliance on international adoption, which was "by no stretch of the imagination an answer to Korea's enormous child welfare problems." Welfare organizations even seemed optimistic about mixed-race children, speculating that placing them in Korean foster families might help "normalize" such mixed-race families and increase the acceptance of these children.[60]

But too many forces militated against the end of Korean adoption. Foreign adopters continued to demand Korean children.[61] The Korean government relied on international adoption to preserve social order, bring in foreign currency, and provide welfare services. Agencies needed it as a revenue source. Birth parents who relinquished or abandoned their children depended on the orphanages and international adoption system to provide a solution. International adoption also allowed Koreans to continue to resist adoption: "As long as most abandoned and relinquished children are moving overseas, people [in Korea] will continue to believe that this is the only possible road and that Koreans 'aren't ready to adopt.'"[62] Thus, Koreans did not have to confront their beliefs about bloodline purity, kinship, or what they owed one another as citizens of a supposedly homogeneous nation.

Despite its drawbacks, many in Korea believed that intercountry adoption was better than the fate that awaited children who were not adopted at all: life in an institution. Although long-term institutionalization was expensive and potentially detrimental to children's development, resources and services for children continued to be concentrated in orphanages. Knowing this, parents continued to abandon children by the thousands well into the 1990s. Alternatives like SOS Children's Villages could serve only hundreds, and the public foster-care system was small, underregulated, and underfunded.[63]

There was a third option besides institutionalization or adoption: helping children remain with their parents. By the late 1980s, the vast majority of all children emigrating for adoption were the children of single mothers—in 1989, the figure was 77 percent (compared to 36.5 percent in the 1970s, and 18 percent in the 1960s) and it has only risen since. But single motherhood was so discounted that an unmarried woman and her child were not even legally considered a family until 1989 (a divorced woman had no parental rights to her children until 1990, and there is currently no way to force fathers to pay child support). Beginning in 1992, the Korean government offered monthly child support to single mother households, although it is a token amount (about $44 in 2012), half of what adoptive parents receive, and far less than what it provides to children in institutions or foster care.[64] As late as 1993, the services available for unwed mothers and their children were only in the early stages and of "very poor" quality.[65] In the 1990s, as in the 1950s, motherhood outside of the patriarchal, heterosexual family was virtually impossible.

South Korea has periodically announced plans to end international adoption, especially as criticism has mounted, both internally and externally.

North Korea began accusing South Korea of selling orphans to foreign "slavers" as early as 1959. By the early 1970s, it claimed that the south was "selling thousands, tens of thousands, of children . . . to foreign marauders under the name of 'adopted children.'" In response, the Park government in 1976 instituted the Five-Year Plan for Adoption and Foster Care. The initiative aimed to reduce intercountry adoptions by one thousand per year and increase domestic adoptions by five hundred per year through a quota system in which the number of adoptions allowed per year would be based on the number completed the year before. The plan restricted the number of countries it would send children to and included a public relations campaign, sponsorship scheme, and incentives for domestic adopters. The Korean government hoped to gradually reduce foreign adoptions until 1981, when they would be ended, except for those considered hard to place: mixed-race and disabled children.[66]

Of course, international adoption did not end in 1981, and in fact it increased dramatically under Park's successor, Chun Doo Hwan. The Chun administration reversed Park's position on international adoption, continuing it "as part of emigration expansion and 'a good-will ambassador' policy." The number of intercountry adoptions reached a peak of 8,837 in 1985, three years before the Seoul Olympics, a moment that marked South Korea's arrival as a modern, developed nation but was marred by humiliating reports on its baby-exporting business. After the Olympics, the Korean government announced plans to end international adoption by 1996; it has made the same announcement twice since, in 1996 (with a phaseout date of 2015), and again in 2007 (phaseout date of 2012). In each case, the plan has been abandoned because of low domestic adoption rates.[67] In 2003, fifty years after the Korean War ended, South Korea had the dubious distinction of being by far the wealthiest of the top suppliers of children for adoption by Americans.[68]

Korea's transformation into an advanced economy enabled it to join the Organisation for Economic Co-operation and Development (OECD) in 1996, but it still fails to provide its citizens the social and economic support that its peer nations do. In terms of spending on social welfare, it has consistently ranked among the bottom of the OECD member nations, and in 2009 it spent just 0.8 percent of gross domestic product on child welfare (compared to the OECD average of 2.3 percent). Even this small amount of welfare spending represents a dramatic increase since the 1997 financial crisis, and it is expected to trend upward as the government increases care for the elderly and combats plummeting fertility rates by—ironically enough—encouraging people to have babies.[69]

Given the lack of social, economic, or legal support, it is still extremely difficult for an unwed mother to keep and raise her child.[70] Single pregnant women, who are often rejected by their families, have few services available to them other than maternity homes. Most of these are operated by international adoption agencies and have proved to be such a pipeline into international adoption that the agencies will no longer be able to operate them beginning in 2015.[71] In 2007, 96 percent of unwed mothers in Korea chose abortion, and 70 percent of those who did give birth relinquished their children for adoption. The children of these women now account for more than 90 percent of children adopted internationally.[72] Unwed mothers continue to face severe ostracism and hostility and to suffer coercion and fraud. Some report that social workers take their babies away shortly after they are born, preventing women from seeing their babies or changing their minds. Birth mothers who attempt to retrieve their children are charged a "ransom": medical and foster care expenses that the government subsidizes for babies relinquished for adoption.[73]

Adoptees searching for their own histories have been critical to uncovering the history of Korean adoption, especially some of its less savory aspects. They have found that international adoption agencies and orphanages protected their "supply chains" through a range of unethical practices, from accepting unclear relinquishments to document forgery and lying to birth parents about the whereabouts of their children. A small but significant number of adult adoptees have repatriated and formed important connections with unwed mothers and birth mothers to advocate for adoption reform and family preservation. Their combined efforts have produced important changes in patriarchal laws and policies and focused attention on the need for better welfare services for women and children.[74] In part because of this activism, the Korean government, which has treated international adoption as both a national shame and a necessary evil for most of the country's postwar history, now seems committed to ending the practice. It continues to promote domestic adoption along with the support of nongovernmental agencies and even Korean celebrities (see Figure 6.2). Despite these efforts, the number of in-country adoptions remains stuck between 1,000 and 1,500 per year—and in fact it dropped to 686 in 2013. Although the number of unwed mothers who keep and raise their children

FIGURE 6.2 Since 2003, Korean photographer Seihon Cho has recruited celebrities like Yoon Eun Hye to pose with children waiting for adoption as part of his annual exhibition, *Letters from Angels* (천사들의 편지). The project aims to promote domestic adoption in Korea.
SOURCE: Courtesy of Seihon Cho.

is small, it is rising every year, along with the legal and social recognition that legitimate families exist in many forms.[75]

Conclusion

Beginning in the 1960s, the Korean adoption industry developed into an efficient business in tandem with the country's larger modernization. By the 1980s, its international adoption program was widely considered the gold standard for its supposed transparency, speed, and professionalism. But just

FIGURE 6.3 These faces represent just a small proportion of the unknown number of Korean children sent overseas for adoption since the 1950s. Collage by Layne Fostervold, 2013.
SOURCE: Courtesy of Layne Fostervold.

as Korea's so-called economic miracle was actually built on the backs of its workers, its highly regarded international adoption industry exacted a high price from some of its most vulnerable members: its poor families and single birth mothers, and the children they sent overseas.[76]

Since its peak in the 1980s, adoption from Korea has slowly but steadily declined. The country sent fewer than 2,500 children abroad each year through the 1990s; by the late 2000s, that number was in the 1,000s. Starting in 2010, Americans adopted Korean children in the hundreds rather than the thousands for the first time since the 1960s. This decrease is part of an overall decline in international adoption in the United States, which has fallen from a high of almost twenty-three thousand children in 2004 to fewer than ten thousand in 2011.[77]

Although sending children abroad for adoption helped Korea solve the problems of racial mixture, poverty, and single motherhood over the past six decades, it is unlikely that it will be as easy to export South Korea's new reality: that it is becoming a multicultural society.[78] One ironic consequence of Korea's economic development and purposeful globalization is its new position as a receiving country for immigrants, primarily migrant workers and brides from less-developed countries in South and Southeast Asia. How to go about integrating them and their mixed-race "Kosian" (Korean Asian) children has been the subject of much public debate.[79] The Korean state has implemented policies to embrace multiculturalism, but ethnic nationalism and talk of bloodlines and purity has led to discrimination and hostility toward non-Koreans and their mixed-race children. How the modern Korean nation responds to this new challenge remains to be seen.

Conclusion

The Korean Origins of International Adoption

> Small stories in so-called hidden places matter because they implicate and complicate what we consider to be the larger story, which is the story of people who do have political and economic powers.
>
> —Louise Erdrich[1]

The International Adoption Complex

In 1961, Canadian missionary and social worker Anne Davison, who had been working in relief and welfare projects in Korea since 1953, shared with a friend her concerns regarding the emerging practice of international adoption:

> Parents in economically depressed areas are made to feel they are standing in the way of the future of their children by trying to continue to care for them. The negative effect of this can be seen by any thoughtful person. We cannot permit the United States in her policy to use its superior economic advantages to encourage indiscriminate importation of children as we might import some commodity in short supply. Any plan of emigration must go hand in hand with a policy of strengthening family life in the poor country. If we indulged in any extensive way, in shuffling children around the world for reasons of poverty alone, we would have to take a new look at the Christian home, the responsibility of parents, and the rights and privileges of parenthood.[2]

Davison's was a minority opinion but one that has proved prescient. She anticipated the potentially negative impact of systematic international adoption on families in sending countries, the role of economic power and commodification in adoption, and how globalization might lead to or require new definitions of kinship. And yet at the time she wrote these ominous words, the "shuffling" of children around the world had already begun.

In the years after the Korean War, a matrix of Korean and American adoption agencies, forms, procedures, standards, and laws emerged, and provided the foundation for the flourishing of Korea-US adoption in the decades to come. Korean adoption became international adoption beginning in the late 1960s as the practice spread to other sending and receiving countries around the world, creating what is today a multibillion dollar global industry. But international adoption is not just an industry, a marketplace in which commodities are exchanged for money. Rather, what has become the worldwide phenomenon of international adoption today comprises an interconnected set of structures and ideologies—an "international adoption complex."

The *structures* of this international adoption complex (IAC) include the machinery that makes international adoption possible: for example, agencies, immigration laws, child welfare institutions, transportation mechanisms, sponsorship programs, and social work procedures. Profit motives are involved, even if they are not the main engine of activity. These are the practical aspects of international adoption that are often described with market analogies.

The *ideologies* of the IAC include racial logics that make it possible for certain children to be imagined as family members and members of the nation; gendered and racialized nationalisms; and various forms of sentimentality, humanitarianism, anticommunism, and religious belief. These components provide tropes for the way Americans think and talk about international adoption, justify the conditions that make it possible, and deflect or minimize the corruption and consumerism that accompany it.

Although these structures and ideologies developed in the context of Korea-US adoption, they have been flexible enough to adapt to the specific cultural, economic, and social circumstances of various other sending and receiving countries and the particular relationships between them. As Americans discovered new sources of adoptable children, they transposed the IAC from Korea to other sending countries: to Vietnam and several Central and Latin American countries in the 1970s; India in the 1980s; and Romania, Russia, and China in the 1990s. These are only the most significant examples, of course, since Americans have adopted from dozens of countries around the world in the last half-century. And although Americans pioneered international adoption, they were not its only practitioners. International adoption is now a popular way to create families in Canada, Australia, and many countries in Europe.

The IAC tends to become established in a systematic fashion. After the initial humanitarian response to a crisis, after children are evacuated from an earthquake or a war, adoption agencies open outposts, locate "orphans," and begin channeling them to families in wealthy Western nations that are experiencing falling fertility rates and a decreased supply of desirable children to adopt. Although wars and natural disasters historically spurred this chain of events, the precipitating crisis has come to be so broadly construed that children are now seen as needing rescue from general social and political disarray. In fact, it has become "self-evident" to some Americans that poverty is a sufficient reason to remove children permanently from their birth families.[3]

The corruption that stems from the unavoidable market dynamics of international adoption shadows the IAC wherever it goes. As international adoption became increasingly systematized in the 1970s and 1980s, demand for children from Western countries proved to flow like water from one place to the next. After a crisis produced a supply of orphans, the IAC followed, but then so did reports of nefarious tactics for procuring children for adoption. An outcry would prompt a sending or receiving country to suspend or limit adoption, and agencies and their clients would begin looking for children elsewhere. The fact that it was relatively easy to divert adoptive parents from one country to another should prompt us to look critically at the role of demand and supply, and humanitarianism and capitalism in the growth of international adoption. Although many of the individuals who facilitated and participated in international adoption had the best of intentions, the fact remains that thousands of individual adoptions added up to a public market in which children were commodified, sourced, and shipped overseas like packages. This is the underside of international adoption for which the soulless language of the market can be fitting.[4]

As the IAC took root in different sending countries, it replicated some of the problems that were seen in Korean adoption. We see the problems around us today. Foreign sponsorship dollars continue to make orphanages in many countries much wealthier than the communities that surround them, encouraging poor parents to relinquish their children so they can have access those resources. Welfare services for poor women and children are oriented toward international adoption rather than domestic solutions. Children are made into orphans a little too quickly and efficiently, with minimal effort devoted to finding extended family or other caregivers. Women are caught between clashing state policies and cultural or familial imperatives regarding their wombs. And birth families still approach international adoption from a position of extreme inequality and vulnerability. Furthermore, the various sensational stories that annually emerge about selling, buying, coercion, fraud, kidnapping, and trafficking in countries from Guatemala to Cambodia to Haiti—and completely unregulated practices within the United States, of adoptive parents "re-homing" children, often across state lines—remind us that many holes remain in international adoption's patchwork of policies, rules, and oversight, not to mention serious but unresolved questions about the ethics of international adoption, both in the abstract and in actual practice.[5]

The 1993 Hague Convention on the Protection of Children and Co-operation in Respect of Inter-Country Adoption represents the international community's effort to combat the irregularities of international adoption by imposing worldwide uniform procedures and guidelines. It aims to protect the rights and best interests of children in international adoption and to prevent abuses such as child kidnapping, selling, and trafficking. The convention makes explicit that it is the state's responsibility to ensure that children can remain with their birth families and that international adoption should be a last resort after other options have been exhausted. Naturally, sending countries claim that they would rather care for their own children than send them abroad, but too often this has been mere lip service. More than fifty countries have signed the convention, which has been in force in the United States since 2008; Korea has signed but not ratified it.

Storytelling and Binary Thinking

Telling stories, of course, helps us understand our lives and our world. In adoption, stories and storytelling take on a special significance. "Telling" in adoption is most associated with the act of revealing to a child that she was adopted—which was not an issue for white families with adopted Korean children—but stories are integral to adoption from start to finish. Birth mothers and adoptive applicants told their stories to social workers, who compiled them into the case files that themselves represent stories. Adoptive parents told stories—perhaps of red threads, of luck, of destiny, of chosenness—to explain to their child why she was born to one person in one place but raised by other people in another place. And storytelling can also mean, from the adoptee's point of view, fashioning a coherent narrative of her own life that helps her make sense of her identity. For her, there are holes in her story that may never be filled, answers never provided to questions as simple as who she looks like or where her hometown is, or those as complex as how and why she came to be adopted. The birth searches that adoptees undertake are not just efforts to find their roots or acquire genetic information, but quests for elemental knowledge of who they are.

The story of international adoption is a multitude of stories. It is hundreds of thousands of stories of birth parents and how they came to be separated from their children, and the stories of the hundreds of thousands of Americans who came to see those children as their own. It is a kaleidoscopic array of stories of war, infertility, poverty, despair, cruelty, compassion, and love. Each individual story of Korean adoption has at its center an intense core of human emotion and experience. But when the lens zooms out, those very individual, highly personal stories merge into something else, like a poster of a city skyline that is actually composed of thousands of small images. At this degree of magnification, it is not the individual stories but the grander, public movement that dominates.

Competing narratives characterize international adoption as either profit-driven baby trade or highly sentimental love story. Some of the current criticism reduces the practice wholly to market terms, describing children as property, forms of "embodied value" or subjects or objects entangled in transnational flows of capital and labor, whereas adoptive parents are depicted as consumers, selecting goods "from an internationalized market in children."[6] Others compare international adoption to child laundering, or slavery.[7] And some emphasize how blurred the line has become between adoption humanitarianism—a questionable motivation to begin with—and adoption consumerism.[8] These kinds of formulations challenge us to think critically about the commodification of foreign children, the role of the profit motive in the international adoption industry, and how these dynamics developed over time. But many of those who created Korean and international adoption—the social workers and missionaries, the adoptive parents, the orphanage directors, and the politicians—acted out of genuine concern for children and went to great lengths and made huge personal sacrifices on their behalf. We should not equate or conflate what happened at the ground level with the structures and ideologies that emerged at a larger level. Market metaphors may fit, but to reduce international adoption simply to a series of cold transactions is unfair.

Then again, reducing the fraught chain of events that comprise international adoption to fairy tales of "meant to be" adoptive families denies the complexity and violence of international adoption. To say that destiny brought children and their "forever families" together erases birth parents. To claim that love sees no color denies the reality of life in a racialized society for children who are labeled as different from the people around them, including their own families. To claim that love will conquer all demonstrates ignorance of the potential long-term ramifications of the emotional and physical traumas of abandonment, separation, institutionalization, and the adoption process itself.

At the center of the fairy tale is, of course, the orphan. Although a significant proportion (perhaps the majority) of Korean children adopted overseas were never actually orphans, their representation as orphans persisted—and persists—because it served the interests of too many people. Birth parents made their children into social orphans so they could be admitted to orphanages or be adopted. Social workers and adoption agencies labeled children as orphans to facilitate placement. The Korean government represented children as orphans so they could attribute international adoption to an orphan problem rather than admit its failure to provide social welfare and other support that would have allowed children to remain with their parents. And adoptive parents imagined these children as orphans because a child without family ties does not come trailing moral and ethical questions or birth parents who might want her back.

Indeed, despite open acknowledgment that international adoption is no longer primarily about finding homes for parentless children, Americans continue to promote the "lie we love": untrue claims about a global orphan crisis, of millions of children around the world who need rescue.[9] The vast majority of so-called orphans around the world are not really orphans, and experts agree that it is best to keep these children with their families and in their countries of birth, a belief codified in the Hague Convention. But Americans—especially those involved in the resurgent evangelical adoption movement—continue to justify international adoption with narratives of child saving and neediness.[10] Besides not being true—the children in greatest need are not the ones who are being adopted—this is a problem because it is centered on privileged Westerners' ideals of what childhood should look like and what one scholar has described as an American "consumer-related entitlement as it applies to motherhood."[11] And more troubling, this story relies on willful ignorance of other stories: the legacies of war and colonialism; the ongoing effects of capitalism, neocolonialism, misogyny, and racism; and the massive global inequalities that make possible the systematic transfer of children from poor countries to rich countries.

In many ways, international adoption is a story of dualisms. Procedurally and ideologically, Korean and international adoption operated simultaneously at two levels: the national and the individual, the public and the private, the global and the everyday. Bridging these levels of experience in our historical analysis allows us to attain a fuller understanding of each, as well as the linkages between them. The everyday is "where macro-level phenomena—politics, economics, ideologies—are lived," and the everyday feeds back into the global. Consider, for example, the mundane act of a woman buying a pound of sugar: it "not only expresses but makes possible a global structure of imperialist politics and labor relations that racialize consumption as well as production." Witnessing a couple who has struggled with the heartbreak of infertility finally receive the child they always wanted and a chance to build the family they envisioned, only a cynical observer would wonder about the invisible price tag on that baby's toe. But just as the seemingly simple gesture of buying a bag of sugar is actually inscribed with enormous and complicated meanings, a white American couple cradling their newly arrived Korean (or Chinese, Guatemalan, or Russian) baby crystallizes both the unique elements of their particular story and more universal economic, social, and political forces.[12]

And yet, although so much of the history of international adoption is recounted in binary terms, we should try to push beyond them in trying to fully make sense of it. A great deal of discussion about international adoption revolves around stark polarities—good or bad, demand or supply, love or money, rescue or kidnap, angry or happy adoptee, adopt a child or leave her to starve in an orphanage—but approaching it from a standpoint of either-or does not help us comprehend how and why international adoption can look so different at the macro and micro levels, or understand the myriad dynamics implicated in the IAC: the role of racial ideologies (mixture, purity, triangulation, flexibility, hierarchies of desirability), visions of families and nations and who can be included in them, and what it means to serve "the best interests of the child." Rather, it is more productive for us to try to hold these ambiguities and tensions together, uncomfortably, and weave a messier but more nuanced and honest story about international adoption: its origins, its meanings, its morality. The ability to tell a story, after all, is one of things that makes us human.

Notes

INTRODUCTION

1. Ginger Thompson, "After Haiti Quake, the Chaos of U.S. Adoptions," *New York Times*, 3 Aug. 2010, http://www.nytimes.com/2010/08/04/world/americas/04adoption.html?pagewanted=all&_r=0.

2. In January 2013, the US Congress passed the North Korean Child Welfare Act. For critiques of it, see Christine Hong, "The Fiction of the North Korean Orphan," *38 North*, 19 Sept. 2012, http://38north.org/2012/09/chong091912/; Jennifer Kwon Dobbs, "Baby Scooping 'Stateless' Children," *Foreign Policy in Focus*, 21 Sept. 2012, http://www.fpif.org/articles/baby_scooping_stateless_children; Christine Hong and Jennifer Kwon Dobbs, "The Case Against the North Korean Refugee Adoption Act of 2011," *Korea Policy Institute*, 24 Sept. 2012, http://www.kpolicy.org/documents/policy/120924christinehongjenniferkwondobbscaseagainstnkraa.html.

3. Laura Briggs, "Mother, Child, Race, Nation: The Visual Iconography of Rescue and the Politics of Transnational and Transracial Adoption," *Gender & History* 15, no. 2 (Aug. 2003): 179–200.

4. The numbers on how many children Korea has sent abroad for adoption, and how many adopted (or to be adopted) Korean children have entered the United States, are extraordinarily incomplete.

5. "International Adoption: Statistics," Holt International, http://www.holtinternational.org/insstats.shtml.

6. US Department of State, Bureau of Consular Affairs, "Immigrant Visas Issued to Orphans Coming to the U.S.," http://www.travel.state.gov/family/adoption/stats/stats_451.html. All statistics are given for the State Department's fiscal year, which ends on September 30.

7. Sarah Potter, *Everybody Else: Adoption and the Politics of Domesticity* (Athens: University of Georgia Press, 2014), 18; Ellen Herman, *Kinship by Design: A History of Adoption in the Modern United States* (Chicago: University of Chicago Press, 2008); Barbara Melosh, *Strangers and Kin: The American Way of Adoption* (Cambridge, MA: Harvard University Press, 2002).

8. House of Representatives, Committee on the Judiciary, *Alien Adopted Children: Hearing before the Subcommittee on Immigration, Citizenship, and International Law*, 95th Cong., 1st sess., 15 June 1977 (Washington: GPO, 1978), 46–50; Karen A. Balcom, *The Traffic in Babies: Cross-Border Adoption and Baby-Selling Between the United States and Canada, 1930–1972* (Toronto: University of Toronto Press, 2011), 62.

9. Moira J. Maguire, "Foreign Adoptions and the Evolution of Irish Adoption Policy," *Journal of Social History* 36, no. 2 (Winter 2002): 387; Mike Milotte, *Banished Babies: The Secret History of Ireland's Baby Export Business* (Dublin: New Island Books, 1997). See also Mike Milotte, "The Baby Black Market," *Irish Times*, 28 June 2014, http://www.irishtimes.com/news/social-affairs/the-baby-black-market-1.1847804; Adoption Rights Now!, "Report into the History of Adoption in Ireland Since 1922," *A Romanian Adoptee* (blog), 28 Aug. 2013, http://gamacavei.wordpress.com/2013/08/28/report-into-the-history-of-adoption-in-ireland-since-1922-by-adoption-rights-now/.

10. For more on refugee policy, see Mae M. Ngai, *Impossible Subjects: Illegal Aliens and the Making of Modern America* (Princeton, NJ: Princeton University Press, 2004); Michael Gill Davis, "The Cold War, Refugees, and U.S. Immigration Policy" (PhD diss., Vanderbilt University, 1996); Carl Bon Tempo, *Americans at the Gate: The United States and Refugees During the Cold War* (Princeton, NJ: Princeton University Press, 2008); Gil Loescher and John A. Scanlan, *Calculated Kindness: Refugees and America's Half-Open Door, 1945–Present* (New York: Free Press, 1986); Steven Porter, "Defining Public Responsibility in a Global Age: Refugees, NGOs, and the American State" (PhD diss., University of Chicago, 2009).

11. The Catholic Committee for Refugees (CCR) placed 231 Polish orphans with American families, and the US Committee for the Care of European Children brought nearly 1,400 orphans to the United States after World War II. Gertrude D. Krichefsky, "Immigrant Orphans," *I&N Reporter* (Oct. 1958), 19.

12. Gertrude D. Krichefsky, "Alien Orphans," *I&N Reporter* (Apr. 1961), 45; Rachel Winslow, "Colorblind Empire: International Adoption, Social Policy, and the American Family, 1945–1976" (PhD diss., University of California, Santa Barbara, 2012), 101; Susan S. Forbes and Patricia Weiss Fagen, "Unaccompanied Refugee Children: The Evolution of U.S. Policies—1939 to 1984" (Washington, DC: Refugee Policy Group, 1984), 17; Mark Wyman, *DP: Europe's Displaced Persons, 1945–1951* (Philadelphia: Balch Institute Press, 1989), 199; Matthew Jacob-

son, *Whiteness of a Different Color: European Immigrants and the Alchemy of Race* (Cambridge, MA: Harvard University Press, 1998); Cathy Choy, *Global Families: A History of Asian International Adoption in America* (New York: New York University Press, 2013), chapter 2; John E. Adams and Hyung Bok Kim, "A Fresh Look at Intercountry Adoptions," *Children* (November–December 1971), 217; Lourdes G. Balanon, "Foreign Adoption in the Philippines: Issues and Opportunities," *Child Welfare* 68, no. 2 (Mar.–Apr. 1989): 241–254.

13. Soon Ho Park, "Forced Child Migration: Korea-Born Intercountry Adoptees in the United States" (PhD diss., University of Hawaii, 1994), 30; Howard Altstein and Rita Simon, *Intercountry Adoption: A Multinational Perspective* (New York: Praeger, 1990) 14–15; Lloyd B. Graham, "Children from Japan in American Adoptive Homes," *Casework Papers from the National Conference on Social Welfare* (1975): 130–131.

14. Although some of the half-black children were fathered by Algerian, Moroccan, and Senegalese soldiers in the French army, they were constructed as an American problem. Heide Fehrenbach, "Of German Mothers and 'Negermischlingskiner': Race, Sex, and the Postwar Nation," in *The Miracle Years: A Cultural History of West Germany, 1949–1968*, ed. Hanna Schissler (Princeton, NJ: Princeton University Press, 2001), 165.

15. Brenda Gayle Plummer, *Rising Wind: Black Americans and U.S. Foreign Affairs, 1935–1960* (Chapel Hill: University of North Carolina Press, 1996), 208–209; Michael Cullen Green, *Black Yanks in the Pacific: Race in the Making of American Military Empire After World War II* (Ithaca, NY: Cornell University Press, 2010).

16. Yukiko Koshiro, *Trans-Pacific Racisms and the U.S. Occupation of Japan* (New York: Columbia University Press, 1999); Heide Fehrenbach, "Rehabilitating Fatherland: Race and German Remasculinization," *Signs* 24, no. 1 (Autumn 1998): 121, 123.

17. Yara-Colette Lemke Muniz de Faria, "'Germany's 'Brown Babies' Must Be Helped! Will You?' U.S. Adoption Plans for Afro-German Children, 1950–1955," *Callaloo* 26, no. 2 (spring, 2003): 342–362; Plummer, *Rising Wind*, 208; Heide Fehrenbach, *Race After Hitler: Black Occupation Children in Postwar Germany and America* (Princeton, NJ: Princeton University Press, 2005), 133.

18. Fehrenbach, "Rehabilitating Fatherland," 123–124; Fehrenbach, "Of German Mothers," 178.

19. Koshiro, *Trans-Pacific Racisms*, 188; Robert A. Fish, "The Heiress and the Love Children: Sawada Miki and the Elizabeth Saunder Home for Mixed-Blood Orphans in Postwar Japan" (PhD diss., University of Hawaii, 2002), 69, 236; William R. Burkhardt, "Institutional Barriers, Marginality, and Adaptation Among the American-Japanese Mixed Bloods in Japan," *Journal of Asian Studies*

42, no. 3 (May 1983): 538–539; Graham, "Children from Japan"; Lloyd B. Graham, "The Adoption of Children from Japan by American Families, 1952–1955" (DSW thesis, University of Toronto, 1958); Lily Anne Yumi Welty, "Advantage Through Crisis: Multiracial American Japanese in Post–World War II Japan, Okinawa and America 1945–1972" (PhD diss., University of California Santa Barbara, 2012).

20. Plummer, *Rising Wind*; Mary Dudziak, *Cold War Civil Rights: Race and the Image of American Democracy* (Princeton, NJ: Princeton University Press, 2000); Penny Von Eschen, *Satchmo Blows Up the World: Jazz Ambassadors Play the Cold War* (Cambridge, MA: Harvard University Press, 2006); Thomas Borstelmann, *The Cold War and the Color Line: American Race Relations in the Global Arena* (Cambridge, MA: Harvard University Press, 2003); Christina Klein, *Cold War Orientalism: Asia in the Middlebrow Imagination, 1945–1961* (Berkeley: University of California Press, 2003); Charlotte Brooks, *Alien Neighbors, Foreign Friends: Asian Americans, Housing, and the Transformation of Urban California* (Chicago: University of Chicago Press, 2009); Ellen D. Wu, *The Color of Success: Asian Americans and the Origins of the Model Minority* (Princeton, NJ: Princeton University Press, 2013); Cindy I-Fen Cheng, *Citizens of Asian America: Democracy and Race During the Cold War* (New York: New York University Press, 2013); Sara Fieldston, "Little Cold Warriors: Child Sponsorship and International Affairs," *Diplomatic History* 38, no. 2 (2014): 240–250; Sara Fieldston, *Raising the World: Child Welfare in the American Century* (Cambridge, MA: Harvard University Press, 2015); Winslow, "Colorblind Empire."

21. Elaine Tyler May, *Homeward Bound: American Families in the Cold War Era*, rev. ed. (1999; New York: Basic Books, 2008).

22. Elaine Tyler May, *Barren in the Promised Land: Childless Americans and the Pursuit of Happiness* (New York: Basic Books, 1995); Laura Briggs, *Somebody's Children: The Politics of Transracial and Transnational Adoption* (Durham, NC: Duke University Press, 2012); Choy, *Global Families*; Balcom, *Traffic in Babies*; Melosh, *Strangers and Kin*; Herman, *Kinship by Design*; Karen Dubinsky, *Babies Without Borders: Adoption and Migration Across the Americas* (New York: New York University Press, 2010); Anne Fessler, *The Girls Who Went Away: The Hidden History of Women Who Surrendered Children for Adoption in the Decades Before* Roe v. Wade (New York: Penguin, 2006); Rickie Solinger, *Wake Up Little Susie: Single Pregnancy and Race Before* Roe v. Wade (1992; New York, Routledge, 2000); Potter, *Everybody Else*.

23. Rickie Solinger, *Beggars and Choosers: How the Politics of Choice Shapes Adoption, Abortion, and Welfare in the United States* (New York: Hill and Wang, 2002); Hawley Fogg-Davis, *The Ethics of Transracial Adoption* (Ithaca, NY: Cornell University Press, 2002); Barbara Yngvesson, *Belonging in an Adopted World:*

Race, Identity, and Transnational Adoption (Chicago: University of Chicago Press, 2010); Jessaca Leinaweaver, *The Circulation of Children: Kinship, Adoption, and Morality in Andean Peru* (Durham, NC: Duke University Press, 2008); Sandra Patton, *Birthmarks: Transracial Adoption in Contemporary America* (New York: New York University Press, 2000); Dorothy E. Roberts, *Shattered Bonds: The Color of Child Welfare* (New York: Civitas, 2002). See also the three-part *Adoption and Ethics* series published by the Child Welfare League of America.

24. See, for example, Gary Gerstle, *American Crucible: Race and Nation in the Twentieth Century* (Princeton, NJ: Princeton University Press, 2001); Gary Gerstle, "The Protean Character of American Liberalism," *American Historical Review* 99, no. 4 (Oct. 1994): 1043–1073; Ruth Feldstein, *Motherhood in Black and White: Race and Sex in American Liberalism, 1930–1965* (Ithaca, NY: Cornell University Press, 2000); Alan Brinkley, *The End of Reform: New Deal Liberalism in Recession and War* (New York: Vintage Press, 1995); Philip Gleason, "Americans All: World War II and the Shaping of American Identity," *Review of Politics* 43, no. 4 (Oct. 1981): 483–518; Thomas J. Sugrue, *Sweet Land of Liberty: The Forgotten Civil Rights Struggle in the North* (New York: Random House, 2008).

25. Wu, *Color of Success*; Charlotte Brooks, "In the Twilight Zone Between Black and White: Japanese American Resettlement and Community in Chicago, 1942–1945," *Journal of American History* 86 (Mar. 2000): 1655–1687; Scott Kurashige, *The Shifting Grounds of Race: Black and Japanese Americans in the Making of Multiethnic Los Angeles* (Princeton, NJ: Princeton University Press, 2010); Peggy Pascoe, *What Comes Naturally: Miscegenation Law and the Making of Race in America* (New York: Oxford University Press, 2010).

26. Claire Jean Kim, "The Racial Triangulation of Asian Americans" *Politics and Society* 27, no. 1 (Mar. 1999): 105–138.

27. Katharine Moon, *Sex Among Allies: Military Prostitution in US-Korea Relations* (New York: Columbia University Press, 1997); Ji-Yeon Yuh, *Beyond the Shadow of Camptown* (New York: New York University Press, 2004); Soojin Pate, *From Orphan to Adoptee: US Empire and Genealogies of Korean Adoption* (Minneapolis: University of Minnesota Press, 2014); Anne Laura Stoler, "Tense and Tender Ties: The Politics of Comparison in North American History and (Post) Colonial Studies," *Journal of American History* 88, no. 3. (Dec. 2001): 829–865; Susie Woo, "'A New American Comes Home': Race, Nation, and the Immigration of Korean War Adoptees, 'GI Babies,' and Brides" (PhD diss., Yale University, 2010).

CHAPTER 1

1. Russell Lloyd Blaisdell, with John Patrick Kennedy, *Kids of the Korean War: Father of a Thousand: Memoirs* (Seoul: Sejong Publishers, 2008), 327.

2. Anne O. Krueger, *The Developmental Role of the Foreign Sector and Aid* (Cambridge, MA: Harvard University Press Council on East Asian Studies, 1979), 8–9; David C. Cole and Princeton N. Lyman, *Korean Development: The Interplay of Politics and Economics* (Cambridge, MA: Harvard University Press, 1971), 18–19; Charles J. Hanley, Sang-Hun Choe, and Martha Mendoza, *The Bridge at No Gun Ri: A Hidden Nightmare from the Korean War* (New York: Henry Holt, 2001), 64; Steven Hugh Lee, *The Korean War, Seminar Studies in History* (London: Pearson Education, 2001), 33.

3. The historiography on the Korean War is huge. Major histories consulted include Bruce Cumings, *Origins of the Korean War: Liberation and the Emergence of Separate Regimes, 1945–47* (Princeton, NJ: Princeton University Press, 1981) (hereafter *Origins I*); *Origins of the Korean War, Vol. 2: The Roaring of the Cataract, 1947–1950* (Princeton, NJ: Princeton University Press, 1990) (hereafter *Origins II*); *Korea's Place in the Sun: A Modern History* (New York: Norton, 1997), and *The Korean War: A History* (New York: Modern Library, 2011). Other works include Allan R. Millett, "Introduction to the Korean War," *Journal of Military History* 65, no. 4 (Oct. 2001): 921–935; Carter Malkasian, *The Korean War, 1950–1953*, Essential Histories (Chicago: Fitzroy Dearborn, 2001); William Stueck, *The Korean War: An International History* (Princeton, NJ: Princeton University Press, 1995).

4. Sahr Conway-Lanz, "Beyond No Gun Ri: Refugees and the United States Military in the Korean War," *Diplomatic History* 29, no. 1 (Jan. 2005), 79; Andrei Lankov, "Korean Civilians North and South, 1950–1953," in *Daily Lives of Civilians in Wartime Asia: From the Taiping Rebellion to the Vietnam War*, ed. Stewart Lone (Westport, CT: Greenwood Press, 2007), 202. Lankov, "Korean Civilians," 204, states that there were five hundred thousand refugees in Pusan by February 1951. Hanley, Choe and Mendoza state that the Pusan perimeter contained 750,000 refugees. Hanley, Choe, and Mendoza, *Bridge at No Gun Ri*, 146. *Time* magazine reported that Pusan (population 400,000) became home to 225,000 refugees in January 1951. "The Greatest Tragedy," *Time*, 15 Jan. 1951.

5. Cumings, *Origins I*, xix; Stueck, *Korean War*, 361; Conway-Lanz, "Beyond No Gun Ri," 51, 80; Lankov, "Korean Civilians," 174, 192; Hanley, Choe, and Mendoza, *Bridge at No Gun Ri*, 208–209, 223, 242; Millett, "Introduction to the Korean War," 924; Malkasian, *Korean War*, 88; Harry Summers Jr., "Through American Eyes: Combat Experiences and Memories of Korea and Vietnam," in *America's Wars in Asia: A Cultural Approach to History and Memory*, ed. Steven I. Levine, Jackie Hiltz, and Philip West (Armonk, NY: East Gate, 1998), 173; Stueck, *Korean War*, 361.

6. *Life* had a readership of about twenty million, which made it "the main source of visual news for Americans during the 1940s and 1950s." Wendy Kozol, "'Good Americans': Nationalism and Domesticity in *LIFE* Magazine, 1945–

1960," in *Bonds of Affection: Americans Define Their Patriotism*, ed. John Bodnar (Princeton, NJ: Princeton University Press, 1996), 231–232.

7. See, for example, Harold Fey's 1952 five-part series on the Korean War, published in *Christian Century*, and Robert H. Mosier, "The GI and the Kids of Korea," *National Geographic*, May 1953, 635–664.

8. "Orphans in Korea," *North Pacific Union Gleaner*, 23 Feb. 1953, 5; John Ford, *This Is Korea!* (1951; South Bend, IN: Non Fiction Video, 1992), DVD.

9. Mosier, "GI and the Kids of Korea," 656; Jeanne Rondot, *The Role of Governmental and Non-Governmental Organisations in Supervising the Placement in Europe of Children from the Third World* (Strasbourg: Council of Europe, 1980), 9; American Korean Foundation, *Report of the Rusk Mission to Korea, March 11–18, 1953* (New York: American Korean Foundation, 1953); William Asbury, "Military Help to Korean Orphanages: A Survey Made for the Commander-in-Chief, United Nations Forces, Far East, and for the Chief of Chaplains of the United States Army," 1954, George Drake personal collection (hereafter Drake Collection); Hanley, Choe, and Mendoza, *Bridge at No Gun Ri*, 243. The estimated number of GI babies comes from the US embassy in Korea and is cited in "Amendment of Refugee Relief Act of 1953," *Congressional Record*, 84th Cong., 2nd sess., vol. 102, pt. 6 (30 Apr. 1956): 7247–7249.

10. GIs had participated in humanitarian activities aimed at local children throughout the twentieth century. For example, in 1918, *Stars and Stripes* launched a program in France through which soldiers could adopt as a mascot a child whose father had died in war or was unable to work because of war-related injuries. The program was the "brainchild" of Harold Ross (a private who would later found the *New Yorker*). Soldiers paid five hundred francs (eighty-eight dollars) to "adopt" a child. The money went to the Red Cross, which provided updates on how the money helped a boy's education. By the end of the war, American soldiers had donated two million francs, individually and in units, and were helping to support 3,444 French children. Jennifer D. Keene, *World War I* (Westport, CT: Greenwood Press, 2006), 71.

11. Together with the UN Korea Reconstruction Agency (UNKRA), KCAC (formerly known as the UN Civil Assistance Command) was considered one of the most effective aid organizations in postwar Korea. KCAC was phased out in 1955 and its responsibilities taken over by Office of the Economic Coordinator, UN Command. AFAK was established in November 1953.

12. American Korean Foundation, *Report of the Rusk Mission to Korea*, 8; Asbury, "Military Help to Korean Orphanages."

13. Mosier, "GI and the Kids of Korea," 643; F [to Mom and Dad], 29 Dec. 1955, Case 40043, Social Welfare History Archive, University of Minnesota (hereafter "ISS case files"); Robert King, "Images of Orphans Haunt Veteran,"

St. Petersburg (FL) *Times*, 27 July 2003, http://www.sptimes.com/2003/07/27/Korea/Images_of_orphans_hau.shtml; Blaisdell, *Kids of the Korean War*.

14. Tammy Cournoyer, "Orphans Found Solace with U.S. Troops," *Stars and Stripes*, 18 June 2000, http://www.stripes.com/orphans.htm; "Little Children War's Biggest Casualty," *Pacific Stars and Stripes*, 6 June 1951; Paull H. Shin, "Senator Paull H. Shin: His Story," speech given at conference of Global Overseas Adoptees' Link, Aug. 1999, http://www.goal.or.kr/english/adoptionissues/shin1999a.htm.

15. For example, see King, "Images of Orphans Haunt Veteran"; Jorge Sanchez, "GI Gave Shelter to the Children of War," *St. Petersburg* (FL) *Times*, 25 July 2003, http://www.sptimes.com/2003/7/25/news_pf/Korea/GI_gave_shelter_to_th.shtml; Cournoyer, "Orphans Found Solace with U.S. Troops"; "Kids Live in Hole in Earth," *Stars and Stripes*, 7 Dec. 1951; "5th AF Aid Exceeds $200,000 in 1953," *Stars and Stripes*, 22 Jan. 1954.

16. Elaine Tarello, "A Christmas Story . . . Chaplain Saves Orphans During Dark Days of Korean War," *Airman*, Dec. 2000, http://www.af.mil/news/airman/1200/kids.htm. See also Blaisdell, *Kids of the Korean War*.

17. Craig S. Coleman, *American Images of Korea* (Elizabeth, NJ: Hollym International, 1990), 149–150; Michael Rougier, "The Little Boy Who Wouldn't Smile," *Life*, 23 July 1951, 92; William J. Lederer and Nelle Keys Perry, "Operation Kid-Lift," *Ladies Home Journal*, 12 Dec. 1952, 48–49.

18. Hye Seung Chung, "Hollywood Goes to Korea: Biopic Politics and Douglas Sirk's *Battle Hymn*," *Historical Journal of Film, Radio and Television* 25, no. 1 (Mar. 2005): 74; Howard A. Rusk, "Voice from Korea: 'Won't You Help Us off Our Knees?'" *Life*, 7 June 1954, 184; Mosier, "GI and the Kids of Korea," 638, 652.

19. "Dr. Verent J. Mills, Christian Children's Fund Executive Director, 1970–1981, remembers his visits to Pusan in 1950," Drake Collection; Hanley, Choe, and Mendoza, *Bridge at No Gun Ri*, 178.

20. Sydne Didier, "'Just a Drop in the Bucket': An Analysis of Child Rescue Efforts on Behalf of Korean Children, 1951 to 1964" (MA thesis, Portland State University, 1998), 13, 18, 25; Mosier, "GI and the Kids of Korea," 640; Case 36568, ISS case files; Gregory Votaw to Ohio CROP c/o CWS, 13 Oct. 1954, Box 103, Folder "Korea (1)," RG 8, Presbyterian Historical Society (PHS), Philadelphia, PA; Memo to Commanding Officer, 326th Communication Reconnaissance Company, 22 Jan. 1953, Drake Collection. Leaf's letter was printed on 29 December 1952, in the *Observer-Dispatch*, Utica, NY; "Korean Children Saved from Cave Get New Help," *New York Times*, 2 Jan. 1954; "Church Asks Goods for Korea Orphans Under Care of GIs," *Jackson Citizen Patriot* (MI), 9 Apr. 1953; "GI's Appeal Through U.S. Paper Brings Stream of Cash and Gifts," *Korean Republic*, 21 Dec. 1953; Mariella T. Provost, annual report, May 1957, Box 10,

Folder 15, RG 140, PHS; George Drake, unsigned form letter, Jan. 1953, Drake Collection; George Grim, "I Like It Here," *Minneapolis Star-Tribune*, 1 Apr. 1953, Drake Collection; "Rotterdam Soldier, 'Dad' to 274 Korean Waifs, Pens Plea for Aid in 'Fathering Needy Family,'" *Schenectady Union-Star* (NY), 19 Mar. 1953, Drake Collection; "Troops Aiding Korean Needy, *Philadelphia Evening Bulletin*, [1953], Drake Collection; "Good Samaritans in Uniform" *Pacific Stars and Stripes*, 15 Dec. 1953.

21. The American Korean Foundation declared that American soldiers had given $13 million in aid; a year later, *Life* magazine quoted a figure—provided by AKF—of more than $25 million. These amounts were probably exaggerated, but as CCF's Asbury put it, qualifications of the figures made them "no less impressive nor less important." Rusk, "Voice from Korea," 184; "Yanks in Korea Give $13 Million in Aid," *Pacific Stars and Stripes*, 7 June 1953; Asbury, "Military Help to Korean Orphanages," sec. 3.

22. Cournoyer, "Orphans Found Solace with U.S. Troops"; "44th ECB Donates $2000 for Youth," *Stars and Stripes*, 3 Dec. 1951; "Tankers Give $1,561 for Korean Amputees," *Pacific Stars and Stripes*, 2 Nov. 1952; "187th Troopers Donate $5,000 for Orphanage," *Pacific Stars and Stripes*, 14 Dec. 1952; Margaret Valk to Mrs. C, 7 Jan. 1954, Case 35341, ISS case files; Case 37462, ISS case files; "Rugged GIs Weep as 'Mascots' Depart," *Pacific Stars and Stripes*, 14 May 1951; Asbury, "Military Help to Korean Orphanages"; Case 36568, ISS case files.

23. Cournoyer, "Orphans Found Solace with U.S. Troops"; Mosier, "GI and the Kids of Korea," 636; Asbury, "Military Help to Korean Orphanages," sec. 3; Marion E. Hartness, annual report, May 1955, 2, Box 10, Folder 13, RG 140, PHS; Chan-ho Lee, "Ethiopians Seek Lost Orphans," *JoongAng Daily* (Seoul), 9 June 2004; "Turks Support Home for 160 Korean Orphans," *Pacific Stars and Stripes*, 19 Apr. 1954; Sun Yup Paik, *From Pusan to Panmunjom: Wartime Memoirs of the Republic of Korea's First Four Star General* (Dulles, VA: Potomac Books, 2007).

24. Cournoyer, "Orphans Found Solace with U.S. Troops"; "Little Children War's Biggest Casualty"; author interview with Molly Holt, 11 Apr. 2007; Christina Klein, *Cold War Orientalism: Asia in the Middlebrow Imagination, 1945–1961* (Berkeley, CA: University of California Press, 2003), 37; Charles Vogel, "Seoul Shows Calloused Attitude in Child's Plight," *Pacific Stars and Stripes*, 8 Aug. 1952; Charles Vogel, "Little Seoul Girl Covered with Maggots Found Dead," *Pacific Stars and Stripes*, 16 Aug. 1952; Cumings, *Origins II*, 695.

25. Author interview with Molly Holt, 11 Apr. 2007; Mosier, "GI and the Kids of Korea," 640, 656; Donna Alvah, *Unofficial Ambassadors: American Military Families Overseas and the Cold War, 1946–1965* (New York: New York University Press, 2007), 53.

26. Alvah, *Unofficial Ambassadors*, 57–58.

27. Asbury, "Military Help to Korean Orphanages," sec. 1, para. 2.

28. "Eighth Chief Sends Cookies to Orphans," *Pacific Stars and Stripes*, 23 Nov. 1951; "728th MPs Plan Fete for 260 Korean Kids," *Pacific Stars and Stripes*, 12 Dec. 1951; "Yanks Befriend Korean Orphan," *Pacific Stars and Stripes*, 12 Feb. 1951; American Korean Foundation, *Report of the Rusk Mission*, 8; Hanley, Choe, and Mendoza, *Bridge at No Gun Ri*, 103.

29. Edgar S. Kennedy, *Mission to Korea* (London: D. Verschoyle, 1952); Cumings, *Origins II*, 691, 695; John Dower, *War Without Mercy: Race and Power in the Pacific War* (New York: Pantheon, 1986); Mark Gayn, *Japan Diary* (Rutland, VT: Charles E. Tuttle Company, 1981), 349; Hanley, Choe, and Mendoza, *Bridge at No Gun Ri*, 71, 79; Hastings, cited in Katharine Moon, "Citizen Power in Korean-American Relations" in *Korean Attitudes Towards the United States: Changing Dynamics*, ed. David Steinberg (Armonk, NY: East Gate, 2005), 234; Reginald Thompson, *Cry Korea: The Korean War: A Reporter's Notebook* (1951; London: Reportage, 2009); David Curtis Skaggs, "The KATUSA Experiment: The Integration of Korean Nationals into the U.S. Army, 1950–1965," *Military Affairs* 38, no. 2 (Apr. 1974): 57. For more on Korean Augmentation to the US Army (KATUSA), see Terrence J. Gough, *US Army Mobilization and Logistics in the Korean War: A Research Approach* (Washington, DC: Center of Military History, 1987), 47–55; Roy E. Appleman, *South to the Naktong, North to the Yalu* (Washington, DC: Center of Military History, 1961), 385–389; Dong-Choon Kim, *The Unending Korean War: A Social History* (Larkspur, CA: Tamal Vista Publications, 2000), 273nn43–44.

30. Conway-Lanz, "Beyond No Gun Ri"; Hanley, Choe, and Mendoza, *Bridge at No Gun Ri*, 189; Cumings, *Origins II*, 690. See also Thompson, *Cry Korea*; Philip D. Chinnery, *Korean Atrocity! Forgotten War Crimes, 1950–1953* (Annapolis, MD: Naval Institute Press, 2000); Bruce Cumings, *The Korean War: A History* (New York: Modern Library, 2010); Kim, *Unending Korean War*, especially chapter 4.

31. Hanley, Choe, and Mendoza, *Bridge at No Gun Ri*, 177; Thompson, *Cry Korea*; Cumings, *Origins II*, 701.

32. Joseph Anthony, *The Rascal and the Pilgrim: The Story of a Boy From Korea* (New York: Farrar, Straus & Cudahy, 1960), 95; "Sung Yong Park: Tasting America" in *East to America: Korean American Life Stories*, ed. Elaine H. Kim and Eui-Young Yu (New York: New Press, 1996), 107–113; Tessa Morris-Suzuki, "Post-War Warriors: Japanese Combatants in the Korean War," *Asia-Pacific Journal* 10, no. 1 (30 July 2012), http://www.japanfocus.org/-Tessa-Morris_Suzuki/3803.

33. Fairfax Downey, *Mascots* (New York: Coward-McCann, 1954); Keene, *World War I*, 70–71.

34. Albert A. Nofi, *A Civil War Treasury: Being a Miscellany of Arms & Artillery, Facts & Figures, Legends & Lore, Muses & Minstrels, and Personalities & People* (Conshohocken, PA: Combined Books, 1992), 107–108. Female camp followers, or vivandières, functioned as "den mother, nurse and mascot" to French troops beginning in the eighteenth century. Ibid., 117.

35. Didier, "Just a Drop in the Bucket"; "Adopted a French Lad," *Harvard Alumni Bulletin* 20 (1910), 414; F. McKelvey Bell, *The First Canadians in France: The Chronicle of a Military Hospital in the War Zone* (New York: George H. Doran Company, 1917); Harry Spring, *An Engineer's Diary of the Great War*, ed. Terry M. Bareither (West Lafayette, IN: Purdue University Press, 2002); Kathryn Close, *Transplanted Children: A History* (New York: US Committee for the Care of European Children, 1953), 37; Mark Kurzem, Lina Caneva, and Rosie Jones, *The Mascot* (New York: Filmmakers Library, 2002), VHS; Thomas Buergenthal, *A Lucky Child: A Memoir of Surviving Auschwitz as a Young Boy* (London: Profile, 2009); Lee Kennett, *GI: The American Soldier in World War II* (Norman: University of Oklahoma Press, 1987); Kennedy, *Mission to Korea*, 128–129; Andrew Geer, "Reckless—Marines War Horse," *Saturday Evening Post*, 17 Apr. 1954.

36. In a number of cases, units provided their physically handicapped mascots with artificial limbs. Soldiers gave "Sammy Hop-a-long" a "peg leg and dressed him in a uniform, complete with combat badge." "Crippled Mascot, 11, Sees IG On Orphanage Worry," *Pacific Stars and Stripes*, 24 May 1953.

37. "Sergeant Yo-Yo Proves Snappy Mascot for MPs: Youth Found in Gutter 'True' Unit Member," *Pacific Stars and Stripes*, 29 Mar. 1953.

38. Case 37462, ISS case files.

39. Mosier, "GI and the Kids of Korea," 635.

40. Ibid., 635.

41. "Devildogs Want Tot: ROK Orphan Saved Pair," *Pacific Stars and Stripes*, 7 Oct. 1950; Anthony, *Rascal and the Pilgrim*, 71.

42. Cournoyer, "Orphans Found Solace with U.S. Troops"; "Little Children War's Biggest Casualty"; Link S. White, *Chesi's Story: One Boy's Long Journey from War to Peace* (Tallahassee, FL: Father & Son, 1995), 28–29, 36, 63–77.

43. Cournoyer, "Orphans Found Solace with U.S. Troops"; photo caption, *Pacific Stars and Stripes*, 30 Aug. 1951; "Adopted Korea Lad Gets GI Upbringing," *Pacific Stars and Stripes*, 22 Jan. 1951; "General's Stars Pinned on 'Skoshi,' Korean Tot," *Pacific Stars and Stripes*, 31 Aug. 1952; "Sergeant Yo-Yo Proves Snappy Mascot for MPs"; "UN Mascots," 14 Dec. 1953, *Stars and Stripes*; "2 'Dads' of Korean Orphan Mike Find PTA Meeting Fun, Difficult," *Pacific Stars and Stripes*, 13 Apr. 1953.

44. Chung, "Hollywood Goes to Korea," 74.

45. Samuel Fuller, *The Steel Helmet* (Lippert Productions [Criterion], 1951), DVD.

46. Cournoyer, "Orphans Found Solace with U.S. Troops"; Journal, 10 Feb. 1953, Box 1438, Folder "Civil Affairs Staff Section Report February 1953," Records Group (RG) 338, National Archives, College Park, MD (hereafter "Archives II"); Morris-Suzuki, "Post-War Warriors."

47. F [to mom and dad], 29 Dec. 1955; Cpl. Peter Steele Bixby, "No. 1 Sargy, Sambo Plan Life Together," *Pacific Stars and Stripes*, 30 Oct. 1950; White, *Chesi's Story*, 101; Andrew Huebner, "Kilroy Is Back: Images of American Soldiers in Korea, 1950–1953" *American Studies* 45, no. 1 (2004): 103–129; "GI Buddies," *Pacific Stars and Stripes*, 30 June 1951; "Tan Yank and Korean Waif Adopt Each Other," *Chicago Defender*, 18 Nov. 1950.

48. White, *Chesi's Story*, 72. Men serving in the Vietnam War adopted dogs, which served as an emotional outlet and something to trust: "The GIs could own, name, and control the dogs but the real 'gooks'—the people—could not be so easily managed . . . unlike the people, the puppies were malleable." Domestic labor was performed not by houseboys but by "hootch girls," Vietnamese women hired by Americans to do housekeeping tasks. Women who also offered sexual services were paid more. Christian Appy, *Working Class War: American Combat Soldiers in Vietnam* (Chapel Hill: University of North Carolina Press, 1993), 262, 290. The male counterpart of the prostitute was actually not the houseboy but the "slickyboy," Korean men in their late teens or early twenties who were described as male camp followers and understood as "punks, hoods, trouble makers, and black market dealers" who stole goods from bases. But trustworthy houseboys and thieving slickyboys were sometimes seen as two sides of the same coin, and the line between them could be blurred quite easily given the racialized stereotypes about Koreans' penchant for stealing from American bases. Whitney Taejin Hwang, "Borderland Intimacies: GIs, Koreans, and American Military Landscapes in Cold War Korea" (PhD diss., University of California, 2010), 71–72.

49. "24th Div. Sergeant Plans Adoption of 'Wild Bill,'" *Stars and Stripes*, 7 July 1954; "Yank, Korean Son Leave for States After Long Wait," *Pacific Stars and Stripes*, 29 Jan. 1955.

50. Untitled articles in *Stars and Stripes*, 12 Mar. and 5 May 1952.

51. Untitled, *Stars and Stripes*, 19 Oct. 1953; Robert L. Brown, "Orphan, 7, Leaves Korea for New Home in Texas," *Stars and Stripes*, 15 June 1954.

52. Kenneth Anderson, "Veteran Greets Adopted Korea Orphan in U.S." *Stars and Stripes*, 23 Nov. 1953; untitled article, *Stars and Stripes*, 9 Dec. 1953.

53. "The Chief's Son," *Time*, 2 Nov. 1953; "Wow!" *Time*, 23 Nov. 1953; "A New American Comes 'Home,'" *Life*, 30 Nov. 1952; "Sailor, Korean Son Fly to Tokyo for U.S. Visa," *Stars and Stripes*, 24 Oct. 1953; "The Americanization of Lee

Kyung Soo," *Stars and Stripes*, 9 Jan. 1954; "Navy Chief and Adopted Korean Boy Arrive," *Stars and Stripes*, 11 Nov. 1953; "A Big New Family Hugs War Orphan," *New York Times*, 22 Dec. 1953.

54. "'So Nice to See You Again . . . ,'" *Stars and Stripes*, 19 June 1956; "Troops Like Mountaintop Life," *Stars and Stripes*, 29 Aug. 1956; "Adopted Brother," *Stars and Stripes*, 1 Feb. 1958; untitled caption, *Stars and Stripes*, 22 Jan. 1956; "Welcome!" *Stars and Stripes*, 14 July 1952; "U.S. Officer's Parents Adopting Korea Waif," *Stars and Stripes*, 21 July 1956; F to Mom and Dad, 12 Dec. 1955, 1, Case 40043, ISS case files.

55. F [to mom and dad], 5 Jan. 1956, Case 40043, ISS case files; White, *Chesi's Story*, 68, 182–183; Kennedy, *Mission to Korea*, 128–129; Paul S. Crane, *Korean Patterns* (Seoul: Hollym, 1967), 163; Margaret Valk to Marie Haefner, 2 Mar. 1955, 1, Case 37097, ISS case files.

56. An ISS social worker summed up a typical assessment in a scribbled note on a case file: "Child has unfortunately become an Army mascot and would in any case have grave difficulties in adjusting to American family life." Handwritten notation, Feb. 1955, Case 36441, ISS case files; Helen McKay to Margaret Valk, 29 Feb. 1956, Case 39852, ISS case files.

57. Margaret Valk to Letitia DiVirgilio, 5 Feb. 1960, 1, Case 37462, ISS case files.

58. Kennedy, *Mission to Korea*, 81.

59. 24 Apr. 1958, Virginia Baumgartner to [no first name] Joseph (ISS American Branch), Case 58316, ISS case files.

60. Robert Teigrob, *Warming Up to the Cold War: Canada and the United States' Coalition of the Willing, from Hiroshima to Korea* (Toronto: University of Toronto Press, 2009), 168–169.

61. Child Placement Service, "Investigation," 19 Jan. 1955, Case 36441, ISS case files.

62. I only found one case of a girl mascot but it is not clear if she was actually a mascot or just left in the care of a potential adoptive father's military buddies while he returned to the US and arranged for her adoption. Case 38498, ISS case files. Servicemen did take care of little girls, but only long enough to nurse them back to health and then turn them over to an orphanage. See for example, "Redlegs Adopt Korean Pin-up," *Pacific Stars & Stripes*, 26 Feb. 1951.

63. American Korean Foundation, Press Release, [1954], File 378, Syngman Rhee Papers, Yonsei University, Seoul, Korea; "Korean Orphan, 9, Gets Fresh Start" *New York Times*, 21 Jan. 1958; Margaret Valk, handwritten notation, 22 Sept. 1960, Case 37462, ISS case files. Original emphasis; Margaret Valk to Letitia DiVirgilio, 5 Feb. 1960, 1, Case 37462, ISS case files.

64. Case 58316, ISS case files; Margaret Valk to Oak Soon Hong, 12 Nov. 1954, Case 36441, ISS case files; "'Adopted' Korean Girl Loves, Officer, Now Happy,"

Pacific Stars and Stripes, 24 July 1951; "Rugged GIs Weep as 'Mascots' Depart"; "Soldiers Get Warning on Waifs' Fondness," *Pacific Stars and Stripes*, 21 Aug. 1951; Eva Kelley to Virginia Baumgartner, 20 Oct. 1958, Case 58316, ISS case files.

65. Department of Defense, *Manual on Intercountry Adoption* (Washington, DC: US GPO, 1959); Elaine Tyler May, *Barren in the Promised Land: Childless Americans and the Pursuit of Happiness* (New York: Basic Books, 1995), 145–146.

66. Case 37013, ISS case files; "Three Star," *Stars and Stripes*, 2 Dec. 1956; "Year Old Korea Orphan Going Home to Indiana," *Stars and Stripes*, 19 Apr. 1956; "Mother Meets Adopted Children for First Time," *Stars and Stripes*, 14 Dec. 1957. Alternatively, a husband might send photos of a few different children, from which his wife would select the one she wanted. Untitled caption. *Stars and Stripes*, 19 Mar. 1955.

67. Military couples stationed in Japan also traveled to Korea to adopt children, sometimes on transportation provided by the military. Richard H. Baird to Henry Little, 17 Aug. 1960, Box 1, Folder 19, RG 197, PHS; "1st Air Force Couple Flies to Korea from Fuchu, Adopts 5 Year Old," *Stars and Stripes*, 8 Aug. 1956.

68. May, *Barren in the Promised Land*.

69. Klein, *Cold War Orientalism*, 30, 54; Richard S. Kim, *The Quest for Statehood: Korean Immigrant Nationalism and U.S. Sovereignty, 1905–1945* (New York: Oxford University Press, 2011).

70. Donald Clark, *Living Dangerously in Korea: The Western Experience, 1900–1950* (Norwalk, CT: Pacific Century Press, 2003); LeRoy Bowman, Benjamin A. Gjenvick, and Eleanor T. M. Harvey, *Children of Tragedy: Church World Service Survey Team Report on Intercountry Orphan Adoption* (New York: Office of Publication and Distribution, National Council of the Churches of Christ in the USA, 1961); Cumings, *Korea's Place in the Sun*, 306.

71. Some of the UN organizations were the UN Civil Assistance Command, the UN Korean Reconstruction Agency, and the UN Commission for the Unification and Rehabilitation of Korea.

72. Bowman, Gjenvick, and Harvey, *Children of Tragedy*, 22–23; John Coventry Smith to Edward Adams, 26 Jan. 1955, Box 1, Folder 8, RG 197, PHS; "An Analysis of the United Presbyterian Position on Orphans in Korea," May 1961, Box 65, Folder 22, Montreat Files, Korea Mission Records, PHS.

73. Advertisements found in various editions of the *Christian Century*, 1953.

74. Christina Klein, "Family Ties and Political Obligation: The Discourse of Adoption and the Cold War Commitment to Asia," in *Cold War Constructions: The Political Culture of United States Imperialism, 1945–1966*, ed. Christian Appy (Amherst: University of Massachusetts Press, 2000), 50; Klein, *Cold War Orientalism*, 152; Sara Fieldston, *Raising the World: Child Welfare in the American Century* (Cambridge, MA: Harvard University Press, 2015).

75. Jane Hunter, *The Gospel of Gentility: American Missionaries in Turn-of-the-Century China* (New Haven, CT: Yale University Press, 1984); Kenneth Scott Latourette, "Missionaries Abroad," *Annals of the American Academy of Political and Social Science* 368 (Nov. 1966): 21–30; Dana Robert, "The Influence of American Missionary Women on the World Back Home," *Religion and American Culture* 12, no. 1 (Winter 2002): 73, 60, 77; Peter Conn, *Pearl Buck: A Cultural Biography* (New York: Cambridge University Press, 1996).

76. Robert Shaffer, "Women and International Relations: Pearl S. Buck's Critique of the Cold War," *Journal of Women's History* 11, no. 3 (Autumn 1999): 151–175; Robert, "American Missionary Women," 75; Foreman biographical file, PHS; "An Analysis of the United Presbyterian Position on Orphans in Korea"; John Coventry Smith, "Concerning the Support of Orphans in Korea," 30 July 1952, Box 16, Folder 43, RG 140, PHS; Robert, "American Missionary Women," 59.

77. Robert, "American Missionary Women," 59.

78. See Cases 37099 and 60020, ISS case files; Marion E. Hartness, Annual Report, May 1955, 3, Box 10, Folder 13, RG 140, PHS; Home study, [Fall 1955], 6, Case 37182, ISS case files.

79. Kim, *Quest for Statehood*; Lee Houchins and Chang-su Houchins, "The Korean Experience in America, 1903–1924," *Pacific Historical Review* 43, no. 4 (Nov. 1974): 564.

80. "Travel Letter from Charles T. Leber No. 16," 9 Nov. 1957, 12, Box 40, Folder 1, RG 8, PHS.

81. Wayne Patterson, *The Ilse: First-Generation Korean Immigrants in Hawaii, 1903–1973* (Honolulu: University of Hawaii Press, 2000); Eui-Young Yu, "Korean Communities in the United States," in *Korea and the United States: A Century of Cooperation*, ed. Youngnok Koo and Dae-Sook Suh (Honolulu: University of Hawaii Press, 1984), 281–318; Illsoo Kim, *New Urban Immigrants: The Korean Community in New York* (Princeton, NJ: Princeton University Press, 1981), 21.

82. Houchins and Houchins, "Korean Experience in America," 564.

83. Untitled photo, *Korean Republic*, 22 Dec. 1953.

84. According to the *Korean Republic*, 622 Korean students went abroad to study in 1953, mostly to the United States (571). Next was France, with 17 students. In 1951, 144 students went abroad, and 426 in 1952. Before the Korean War, about 300 students went abroad each year. "622 Go Abroad to Study," *Korean Republic*, 23 Dec. 1953.

CHAPTER 2

1. Pearl S. Buck and Theodore F. Harris, *For Spacious Skies: Journey in Dialogue* (New York: John Day, 1966), 8.

2. Young Han Choo, Weekly Report, 28 Jan. 1954, 4, File 545, Syngman Rhee Presidential Papers, Yonsei University, Seoul, South Korea (hereafter "Rhee papers").

3. Yukiko Koshiro, *Trans-Pacific Racisms and the U.S. Occupation of Japan* (New York: Columbia University Press, 1999); Donna Alvah, *Unofficial Ambassadors: American Military Families Overseas and the Cold War, 1946–1965* (New York: New York University Press, 2007); Mire Koikari, "Rethinking Gender and Power in the US Occupation of Japan, 1945–1952," *Gender and History* 11, no. 2 (July 1999): 313–335; John Dower, *Embracing Defeat: Japan in the Wake of World War II* (New York: W. W. Norton, 1999); Maria Hohn, *GIs and Fräuleins: The German-American Encounter in 1950s West Germany* (Chapel Hill: University of North Carolina Press, 2002); Heide Fehrenbach, "Of German Mothers and 'Negermischlingskiner': Race, Sex, and the Postwar Nation," in *The Miracle Years: A Cultural History of West Germany, 1949–1968*, ed. Hanna Schissler (Princeton, NJ: Princeton University Press, 2001), 164–186; Heide Fehrenbach, "Rehabilitating Fatherland: Race and German Remasculinization," *Signs* 24, no. 1 (Autumn 1998): 107–127; Sabine Lee, "A Forgotten Legacy of the Second World War: GI Children in Post-War Britain and Germany," *Contemporary European History* 20, no. 2 (2011): 157–181; Petra Goedde, *GIs and Germans: Culture, Gender, and Foreign Relations, 1945–1949* (New Haven, CT: Yale University Press, 2002); Naoko Shibusawa, *America's Geisha Ally: Reimagining the Japanese Enemy* (Cambridge, MA: Harvard University Press, 2010); Sarah Kovner, *Occupying Power: Sex Workers and Servicemen in Postwar Japan* (Stanford, CA: Stanford University Press, 2012); Mary Louise Roberts, *What Soldiers Do: Sex and the American GI in World War II France* (Chicago: University of Chicago Press, 2013); Seungsook Moon and Maria Hohn, eds., *Over There: Living with the U.S. Military Empire from World War Two to the Present* (Durham, NC: Duke University Press, 2010).

4. Na Young Lee, "The Construction of U.S. Camptown Prostitution in South Korea: Trans/formation and Resistance" (PhD diss., University of Maryland, College Park, 2006); Katharine Moon, *Sex Among Allies: Military Prostitution in U.S.-Korea Relations* (New York: Columbia University Press, 1997); Brenda Stoltzfus and Saundra Pollock Sturdevant, *Let the Good Times Roll: Prostitution and the U.S. Military in Asia* (New York: New Press, 1992); Margo Okazawa-Rey, "Amerasian Children of GI Town: A Legacy of U.S. Militarism in South Korea," *Asian Journal of Women's Studies* 3 (1997): 71–102; Janet Graff Valentine, "The American Combat Solder in the Korean War" (PhD diss., University of Alabama, 2002), 132; Edgar S. Kennedy, *Mission to Korea* (London: Derek Verschoyle, 1952), 155; Heisoo Shin, "Women's Sexual Services and Economic Development: The Political Economy of the Entertainment Industry and South Korean Dependent Development" (PhD diss., Rutgers University, 1991); author interview with Molly

Holt, 11 Apr. 2007; Su-Je Lee Gage, "Pure Mixed Blood: The Multiple Identities of Amerasians in South Korea" (PhD diss., Indiana University, 2007); Charles J. Hanley, Sang-Hun Choe, and Martha Mendoza, *The Bridge at No Gun Ri: A Hidden Nightmare from the Korean War* (New York: Henry Holt, 2001), 189; Bruce Cumings, *Origins of the Korean War*, vol. 2, *The Roaring of the Cataract, 1947–1950* (Princeton, NJ: Princeton University Press, 1990), 706.

5. Bruce Cumings, "Silent but Deadly: Sexual Subordination in the U.S.-Korean Relationship," in *Let the Good Times Roll*, ed. Brenda Stoltzfus and Saundra Pollock Sturdevant (New York: New Press, 1992), 171, 173; Ji-Yeon Yuh, *Beyond the Shadow of Camptown: Korean Military Brides in America* (New York: New York University Press, 2004), 40–41; Eleanor C. Van Lierop, Annual Report 1959, 5, Box 10, Folder 17, RG 140, Presbyterian Historical Society, Philadelphia, PA (hereafter "PHS"); Whitney Taejin Hwang, "Borderland Intimacies: GIs, Koreans, and American Military Landscapes in Cold War Korea" (PhD diss., University of California, Berkeley, 2010), 94; Moon, *Sex Among Allies*, 3, 30; Hanley, Choe, and Mendoza, *Bridge at No Gun Ri*, 243; Andrei Lankov, "Korean Civilians North and South, 1950–1953," in *Daily Lives of Civilians in Wartime Asia: From the Taiping Rebellion to the Vietnam War*, ed. Stewart Lone (Westport, CT: Greenwood Press, 2007), 206; John Lie, "The Transformation of Sexual Work in 20th Century Korea," *Gender and Society* 9, no. 3 (June 1995): 316; Branch Director, USIS, Seoul to Director, USIS, Korea, Weekly Evaluation Report 23–29 Dec. 1951. Forwarded with Despatch from US Embassy Pusan to State Dept, Washington, DC, 13 Feb. 1952, 1, Box 5697, Records Group (RG) 59, National Archives, College Park, MD (hereafter "Archives II").

6. David T. Fautua, "The 'Long Pull' Army: NSC-68, the Korean War, and the Creation of the Cold War U.S. Army," *Journal of Military History* 61, no. 1 (Jan. 1997): 93–120; Andrew J. Huebner, "Kilroy Is Back: Images of American Soldiers in Korea, 1950–1953," *American Studies* 45, no. 1 (2004): 103–129; David W. Tarr, "The Military Abroad," *Annals of the American Academy of Political and Social Science* 368 (Nov. 1966): 31–42; Eugenie Hochfeld and Margaret A. Valk, *Experience in Inter-Country Adoptions* (New York: International Social Service, American Branch, 1953); US Department of Defense, *Manual on Intercountry Adoption* (Washington, DC: GPO, 1959); Moon, *Sex Among Allies*, 36.

7. Yuh, *Beyond the Shadow of Camptown*, 32. In the 1960s a GI returning to the United States at the end of a tour "could sell the 'package'—'the hooch, complete with furniture and moose, to an incoming soldier' for $200 to $300." The terms used to describe these arrangement demonstrate the continuities between GI fraternization in Japan and Korea after World War II: "moose" is a corruption of *musume*, the Japanese word for girl, while "hooch" comes from the Japanese word *uchi* (house)." Hwang, "Borderland Intimacies," 61.

8. Anne Davison, "The Mixed Racial Child," undated, 1, Folder: Korea—Adoptions to '62, Box 34, International Social Service, American Branch Records, Social Welfare History Archives, University of Minnesota (hereafter "ISS records"); Harry Holt to Richard Neuberger, 16 Jan. 1960, Box 11, Folder 26, Richard Neuberger Papers, Ax 078, Special Collections and University Archives, University of Oregon Libraries, Eugene, OR; Kim, *Who Will Answer*, 5; Yuh, *Beyond the Shadow of Camptown*, 39; Olivette Swallen, Personal Report, 1958–1959, 2, Folder 17, Box 10, RG 140, PHS, original emphasis.

9. Kim, *Who Will Answer*, 5; Yuh, *Beyond the Shadow of Camptown*; David W. Tarr, "The Military Abroad," *Annals of the American Academy of Political and Social Science* 368 (Nov. 1966): 31–42; Koshiro, *Trans-Pacific Racisms*; Davison, "Mixed Racial Child," 1; US Command Headquarters, US Forces Korea, EUSA, "Report—The Amerasian in Korea: Present Problems and Future Prospects," 1977 [courtesy of Whitney Taejin Hwang, in author's possession]; Hi Taik Kim and Elaine Reid, "After a Long Journey: A Study on the Process of Initial Adjustment of the Half and Full Korean Children Adopted by American Families, and the Families' Experiences with These Children During the Transitional Period" (MA thesis, University of Minnesota, 1970), 38–39. For a general history of military marriages, see Susan Zeiger, *Entangling Alliances: Foreign War Brides and American Soldiers in the Twentieth Century* (New York: New York University Press, 2010).

10. Anne Davison, "Mixed Racial Child," 1; Louis O'Conner, "The Adjustment of a Group of Korean and Korean-American Children Adopted by Couples in the United States" (MA thesis, University of Tennessee, 1964), 18; Okazawa-Rey, "Amerasian Children of GI Town"; Bong Soo Park, "Intimate Encounters, Racial Frontiers: Stateless GI Babies in South Korea and the United States, 1953–1965" (PhD diss., University of Minnesota, 2010); Yuri W. Doolan, "Being Amerasian in South Korea: Purebloodness, Multiculturalism, and Living Alongside the U.S. Military Empire" (Honors thesis, Ohio State University, 2012). For more on statelessness, see Linda Kerber, "The Stateless as the Citizen's Other: A View from the United States," *American Historical Review* 112, no. 1 (Feb. 2007): 1–34.

11. "An Analysis of the United Presbyterian Position on Orphans in Korea," [1961–1962], 5, Box 65, Folder 22, Montreat Files, Korea Mission Records, PHS, original emphasis; Margaret Valk to Missouri Department of Social Welfare, 2 May 1958, 1, Case 58862, ISS Adoption Case Files, Social Welfare History Archive, University of Minnesota (hereafter "ISS case files"); Margaret A. Valk, *Korean-American Children in American Adoptive Homes* (New York: Child Welfare League of America, 1957), 4; Phyllis Woodley to Howard Rusk, 24 Nov. 1953, 1, File 548, Rhee papers.

12. Valk, *Korean-American Children,* 6; O'Conner, "Adjustment of a Group of Korean and Korean-American Children," 19–21, 6, 11; Bertha Holt, *The Seed from the East* (Eugene, OR: Holt International Children's Services, 1956), 2.

13. Carl Strom to Robert J. G. McClurkin, 2 Mar. 1955, File 795, 795B, 895, 895B, 995, 995B, Records of the US State Dept. relating to Internal Affairs of Korea, 1955–59, accessed at National Assembly Library, Seoul, Korea (hereafter "NAL"); Margaret Valk, "Adoption Program—Korea," undated [visit was 21–30 Nov. 1956], 3–4, Box 34, Folder "Korea—Adoptions to '62," ISS records; Minutes of Extra-ordinary Meeting of the Joint ROK/KCAC/UNKRA Committee for Child Welfare, [received 25 Oct. 1954], 2, Box 153, Folder 4882, Collection 23B, Center for Migration Studies, Staten Island, NY (hereafter "CMS"); Edward Swanstrom to Bruce Mohler, 17 Jan. 1958, Box 12, Folder "Children—Polish, Navajo, etc.," Collection 23, CMS.

14. Lucile Chamberlin to Susan Pettiss, 23 Mar. 1956, 2; Helen McKay to Susan Pettiss, 20 Feb. 1956, 1, Box 10, Folder "Children—Independent Adoption Schemes. World Vision," ISS records; Bertha Holt, *Bring My Sons from Afar* (Eugene, OR: Holt International Children's Services, 1986), 31.

15. Richard Steinman to Joseph Reid, 13 Jan. 1954, Box 675, Folder 7-3-1-3, Jan. 1954, RG 102, Archives II; Grace Rue to Bessie Irvin, [Jan. 1954], Box 675, Folder 7-3-1-3, Jan. 1954, RG 102, Archives II; Rose Marie and Lee Callaway to President and Mrs. Eisenhower, 26 Dec. 1953, Box 676, Folder 7-3-1-3, Feb. 1955, RG 102, Archives II; Syngman Rhee reported that his consul in San Francisco received four hundred requests, while other correspondence noted five hundred requests. The number 608 comes from Penny Young Sook Kim, Richard A. Schaefer, and Charles Mills, *Though Bombs May Fall: The Extraordinary Story of George Rue, Missionary Doctor to Korea* (Nampa, ID: Pacific Press Publishing Association, 2003), 116. CCF received "a few requests" every day for adoptions. CCF's director Clarke speculated that if word got out that more Korean children were available for adoption, he "would receive an avalanche of inquiries." J. Calvitt Clarke to Noel Braga, 17 Jan. 1955, 1–2; Noel Braga to J. Calvitt Clarke, 14 Jan. 1955, 1, Microfilm Roll 19, RG 59, Archives II.

16. "First Korean War Baby Brought Here by Nurse," *Los Angeles Times,* 21 Dec. 1953; Richard Steinman to Joseph Reid, 13 Jan. 1954; Grace Rue to Bessie Irvin, [Jan. 1954], Box 675, Folder 7-3-1-3, Jan. 1954, RG 102, Archives II.

17. Bruce Cumings, *Korea's Place in the Sun: A Modern History* (New York: Norton, 1997), 31; Gi-Wook Shin, *Ethnic Nationalism in Korea: Genealogy, Politics, And Legacy* (Stanford, CA: Stanford University Press, 2006), 3–4, 99–102; Nadia Kim, *Imperial Citizens: Koreans and Race from Seoul to LA* (Stanford, CA: Stanford University Press, 2008); Gi-Wook Shin and Paul Y. Chang, "The Politics

of Nationalism in U.S.-Korean Relations," *Asian Perspective* 28, no. 4 (2004): 121, 126; Frank Dikotter, Introduction to *The Construction of Racial Identities in China and Japan: Historical and Contemporary Perspectives*, ed. Frank Dikotter (Honolulu: University of Hawaii Press, 1997), 4; Carter Eckert, Ki-baik Lee, Young Ick Lew, Michael Robinson, and Edward W. Wagner, *Korea Old and New: A History* (Cambridge, MA: Ilchokak, Publishers for Korea Institute, Harvard University, 1990), 407; Henry Em, *The Great Enterprise: Sovereignty and Historiography in Modern Korea* (Durham, NC: Duke University Press, 2013); Social Welfare Society, *The 5 Decades of SWS: A Love Nest (Since 1954–2003)* (Seoul: Social Welfare Society, 2004), 38–39.

18. Memorandum of Conversation, 25 Jan. 1955, File 795, 795B, 895, 895B, 995, 995B, Records of the US State Dept. relating to Internal Affairs of Korea, 1955–59, NAL; Office of the President to Young Han Choo, 5 Feb. 1954, File 545, Rhee papers; Valk, "Adoption Program—Korea," 3; Pearl Buck quoted in Clare Golden to Orville Crays, 30 Jan. 1959, Box 884, Folder 7-3-1-3, Sept. 1960, RG 102, Archives II; William Kirk to Eugene Carson Blake, 17 June 1958, 2, Box 10, Folder "Holt, Harry Vol. 2," ISS records; State Department of Social Welfare Office Memorandum, Program Memo No. 50 (RRA), 30 June 1955, 3, Box 675, Folder 7-3-1-3, Oct. 1955, RG 102, Archives II; Augusta Mayerson to Helen Wilson, 25 Feb. 1953, 1, Box 35, Folder "Korea—Correspondence Vol. 1," ISS records.

19. Memorandum of Conversation re: Entry of Korean War Orphans into the United States, 17 July 1953, File 895, Records of the US Dept. of State relating to Internal Affairs of Korea, 1950–54, NAL; Catholic Committee for Refugees and ISS, "The Problem of Transportation Costs for Korean Orphans Immigrating to the United States Under the Refugee Relief Act," undated, enclosed with Emil Komora to David Rolbein, 30 Jan. 1956, 3, Folder 4882, Box 153, Collection 23B, CMS; David Rolbein to John Coulter, 31 Jan. 1956, 1, Folder 4882, Box 153, Collection 23B, CMS.

20. Syngman Rhee to Young Han Choo, 3 Dec. 1953, File 547, Rhee papers; Leonard Mayo to Howard Rusk, Jack Taylor, and Palmer Bevis, 5 Jan. 1954, 4, File 548, Rhee papers; J. Calvitt Clarke to Noel Braga, 17 Jan. 1955, 2; Grace Rue to Bessie Irvin, [1953 or 1954], Box 35, Folder "Korea—Correspondence. Vol. 1," ISS records.

21. Bum-Ju Whang, *50-Year History of Holt Children's Services, Inc.* (Seoul: Holt Children's Service, 2005), 143; The Rhee government tried unsuccessfully to propose an orphan adoption bill in July 1955, June 1956, June 1958, January and February 1959, December 1960, and January 1961. Won, "A Study on Korean Adoption Policy," 21.

22. David C. Cole and Princeton N. Lyman, *Korean Development: The Interplay of Politics and Economics* (Cambridge, MA: Harvard University Press, 1971),

27, 79; Won, "Study on Korean Adoption Policy"; Eckert et al., *Korea Old and New*, 352–353.

23. Tobias Hubinette, "Comforting an Orphaned Nation: Representations of International Adoption and Adopted Koreans in Korean Popular Culture" (PhD diss., Stockholm University, 2005), 59–60; Won, "A Study on Korean Adoption Policy," 20; Whang, *50-Year History of Holt*, 123; Ministry of Foreign Affairs, ROK to US Embassy, Seoul, 31 July 1954, 1, Box 153, Folder 4882, Collection 23B, CMS.

24. ISS, "With Regard to Korean Adoption Procedure," undated, 1. Attached to "Korean Adoption Law," Box 882, Folder 7-3-1-3, June 1962, RG 102, Archives II; State Department of Social Welfare Office Memorandum, Program Memo No. 50 (RRA) Subject: Summary of Meeting with Miss Violet Choi from Korea (1 June 1955), 30 June 1955, 3, Box 675, Folder "7-3-1-3 Oct. 1955 Interstate Placement, Non-Resident Problems, Juvenile Immigration, Transient Boys," RG 102, Archives II.

25. Carl Strom to Charles C. Diggs Jr., 3 Mar. 1955, Microfilm Roll 19, RG 59, Archives II; Noel Braga to J. Calvitt Clarke, 14 Jan. 1955, 1; Minutes of Extraordinary Meeting of the Joint ROK/KCAC/UNKRA Committee for Child Welfare, [received 25 Oct. 1954], 1, Box 153, Folder 4882, Collection 23B, CMS; Kim, *Who Will Answer*; Carl Strom to William G. Jones, 3 Mar. 1955, Microfilm Roll 19, RG 59, Archives II; Valk, "Adoption Program—Korea," 5.

26. Memo for the Record, "Notes on the Meeting of the Adoption Committee Held at the UNKRA Club . . ." [meeting was 16 Sept. 1954]; Memo for the Record, [meeting was 30 Aug. 1954]; "Minutes of Extra-ordinary Meeting of the Joint ROK/KCAC/UNKRA Committee for Child Welfare," [received 25 Oct. 1954]; "Minutes of the 28th Meeting of joint ROK/KCAC/UNKRA . . ." [meeting was 10 July 1954]; "Minutes of Meeting on Placement Service for Korean Children," 13 July 1954, all in Box 153, Folder 4882, Collection 23B, CMS; Valk, "Adoption Program—Korea," 6–7; Memo for the Record, "Notes on the Meeting of the Adoption Committee Held at the UNKRA Club," [received 25 Oct. 1954], 2, Box 153, Folder 4882, Collection 23B, CMS; Peter Kent Malone to John Rieger, 17 Dec. 1955, Box 27, Folder: Seoul Area [folder 2/2], RG 59, Archives II.

27. Susan Pettiss, Memo to Files, 10 Feb. 1956, 3, Box 10, Folder "Children—Independent Adoption Schemes. World Vision," ISS records; author interview with Molly Holt, 11 Apr. 2007; Valk, "Adoption Program—Korea," 3.

28. Valk, "Adoption Program—Korea," 4.

29. "United Nations, Third Addendum to the Report of the Agent General of the United Nations Korean Reconstruction Agency," cited in William Asbury to J. Calvitt Clarke, 17 Sept. 1953, 5, George Drake personal collection (hereafter "Drake collection"); "Facts About the Aid Program in Korea," undated, 47, Box 1,

Folder "500 Aid Program 1953–1954–1955," RG 84, Archives II; William Asbury, "Military Help to Korean Orphanages: A Survey Made for the Commander-in-Chief, United Nations Forces, Far East, and for the Chief of Chaplains of the United States Army," 1954, sec. 9, para. 150, Drake collection.

30. Sidney Talisman, "Report on Visit to Korea—June 24 to July 2, 1968," Box 34, Folder "Korea—Administrative Correspondence," ISS records.

31. Valk, "Adoption Program—Korea," 9. Valk reported that funds for the building came from AFAK, which she spelled out as "American Forces Aid to Korea." She probably meant Armed Forces Assistance to Korea. A special wing of this building was funded in part by CCF; a Texas benefactor; and Mrs. L. L. Lemnitzer, the wife of the former commander of the UN Command in Korea. That wing, the Lemnitzer-Doughty-Clarke Wing, housed the mixed-race children that ISS and CPS would send abroad for adoption. Seungil Shin, "Mixed Blood Orphans Await Foster Parents," *Korean Republic*, 11 Mar. 1962, Box 35, Folder "Korea—General, Discard," ISS Records.

32. Asbury, "Military Help to Korean Orphanages," sec. 8, para. 137.

33. Arnold Vaught, "Relief and Reconstruction in Korea: A Report to the Department of Church World Service by Arnold B. Vaught," [received 19 Feb. 1953], 4, Box 102, Folder "Vaught—Asia Trip; Personal," RG 8, PHS, original emphasis.

34. American Korean Foundation, *Report of the Rusk Mission to Korea, March 11–18, 1953* (New York: American-Korean Foundation, 1953), 5.

35. William F. Asbury to J. Calvitt Clarke, 17 Sept. 1953, 2, Drake collection.

36. Valk, "Adoption Program—Korea," 1–2.

37. Valk, "Adoption Program—Korea," 2; Won, "A Study on Korean Adoption Policy," 20; Asbury, "Military Help to Korean Orphanages," sec. 8, paras. 130, 128; Valk, "Adoption Program—Korea," 1.

38. Kwang Choi and Soonwon Kwon, "Social Welfare and Distribution Policies," in *The Korean Economy 1945–1995: Performance and Vision for the 21st Century*, ed. Dong-Se Cha, Kwang Suk Kim, and Dwight H. Perkins (Seoul: Korea Development Institute, 1997), 544; Won, "Study on Korean Adoption Policy," 20.

39. Asbury, "Military Help to Korean Orphanages," sec. 8, para. 131. During the reconstruction period (1953–1961), 25.9 percent of Korean government expenditures went to social development, including 5.6 percent for health and welfare. Irma Adelman, "Social Development in Korea, 1953–1993," in *The Korean Economy 1945–1995: Performance and Vision for the 21st Century*, ed. Dong-Se Cha, Kwang Suk Kim, and Dwight H. Perkins (Seoul: Korea Development Institute, 1997), 513.

40. Asbury, "Military Help to Korean Orphanages," sec. 8, para. 129.

41. During the Korean War, South Korea received $330 million in grant aid from various organizations in the United States and from UNKRA. Grant aid

peaked during the postwar reconstruction period, during which UNKRA provided $120 million. In this period, US official aid reached $1.745 billion, including Pub. L. No. 480 (food aid program) funds for food assistance. Choi and Kwon, "Social Welfare and Distribution Policies," 13.

42. American Embassy Seoul to Department of State, Washington, 26 Feb. 1958, 4, File 795, 795B, 895, 895B, 995, 995B, Records of the US Dept. of State relating to Internal Affairs of Korea, 1955–59, NAL. In 1957, foreign relief aid accounted for 105 percent of Korean government spending on social welfare; 75 percent in 1958, 78 percent in 1959, and 40 percent in 1960. Dong-Myeon Shin, *Social and Economic Policies in Korea: Ideas, Networks and Linkages* (London: Routledge Curzon, 2003), 49–50.

43. Cumings, *Korea's Place in the Sun*, 306; Vaught, "Relief and Reconstruction in Korea," 4; Asbury, "Military Help to Korean Orphanages," sec. 3b, para. 28; Paul R. Cherney, "Visit to Korea, June 23 to July 9, 1965," 20 July 1965, 16, Box 35, Folder "Korea: Child Placement Service, General, 1964–65," ISS records; William A. Douglas, "South Korea's Search for Leadership," *Pacific Affairs* 37, no. 1 (Spring 1964): 24; LeRoy Bowman, Benjamin A. Gjenvick, and Eleanor T. M. Harvey, *Children of Tragedy: Church World Service Survey Team Report on Intercountry Orphan Adoption* (New York: National Council of the Churches of Christ in the USA, 1961), 26; Eva Kelley to Alice Folsom, 4 Nov. 1959, 1, Case 58899, ISS case files; author interview with Molly Holt, 11 Apr. 2007; Gardner Munro to Danica Adjemovitch, 26 Aug. 1964, Case 632143, ISS case files; Case 66852, ISS case files.

44. Richard Baird, "Observations Regarding Korean Orphanages," Apr. 1961, 7, Box 16, Folder 44, RG 140, PHS.

45. Baird, "Observations Regarding Korean Orphanages," 1.

46. Excerpt of letter from Anne Davison to Arnold B. Vaught, 25 Jan. 1955, 1, Box 103, Folder "Korea (2)," RG 8, PHS.

47. Baird, "Observations Regarding Korean Orphanages," 4–6.

48. Helen Miller, "Korea's International Children," *Lutheran Social Welfare*, Summer 1971, 18.

49. Richard Baird to Henry Little, 10 Feb. 1959, Box 1, Folder 15, RG 197, PHS; Boyd B. Lowry to James MacCracken, 29 June 1965, Box 40, Folder 3, RG 8, PHS; Baird, "Observations Regarding Korean Orphanages," 7–8.

50. Melosh, *Strangers and Kin*, 17; Anne Davison to Una Schreiber, 27 July 1960, Case 41351, ISS case files; Oak Soon Hong to Susan Pettiss, 27 Dec. 1954, Case 36489, ISS case files; Asbury, "Military Help to Korean Orphanages," sec. 9, para. 149; Gregory Votaw to Dr. [Homer] Gamboe, 23 Feb. 1955, Box 103, Folder "Korea (2)," RG 8, PHS; Case 63662, ISS case files; Shin, "Women's Sexual Services and Economic Development," 61.

51. Anne Davison to Letitia DiVirgilio, 30 Apr. 1961, Case 602221, ISS case files; Larry E. Tise, *A Book About Children Christian Children's Fund, 1938–1991* (Falls Church, VA: Hartland Publishing), 66.

52. Carl Strom to Robert J. G. McClurkin, 2 Mar. 1955, File 795, 795B, 895, 895B, 995, 995B, Records of the US State Dept. relating to Internal Affairs of Korea, 1955–59, NAL; Noel Braga to J. Calvitt Clarke, 14 Jan. 1955, 2; "Minutes of Meeting on Placement Service for Korean Children, 13 July 1954," 1, Box 35, Folder "Korea—Correspondence. Vol. 1," ISS records; author interview with Hyun Sook Han, 16 June 2006.

53. Y. T. Pyun to Myo Mook Lee, 5 July 1955, File 553, Rhee papers; Memo of Conversation, 25 Jan. 1955, 2, File 795, 795B, 895, 895B, 995, 955B, US State Dept. relating to the Internal Affairs of Korea, 1955–59, NAL; Rosemary C. Sarri, Penoak Baik, and Marti Bombyk, "Goal Displacement and Dependency in South Korean–United States Intercountry Adoption," *Children and Youth Services Review* 20, nos. 1–2 (1998): 91.

54. William T. Kirk to Leonard Mayo, 19 June 1954, 1–2, Box 35, Folder "Korea—Correspondence. Vol. 1," ISS records.

55. Helen Wilson to Augusta Mayerson, 21 Jan. 1953, 2, Box 35, Folder "Korea—Correspondence. Vol. 1," ISS Records; Augusta Mayerson to Helen Wilson, 25 Feb. 1953, 2, Box 35, Folder "Korea—Correspondence. Vol. 1," ISS records; Mayo to Rusk, Taylor, and Bevis, 5 Jan. 1954, 2.

56. Excerpt of letter from Davison to Vaught, 1; "World Vision Incorporated," 26 Sept. 1955, attached to Andrew Juras to Martin Gula, 3 Nov. 1955, 2, Box 675, Folder 7-3-1-3, Oct. 1955, RG 102, Archives II; author interview with Hyun Sook Han, 16 June 2006.

57. Wilson to Mayerson, 2; Mayo to Rusk, Taylor, and Bevis, 2; Memo for the Record, "Notes on the Meeting of the Adoption Committee Held at the UNKRA Club . . . ," [16 Sept. 1954], Box 153, Folder 4882, Collection 23B, CMS; J. Calvitt Clarke to Noel Braga, 17 Jan. 1955.

58. Catholic Committee for Refugees and ISS, "The Problem of Transportation Costs for Korean Orphans Immigrating to the United States Under the Refugee Relief Act," undated, 1, enclosed with Emil Komora to David Rolbein, 30 Jan. 1956, Box 153, Folder 4882, Collection 23B, CMS; John B. Coulter to David Rolbein, 23 Feb. 1956, Box 153, Folder 4882, Collection 23B, CMS; Susan Pettiss, "Report: Trip to the West Coast and Ohio," 13 Mar. 1956, enclosed in Susan Pettiss to Frank Phillips, 16 Mar. 1956, Box 10, Folder "Children—Independent Adoption Schemes. World Vision," ISS Records; Helen Wilson to Augusta Mayerson, 21 Jan. 1953, 2.

59. Mayo to Rusk, Taylor, and Bevis, 3.

60. Mayo to Rusk, Taylor, and Bevis, 4; Howard Rusk to Phyllis Woodley, 20 Jan. 1954, File 548, Rhee papers.

61. Michael Omi and Howard Winant, *Racial Formation in the United States: From the 1960s to the 1990s* (New York: Routledge, 1994); Thomas C. Holt, *The Problem of Race in the Twenty-First Century* (Cambridge, MA: Harvard University Press, 2000); Benedict Anderson, *Imagined Communities: Reflections on the Origin and Spread of Nationalism* (1983; London: Verso, 1991); Bonnie Honig, *Democracy and the Foreigner* (Princeton, NJ: Princeton University Press, 2001).

62. Mary Dudziak, *Cold War Civil Rights: Race and the Image of American Democracy* (Princeton, NJ: Princeton University Press, 2000).

63. As of the 1953 armistice, American troops constituted 32.4 percent of the total UN Command and 88.5 percent of the non-Korean UN Command. Troops from sixteen countries fought under the UN Command during the Korean War. US Forces Korea, Public Affairs Office, "Backgrounder No. 1: United Nations Command," http://www.korea.army.mil/pao/backgrounder/BG1.htm.

64. Case 601213, ISS case files.

65. Peggy Pascoe, "Miscegenation Law, Court Cases, and Ideologies of 'Race' in Twentieth-Century America," *Journal of American History* 83, no. 1 (June 1996): 44–69; David Hollinger, "Amalgamation and Hypodescent: The Question of Ethnoracial Mixture in the History of the United States," *American Historical Review* 108, no. 5 (Dec. 2003): 1363–1390; Ian Haney-Lopez, *White by Law: The Legal Construction of Race* (1996; New York: New York University Press, 2006).

66. John P. Smith to Senator Langer, 11 July 1957, quoted in "Admission of Alien Orphans Adopted by American Families," *Congressional Record* (hereafter "CR"), 85th Cong., 1st sess., Vol. 103 (24 July 1957): 12530; Molly Holt, quoted in Gage, "Pure Mixed Blood," 100.

67. These biological arguments and images held such force that they continued to be deployed into the 1980s, in support of immigration legislation for Amerasians, "the flesh of our flesh, the blood of our blood—American flesh and blood—our own sisters and brothers in Asia." John Shade, *America's Forgotten Children: The Amerasians* (Perkasie, PA: Pearl S. Buck Foundation, 1980), 30.

68. This understanding of children as belonging to their fathers was so powerful that until the end of the twentieth century custody of children was automatically awarded to their fathers in divorce cases. Kyung Ae Park, "Women and Development: The Case of South Korea," *Comparative Politics* 25, no. 2 (Jan. 1993): 134–135.

69. Harry Holt to Richard Neuberger, 3 July 1957, quoted in "Private Relief Legislation," *CR*, 85th Cong., 1st sess., Vol. 103 (16 July 1957): 11828; "Case Study Records," 3, Case 66575, ISS case files; "Social History of ——," 8 Mar. 1955, 2, Case 37220, ISS case files.

70. Kim, *Who Will Answer*, 2, 5, 3, 113; Okazawa-Rey, "Amerasian Children of GI Town"; Sveinung J. Moen, *The Amerasians: A Study and Research on Interracial*

Children in Korea (Seoul: Taewon Publishing, 1974); Grace Yoon Kyung Lee and Diana S. Lee, *Camp Arirang* (Camp Arirang Productions, 1995), VHS.

71. Edward Said famously argued that the relationship between the Occident and the Orient has long been figured as a male-female dynamic of power and sexual relations. Western colonial discourse has historically justified and naturalized the power discrepancies and exploitation present in the colonial relationship through familial metaphors that position the metropole's relationship to the colony as one of father to child, older brother to younger brother, and husband to wife. Edward W. Said, *Orientalism* (New York: Vintage, 1979).

72. See, for example, Ann Laura Stoler, "Tense and Tender Ties: The Politics of Comparison in North American History and (Post)Colonial Studies," *Journal of American History* 88, no. 3. (Dec. 2001): 829–865; Ann Laura Stoler, *Carnal Knowledge and Imperial Power: Race and the Intimate in Colonial Rule* (Berkeley: University of California Press, 2002); Ann Laura Stoler, ed., *Haunted by Empire: Geographies of Intimacy in North American History* (Durham, NC: Duke University Press, 2006); Frederick Cooper and Ann Laura Stoler, *Tensions of Empire: Colonial Cultures in a Bourgeois World* (Berkeley: University of California, 1997); Françoise Vergès, *Monsters and Revolutionaries: Colonial Family Romance and Métissage* (Durham, NC: Duke University Press, 1999); Julia Clancy-Smith and Frances Gouda, eds., *Domesticating the Empire: Race, Gender, and Family Life in French and Dutch Colonialism* (Charlottesville: University of Virginia Press, 1998); Robert Shaffer, "Women and International Relations: Pearl S. Buck's Critique of the Cold War," *Journal of Women's History* 11, no. 3 (Autumn 1999): 151–175; Emma Jinhua Teng, *Eurasian: Mixed Identities in the United States, China, and Hong Kong, 1842–1943* (Berkeley: University of California Press, 2013).

73. William R. Burkhardt, "Institutional Barriers, Marginality, and Adaptation Among the American-Japanese Mixed Bloods in Japan," *Journal of Asian Studies* 42, no. 3 (May 1983): 540; Marilyn T. Trautfield, "America's Responsibility to Amerasian Children: Too Little, Too Late," *Brooklyn Journal of International Law* 10 (1984): 75; Joseph M. Ahern, "Out of Sight, Out of Mind: United States Immigration Law and Policy as Applied to Filipino-Amerasians," *Pacific Rim Law and Policy Association* 1, no. 1 (1992): 105–126.

74. Burkhardt, "Institutional Barriers," 534.

75. Christina Firpo, "Lost Boys: 'Abandoned' Eurasian Children and the Management of the Racial Topography in Colonial Indochina, 1939–1945," *French Colonial History* 8 (2007): 204, 209, 216, 211; Christina Firpo, "Crises of Whiteness and Empire in Colonial Indochina: The Removal of Abandoned Eurasian Children from the Vietnamese Milieu 1890–1956," *Journal of Social History* 43, no. 3 (Spring 2010): 593.

76. Firpo, "Lost Boys," 204; Firpo, "Crises of Whiteness," 600.

77. Firpo, "Crises of Whiteness," 602–3, 606; Bonnie Kae Grover, "Aren't These Our Children? Vietnamese Amerasian Resettlement and Restitution," *Virginia Journal of Social Policy and the Law* 2, no. 2 (Spring 1995): 250–253; US Senate, Comm. on the Judiciary, *Amerasian Immigration Proposals. Hearing Before the Subcommittee on Immigration and Refugee Policy*, 21 June 1982, 97th Cong., 2nd sess. (Washington: US GPO, 1982), 82; Robin S. Levi, "Legacies of War: The United States' Obligation Toward Amerasians," *Stanford Journal of International Law* 29 (1992–1993): 477–478; Trautfield, "America's Responsibility to Amerasian Children," 69–72.

78. Mary Lee, "Mixed Race Peoples in the Korean National Imaginary and Family," *Korean Studies* 32 (2009): 72.

79. "Letters to the Times: Entry for Orphans Urged," *New York Times*, 24 June 1957.

80. Stoler, "Sexual Affronts and Racial Frontiers"; Vergès, *Monsters and Revolutionaries*, especially chap. 3.

81. David Pomfret, "'Child Slavery' in British and French Far-Eastern Colonies 1880–1945," *Past and Present* 201, no. 1 (Nov. 2008): 202.

82. Noel Braga to J. Calvitt Clarke, 14 Jan. 1955, 2; J. Calvitt Clarke to Noel Braga, 17 Jan. 1955, 1.

83. Elfrieda Kraege to John Coventry Smith, 22 Nov. 1955, 2, Box 1, Folder 7, RG 197, PHS; Ellen D. Wu, *The Color of Success: Asian Americans and the Origins of the Model Minority* (Princeton, NJ: Princeton University Press, 2013), chap. 7; Memo re: Conversation with R. W. Kenney, 27 Jan. 1955, Box 35, Folder "Countries: Korea," ISS Records; Handwritten Note on News Release, 15 Nov. 1954, Box 1, Folder "Adoptions (General), Various," Collection 23, CMS.

84. Susan Pettiss to Marcia Williams, 9 Jan. 1958, 2, Box 34, Folder "ISS Branches. Korea Adoption Jan–Dec 1958," ISS records; Syngman Rhee to Young Han Choo, 24 Aug. 1955, File 578, Rhee papers; Carl W. Strom to William G. Jones, 3 Mar. 1955; Carl W. Strom to Charles C. Diggs Jr., 3 Mar. 1955, Microfilm Roll 19, RG 59, Archives II; "Drive to Adopt Korean GI Tots," *Chicago Defender*, 19 Mar. 1955; Noel Braga to J. Calvitt Clarke, 14 Jan. 1955, 2.

85. Syngman Rhee to Young Han Choo, 3 Dec. 1953; Phyllis Woodley to Howard Rusk, 24 Nov. 1953, File 548, Rhee papers.

CHAPTER 3

1. Harry Holt, "Dear Friends" letter, 27 Dec. 1956, 3–4, Box 10, Folder "Holt, Harry Vol. I," International Social Service, American Branch Records, Social Welfare History Archives, University of Minnesota (hereafter "ISS records").

2. Robert and Dora Bersagel to Wayne Morse, 20 July 1956, in "Needed Revision of the McCarran-Walter Act," *Congressional Record* (hereafter *CR*), 84th Cong., 2nd sess., Vol. 102 (23 July 1956): 13979.

3. Crystal J. Gates, "China's Newly Enacted Intercountry Adoption Law: Friend or Foe?" *Indiana Journal of Global Legal Studies* 7 (Fall 1999): 370; Martin E. Marty, *Modern American Religion*, vol. 3, *Under God, Indivisible, 1941–1960* (Chicago: University of Chicago Press, 1996), 294; A. Roy Eckardt, "The New Look in American Piety," *Christian Century*, 17 Nov. 1954, 1396.

4. Bertha Holt, *Bring My Sons from Afar* (Eugene, OR: Holt International Children's Services, 1986), 9, 11.

5. Mary Dudziak, *Cold War Civil Rights: Race and the Image of American Democracy* (Princeton, NJ: Princeton University Press, 2000); Penny Von Eschen, *Satchmo Blows Up the World: Jazz Ambassadors Play the Cold War* (Cambridge, MA: Harvard University Press, 2004); Christina Klein, *Cold War Orientalism: Asia in the Middlebrow Imagination, 1945–1961* (Berkeley: University of California Press, 2003).

6. Bruce Cumings, "Occurrence at Nogun-Ri Bridge: An Inquiry into the History and Memory of a Civil War," *Critical Asian Studies* 33, no. 4 (Dec. 2001): 521; Craig S. Coleman, *American Images of Korea* (Elizabeth, NJ: Hollym International, 1990); see also Hannah Kim, "Ties That Bind: People, Policy, and Perception in US-Korean Relations" (PhD diss., University of Delaware, 2011).

7. Howard A. Rusk, "Voice from Korea: 'Won't You Help Us Off Our Knees?'" *Life*, 7 June 1954, 184, 187.

8. About 2 percent of South Koreans were Protestants in 1950. Vladimir Tikhonov, "South Korea's Christian Military Chaplaincy in the Korean War—Religion as Ideology?" *Asia-Pacific Journal* 11, no. 1 (6 May 2013); See Harold E. Fey's five-part series on the Korean War, published in *Christian Century*, January–February, 1952.

9. Michael Rougier, "The Little Boy Who Wouldn't Smile," *Life*, 23 July 1951, 93; Bertha Holt, *The Seed from the East* (Eugene, OR: Holt International Children's Services, 1956), 20; Bill Stapleton, "Little Orphan Island," *Collier's*, 14 July 1951, 51; Sydne Didier, "'Just a Drop in the Bucket': An Analysis of Child Rescue Efforts on Behalf of Korean Children, 1951 to 1964" (MA thesis, Portland State University, 1998), 13.

10. Wendy Kozol, *Life's America* (Philadelphia: Temple University Press, 1994); Elaine Tyler May, *Homeward Bound: American Families in the Cold War Era* (1988; New York: Basic Books, 1999).

11. Christina Klein, "Family Ties and Political Obligation: The Discourse of Adoption and the Cold War Commitment to Asia," in *Cold War Constructions: The Political Culture of United States Imperialism, 1945–1966*, ed. Christian Appy (Amherst: University of Massachusetts Press, 2000), 35, 42.

12. Opening editorial, *Life*, 26 Dec. 1955, 13.

13. "The Testimony of a Devout President," *Life*, 26 Dec. 1955, 12.

14. "An Unprecedented Wave of Religious Observance Sweeps over the U.S," *Life*, 26 Dec. 1955, 46; May, *Homeward Bound*, 20; Marty, *Modern American Religion*, 293; Jonathan P. Herzog, *The Spiritual-Industrial Complex: America's Religious Battle Against Communism in the Early Cold War* (New York: Oxford University Press, 2011); Seth Jacobs, "'Our System Demands the Supreme Being': The U.S. Religious Revival and the 'Diem Experiment,' 1945–55," *Diplomatic History* 25, no. 4 (Fall 2001): 589–624.

15. Eckardt, "New Look in American Piety," 1395–1396. *Christian Century* and *Christianity and Crisis* are two nondenominational Christian periodicals that were widely read at the time.

16. In 1955, *Life* published several special issues on the topic of "The World's Great Religions." "The World's Important Religions," *Christianity and Crisis*, 13 June 1955, 79.

17. Marty, *Modern American Religion*, 294.

18. "Admission of Refugee Orphans to Citizenship in United States," *CR*, 85th Cong., 2nd sess., vol. 104 (19 Feb. 1958): 2398.

19. Henry R. Luce, "The American Century," *Life*, 17 Feb. 1941, 61–65.

20. Harold Fey, "Will Korea Perish?" *Christian Century*, 16 Jan. 1952, 66; Klein, "Family Ties and Political Obligation," 40.

21. "Testimony of a Devout President," 13.

22. Rusk, "Voice from Korea," 187.

23. In case readers missed this message, editors were conscientious about spelling it out in photo captions that dubbed them "innocent victims of war." William J. Lederer and Nelle Keys Perry, "Operation Kid-Lift," *Ladies' Home Journal*, 12 Dec. 1952, 49.

24. Marvin Koner, "Korea's Children: The Old in Heart," *Collier's*, 25 July 1953, 24–25.

25. "Increase in Number of Visas to Be Issued to Orphans Under the Refugee Relief Act of 1953," *CR*, 84th Cong., 2nd sess., vol. 102 (26 July 1956): 14741–14743; [no first name noted] Adair to Arthur Watkins, 19 Sept. 1953, Box 58, Folder "I&N Act—Adopted Children," RG 46, National Archives, Washington, DC (hereafter "Archives I").

26. "Increase in Number of Visas to Be Issued to Orphans," 14742; Pearl S. Buck, *Children for Adoption* (New York: Random House, 1964), 167; "Author Pearl Buck to Adopt Part-Negro Orphan," *Chicago Defender*, 5 Apr. 1958.

27. Elaine Tyler May, "Cold War—Warm Hearth: Politics and the Family in Postwar America," in *The Rise and Fall of the New Deal Order, 1930–1980*, ed. Steve Fraser and Gary Gerstle (Princeton, NJ: Princeton University Press, 1989), 153–181.

240   Notes to Chapter 3

28. "The Forgotten People," *Time*, 15 July 1951.

29. Rougier, "Little Boy Who Wouldn't Smile," 92.

30. Louis O'Conner, "The Adjustment of a Group of Korean and Korean-American Children Adopted by Couples in the United States" (MA thesis, University of Tennessee, 1964), 28; "A Famous Orphan Finds a Happy Home," *Life*, 15 May 1956, 129.

31. After *The Seed from the East*, Bertha Holt wrote three more books: *Outstretched Arms* (1972), *Created for God's Glory* (1982), and *Bring My Sons from Afar* (1986). All of these books describe different aspects of the Holt agency's work with orphans in Korea and around the world. Proceeds from their sale fund Holt International Children's Services.

32. Pierce, a deeply religious Christian, created World Vision in 1950 specifically to help children orphaned in the Korean War. By 1953, World Vision had established a child sponsorship program, through which monthly sponsorship funds were used to provide children with food, education, health care, and vocational training. Bob Pierce and Ken Anderson, *The Untold Korea Story* (Grand Rapids, MI: Zondervan Publishing, 1951); Bob Pierce and Dorothy C. Haskin, *Orphans of the Orient: Stories That Will Touch Your Heart* (Grand Rapids, MI: Zondervan Publishing, 1964).

33. Holt, *Seed from the East*, 44.

34. Holt, *Bring My Sons from Afar*, 9.

35. Holt, *Seed from the East*, 55.

36. Holt, *Bring My Sons from Afar*, 9.

37. Bertha Holt Oral History, 17 Nov. 1992, Tape 6, Oregon Historical Society (hereafter "OHS").

38. Ron Moxness, "Good Samaritan of Korea," *American Mercury*, Oct. 1956, 88.

39. Holt, *Seed from the East*, 64. The Holt Bill (S. 2312) was introduced on 24 June 1955, and passed on 29 July 1955. See "Relief of Certain Korean War Orphans," *CR*, 84th Cong., 1st sess., vol. 101 (24 June 1955): 9154; "Korean War Orphans," *CR*, 84th Cong., 1st sess., vol. 101 (29 July 1955): 12078.

40. In introducing the bill in June 1955, Neuberger asserted his belief that the Holts were "well prepared to provide a wholesome Christian home" for the eight children. He supported this statement with seventy-nine letters of recommendation from the Holts' friends and neighbors. "Relief of Certain Korean War Orphans," 9154.

41. Moxness, "Good Samaritan of Korea," 84; Holt, *Seed from the East*, 192.

42. Holt, *Seed from the East*, 200–201, 205, 219.

43. Holt, *Seed from the East*, 51; Moxness, "Good Samaritan of Korea," 84–88; "Amendment of Refugee Relief Act of 1953," *CR*, 84th Cong., 2nd sess., vol. 102

(30 Apr. 1956): 7247. Two years later, Neuberger expanded the sobriquet to include the entire family: "I know of no family which has better symbolized the Biblical Good Samaritan." "Admission of Refugee Orphans to Citizenship in United States," 2397.

44. "Mr. Holt 'Moves the World,'" *Oregonian*, 9 Apr. 1956; "Admission of Refugee Orphans to Citizenship in United States," 2397.

45. May, *Homeward Bound*, 49.

46. David Hyungbok Kim, *Who Will Answer . . .* (2001; Eugene, OR: Holt International Children's Services, 2006), 124, 126.

47. For more on the fight over proxy adoption between Holt and HAP and the mainstream social work establishment, see Arissa Oh, "Into the Arms of America: The Korean Roots of International Adoption" (PhD diss., University of Chicago, 2008), chapters 5 and 6.

48. "Dear Friends" letter, 14 Dec. 1955; "Family Information" form attached to "Dear Friends" letter, 14 Dec. 1955; Executive Committee, Korea Mission, Commission on Ecumenical Mission and Relations of the United Presbyterian Church in the USA, "Report on Proxy Adoptions of Mixed-Blood Children," Apr. 1959, 13, Box 10, Folder "Korean Refugees," RG 46, Archives I.

49. Buck, *Children for Adoption*, 152–155. Buck established Welcome House, an adoption agency, in 1949. Unlike the Holts, she set out to help Amerasian children who were compelled to remain in Asia. Her focus later changed to placing Amerasians for intercountry adoption. By the end of the century, her agency had placed about five thousand children for adoption. Peter Conn, *Pearl S. Buck: A Cultural Biography* (New York: Cambridge University Press, 1996).

50. "Dear Friends" letter, 14 Dec. 1955, 1; "Dear Friends" letter, 17 Sept. 1957, 1, Folder: Holt, Harry Vol. 1, Box 10, ISS records.

51. "Dear Friends" letter, [1958], attached to Mrs. Edward Gresham to Laurin Hyde, 27 May 1958, Box 10, Folder "Holt, Harry Vol. 2," ISS records; Bertha Holt, *Outstretched Arms* (Eugene, OR: Holt International Children's Services, 1972), 283; "New Faces," *Time*, 23 Dec. 1957, 16; "Dear Friends" letter, February 1957, Box 153, Folder 4884, Collection 23B, Center for Migration Studies, Staten Island, NY (hereafter "CMS").

52. "Dear Friends" letter, 27 Dec. 1956; Bertha Holt Oral History, Tape 6, OHS.

53. Kim, *Who Will Answer*, 121; Kenneth Joseph Foreman Jr. Ninth Annual Report for the Board of Foreign Missions, [received 4 Nov. 1957], Box 10, Folder 15, RG 140, Presbyterian Historical Society, Philadelphia, PA; Bertha Holt Oral History, Tape 6, OHS; "Dear Friends" letter, 17 Sept. 1957, 2.

54. "Dear Friends" letter, 17 Sept. 1957, 3.

55. Bertha Holt Oral History, Tape 6, OHS.

56. The ASB provided a "special narrative personnel report" for Holt, and at the reduced rate of $6 per report "because of the fine work he was doing." Katherine Kuplan to Susan Pettiss, 20 Sept. 1956, 1, Box 10, Folder "Children—Independent Adoption Schemes. Holt, Harry. 1955–1957 Vol. 1," ISS records.

57. Margaret Valk to Rev. John Kirkpatrick, 18 Dec. 1957, Box 10, Folder "Children—Independent Adoption Schemes. Holt, Harry. 1955–1957 Vol. 1," ISS records.

58. Bum-Ju Whang, *50-Year History of Holt Children's Services, Inc.* (Seoul: Holt Children's Service, 2005), 160, 163; Kim, *Who Will Answer*.

59. Kim, *Who Will Answer*, 201–202; Arnold Lyslo, "A Few Impressions on Meeting the Harry Holt Plane, the 'Flying Tiger,' Which Arrived in Portland, Oregon, December 27, 1958," 1, Box 10, Folder "Children—Independent Adoption Schemes, Holt, Harry, Vol. 2 1958–1959," ISS records.

60. Mrs. Warren C. Eveland to Susan Pettiss, 22 May 1958, Box 34, Folder "ISS, Branches Korea Adoptions Jan. 1958–Dec. 1958," ISS records.

61. According to Holt Adoption Program, there were fifty children on this flight.

62. Mrs. Warren C. Eveland to Susan Pettiss, 22 May 1958; Susan Pettiss, Memo to Files, 6 June 1958, Box 34, Folder "ISS, Branches Korea Adoptions Jan. 1958–Dec. 1958," ISS records.

63. Of the 107 children on a 27 December 1958 flight, an eyewitness noted that all were thin but did not seem sickly, although many of them had coughs and colds, and 13 needed hospitalization. Lyslo, "A Few Impressions."

64. Kim, *Who Will Answer*, 157–162.

65. Case 37013, ISS Adoption Case Records, Social Welfare History Archive, University of Minnesota (hereafter "ISS case files"); ISS NY to ISS Korea, 19 Nov. 1958, Box 35, Folder "Korea 'Oxford Committee for Famine Relief' 1957–1966," ISS records; Case 58900, ISS case files; Holt, *Bring My Sons from Afar*, 37.

66. Whang, *50-Year History of Holt*; Kim, *Who Will Answer*, 145, 117.

67. These are captions from the *Chicago Defender* on 10 Apr. 1956; 19 Dec. 1956; and 8 Feb. 1958.

68. Lyslo, "A Few Impressions." Korean residents of Hawaii also greeted Holt flights that stopped over in Hawaii with food and provided for the escorts a respite from the burdens of around-the-clock child care. Kim, *Who Will Answer*.

69. Lyslo, "A Few Impressions," 2.

70. Ibid., 2–3.

71. Alsi Robinette to ISS, 31 July 1959, Case 37176, ISS case files.

72. Louis O'Conner and Dong Soo Kim completed two of the earliest social work studies of how Korean children were adjusting to their adoptive American

homes in 1964 and 1976, respectively. Their findings fall in line with other similar studies. I have made general statements here based on information available in all these sources.

73. Dong Soo Kim, "Intercountry Adoptions" (PhD diss., University of Chicago, 1976), 107; Holt, *Seed from the East*, 236. It is striking that Bertha Holt put "retarded" and "oriental" together in the same category, as these were two of the categories of children that American social workers considered unadoptable.

74. Jean E. Privat to Richard Neuberger, 1 Apr. 1958, Box 11, Folder 26, Neuberger Papers Richard Neuberger Papers, Special Collections and University Archives, University of Oregon Libraries, Eugene, OR (hereafter "Neuberger papers"); Holt, *Seed from the East*, 200–5; Holt, *Bring My Sons from Afar*, 29, 44; Didier, "Just a Drop in the Bucket," 115.

75. Raymond W. Riese to Paul H. Martin, 13 May 1958, 1, Box 10, Folder "Holt, Harry. Vol. 2," ISS records; Lois McCarty to Carl Adams, 30 Aug. 1957, Box 10, "Folder: Holt, Harry, Vol. 1," ISS records; Margaret Valk to Elinor Westerfield, 11 July 1956, 1, Case 38332, ISS case files.

76. Harry Holt to Richard Neuberger, 5 June 1959 and 16 Jan. 1960, Box 11, Folder 26, Neuberger papers; Kim, *Who Will Answer*, 366; LeRoy Bowman, Benjamin A. Gjenvick, and Eleanor T. M. Harvey, *Children of Tragedy: Church World Service Survey Team Report on Intercountry Orphan Adoption* (New York: National Council of the Churches of Christ in the USA, 1961), 78.

77. Buck, *Children for Adoption*, 157; Holt, *Bring My Sons from Afar*, 9.

78. Susan Pettiss, "Report: Trip to the West Coast and Ohio," 13 Mar. 1956, enclosed in Susan Pettiss to Frank Phillips, 16 Mar. 1956, 3, Box 10, Folder "Children—Independent Adoption Schemes. World Vision," ISS records.

79. Pettiss, "Report: Trip to the West Coast and Ohio," 4.

80. David Hollinger, "Amalgamation and Hypodescent: The Question of Ethnoracial Mixture in the History of the United States," *American Historical Review* 108, no. 5 (Dec. 2003); Henry Yu, "Tiger Woods Is Not the End of History: Or, Why Sex Across the Color Line Won't Save Us All," *American Historical Review* 108, no. 5 (Dec. 2003): 1406–1414; Ellen D. Wu, *The Color of Success: Asian Americans and the Origins of the Model Minority* (Princeton, NJ: Princeton University Press, 2014), chapter 7.

81. Matthew Pratt Guterl, *Josephine Baker and the Rainbow Tribe* (Cambridge, MA: Belknap Press of Harvard University Press, 2014).

82. Other notable celebrities who adopted mixed-race Asian children in this period include Buck's friends Oscar Hammerstein and James Michener, and Roy and Dale Rogers.

83. Guterl, *Josephine Baker*, 103; "Life Visits a One-Family U.N.," *Life*, 12 Nov. 1951, 157; Helen Doss, *The Family Nobody Wanted* (1954; Boston: Northeastern

University Press, 2001); Joseph P. Blank, *19 Steps up the Mountain: The Story of the DeBolt Family* (Philadelphia: J. B. Lippincott, 1976); Rebecca Trounson, "Dorothy DeBolt Dies at 89; Adoption Advocate Raised 20 Children" *Los Angeles Times*, 12 Mar. 2013, http://articles.latimes.com/2013/mar/12/local/la-me-dorothy-debolt-20130312; Dorothy DeBolt and John Korty, *Who Are the DeBolts? (And Where Did They Get 19 Kids?)* (Docurama, 1977), DVD.

84. Mr. and Mrs. Jacob Warkentin to Wayne Morse, 21 July 1956, quoted in "Increase in Number of Visas to be Issued to Orphans," 14743.

85. In his 1976 study of self concept among Holt adoptees, Dong Soo Kim analyzed questionnaires completed by 406 adoptive families. One of the questions asked was, "What do you believe was your *primary motivation* to seek the adoption of this child?" Kim discovered that the leading reasons behind the adoptions—as reported by these 406 families—were love of children and parenting (32.7 percent of respondents), humanitarian and/or religious concern (30.9 percent), and responsibility for and interest in Korea (10.3 percent). These findings suggest that Christian Americanist concerns—as suggested by the second and third most popular reason—did play a small but significant role in the adoption decisions. Other less popular reasons were sterility (9.9 percent); compensation or completion for family (8.8 percent); others (6.3 percent); and population explosion (1.1 percent). Approximately half of the 406 respondents had adopted between 1956 and 1962, while the other half adopted between 1962 and 1972. Kim, "Intercountry Adoptions," 87, 90–91.

86. O'Conner, "Adjustment of a Group of Korean and Korean-American Children," 29.

87. "Increase in Number of Visas to be Issued to Orphans Under the Refugee Relief Act of 1953," 14743; Mr. and Mrs. Luke Knowlton to Wayne Morse, 20 July 1956, quoted in "Refugee Relief Act Must Be Amended to Assist War Orphans," *CR*, 84th Cong., 2nd sess., vol. 102 (23 July 1956): 13982.

88. Elaine Tyler May, *Barren in the Promised Land: Childless Americans and the Pursuit of Happiness* (New York: Basic Books, 1995); Barbara Melosh, *Strangers and Kin: The American Way of Adoption* (Boston: Harvard University Press, 2002); Julie Berebitsky, *Like Our Very Own: Adoption and the Changing Culture of Motherhood, 1851–1950* (Lawrence: University Press of Kansas, 2000); Bruce H. Berry, "Legislation," *Brooklyn Law Review* 28, no. 2 (Apr. 1962): 324.

89. Warkentin to Morse, 21 July 1956; Mrs. C. O. Alford to Wayne Morse, 19 July 1956, quoted in "Refugee Relief Act Must Be Amended to Assist War Orphans," 13981.

90. Mr. and Mrs. Bruce R. Sexton to Wayne Morse, 29 July 1956, quoted in "Refugee Relief Act Must Be Amended to Assist War Orphans," 13982; Warkentin to Morse, 21 July 1956.

91. Jessie Bennett Sams won the *Saturday Review*'s Anisfield-Wolf Award in Race Relations for her memoir *White Mother* in 1958. Buck was on the judging committee. Klein, "Family Ties and Political Obligation," 62–63.

92. Peggy Pascoe, "Miscegenation Law, Court Cases, and Ideologies of 'Race' in Twentieth-Century America," *Journal of American History* 83 (June 1996): 48.

93. Klein, "Family Ties and Political Obligation," 63–64.

94. Holt, *Seed from the East*, Preface; Klein, "Family Ties and Political Obligation," 60.

CHAPTER 4

1. Statement by [birth mother], 7 Jan. 1955, Case 36489, ISS Adoption Case Files, Social Welfare History Archive, University of Minnesota (hereafter "ISS case files"). As the errors in her statement suggest, this birth mother was presumably not a fluent English speaker.

2. ISS Case 64815, ISS case files.

3. Lucile Chamberlin to Susan Pettiss, 23 Mar. 1956, Box 10, Folder "Children—Independent Adoption Schemes. World Vision. 1955–1960," International Social Service, American Branch Records, Social Welfare History Archives, University of Minnesota (hereafter "ISS records").

4. Won Moo Hurh, "Marginal Children of War: An Exploratory Study of American-Korean Children," paper presented at joint meeting of Midwest and Ohio Valley Sociological Societies, 3 May 1969.

5. Barbara Melosh, *Strangers and Kin: The American Way of Adoption* (Cambridge, MA: Harvard University Press, 2002), 3; Julie Berebitsky, *Like Our Very Own: Adoption and the Changing Culture of Motherhood, 1851–1950* (Lawrence: University Press of Kansas, 2000), 130; Ellen Herman, "The Paradoxical Rationalization of Modern Adoption," *Journal of Social History* 36, no. 2 (Winter 2002): 360.

6. Melosh, *Strangers and Kin*, 211; Berebitsky, *Like Our Very Own*, 12–13.

7. Regina Kunzel, *Fallen Women, Problem Girls: Unmarried Mothers and the Professionalization of Social Work 1890–1945* (New Haven, CT: Yale University Press, 1993); Berebitsky, *Like Our Very Own*, 8; Melosh, *Strangers and Kin*; Herman, "Paradoxical Rationalization of Modern Adoption," 340–341, 347; US Department of Health, Education, and Welfare, Social Security Administration, Children's Bureau, "Protecting Children in Adoption," Children's Bureau publication 354, 1955, 26, quoted in Laurin and Virginia Hyde, "A Study of Proxy Adoptions," Box 11, Folder "Proxy Adoption, Study On, 1959," ISS records.

8. Kunzel, *Fallen Women, Problem Girls*; Melosh, *Strangers and Kin*, 109; Berebitsky, *Like Our Very Own*, 129; Bruce H. Berry, "Legislation," *Brooklyn Law Review* 28, no. 2 (Apr 1962): 324n4; Herman, "Paradoxical Rationalization of Modern Adoption"; Hyde and Hyde, "A Study of Proxy Adoptions," appendix A.

9. Berebitsky, *Like Our Very Own*, 135; "Results of Leadership, Demonstrations, and Training In South Korea by International Social Service 1954–1966," undated, Box 34, Folder "Korea—Administrative Correspondence," ISS records; Bertha Holt, *Bring My Sons from Afar* (Eugene, OR: Holt International Children's Services, 1986), 12.

10. For more on home studies, see Sarah Potter, *Everybody Else: Adoption and the Politics of Domestic Diversity in Postwar America* (Athens: University of Georgia Press, 2014).

11. Report of home study, 18 Nov. 1954, 2, Case 37099, ISS case files. For more on motivations behind domestic adoptions, see Melosh, *Strangers and Kin;* Berebitsky, *Like Our Very Own*; Herman, *Kinship by Design*; Elaine Tyler May, *Barren in the Promised Land: Childless Americans and the Pursuit of Happiness* (New York: Basic Books, 1995); "Adoptive Home Study," [forwarded to ISS 19 Sept. 1963], 1, Case 621887, ISS case files; Ilona Zucker to Danica Adjemovitch, 8 Aug. 1957, 2, Case 571120, ISS case files; Home Study, 3 June 1955, 4, Case 37827, ISS case files.

12. Margaret Valk to Elsie Charls, 18 Feb. 1955, 2, Case 37362, ISS case files; Melosh, *Strangers and Kin*, 38; Valk to Charls, 18 Feb. 1955, 2; Helen Miller, "Korea's International Children," *Lutheran Social Welfare*, Summer 1971, 15.

13. As of 1961, four Korean universities offered social work degree programs. There were no graduate programs in social work. LeRoy Bowman, Benjamin A. Gjenvick, and Eleanor T. M. Harvey, *Children of Tragedy: Church World Service Survey Team Report on Intercountry Orphan Adoption* (New York: National Council of the Churches of Christ in the USA, 1961), 33; author interview with Hyun Sook Han, 16 June 2006.

14. Determining a child's orphan status has historically been a problem in US domestic adoptions as well. At the turn of the century, only 10–15 percent of children in institutions were "full orphans." Berebitsky, *Like Our Very Own*, 34.

15. Jodi Kim calls this the "social death" of the child and her Korean birth parents. Kim, "An "Orphan" with Two Mothers: Transnational and Transracial Adoption, the Cold War, and Contemporary Asian American Cultural Politics," *American Quarterly* (2009): 857; Eleana Kim, "Our Adoptee, Our Alien: Transnational Adoptees as Specters of Foreignness and Family in South Korea," *Anthropological Quarterly* 80, no. 2 (Spring 2007): 497–531. The term *paper orphan* comes from Jane Jeong Trenka, "My Adoption File," *Jane's Blog*, http://jjtrenka.wordpress.com/about/adoption-file/.

16. Thomas Park Clement, *The Unforgotten War (Dust of the Streets)* (Bloomfield, IN: Truepeny Publishing, 1998), 6; Hi Taik Kim and Elaine Reid, "After a Long Journey: A Study on the Process of Initial Adjustment of the Half and Full Korean Children Adopted by American Families, and the Families' Experiences

with these Children During the Transitional Period" (MA thesis, University of Minnesota, 1970).

17. Myoung H. Rhee to Margaret Valk, 9 June 1958, Case 37176, ISS case files; Oak Soon Hong to Susan Pettiss, 27 Dec. 1954, 1, Case 36489, ISS case files.

18. Han, *Many Lives Intertwined*, 109; Case 36489, ISS case files.

19. Author interview with Molly Holt, 11 Apr. 2007; David Hyungbok Kim, *Who Will Answer . . . ?* (2001; Eugene, OR: Holt International Children's Services, 2006), 125, 132, 192; Dorothy Frost, Memo for the Record, 25 Nov. 1958, 1, Box 10, Folder "Holt, Harry. Vol. 2," ISS records.

20. Bum-Ju Whang, *50-Year History of Holt Children's Services, Inc.* (Seoul: Holt Children's Service, 2005), 145.

21. Whang, *50-Year History of Holt*, 150; author interview with Molly Holt; Kim, *Who Will Answer*, 122, 157, 166, 220, 258; Bertha Holt Oral History, 17 Nov. 1992, Tape 7, Oregon Historical Society (hereafter "OHS"); Case 581243, ISS case files; Minutes of Extra-ordinary Meeting of the Joint ROK/KCAC/UNKRA Committee for Child Welfare, [received 25 Oct. 1954], 2, Box 153, Folder 4882, Collection 23B, Center for Migration Studies, Staten Island, NY (hereafter "CMS").

22. Hyun Sook Han, *Many Lives Intertwined* (St. Paul, MN: Yeong & Yeong, 2004), 99–100; Holt, *Bring My Sons from Afar*, 12.

23. Han, *Many Lives Intertwined*, 100–101; Memo for the Record, "Notes on the Meeting of the Adoption Committee Held at the UNKRA Club," [received 25 Oct. 1954], 1, Box 153, Folder 4882, Collection 23B, CMS; Peter Kent Malone to John Rieger, Country Chief's Monthly Narrative Report, 17 Dec. 1955, Box 27, Folder "Seoul Area [folder 2/2], RG 59, National Archives, College Park, MD (hereafter "Archives II").

24. Susan Pettiss, Memo to Files, 6 June 1958, Box 34, Folder "ISS, Branches Korea Adoptions Jan. 1958–Dec. 1958," ISS records; Marcia Williams to Althea Knickerbocker, 28 Mar. 1958, Case 36608, ISS case files; William Hilliard, "Thieves Further Delay Korean Baby Airlift, Already Harassed [*sic*] by Redtape," *Oregonian*, 16 Dec. 1956.

25. Virginia Baumgartner to Margaret Valk, 2 June 1958, Case 58863, ISS case files.

26. Virginia Baumgartner to Susan Pettiss, 2 Dec. 1959, 1, Box 34, Folder "Korea—Adoptions to 1962 Rejections—Non Policy," ISS records; Kim, *Who Will Answer*; "Measures for the Welfare of Mixed-Blood Children in Korea," 8 Aug. 1967, 6, Box 35, Folder "Korea—Correspondence. Vol. 1," ISS records; American Embassy Consular Section, Seoul, Korea, "Adoption and Visas for Korean Orphans: Public Law 85-316, The Immigration Act of September 11, 1957," [1958], Box 34, Folder "ISS, Branches Korea Adoptions Jan. 1958–Dec. 1958," ISS records. ISS and CPS merged in 1966.

27. Marcia Williams to Susan Pettiss, 2 May 1958, 1, Box 34, Folder "ISS, Branches Korea Adoptions Jan. 1958–Dec. 1958," ISS records; Baumgartner to Pettiss, 2 Dec. 1959, 2; Margaret Valk, "Report: International Social Service: Inter-Country Adoption Program with Korea (1953–1958)," [1958], 9, Box 34, Folder "ISS, Branches Korea Adoptions Jan. 1958–Dec. 1958," ISS records; author interview with Molly Holt, 11 Apr. 2007; Marcia Williams to Susan Pettiss, 10 Mar. 1958, 1–2, Box 34, Folder "ISS, Branches Korea Adoptions Jan. 1958–Dec. 1958," ISS records; Marcia Speers to Susan Pettiss, 26 Nov. 1957, 2, Box 34, Folder "ISS, Branches Korea Adoptions Jan. 1958–Dec. 1958," ISS records.

28. Herman, "Paradoxical Rationalization of Modern Adoption," 340; Melosh, *Strangers and Kin*; Berebitsky, *Like Our Very Own*; Rickie Solinger, *Wake Up Little Susie: Single Pregnancy and Race Before* Roe v. Wade (1992; New York: Routledge, 2000).

29. Kim, *Who Will Answer*, 4, 3; Han, *Many Lives Intertwined*, 107; "Report of Investigation," 27 Dec. 1954, Case 36489, ISS case files; Kim and Reid, "After a Long Journey."

30. Harry Holt to Mrs. P, 7 Apr. 1958, Case 36608, ISS case files; Althea Knickerbocker to Kathryn Gordon, 29 Apr. 1958, 2, Case 36608, ISS case files; Excerpt from a letter from Harry to Bertha Holt, 18 Aug. 1955, quoted in Whang, *50-Year History of Holt*, 135.

31. Dong Soo Kim, "From Women to Women with Painful Love: A Study of Maternal Motivation in Intercountry Adoption Process," in *Korean Women in a Struggle for Humanization*, ed. Harold Hakwon Sunoo and Dong Soo Kim (Memphis: Association of Korean Christian Scholars in North America, 1978); Kim and Reid, "After a Long Journey."

32. Anne Davison, "The Mixed Racial Child," undated, 2, Box 34, Folder "Korea—Adoptions to '62," ISS records; Kim, "From Women to Women with Painful Love," 137–138, 141.

33. Kim and Reid, "After a Long Journey," 33; Davison, "The Mixed Racial Child," 2; Holt, *Bring My Sons from Afar*, 12; Han, *Many Lives Intertwined*, 100.

34. Untitled report, [1957 or 1958], Case 42331, ISS case files; Virginia Baumgartner to Margaret Valk, 2 June 1958, Case 58863, ISS case files.

35. Holt, *Bring My Sons from Afar*, 13.

36. Virginia Baumgartner to Mary Davis, 11 Aug. 1959, Case 591535, ISS case files.

37. Case 60825, ISS case files; Anne Davison to Valeen Pon, 27 June 1960, Case 67230, ISS case files; Case 60825, ISS case files.

38. Virginia Baumgartner to Margaret Valk, 2 June 1958, Case 58863, ISS case files; "PRC's [Paul Cheney] Notes on Field Visit—ISS Korea Staff," [1962], 19, Box 35, Folder "Korea—General, Discard," ISS records.

39. "PRC's [Paul Cheney] Notes on Field Visit—ISS Korea Staff," [1962], 19, Box 35, Folder "Korea—General, Discard," ISS records.

40. Kim, "From Women to Women with Painful Love," 137.

41. Pearl S. Buck, *Children for Adoption* (New York: Random House, 1964), 157; *Adoption of Oriental Children by American White Families: An Interdisciplinary Symposium* (New York: Child Welfare League of America, 1960), 11; home study [forwarded to ISS on 6 July 1966], 4, Case 65906, ISS case files.

42. Geoffrey Keleher to Jean Bamford Keleher, 20 May 1956, Microfilm Roll 19, RG 59, Archives II; Buck, *Children for Adoption*; *Adoption of Oriental Children*, 11.

43. Although matching included intelligence and religion, social workers placed most emphasis on racial matching by midcentury. Melosh, *Strangers and Kin*, 93. For more on religious matching, see Ellen Herman, "Paradoxical Rationalization of Modern Adoption"; Ellen Herman, "The Difference Difference Makes: Justine Wise Polier and Religious Matching in Twentieth-Century Child Adoption," *Religion and American Culture* 10, no. 1 (Winter 2000): 57–98.

44. An invisible adoption would also spare both the birth mother and adoptive mother the stigma of having transgressed contemporary gender norms and revealing themselves to be unfeminine: by becoming pregnant out of wedlock, on the one hand, and being infertile, on the other. Women were usually blamed for marital infertility. Melosh, *Strangers and Kin*, 112, 120, 152, 209–210. Elaine Tyler May discusses infertility and adoption in *Barren in the Promised Land*, and E. Wayne Carp examines the history of secrecy in adoption in *Family Matters: Secrecy and Disclosure in the History of Adoption* (Cambridge, MA: Harvard University Press, 1998).

45. Brian Paul Gill, "Adoption Agencies and the Search for the Ideal Family, 1918–1965," in *Adoption in America: Historical Perspectives*, ed. E. Wayne Carp (Ann Arbor: University of Michigan Press, 2002), 160–180.

46. Eleana Kim, "Erasures of Empire: The Disavowals of Race in Transnational Korean Adoption," 2011, unpublished paper in author's possession, 11.

47. Bertha Holt, *Outstretched Arms* (Eugene, OR: Holt International Children's Services, 1972), 283–284; author interview with Molly Holt, 11 Apr. 2007.

48. Melosh, *Strangers and Kin*, 102; Mrs. Douglass A. Young to Muriel Webb, 25 Mar. 1958, Box 10, Folder "Holt, Harry. Vol. 2," ISS records; Susan Pettiss to Muriel Webb, 18 Apr. 1958, Box 10, Folder "Holt, Harry. Vol. 2," ISS records.

49. Buck, *Children for Adoption*; Pearl S. Buck, *The Hidden Flower* (New York: Pocket Books, 1952); Melosh, *Strangers and Kin*, 94; Case 571339, ISS case files; Photos 142, 172, 190, 193, and 194, Collection 23B, CMS; Margaret Valk to Sam Karelitz, 14 Sept. 1960, Box 34, Folder "Korea—Adoptions to 1962 Rejections—Non Policy," ISS records; Sam Karelitz to Margaret Valk, 20 Sept.

1960, Box 34, Folder "Korea—Adoptions to 1962 Rejections—Non Policy," ISS records.

50. Han, *Many Lives Intertwined*, 114.

51. Eva Kelley to Lillian Lewis, 18 Sept. 1964, Case 41811, ISS case files; Helen McKay to Margaret Valk, [July 1956], Case 41811, ISS case files; Albert Beck to CA Department of Social Welfare, [received 11 Mar. 1955], 2, Case 37651, ISS case files.

52. Nadia Kim, *Imperial Citizens: Koreans and Race from Seoul to LA* (Stanford, CA: Stanford University Press, 2008); Eleanor Linse to St. Louis County Welfare Office, 11 Mar. 1957, 1–2, Box 10, Folder "Holt, Harry Vol. 1," ISS records; Clement, *Unforgotten War*, 12; Margaret Valk to Elsie Charls, 18 Feb. 1955, Case 37362, ISS case files; Noel Braga to J. Calvitt Clarke, 14 Jan. 1955, Microfilm Roll 19, RG 59, Archives II.

53. Susan Pettiss to Marcia Williams, 9 Jan. 1958, 2, Box 34, Folder "ISS Branches. Korea Adoption Jan.–Dec. 1958," ISS records; Melosh, *Strangers and Kin*, 54; Holt, *Bring My Sons from Afar*, 27, 103, 167; "New Faces," *Time*, 23 Dec. 1957, 16; Bertha Holt, *The Seed from the East* (Eugene, OR: Holt International Children's Services, 1956), 236.

54. "State Department Seeks to Help 'Ostracized' Korea Brown Babies," *Jet*, 24 Mar. 1955, 16–17. Box 11, Folder "Brown Baby file," RG 59, Archives II. Thanks to Madeline Hsu for drawing my attention to this source.

55. Kori Graves, "Domesticating Foreign Affairs: The African-American Family, Korean War Orphans, and Cold War Civil Rights" (PhD diss., University of Wisconsin–Madison, 2011).

56. Ethel Payne, "PARENTS WANTED! Why Not Adopt a Baby?" *Chicago Defender*, 12 Apr. 1952; Ethel Payne, "PARENTS WANTED! Why Not Adopt a Baby?" installment 2, *Chicago Defender*, 19 Apr. 1952; Ethel Payne, "PARENTS WANTED! Why Not Adopt a Baby?" installment 3, *Chicago Defender*, 26 Apr. 1952; "Why Negroes Don't Adopt Children," *Ebony*, July 1952, 31; "Attitudes of Negro Professional and Business Men Toward Adoption," vol. 1 (collected MSW theses, University of Buffalo School of Social Work, 1960).

57. Ilona Zucker to Margaret Valk, 29 Apr. 1957, 1, Case 571120, ISS case files. The Spence-Chapin agency, a private agency in New York, recruited prominent African Americans in its home-finding program, which it aimed at the "Black 400." "Why Negroes Don't Adopt Children," 34; Melosh, *Strangers and Kin*, 101. For more on the National Urban League's drive to promote African American adoption, see Graves, "Domesticating Foreign Affairs."

58. Ilona Zucker to Crystal Breeding, 13 Dec. 1957, Case 42334, ISS case files; Letitia DiVirgilio to Margaret Valk, 5 Nov. 1958, 1, Case 571339, ISS case

files; Andrew Juras to William Kirk (Attn Pettiss), 4 May 1956, 2, Box 10, Folder "Holt, Harry Vol. 1," ISS records; Kim, "Erasures of Empire," 10.

59. Letitia DiVirgilio to Margaret Valk, 5 Nov. 1958, 2, Case 571339, ISS case files. The BCSA's own policy was that parents adopting internationally should not pay more than they would if they were adopting domestically. In the case of domestic adoptions, BCSA used a sliding scale, based on family income, to calculate costs, and waived or adjusted payments on a case-by-case basis. For almost all the international adoptions, BCSA waived the cost for its own services or charged a token fee.

60. DiVirgilio to Valk, 5 Nov. 1958, 2.

61. Margaret Valk, handwritten notation, Mar. 1956 on Grace Louise Hubbard to Margaret Valk, 20 Sept. 1955, Case 36746, ISS case files; Margaret Valk to Grace Rue, 25 June 1956, Case 36746, ISS case files.

62. Melosh, *Strangers and Kin*, 149–150; Margaret Valk to VA Department of Public Welfare, 10 Apr. 1956, Case 38038, ISS case files; "Why Negroes Don't Adopt Children," 31. For more on domestic and international African American adoption, see Graves, "Domesticating Foreign Affairs"; Potter, *Everybody Else*.

63. "Why Negroes Don't Adopt Children"; Melosh, *Strangers and Kin*; DiVirgilio to Valk, 5 Nov. 1958, 1–2; Graves, "Domesticating Foreign Affairs," 21.

64. Susan Pettiss to Marcia Williams, 9 Jan. 1958, 3, Box 34, Folder "ISS Branches. Korea Adoption Jan–Dec. 1958," ISS records; Nellie Loomis to Crystal Breeding, 18 Jan. 1957, Case 42234, ISS case files; NJ Board of Child Welfare to Mrs. M, 18 July 1955, 1–2, Case 38291, ISS case files.

65. Eleanor Linse to St. Louis County Welfare Office, 11 Mar. 1957, 1–2, Box 10, Folder: Holt, Harry Vol. 1, ISS records; Ilona Zucker to Crystal Breeding, 3 June 1957, 1, Case 42334, ISS case files; Mrs. M to Child Placement Service, 3 May 1955, Case 38291, ISS case files; Melosh, *Strangers and Kin*, 96–7; Ilona Zucker to Crystal Breeding, 18 June 1957, 1, Case 42334, ISS case files.

66. Ilona Zucker to Margaret Valk, 29 Apr. 1957, 1, Case 571120, ISS case files; Letitia DiVirgilio to Danica Adjemovitch, 16 June 1958, 1, Case 571120, ISS case files.

67. Letitia DiVirgilio to Danica Adjemovitch, 13 May 1958, 1, Case 571120, ISS case files; Danica Adjemovitch to ISS Korea, 12 June 1958, Case 571120, ISS case files; DiVirgilio to Adjemovitch, 16 June 1958, 1.

68. Letitia DiVirgilio to Danica Adjemovitch, 6 June 1958, 2, Case 571120, ISS case files; DiVirgilio to Adjemovitch, 16 June 1958, 1.

69. Melosh, *Strangers and Kin*, 99; Margaret Valk to Virginia Baumgartner, 24 June 1958, Box 34, Folder "ISS, Branches Korea Adoptions Jan. 1958–Dec. 1958," ISS records; Graves, "Domesticating Foreign Affairs," 92–93. The social worker did not specify whether the dark brown sample was of hose, paper, or

crayon. Personal email from Kori Graves, 17 Jan. 2013, in author's possession; Evelyn McKee to Harriet Soulen, 5 Dec. 1963, Case 571026, ISS case files; Haesong Chun to Harriet Soulen, 8 Jan. 1964, 1, Case 571026, ISS case files.

70. *Adoption of Oriental Children by American White Families*, 26, 32, 34; Sydne Didier, "'Just a Drop in the Bucket': An Analysis of Child Rescue Efforts on Behalf of Korean Children, 1951 to 1964" (MA thesis, Portland State University, 1998), 99; Peggy Pascoe, "Miscegenation Law, Court Cases and Ideologies of 'Race' in Twentieth-Century America," *Journal of American History* 83, no. 1 (June 1996): 44–69.

71. Margaret Valk to Willella Kennedy, 11 Mar. 1955, 1, Case 37099, ISS case files.

72. Report on visit, Nov. 1964, Case 621887, ISS case files; Cheri Register, *Beyond Good Intentions: A Mother Reflects on Raising Internationally Adopted Children* (St. Paul, MN: Yeong & Yeong, 2005).

73. Margaret Valk to Elsie Charls, 18 Feb. 1955, 2, Case 37362, ISS case files; home study, [late 1950s], 3, Case 581935, ISS case files; home study, 22 June 1955, 19, Case 37217, ISS case files.

74. [State] Department of Social Work to Margaret Valk, 5 May 1955, Case 37827, ISS case files; [State] DSW to Margaret Valk, 3 June 1955, 3, Case 37827, ISS case files; "Foster home evaluation," enclosed with [State] DSW to Margaret Valk, 3 June 1955, 3, Case 37827, ISS case files.

75. California Department of Social Welfare to Althea Knickerbocker, 15 Dec. 1961, 1, Case 61207, ISS case files; Patricia Seavers to ISS, 10 Jan. 1957, 2, Case 37182, ISS case files; home study, 22 June 1955, 19, Case 37217, ISS case files.

76. Home study, undated, enclosed with Cerise Klepper to Dorothy Sills, 16 May 1955, Case 36585, ISS case files; Case 60209, ISS case files; Mamie Goodman to Susan Pettiss and Margaret Valk, 2 Mar. 1956, Case 37013, ISS case files.

CHAPTER 5

1. Harry C. Stickler, "Orphan Airlift: From Seoul to Brussels with Nine Little Orphans," *Asia Magazine*, 25 Aug. 1974, in *The Unbroken Circle: A Collection of Writings on Interracial and International Adoption*, ed. Betty Kramer (Minneapolis: Organization for a United Response, 1975), 145.

2. Gil Loescher and John A. Scanlan, *Calculated Kindness: Refugees and America's Half-Open Door, 1945–Present* (New York: Free Press, 1986); Carl Bon Tempo, *Americans at the Gate: The United States and Refugees During the Cold War* (Princeton, NJ: Princeton University Press, 2008), 99; Steven Porter, "Defining Public Responsibility in a Global Age: Refugees, NGOs, and the American State" (PhD diss., University of Chicago, 2009); Bryan O. Walsh, "Cuban Refugee Children," *Journal of Interamerican Studies and World Affairs* 13, nos. 3–4

(July–Oct. 1971): 378–415; María de los Ángeles Torres, *The Lost Apple: Operation Pedro Pan, Cuban Children in the U.S., and the Promise of a Better Future* (Boston: Beacon Press, 2004).

3. I thank Ellen Wu for providing me with the language for this point.

4. Ellen Herman, *Kinship by Design: A History of Adoption in the Modern United States* (Chicago: University of Chicago Press, 2008), 8; Laura Briggs, "Making 'American' Families: Transnational Adoption and U.S. Latin America Policy," in *Haunted by Empire: Geographies of Intimacy in North American History*, ed. Ann Laura Stoler (Durham, NC: Duke University Press, 2006), 349.

5. Mae M. Ngai, *Impossible Subjects: Illegal Aliens and the Making of Modern America* (Princeton, NJ: Princeton University Press, 2004).

6. Aristide Zolberg, "The Roots of American Refugee Policy" *Social Research* 55, no. 4 (Winter 1988): 649–678; Bon Tempo, *Americans at the Gate;* Porter, "Defining Public Responsibility"; Loescher and Scanlan, *Calculated Kindness*; Michael Gill Davis, "The Cold War, Refugees, and U.S. Immigration Policy" (PhD diss., Vanderbilt University, 1996); Kathryn Close, *Transplanted Children: A History* (New York: US Committee for the Care of European Children, 1953), 40–41; Beth C. Cohen, *Case Closed: Holocaust Survivors in Postwar America* (New Brunswick, NJ: Rutgers University Press, 2007); Robert Matthews, "The Littlest Immigrants: The Immigration and Adoption of Foreign Orphans" (PhD diss., Virginia Polytechnic Institute and State University, 1989); US Displaced Persons Commission, *Memo to America: The DP Story, the Final Report* (Washington, DC: GPO, 1952), 207–209; Clayton B. Doughty, "Adoption and Immigration of Alien Orphans" *I&N Reporter*, Apr. 1964, 50.

7. Tara Zahra, *The Lost Children: Reconstructing Europe's Families After World War II* (Cambridge, MA: Harvard University Press, 2011); Gertrude D. Krichefsy, "Alien Orphans," *I&N Reporter*, Apr. 1961, 43; US Displaced Persons Commission, *Memo to America*; Matthews, "Littlest Immigrants," 35.

8. Bon Tempo, *Americans at the Gate*, 34.

9. Undated advisory opinions, Box 17, Folder "RRP/FE Advisory Opinion," Records Group (RG) 59, Entry 5496, National Archives, College Park, MD (hereafter "Archives II"); Scott McLeod to the Acting Secretary, 19 Apr. 1954, Box 17, Folder "Orphan Program," RG 59, Archives II.

10. Bon Tempo, *Americans at the Gate*, 40.

11. When the RRA orphan visas were exhausted, hundreds of children in Korea were still awaiting processing. As a short-term solution to the situation, President Eisenhower exercised parole power to admit 925 orphans into the United States. Outerbridge Horsey to Lt. Gen. Earl Barnes, 26 Sept. 1956, Box 9, Folder 1-D/2 "ORM General 1955–56," RG 59, Archives II; "Refugee Relief Act Must Be Amended to Assist War Orphans," *Congressional Record* [hereafter *CR*]

84th Cong., 2nd sess., vol. 102 (21 July 1956): 13980; *Facilitating Entry of Certain Adopted Children* report to accompany HR 8123, HR Report 1199, 85th Cong., 1st sess. (19 Aug. 1957): 6; "Admission of 10,000 Refugee Orphans to the United States," *CR*, 85th Cong., 1st sess., vol. 103 (25 Jan. 1957): 964; "Statement by the President" 26 Oct. 1956, in Pierce Gerety to All Members of Congress, 31 Oct. 1956, Box 9, Folder "1-D/2 ORM General 1955–56," RG 59, Archives II. Although INS sources report that 925 orphans were paroled, other sources report 833 and 839, stated respectively in Helen F. Eckerson, "Report on the Act of September 11, 1957," *I&N Reporter*, Apr. 1959, 48; "Facilitating Entry," 5.

12. Eugenie Hochfeld and Margaret A. Valk, *Experience in Inter-Country Adoptions* (New York: International Social Service, American Branch, 1953); US Department of Defense, *Manual on Intercountry Adoption* (Washington, DC: US GPO, 1959).

13. "Dear Friends" letter, 27 Dec. 1956, 3, Box 10, Folder "Holt, Harry Vol. 1," International Social Service, American Branch Records, Social Welfare History Archives, University of Minnesota (hereafter "ISS records"). For more on the conflict between advocates and opponents of proxy adoption, see Arissa Oh, "Into the Arms of America: The Korean Roots of International Adoption" (PhD diss., University of Chicago, 2008), chapters 5 and 6.

14. "Private Relief Legislation," *CR*, 85th Cong., 1st sess., vol. 103 (16 July 1957): 10683. Bum-Ju Whang, *50-Year History of Holt Children's Services, Inc.* (Seoul: Holt Children's Service, 2005), 126.

15. See, for example, "Needed Revision of the McCarran-Walter Act," *CR*, 84th Cong., 2nd sess., vol. 102 (23 July 1956): 13979–13982.

16. Like many attempts at immigration reform during this period, the Act of 11 September 1957 was imperfect: it did not grant permanent status to Hungarian parolees or liberalize the quota system as President Eisenhower had requested. However, it did modify the 1952 McCarran-Walter Act in important ways by providing a number of non-quota visas for refugees fleeing communism or other forms of tyranny and by facilitating family reunification. "President Requests Revisions in U.S. Immigration Laws," *Congressional Quarterly Almanac*, (1957); Act of 11 September 1957, Public Law 85-316 (71 Stat. 639); Statement by Senator Kennedy, "Amendment of Immigration and Nationality Act," *CR*, 85th Cong., 1st sess., vol. 103 (21 Aug. 1957): 15498.

17. Under the 1957 law, orphans paroled into the United States between the expiration of the RRA and September 1957 were able to have their status adjusted to permanent resident aliens. The 1957 law also shifted responsibility for orphan visas from the State Department, which had administered the RRA, to the attorney general in the Justice Department. This rejection of the social work establishment's proposal to move the orphan program to the Children's Bureau

(part of the Department of Health, Education, and Welfare) indicated that Congress viewed intercountry adoption as primarily an immigration, not a child welfare, issue. Kirsten Lovelock, "Intercountry Adoption as Migratory Practice: A Comparative Analysis of Intercountry Adoption and Immigration Policy and Practice in the United States, Canada and New Zealand in the Post W.W. II Period," *International Migration Review* 34 (Fall 2000): 907–949.

18. S. Rep. 475, "Amending Section 4 and Section 6 of the Act of September 11, 1957," 86th Cong., 1st sess. (1959), 5; Bon Tempo, *Americans at the Gate*, 98; Zolberg, "Roots of American Refugee Policy," 668.

19. The Act of 26 September 1961: PL 87-310, US Statutes at Large. This act marked the first time refugee legislation was incorporated into permanent immigration law. Helen J. Eckerson and Gertrude D. Krichefsky, "Principles of Immigration Law—Part 2," *I&N Reporter*, Apr. 1962, 48.

20. Parents in the four states that did not allow foreign adoptions—California, Minnesota, Ohio, and Michigan—still had to travel to Korea to adopt.

21. Stephanie Sue Padilla, "Adoption of Alien Orphan Children: How United States Immigration Law Defines Family," *Georgetown Immigration Law Journal* 7 (1993): 817–844; Abraham Ribicoff to Emanuel Celler, 13 July 1961, in H.R. Rep. 1086, "Amending the Immigration and Nationality Act and for Other Purposes," 87th Cong., 1st sess. (1961), 9; Daniel J. Steinbock, "The Admission of Unaccompanied Children into the United States," *Yale Law and Policy Review* 7 (1989): 1451; Nancy Ota, "Private Matters: Family and Race and the Post-World-War-II Translation of 'American,'" *International Review of Social History* 46 (2001): 209–234; Martha Gardner, *The Qualities of a Citizen: Women, Immigration, and Citizenship, 1870–1965* (Princeton, NJ: Princeton University Press, 2005).

22. See Oh, "Into the Arms of America," table 3.2, 157; Bill Ong Hing, *Making and Remaking Asian America Through Immigration Policy, 1850–1990* (Palo Alto, CA: Stanford University Press, 1993), table 7, 66.

23. Theodore Sorensen to Russell Palmer, 13 Apr. 1961, Box 377, Folder "Immigration and Naturalization 1-20-61 to 6-25-61," John F. Kennedy Library, Boston (Hereafter "Kennedy Library").

24. "Legislation to Extend Orphan Immigration Program Urgently Needed"; Bertha Holt, *The Seed from the East* (Eugene, OR: Holt International Children's Services, 1956), 205; Bertha Holt, *Bring My Sons from Afar* (Eugene, OR: Holt International Children's Services, 13, 29); Meg Greenfield, "The Melting Pot of Francis E. Walter," *Reporter* (26 Oct. 1961), 24–28; Stephen Wagner, "The Lingering Death of the National Origins Quota System: A Political History of United States Immigration Policy, 1952–1965" (PhD diss., Harvard University, 1986).

25. The number of children admitted under temporary orphan provisions follows: 4,065 under the Displaced Persons Act of 1948; 466 under the act of

29 July 1953; 3,761 under the Refugee Relief Act of 1953; and 8,474 under the Act of 11 September 1957. Together, these four temporary programs allowed the entry of 16,766 immigrant orphans. [Senator Keating speaking about orphan programs], *CR*, 87th Cong., 1st sess., vol. 107 (12 July 1961): 12366.

26. Mr. and Mrs. Luke Knowlton to "the Senators," 20 July 1956, and Mr. and Mrs. Lawrence Lockwood to Wayne Morse, 20 July 1956, in "Needed Revision of the McCarran-Walter Act," *CR*, 84th Cong., 2nd sess., vol. 102 (23 July 1956): 13981–13982; Berta Burch Babb to Wayne Morse, 20 July 1956, and Mr. and Mrs. William A. K. Lammert to Wayne Morse, 23 July 1956, in "Increase in Number of Visas to Be Issued to Orphans Under the Refugee Relief Act of 1953," *CR*, 84th Cong., 2nd sess., vol. 102 (26 July 1956): 14741–14743; "Adoption of Korean Orphans," *CR*, 85th Cong., 1st sess., vol. 103 (3 July 1957): 10879.

27. [Senator Keating speaking about orphan programs], *CR*, 12371.

28. For more on how international adoption policy evolved during this period, see Rachel Winslow, "Colorblind Empire: International Adoption, Social Policy, and the American Family, 1945–1976" (PhD diss., University of California, Santa Barbara, 2012); Karen Dubinsky, *Babies Without Borders: Adoption and Migration Across the Americas* (New York: New York University Press, 2010).

29. The Act of 29 July 1953 explicitly defined the category of "eligible orphan." This definition was used, with minor changes, in all subsequent orphan legislation.

30. Eleana Kim, "Our Adoptee, Our Alien: Transnational Adoptees as Specters of Foreignness and Family in South Korea," *Anthropological Quarterly* 80, no. 2 (Spring 2007): 520; Eleana Kim, *Adopted Territory: Transnational Korean Adoptees and the Politics of Belonging* (Durham, NC: Duke University Press, 2010), 11.

31. Mr. and Mrs. Scott Smith to JFK, 19 June 1961; Lea Oliver to JFK, 22 May 1961; David and Dorothea Chamberlain to JFK, 22 June 1961, all in Box 482, Folder "LE/IM Jan. 20, 1961 through July 10, 1961," Kennedy Library; Mr. and Mrs. Alvie E. Leach to Wayne Morse, 2 May 1961 and Calvin W. Rogers to Wayne Morse, 29 May 1961, in "Mutual Educational and Cultural Exchange Act of 1961," *CR*, 87th Cong., 1st sess., vol. 107 (12 July 1961): 12370. See also letters in "Legislation Needed to Extend Orphan Immigration Law Which Expires June 30, 1959," *CR*, 86th Cong., 1st sess., vol. 105 (15 May 1959): 8248–8251.

32. Kim, *Adopted Territory*, 101; Elaine Tyler May, *Homeward Bound: American Families in the Cold War Era* (1988; New York: Basic Books, 1999); Elaine Tyler May, *Barren in the Promised Land: Childless Americans and the Pursuit of Happiness* (Cambridge, MA: Harvard University Press, 1997); David Eng, "Transnational Adoption and Queer Diasporas," *Social Text*, 21, no. 3 (Fall 2003): 11; Laura Briggs, "Mother, Child, Race, Nation," *Gender and History* 15, no. 2 (Aug. 2003): 182.

33. Bernard Stern to JFK, 21 June 1961; Richard Wayne to JFK, 18 June 1961; Mr. and Mrs. George Wickes to JFK, 22 June 1961; and Dr. and Mrs. Herman Brezing to JFK, 21 June 1961, all in Box 482, Folder "LE/IM Jan. 20, 1961 through July 10, 1961," Kennedy Library; Mrs. Walter E. Crouse to Wayne Morse, 29 May 1961, in "Mutual Educational and Cultural Exchange Act of 1961," *CR*, 12371.

34. Nancy Cott, *Public Vows: A History of Marriage and the Nation* (Cambridge, MA: Harvard University Press, 2000), 197.

35. Mark Jerng, *Claiming Others: Transracial Adoption and National Belonging* (Minneapolis: University of Minnesota Press, 2010), 210; Anne McClintock, *Imperial Leather: Race, Gender and Sexuality in the Colonial Contest* (New York: Routledge, 1995).

36. Wayne Morse to James Eastland, 29 June 1959, in "Amendment of Section 6 of the Act of September 11, 1957," *CR*, 86th Cong., 1st sess., vol. 105 (22 July 1959): 13968.

37. Lillian Llewellyn, Home Study, [1954] 1, 3, Case 37133, ISS Adoption Case Records, Social Welfare History Archive, University of Minnesota (hereafter "ISS case files").

38. Rev. Fenton Strickland to JFK, 19 June 1961, Box 482, Folder "LE/IM Jan. 20, 1961 through July 10, 1961," Kennedy Library; Barbara Joe, "In Defense of Intercountry Adoption," *Social Service Review* 52, no. 1 (Mar 1978): 5.

39. Eng, "Transnational Adoption and Queer Diasporas," 7; Dubinsky, *Babies Without Borders*, 20.

40. Briggs, "Making 'American' Families." For more on the political symbolism of children, see Dubinsky, *Babies Without Borders*.

41. Ellen Wu, *The Color of Success: Asian Americans and the Origins of the Model Minority* (Princeton, NJ: Princeton University Press, 2013); Charlotte Brooks, "In the Twilight Zone Between Black and White: Japanese American Resettlement and Community in Chicago, 1942–1945," *Journal of American History* 86 (Mar. 2000): 1655–1687; Sucheng Chan, *Asian Americans: An Interpretive History* (Boston: Twayne, 1991); Madeline Hsu, "The Disappearance of America's Cold War Chinese Refugees, 1948–1966," *Journal of American Ethnic History* 31, no. 4 (Summer 2012): 12–33; Scott Kurashige, *The Shifting Grounds of Race: Black and Japanese Americans in the Making of Multiethnic Los Angeles* (Princeton, NJ: Princeton University Press, 2010), 202; Caroline Chung Simpson, *An Absent Presence: Japanese Americans in Postwar American Culture, 1945–1960* (Durham, NC: Duke University Press, 2001); Christina Klein, *Cold War Orientalism: Asia in the Middlebrow Imagination, 1945–1961* (Berkeley: University of California Press, 2003); Cindy I-Fen Cheng, *Citizens of Asian America: Democracy and Race During the Cold War* (New York: New York University Press, 2013).

42. John W. Dower, *Embracing Defeat: Japan in the Wake of World War II* (New York: Norton, 1999), 138; Naoko Shibusawa, *America's Geisha Ally: Reimagining the Japanese Enemy* (Cambridge, MA: Harvard University Press, 2006); Klein, *Cold War Orientalism*.

43. Ngai, *Impossible Subjects*, 246; Greenfield, "The Melting Pot of Francis E. Walter," 25.

44. Senate Committee on the Judiciary, *Authorizing Additional Visas for Orphans*, S. Rep. 2684, 84th Cong., 2nd sess., 1956, 3; Bon Tempo, *Americans at the Gate*, 41; Mr. and Mrs. Elmer Enochs to Theodore Francis Green, 21 May 1957, Box 2, Folder "I&N Act—Adopted Children, 2 of 2," RG 46, National Archives, Washington, DC; June Anders to JFK, 17 June 1961; Richard Dommes to JFK, 21 June 1961; and Richard S. Wayne to JFK, 18 June 1961, all in Box 482 WHCFS, Folder "LE/IM Jan. 20, 1961 through July 10, 1961," Kennedy Library.

45. Lynne McTaggart, "How I Sold—and Almost Bought—a Baby," *New York News Magazine*, 13 Apr. 1975, in Senate Committee on Labor and Public Welfare, *Adoption and Foster Care, 1975: Hearings Before the Subcommittee on Children and Youth*, 94th Cong., 1st sess., 28–29 Apr., 14 and 18 July 1975 (Washington DC: GPO, 1975), 6, 74; Wayne King, "Adoption Agencies Report Shortage of White Infants," *New York Times*, 7 Dec. 1970.

46. Eve Edstrom, "Black Market Baby Traffic Told at Probe," *Washington Post*, 20 Nov. 1953, 1; Karen Balcom, *The Traffic in Babies: Cross-Border Adoption and Baby-Selling Between the United States and Canada, 1930–1972* (Toronto: University of Toronto Press, 2011); Rickie Solinger, *Wake Up Little Susie: Single Pregnancy and Race Before* Roe v. Wade (1992; New York: Routledge, 2000), 166; Marybeth Weinstein, "The Markets—Black and Gray—in Babies," *New York Times*, 27 Nov. 1955; Senate Committee on the Judiciary, *Juvenile Delinquency (Interstate Adoption Practices): Hearings Before the Subcommittee to Investigate Juvenile Delinquency*, 84th Cong., 1st sess., 15–16 July 1955 (Washington, DC: GPO, 1956); *Adoption and Foster Care, 1975*; House Committee on the Judiciary, *Sale of Children in Interstate and Foreign Commerce: Hearings Before the Subcommittee on Criminal Justice*, 95th Cong., 1st sess., 21 Mar. and 25 Apr. 1977 (Washington, DC: US GPO, 1979).

47. Herman, *Kinship by Design*, 242; NABSW, "Position Statement on Trans-Racial Adoptions," Sept. 1972, http://c.ymcdn.com/sites/nabsw.org/resource/collection/E1582D77-E4CD-4104-996A-D42D08F9CA7D/NABSW_Trans-Racial_Adoption_1972_Position_(b).pdf; Laura Briggs, *Somebody's Children: The Politics of Transracial and Transnational Adoption* (Durham, NC: Duke University Press, 2012), chapter 1; Wendell Rawls Jr., "Adoption Abroad Brings Heartache to Some Couples," *New York Times*, 24 June 1978.

48. Herman, *Kinship by Design*, 198, 242, 252; Jooyeon Koo, "In Whose Best Interest? American Adoption of Korean Children in the 1970s" (Scholar of the

College project, Boston College, 2012); Ana Teresa Ortiz and Laura Briggs, "The Culture of Poverty, Crack Babies, and Welfare Cheats: The Making of the 'Healthy White Baby Crisis,'" *Social Text* 21, no. 3 (Fall 2003): 76, 21; Dorothy Roberts, *Shattered Bonds: The Color of Child Welfare* (New York: Basic Civitas Books, 2003); Raka Shome, "'Global Motherhood': The Transnational Intimacies of White Femininity," *Critical Studies in Media Communication* 28, no. 5 (2011), 403; Dawn Davenport, "Born in America, Adopted Abroad," *Christian Science Monitor*, 27 Oct. 2004; Hari Sreenivasan and Nils Kongshaug, "Foreigners Vie to Adopt Black U.S. Babies," *ABC World News*, 5 Mar. 2005; "A Canadian Haven for Black Babies," *Globe and Mail*, 1 Oct. 2005; Virginia Lee Warren, "Unwanted Children Find Parents Across the Sea," *New York Times*, 20 Aug. 1972; Elizabeth Payne, "Florida Moms, Fearing Racism, Sending Babies to Canada for Adoption," *Ottawa Citizen*, 21 July 2014, http://ottawacitizen.com/news/national/sun-sand-adoptions-floridas-surprising-growth-industry; Rebecca Buckwalter-Poza, "America's Unseen Export: Children, Most of them Black," *Pacific Standard*, 24 June 2014, http://www.psmag.com/navigation/politics-and-law/outgoing-adoption-americas-unseen-export-children-black-84084/.

49. Briggs, *Somebody's Children*, chapter 2; Margaret D. Jacobs, "Remembering the 'Forgotten Child': The American Indian Child Welfare Crisis of the 1960s and 1970s," *American Indian Quarterly* 37, nos. 1–2 (Winter–Spring 2013): 140.

50. David Fanshel, *Far from the Reservation: The Transracial Adoption of American Indian Children* (Metuchen, NJ: Scarecrow Press, 1972), 24, 119; Jacobs, "Remembering the 'Forgotten Child,'" 142–143.

51. Fanshel, *Far from the Reservation*, 81–93. See Briggs, *Somebody's Children*, for a discussion of the relationship between the NABSW and Native American responses to transracial adoption. The Church of Jesus Christ of Latter-day Saints' Indian Student Placement Program provided temporary foster care and education. It began in 1954 and at the time of the ICWA's passage was far bigger than the IAP. The Mormon church was able to win an exception for itself to the ICWA. Briggs, *Somebody's Children*, chapter 2; Herman, *Kinship by Design*, chapter 7. For more on the Mormon Indian Student Placement Program, see Lynette Riggs, "The Church of Jesus Christ of Latter-day Saints' Indian Student Placement Service: A History" (PhD diss., Utah State University, 2008).

52. Hosu Kim, "Mothers Without Mothering: Birth Mothers from South Korea Since the Korean War," *International Korean Adoption: A Fifty-Year History of Policy and Practice*, ed. Kathleen Ja Sook Bergquist, M. Elizabeth Vonk, Dong Soo Kim, and Marvin D. Feit (New York: Haworth Press, 2007), 142; Cheri Register, *Are Those Kids Yours?* (New York: Free Press, 1990), 137.

53. Sara Dorow, "Racialized Choices: Chinese Adoption and the 'White Noise' of Blackness," *Critical Sociology* 32, nos. 2–3 (2006): 370; Soojin Pate, "Genealogies of Korean Adoption: American Empire, Militarization, and Yellow

Desire" (PhD diss., University of Minnesota, 2010), 219–223; Jan De Hartog, *The Children: A Personal Record for the Use of Adoptive Parents* (New York: Atheneum, 1969), 210–211.

54. Matthew Frye Jacobson, *Roots Too: White Ethnic Revival in Post–Civil Rights America* (Cambridge, MA: Harvard University Press, 2008); "America Is All They Know, but They're Not Quite at Home," *New York Times*, 1 Mar. 1977.

55. Frances Koh, *Oriental Children in American Homes* (Minneapolis: East-West Press, 1981), 106; De Hartog, *Children*, 53, 67, 68–69, 166, 169; Marjorie Margolies, *They Came to Stay* (New York: Warner, 1976), 122, 132. I am grateful to Jooyeon Koo for bringing the Margolies memoir to my attention.

56. Margolies, *They Came to Stay*, 16, 68, 93, 155, 239; De Hartog, *Children*, 75, 154, 187.

57. Koh, *Oriental Children in American Homes*; Hyun Sook Han, *Understanding My Child's Korean Origins* (St. Paul: Children's Home Society of Minnesota, 1984).

58. Marjorie Kriz, "Flights of Compassion," *Chicago Tribune*, 29 Oct. 1972; Georgia Dullea, "For Korean Lepers' Children, It's America the Beautiful," *New York Times*, 4 Apr. 1977; Andy Burgio, "Our Baby," and Jim Bouton, "Why We Adopted an Interracial Child" [1971], both in *The Unbroken Circle: A Collection of Writings on Interracial and International Adoption*, ed. Betty Kramer (Minneapolis: Organization for a United Response, 1975), 63 and 95.

59. Compare this with a competing body of research, much of it produced by black and Native American social workers who advocated same-race placements, that claimed that transracial adoption damaged children of color. Jane Jeong Trenka, Julia Chinyere Oparah, and Sun Yung Shin, eds., *Outsiders Within: Writing on Transracial Adoption* (New York: South End Press, 2006), 4.

60. Some examples of these studies are Arnold R. Silverman, "Outcomes of Transracial Adoption," *Future of Children* 3, no. 1 (Spring 1993): 104–118; John E. Adams and Hyung Bok Kim, "A Fresh Look at Intercountry Adoptions," *Children* (Nov.–Dec. 1971): 214–221. For an overview of some of these studies, see Howard Altstein and Rita J. Simon, *Intercountry Adoption: A Multinational Perspective* (Westport, CT: Praeger, 1991); Richard M. Lee, "The Transracial Adoption Paradox: History, Research, and Counseling Implications of Cultural Socialization," *Counseling Psychologist* 31, no. 6 (Nov. 2003): 711–744.

Dong Soo Kim did not dissent from this consensus, but he was more critical, questioning what price adoptees were paying (in terms of cultural identity, for example) for their seemingly good adjustment. See Dong Soo Kim, "Intercountry Adoptions" (PhD diss., University of Chicago, 1976); Dong Soo Kim, "Issues in Transracial and Transcultural Adoption," *Social Casework* (Oct. 1978): 477–486;

Dong Soo Kim, "How They Fared in American Homes: A Follow-Up Study of Adopted Korean Children," *Children Today* 6, no. 2 (Mar.–Apr. 1977), 2–6.

61. Kim Park Nelson, "Korean Looks, American Eyes: Korean American Adoptees, Race, Culture and Nation" (PhD diss., University of Minnesota, 2009), 171.

62. Ibid.; Lee, "The Transracial Adoption Paradox."

63. "America Is All They Know, but They're Not Quite at Home," *New York Times*, 1 Mar. 1977.

64. For more on why the model minority stereotype attracted particular attention in the 1960 and 1980s, see Keith Osajima, "Asian Americans as the Model Minority: An Analysis of the Popular Press Image in the 1960s and 1980s," in *Contemporary Asian America*, ed. Min Zhou and James V. Gatewood (New York: New York University Press, 2000), 449–458. For the origins of the model minority stereotype, see Wu, *Color of Success*.

65. The past decade has witnessed an explosion in the number of academic studies and cultural works, particularly memoirs and films, about and by adult Korean adoptees. Some examples are Madelyn Freundlich and Joy Lieberthal, "The Gathering of the First Generation of Adult Korean Adoptees: Adoptees' Perceptions of International Adoption," June 2000, http://www.adoptioninstitute.org/proed/korfindings.html; Sook Wilkinson and Nancy Fox, eds., *After the Morning Calm: Reflections of Korean Adoptees* (Bloomfield Hills, MI: Sunrise Ventures, 2002); Trenka, Oparah, and Shin, *Outsiders Within*; Jo Rankin and Tonya Bishoff, eds., *Seeds from a Silent Tree: An Anthology by Korean Adoptees* (Glendale, CA: Pandal, 1997).

66. For an excellent ethnography of Korean adoptees, see Eleana Kim, *Adopted Territory: Transnational Korean Adoptees and the Politics of Belonging* (Durham, NC: Duke University Press, 2010).

67. Park Nelson, "Korean Looks, American Eyes," 267.

68. My discussion of the figure of the Korean orphan is limited only to the period under consideration and does not examine what she represented for Koreans or the Korean state, or Korean adoptees' own self-identification either as children or as adults. For explorations along these lines and in the contemporary period, see Kim, *Adopted Territory*; So Young Park, "Transnational Adoption, Hallyu and the Politics of Korean Popular Culture," *Biography* 33, no. 1 (Winter 2010): 151–166; Tobias Hubinette, *Comforting an Orphaned Nation: Representations of International Adoption and Adopted Koreans in Korean Popular Culture* (Seoul: Jimoondang, 2006). For a discussion of the construction of the "war orphan" before the Korean War, see Winslow, "Colorblind Empire," chapter 2.

69. Oh, "'A New Kind of Missionary Work"; Mark Jerng, *Claiming Others*. For discussion of the sentimental in Cold War American understandings of Asia,

see Klein, *Cold War Orientalism*. Laura Briggs provides an excellent analysis of the iconography of rescue in "Mother, Child, Race, Nation."

70. Lovelock, "Intercountry Adoption as Migratory Practice," 908; Sidney Talisman to Patricia Nye, 2 Feb. 1973, Box 34, Folder "Korea-Mr. Tahk's Visit, April, 1973," ISS records.

71. Kim, *Adopted Territory*, 73.

72. The phrase "put up for adoption" comes from the orphan trains of the late nineteenth and early twentieth century, which sent poor children from eastern cities to rural communities in the US West and Midwest. Upon arrival, the children were "put up" on platforms to be selected by a foster family. The child would live with the family and work for his or her keep. The most famous orphan train program was run by the Children's Aid Society, but other organizations also sent orphan trains west. The society's orphan trains moved about one hundred thousand children west between 1854 and 1929. For more on orphan trains, see Linda Gordon, *The Great Arizona Orphan Abduction* (Cambridge, MA: Harvard University Press, 2001).

73. Viviana A. Zelizer, *Pricing the Priceless Child: The Changing Social Value of Children* (Princeton, NJ: Princeton University Press, 1985), 11, 13, 15; Dubinsky, *Babies Without Borders*, 103.

74. Besides the United States, other receiving countries were France, Denmark, Sweden, Australia, and Norway. Korean Unwed Mothers Support Network and Korean Women's Development Institute, *Reviewing Issues on Unwed Mothers' Welfare in Korea: Intercountry Adoption, Related Statistics and Welfare Policies of Developed Countries* (Seoul: KUMSN, 2009), 22; Peggy Lindquist, "Letters to the Editor," *Progressive*, Apr. 1988, 6.

75. Judy Foreman, "Adopting from Foreign Countries," *Boston Globe*, 4 June 1981; Connie Lauerman, "Couples Take their Quest for Adoptions Worldwide," *Chicago Tribune*, 14 Jan. 1973; Diane Cole, "The Cost of Entering the Baby Chase," *New York Times*, 9 Aug. 1987.

76. See Karen Balcom, *The Traffic in Babies: Cross-Border Adoption and Baby-Selling Between the United States and Canada, 1930–1972* (Toronto: University of Toronto Press, 2011).

77. "Adoption Groups' Focus Changes to Other Nations," *Wall Street Journal*, 7 Jan. 1977; US Congress, House Committee on the Judiciary, *Alien Adopted Children: Hearing Before the Subcommittee on Immigration, Citizenship, and International Law*, 95th Cong., 1st sess. (15 June 1977), 47–50; Briggs, *Somebody's Children*; Richard H. Weil, "International Adoptions: The Quiet Migration," *International Migration Review* 18, no. 2 (Summer 1984): 276–293.

78. William R. Greer, "The Adoption Market: A Variety of Options," *New York Times*, 26 June 1986; Robert Lindsey, "Adoption Market: Big Demand,

Tight Supply," *New York Times*, 5 Apr. 1987; Cynthia Crossen, "Adopting Abroad: Battling Illness, Bureaucracy, Expenses and Racism," *Wall Street Journal*, 21 May 1985.

79. For more on the origins and development of international adoption from Vietnam, see Winslow, "Colorblind Empire," chapters 5–6; Allison Varzally, "Vietnamese Adoptions and the Politics of Atonement," *Adoption and Culture* 2 (2009): 159–201.

80. Australians, Canadians and parents of various European nationalities also adopted Vietnamese children both before and as a result of Operation Babylift.

81. US Congress, House Committee on the Judiciary, *Report of Special Study Subcommittee of the Committee on the Judiciary to Review Immigration, Refugee, and Nationality Problems*, (Washington, DC: GPO, 1973), 28; Senate Committee on the Judiciary, *Relief and Rehabilitation of War Victims in Indochina, Part II: Orphans and Child Welfare: Hearing Before the Subcommittee to Investigate Problems Connected with Refugees and Escapees*, 93rd Cong., 1st sess. (11 May 1973) (Washington: US GPO, 1973), 19, 87; Mary Kathleen Benet, *The Politics of Adoption* (New York: Free Press, 1976), 123–124, 130; Senate Committee on Foreign Relations, *Vietnam Children's Care Agency* [Hearing], 92nd Cong., 2nd sess., 5 Apr. 1972 (Washington, DC: GPO, 1972), 109–110, 113; Tarah Brookfield, "Maverick Mothers and Mercy Flights: Canada's Controversial Introduction to International Adoption," *Journal of the Canadian Historical Association* 19, no. 1 (2008): 315; Joshua Forkert, "Orphans of Vietnam: A History of Intercountry Adoption Policy and Practice in Australia, 1968–1975" (PhD diss., University of Adelaide, 2012), 92.

82. See Brookfield, "Maverick Mothers," for an account of Canadian adoptions from Vietnam, which she characterizes as a maternalist mission undertaken by "maverick mothers."

83. *Vietnam Children's Care Agency*; Memo to FILE from WRS, 17 July 1967, Box 10, Folder "Children—Independent Adoption Schemes. HOLT, Harry. 1960–1963 Vol. III," ISS records; *Adoption and Foster Care, 1975*, 11.

84. *Relief and Rehabilitation of War Victims in Indochina, Part II*, 33, 36. The figures conflict. At the end of 1973 a report by the special subcommittee stated that Americans adopted 85 children in 1971, and 367 in 1972, and estimated that they would adopt another 500 in 1973. *Report of Special Study Subcommittee*, 26.

85. *Alien Adopted Children*, 116; *Relief and Rehabilitation of War Victims in Indochina, Part II*, 92.

86. *Vietnam Children's Care Agency*, 109.

87. Gloria Emerson, "Operation Babylift," *New Republic*, 26 Apr. 1975; Agency for International Development, *Operation Babylift Report* (Washington, DC: Emergency Movement of Vietnamese and Cambodian Orphans for

Intercountry Adoption, Apr.–June 1975); Edward Zigler, "A Developmental Psychologist's Overview of Operation Babylift," *American Psychologist* 31, no. 5 (May 1976): 329–340; Forkert, "Orphans of Vietnam," chapter 6; Grace Paley, "Other People's Children," *Ms.*, Feb. 1976; Barbara M. Brown, "Comment: Operation Babylift and the Exigencies of War—Who Should Have Custody of 'Orphans'?" *Northern Kentucky Law Review* 7 (1980): 81–91; Susan Zeiger, *Entangling Alliances: Foreign War Brides and American Soldiers in the Twentieth Century* (New York: New York University Press, 2010), 231–234.

88. The class-action lawsuit, *Nguyen Da Yen v. Kissinger*, was filed in 1975. The plaintiffs, guardians who filed the suit on behalf of three airlifted Vietnamese siblings, argued that the children were being illegally detained by the INS in violation of their human rights and their rights under the Fifth Amendment (liberty and due process). The class-action suit was intended to slow down the frenzy to adopt Operation Babylift children by suspending all adoption proceedings until the courts could confirm that all the children were orphaned and available for adoption. As a result of the case, the INS was ordered to investigate the files of all the airlifted children, which led to the court's acknowledgment that not all of the children were orphans and not all had not been properly released into the custody of the adoption agencies that were trying to place them in American homes. Nonetheless, the case was dismissed as a class action in 1976. See Forkert, "Orphans of Vietnam"; Brown, "Comment: Operation Babylift."

89. Barbara Yngvesson, "Placing the 'Gift Child' in Transnational Adoption," *Law and Society Review* 36, no. 2 (2002): 233.

90. Julie Berebitsky, *Like Our Very Own: Adoption and the Changing Culture of Motherhood, 1851–1950* (Lawrence: University Press of Kansas, 2000); Herman, *Kinship by Design*; Zelizer, *Pricing the Priceless Child*, 11; Lovelock, "Intercountry Adoption as Migratory Practice," 908; Dorow, "Racialized Choices," 374.

91. Loey Werking Wells, "Bold Yellow in a Sky of Blue," in *More Voices: A Collection of Works from Asian Adoptees*, ed. Susan Soonkeum Cox (St. Paul, MN: Yeong & Yeong, 2011), 176; William Sluis, "All in a Day: Korean Tots See New Parents," *Chicago Tribune*, 6 July 1972; Park Nelson, "Korean Looks, American Eyes," 105; Kim, "Mothers Without Mothering," 145–147; Yngvesson, "Placing the 'Gift Child'"; Judith Modell, "Freely Given: Open Adoption and the Rhetoric of the Gift," in *Transformative Motherhood: On Giving and Getting in a Consumer Culture*, ed. Linda Layne (New York: New York University Press, 1999), 29–64; Rickie Solinger, *Beggars and Choosers: How the Politics of Choice Shapes Adoption, Abortion, and Welfare in the United States* (New York: Hill and Wang, 2002); Kit Myers, "Love and Violence in Transracial/National Adoption" (MA thesis, University of California, San Diego, 2009); Margolies, *They Came to Stay*, 67, 79.

92. John M. Kirkpatrick to ISS American Branch, 9 Dec. 1957, 2, Box 10, Folder "Holt, Harry, Vol. 1," ISS records; Mr. B to William Kirk, 14 Feb. 1961, Case 601276, ISS case files; Margaret Valk to Lucille Evers, 21 Sept. 1955, Case 38841, ISS case files; Lois McCarty to Carl Adams, 30 Aug. 1957, 3, Box 10, Folder "Holt, Harry, Vol. 1," ISS records; Margaret Valk to Elinor Westerfield, 11 July 1956, 3, Case 38332, ISS case files.

93. Koh, *Oriental Children in American Homes*, 104; Margolies, *They Came to Stay*; Megan Brown, "Yellow in the Bluegrass," in Cox, ed. *More Voices*, 70; Briggs, *Somebody's Children*, 120.

94. Solinger, *Beggars and Choosers*, 26–28; Register, *Are Those Kids Yours?*, 39; Judy McDermott, "Parents Share Experiences of Adoption," *Oregonian*, 20 Nov. 1976; De Hartog, *Children*, 233.

95. Ken Hartnett, "Decade of Despair for an Orphan," *Boston Globe*, 4 May 1975; Case 39176, ISS case files; Register, *Are Those Kids Yours?*; Koh, *Oriental Children in American Homes*, 18; Case 64815, ISS case files; Ursula Gallagher "Intercountry Adoptions," speech given 25 Mar. 1966 at Eastern Regional Conference of the CWLA, Box 1166, Folder "7-3-1-3 Non-resident problems (include juvenile immigration, transient boys), Oct. 67," RG 102, Archives II; Elsie Heller to Paul Cherney [July 1966], 4, Box 35, Folder "Korea: General 1966–67," ISS records.

96. Quoted in Register, *Are Those Kids Yours?*, 212; Solinger, *Beggars and Choosers*, 32.

97. Jacqueline Bhabha, "Moving Babies: Globalization, Markets and Transnational Adoption," *Fletcher Forum of World Affairs* 28, no. 2 (Summer 2004): 181–198; Patricia Nye to Audrey Moser, 3 Oct. 1969, 3, Box 35, Folder "Child Placement Service. General 1968–69," ISS records; Whitney Taejin Hwang, "Borderland Intimacies: GIs, Koreans, and American Military Landscapes in Cold War Korea" (PhD diss., University of California, 2010); *Alien Adopted Children*, 23.

98. Briggs, "Mother, Child, Race, Nation," 181.

99. Dubinsky, *Babies Without Borders*, 3, 14; Liisa Malkki has called children a "tranquilizing convention" that "depoliticize highly political contexts" (cited in Kim, *Adopted Territory*, 75).

CHAPTER 6

1. Peter Maass, "Adoptions: Korea's Disquieting Problem" *Washington Post*, 14 Dec. 1988.

2. Susan Chira, "U.S. Olympic Reporting Hits a Raw Korean Nerve," *New York Times*, 28 Sept. 1988; Bruce Cumings, *Korea's Place in the Sun* (New York: Norton, 1998), 333; Jinwung Kim, "Recent Anti-Americanism in South Korea: The Causes," *Asian Survey* 29, no. 8 (Aug. 1989): 743–763; Nancy K. Rivenburgh,

"National Image Richness in US-Televised Coverage of South Korea During the 1988 Olympics" *Asian Journal of Communication* 2, no. 2 (1992): 1–39.

3. Seungsook Moon, *Militarized Modernity and Gendered Citizenship in South Korea* (Durham, NC: Duke University Press, 2005); Edward S. Mason, Mahn Je Kim, Dwight H. Perkins, Kwang Suk Kim, and David C. Cole, *The Economic and Social Modernization of the Republic of Korea* (Cambridge, MA: Harvard University Press, 1980), 98.

4. Emerson Chapin, "Success Story in South Korea" *Foreign Affairs* 47 (Apr. 1969): 560–574; Mason et al., *Economic and Social Modernization*, 182; Tae-Gyun Park, "Change in U.S. Policy Toward South Korea in the Early 1960s," *Korean Studies* 23 (1999): 99, 102; Anne O. Krueger, *The Developmental Role of the Foreign Sector and Aid* (Cambridge, MA: Harvard University Press and Council on East Asian Studies, 1979), 12, 80; Hallam C. Shorrock Jr., *Is the Emergency Over? A Report About Korea and the Programs of Korea Church World Service During 1959* (Seoul: Korea Church World Service, 1960).

5. Homer Bigart, "New York Is Cited as a Baby Market," *New York Times*, 6 Jan. 1959; "Pearl Buck Upholds Adoptions by Proxy for Waifs in Korea," *New York Times*, 7 Jan. 1959; Paul R. Cherney, "Visit to Korea, June 23 to July 9, 1965," 20 July 1965, 4, Box 35, Folder "Korea: Child Placement Service, General. 1964–65," ISS Administrative Records, Social Welfare History Archive, University of Minnesota (hereafter "ISS records"); Ursula Gallagher, "Field Trip to Korea," [visit was 15–19 Nov. 1965], 4, Box 35, Folder "Korea: Child Placement Service, General. 1964–65," ISS records.

6. Virginia Baumgartner to Margaret Valk, 14 July 1958, Box 35, Folder "Korea Delegation. Manual—Adoption Law, 1953–60," ISS records; Sidney Talisman, "Report on Visit to Korea—June 24 to July 2, 1968," 1, Box 34, Folder "Korea—Administrative Correspondence," ISS records. A 1965 study indicates that poverty was the number-one reason behind child abandonment, cited in 53.4 percent of cases. Other reasons were: child's handicap (18.5 percent), family disorder (11.4 percent), parental neglect (6.7 percent), illegitimacy (5.5 percent), and the mother's work as a prostitute (4.5 percent). Dong Soo Kim, "From Women to Women with Painful Love: A Study of Maternal Motivation in Intercountry Adoption Process," in *Korean Women in a Struggle for Humanization*, ed. Harold Hakwon Sunoo and Dong Soo Kim (Memphis: Association of Korean Christian Scholars in North America, 1978), 120; Charles G. Chakerian, *From Rescue to Child Welfare* (New York: Child Immigration Services, Church World Service, 1968), 37.

7. LeRoy Bowman, Benjamin A. Gjenvick, and Eleanor T. M. Harvey, *Children of Tragedy: Church World Service Survey Team Report on Intercountry Orphan Adoption* (New York: Office of Publication and Distribution, National Council of the Churches of Christ in the USA, 1961), 28; Il SaKong, *Korea in the*

World Economy (Washington, DC: Institute for International Economics, 1993), 44; Byung Hyun Park, "The Development of Social Welfare Institutions in East Asia: Case Studies of Japan, Korea, and the People's Republic of China, 1945–1989" (PhD diss., University of Pennsylvania, 1990); Young Hee Won, "Hanguk ibyang j Ŏngchaeke gwanhan y Ŏngu: Junkaegwaj Ŏng meet munjej Ŏmeul joongshim Ŭlo" [A Study on Korean Adoption Policy: Focusing on Evolution and Problems] (MA thesis, Ewha University, 1990), 25.

8. Chakerian, *From Rescue to Child Welfare*, 36; Bum-Ju Whang, *50-Year History of Holt Children's Services, Inc.* (Seoul: Holt Children's Service, 2005), 120; Minsun Sung Whang, "An Exploratory Descriptive Study of Inter-Country Adoption of Korean Children with Known Parents" (PhD diss., University of Hawaii, 1976), 20; Talisman, "Report on Visit to Korea," 1; Richard H. Weil, "International Adoptions: The Quiet Migration," *International Migration Review* 18, no. 2 (Summer 1984): 282.

9. Soon Ho Park, "Forced Child Migration: Korea-Born Intercountry Adoptees in the United States" (PhD diss., University of Hawaii, 1994), 87–88; Rosemary C. Sarri, Penoak Baik, and Marti Bombyk, "Goal Displacement and Dependency in South Korean–United States Intercountry Adoption," *Children and Youth Services Review* 20, nos. 1–2 (1998): 87–114; Bowman, Gjenvick, and Harvey, *Children of Tragedy*, 23; Gallagher, "Field Trip to Korea," 5.

10. Cherney, "Visit to Korea, June 23 to July 9, 1965," 4, 10–12; Elsie Heller to Paul Cherney, [July 1966], 3, Box 35, Folder "Korea: General 1966–67," ISS records; Richard Baird, "Observations Regarding Korean Orphanages," Apr. 1961, Box 16, Folder 44, Record Group (RG) 140, Presbyterian Historical Society, Philadelphia, PA (hereafter "PHS"); Helen Miller, "Recent Developments in Korean Services for Children" *Children*, Jan.–Feb. 1971, 28.

11. Baird, "Observations Regarding Korean Orphanages"; Ralph Ten Have to Ursula Gallagher, 12 Aug. 1963, Box 1033, Folder "7-3-1-3 1963–1968 Non-Resident Problems (Include Juvenile Immigrant, Transient Boys," RG 102, National Archives, College Park, MD (hereafter "Archives II"); Sydney Byma, "Overseas Adoptions Threaten Development of Local Services," *Canadian Child Welfare News*, May–June 1974, 8; J. Calvitt Clarke to Harry Holt, 30 Apr. 1959, 1, Box 10, Folder "HOLT, Harry Vol. II," ISS records; Penny DeFore, *With All My Love* (Englewood Cliffs, NJ: Prentice-Hall, 1965).

12. "Memorandum on Discussions July 30, 1962 with Anne Davison," 2 Aug. 1962, Box 35, Folder "Korea Delegation. Manual—Adoption Law, 1953–60," ISS records; Bowman, Gjenvick and Harvey, *Children of Tragedy*, 27; Gallagher, "Field Trip to Korea," 4; Cherney, "Visit to Korea, June 23 to July 9, 1965"; Miller, "Recent Developments in Korean Services for Children," 28.

13. Mal-im Chung, "Thoughts of the Times," *Korea Times*, 3 Sept. 1966, quoted in Charles G. Chakerian, *Children of Hope* (New York: Church World

Service; Chicago: McCormick Theological Seminary, 1966), 23; Gallagher, "Field Trip to Korea," 12; Weil, "International Adoptions," 282; Kim, "From Women to Women," 120. Since the late 1970s laws and policies have encouraged birth parents to properly relinquish children rather than abandoning them. Park, "Forced Child Migration," 57, 81.

14. John Coventry Smith to Richard H. Baird, 13 Jan. 1959, Box 1, Folder 16, RG 197, PHS; Anne Davison to Althea Knickerbocker, 12 Dec. 1960, Case 591518, ISS Adoption Case Records, Social Welfare History Archive, University of Minnesota (hereafter "ISS case files"); "Sounds Note of Warning On Adoption of Koreans," *Kansas City Times*, 28 Nov. 1960, Box 34, Folder "Korea—Adoptions to 1962 Rejections—Non Policy," ISS records; Won, "A Study on Korean Adoption Policy," 21; Heller to Cherney, [July 1966]; Virginia Baumgartner to Margaret Valk, 17 July 1958, Case 38838, ISS case files; Margaret Valk to Mrs. B, 14 Mar. 1960, Case 60733, ISS case files; Davison, "Report of my visit to Mr. Harry Holt this afternoon," 30 Oct. 1961, enclosed with Anne Davison to Susan Pettiss, 30 Oct. 1961, Box 34, Folder "Korea—Adoptions to 1962 Rejections—Non Policy," ISS records.

15. Anne Davison to Samuel Moffett, 27 July 1961, 1–2, Box 2, Folder 1, RG 197, PHS.

16. Barbara Joe, "In Defense of Intercountry Adoption," *Social Service Review* 52, no. 1 (Mar. 1978): 9.

17. Kim, "From Women to Women"; Won, "A Study on Korean Adoption Policy," 27; Anne Davison, "ISS Korea: Report for 1 January–31 August, 1961," undated, Folder "Korea—Adoptions to '62," Box 34, ISS records; Whang, *50-Year History of Holt*, 195, 583; Davison, "ISS Korea: Report for 1 January–31 August, 1961"; Youn Taek Tahk to Patricia Nye, [stamped 13 Mar. 1968], 3, Box 35, Folder "Child Placement Service. General 1968–69," ISS records.

18. The Korean government revised the 1961 Extraordinary Adoption Law for Orphans in 1966 and again in 1976. Youn-Taek Tahk, "Intercountry Adoption Program in Korea: Policy, Law and Service," in *Adoption in Worldwide Perspective: A Review of Programs, Policies and Legislation in 14 Countries*, ed. R. A. C. Hoksbergen (Berwyn, PA: Swets North America, 1986), 80; Chin Kim and Timothy G. Carroll, "Intercountry Adoption of South Korean Orphans: A Lawyer's Guide," *Journal of Family Law* 14 (1975–1976): 230; Sarri, Baik, and Bombyk, "Goal Displacement," 94; Jane Jeong Trenka, "Transnational Adoption and the 'Financialization of Everything,'" *Conducive Chronicle*, Aug.–Sept. 2009, http://cchronicle .com/2009/11/transnational-adoption-and-the-%E2%80%9Cfinancialization-of -everything%E2%80%9D/.

19. Helen Miller, "Korea's International Children," *Lutheran Social Welfare*, Summer 1971, 21; Byung Hoon Chun, "Adoption and Korea," *Child Welfare*, Mar.–Apr. 1989, 258.

20. Hyun Sook Han, *Many Lives Intertwined* (St. Paul, MN: Yeong & Yeong, 2004), 117, 133; Chakerian, *From Rescue to Child Welfare*; Miller, "Korea's International Children."

21. Bowman, Gjenvick, and Harvey, *Children of Tragedy*, 25–26; Byma, "Overseas Adoptions"; Won Moo Hurh, "Marginal Children of War: An Exploratory Study of American-Korean Children," paper presented at joint meeting of Midwest and Ohio Valley Sociological Societies, 3 May 1969; Han, *Many Lives Intertwined*, 120, 133; Park, "Forced Child Migration," 115–116.

22. Won, "A Study on Korean Adoption Policy," 28–29; Whang, *50-Year History of Holt*; Chun, "Adoption and Korea," 256; Park, "Forced Child Migration," 20–21.

23. Matthew Rothschild, "Babies for Sale: South Koreans Make Them, Americans Buy Them" *Progressive* 52, no. 1 (1988): 18–23; Jonathan Dickens, "Social Policy Approaches to Intercountry Adoption," *International Social Work* 52, no. 2 (2009): 600–601; Sarri, Baik, and Bombyk, "Goal Displacement"; Patricia Nye to Audrey Moser (ISS HQ), 3 Oct. 1969, 2, Box 35, Folder "Child Placement Service. General 1968–69," ISS records; Byma, "Overseas Adoptions," 9; Chakerian, *From Rescue to Child Welfare*, 55; ISS worker quoted in Eleana Kim, *Adopted Territory: Transnational Korean Adoptees and the Politics of Belonging* (Durham, NC: Duke University Press, 2010), 75.

24. Youn Taek Tahk to Paul Cherney, 17 Nov. 1966, Box 35, Folder "Child Placement Service. General 1968–69," ISS records; Kim, *Adopted Territory*, 74.

25. Munro to Cherney, 31 Aug. 1965, 1, Box 35, Folder "Korea: Child Placement Service. General. 1964–1965," ISS records; Kim, *Adopted Territory*, 73; Kelsey Hye Sun March, "A Market for Children: The Rise of Modern Intercountry Adoption" (MA thesis, University of Washington, 2008).

26. Byma, "Overseas Adoptions," 9.

27. Edna Weber to Mrs. Michael Harris, 29 Aug. 1967, Box 35, Folder "Korea: General 1966–67," ISS records; "Corrections to Report of Visit by Paul R. Cherney," attached to Gardner Munro to Paul Cherney, 9 Aug. 1965, 3, Box 35, Folder "Korea: Child Placement Service. General. 1964–1965," ISS records; Heller to Cherney [July 1966], 3; Youn Taek Tahk to Patricia Nye, 26 Dec. 1967, Box 35, Folder "Child Placement Service. General 1968–69," ISS records; [Josephine Beard], "Conferences with Child Placement Service in Korea During the Period of Time Between April 11th and April 19, 1968," 2, Box 35, Folder "Report on Korea, Child Placement, 1968—Josephine Beard," ISS records.

28. Byma, "Overseas Adoptions," 9; Soon-Duck Ahn, "A Study of the Unwed Mother," *Women's Studies Forum* (31 Dec. 1986): 51 [unpaginated]; Helen Tieszen, "Changes in Services to Children," *Children*, Jan.–Feb. 1966, 28–30.

29. Hosu Kim, "Mothers Without Mothering: Birth Mothers from South Korea Since the Korean War," in *International Korean Adoption: A Fifty-Year*

History of Policy and Practice, ed. Kathleen Ja Sook Bergquist, M. Elizabeth Vonk, Dong Soo Kim, and Marvin D. Feit (New York: Haworth Press, 2007), 141.

30. What I call patriarchal nationalism has elsewhere been described as "androcentric nationalism" and "hypermasculine authoritarianism." Seungsook Moon, "Begetting the Nation: The Androcentric Discourse of National History and Tradition in South Korea," in *Dangerous Women: Gender and Korean Nationalism*, ed. Elaine Kim and Chungmoo Choi (New York: Routledge, 1998); Moon, *Militarized Modernity*; Jongwoo Han and L. H. M. Ling, "Authoritarianism in the Hypermasculinized State: Hybridity, Patriarchy, and Capitalism in Korea," *International Studies Quarterly* 42, no. 1 (Mar. 1998): 53–78.

31. Han and Ling, "Authoritarianism in the Hypermasculinized State," 65; Lee, "Industrialization and Women," 147; Moon, "Begetting the Nation," 57–58.

32. Hyaeweol Choi, "'Wise Mother, Good Wife': A Transcultural Discursive Construct in Modern Korea," *Journal of Korean Studies* 14, no. 1 (Fall 2009): 1–34; Moon, "Begetting the Nation," 41; Moon, *Militarized Modernity*, 83, 89; Chang Pilwha, "Talking About Sexuality," in *Women's Experiences and Feminist Practices in South Korea*, ed. Chang Pilwha and Kim Eun-shil (Seoul: Ewha Womans University Press, 2005), 119; Elaine Kim and Chungmoo Choi, "Introduction," in *Dangerous Women*, 5; Taek Il Kim and Nam Hoon Cho, "Republic of Korea," *Studies in Family Planning* 11, no. 11 (Nov. 1980): 326; Baik and Chung, "Family Policy in Korea." State-led family planning programs remained in place from the 1960s through the 1980s. By 1987, the average birthrate had fallen to 1.6 per woman. Kyung-Sup Chang, "Compressed Modernity and Its Discontents: South Korean Society in Transition," *Economy and Society* 28, no. 1 (1999): 33; In-Joung Whang, "Integration and Coordination of Population Policies in Korea," *Asian Survey* 14, no. 11 (Nov. 1974): 990; Kim, "The Cultural Logic of the Korean Modernization Project." For more on family planning, see John P. DiMoia, *Reconstructing Bodies: Biomedicine, Health, and Nation Building in South Korea Since 1945* (Stanford, CA: Stanford University Press, 2013).

33. Ruth Barraclough, *Factory Girl Literature: Sexuality, Violence, and Repression in Industrializing Korea* (Berkeley: University of California Press, 2012), 62, 68–69, 71–72, 110; Robert F. Spencer, *Yŏgong: Factory Girl* (Seoul: Royal Asiatic Society, Korea Branch, 1988); Eun-shil Kim, "The Cultural Logic of the Korean Modernization Project and Its Gender Politics," *Asian Journal of Women's Studies* 6, no. 2 (June 2000): 50 [unpaginated]; Seung-kyung Kim, "Productivity, Militancy, and Femininity: Gendered Images of South Korean Women Factory Workers," *Asian Journal of Women's Studies* 3, no. 3 (Sept. 1997): 8 [unpaginated]; Lee, "Industrialization and Women," 147; David I. Steinberg, *Foreign Aid and the Development of the Republic of Korea: The Effectiveness of Concessional Assistance* (Washington, DC: US Agency for International Development, 1985), 65; Cyn-

thia Enloe, *The Curious Feminist: Searching for Women in A New Age of Empire* (Berkeley: University of California Press, 2004), chapters 3–4.

34. Laurel Kendall, ed., *Under Construction: The Gendering of Modernity, Class, and Consumption in the Republic of Korea* (Honolulu: University of Hawaii Press, 2001); Kim, "Cultural Logic of the Korean Modernization Project"; Chang, "Compressed Modernity," 33–34.

35. Sarri, Baik, and Bombyk, "Goal Displacement," 94, 99; Seung-Kyung Kim, *Class Struggle or Family Struggle? The Lives of Women Factory Workers in South Korea* (Cambridge: Cambridge University Press, 2009), 71; Spencer, *Yŏgong*, 138–143; Ahn, "A Study of the Unwed Mother"; Jooyeon Koo, "In Whose Best Interest? American Adoption of Korean Children in the 1970s" (Scholar of the College project, Boston College, 2012); Han, *Many Lives Intertwined*, 128.

36. Kim Park Nelson, "Shopping for Children in the International Marketplace," 96 and Jae Ran Kim, "Scattered Seeds," in *Outsiders Within: Writing on Transracial Adoption*, ed. Jane Jeong Trenka, Julia Chinyere Oparah, and Sun Yung Shin (Cambridge, MA: South End Press, 2006); Anders Riel Muller, "Adoptee Justice Is About Social Justice," *Korea Times*, 9 Oct. 2012, http://www.koreatimes.co.kr/www/news/opinon/2012/10/137_121822.html; personal email from Anders Riel Muller, 13 Oct. 2012, in author's possession; Alice Amsden, *Asia's Next Giant: South Korea and Late Industrialization* (New York: Oxford University Press, 1989), 154; Jennifer Kwon Dobbs, "Ending South Korea's Child Export Shame," *Foreign Policy in Focus*, 23 June 2011, http://fpif.org/ending_south_koreas_child_export_shame/; SaKong, *Korea in the World Economy*, 226–227. Gross domestic product figures are from the US Economic Research Service (http://www.ers.usda.gov).

37. In-Jin Yoon, *The Social Origins of Korean Immigration to the United States from 1965 to the Present* (Honolulu: East-West Center, 1993), 31; Illsoo Kim, *New Urban Immigrants: The Korean Community in New York* (Princeton, NJ: Princeton University Press, 1981), 48, 52–54; Linda Mathews, "Despite Popularity, Cute Korean Babies Aren't for Export," *Wall Street Journal*, 7 Jan. 1977.

38. Han Hong-koo, "South Korea and the Vietnam War," in *Developmental Dictatorship and the Park Chung-Hee Era: The Shaping of Modernity in the Republic of Korea*, ed. Lee Byeong-Cheon (Paramus, NJ: Homa & Sekey, 2003), 248–270; Charles K. Armstrong, "Doubly Forgotten: Korea's Vietnam War and the Revival of Memory," in *Ruptured Histories: War, Memory, and the Post-Cold War in Asia*, ed. Sheila Miyoshi Jager and Rana Mitter (Cambridge, MA: Harvard University Press, 2007), 291–306.

39. Barraclough, *Factory Girl Literature*, 74. As Katharine Moon points out, Korea's "tradition of governmental utilization of women and their sexuality for political ends" dates back to the early Koryo dynasty (AD 918–1392). Moon, *Sex*

Among Allies: Military Prostitution in U.S.-Korea Relations (New York: Columbia University Press, 1997), 39.

40. In fact, the *kisaeng* sex workers, like factory girls, were sometimes referred to as "industrial soldiers." Barraclough, *Factory Girl Literature*, 72; Heisoo Shin, "Women's Sexual Services and Economic Development: The Political Economy of the Entertainment Industry and South Korean Dependent Development" (PhD diss., Rutgers University, 1991), 64–73.

41. Diana S. Lee and Grace Yoon Kyung Lee, *Camp Arirang* (San Francisco: National Asian American Telecommunications Association, NAATA, 1995), VHS; C. Sarah Soh, *The Comfort Women: Sexual Violence and Postcolonial Memory in Korea and Japan* (Chicago: University of Chicago Press, 2008), 221; Lee, *Service Economies*, 89; Han and Ling, "Authoritarianism in the Hypermasculinized State," 69. Camptowns were essential to earning foreign exchange for Korea and played a vital role in the country's economic ascent under Park. During their heyday in the 1960s, US troops' spending on women, alcohol, and entertainment contributed 25 percent of South Korea's gross national product. Moon, *Sex Among Allies*, 44; Lee, *Service Economies*, 126.

42. Whitney Taejin Hwang, "Borderland Intimacies: GIs, Koreans, and American Military Landscapes in Cold War Korea" (PhD diss., University of California, 2010), 135–136, 146; Mary Lee, "Mixed Race Peoples in the Korean National Imaginary and Family," *Korean Studies* 32 (2008): 56–85; Mildred Arnold to Mrs. Angle [no first name given], 1; Sveinung J. Moen, *The Amerasians: A Study and Research on Interracial Children in Korea* (Seoul: Taewon Publishing, 1974), 83; US Command Headquarters, US Forces Korea, EUSA, "Report—The Amerasian in Korea: Present Problems and Future Prospects," 1977 [in author's possession], 8, 10; Minutes, KAVA Social Welfare Committee Meeting, 15 Sept. 1965, Box 35, Folder "Non-ISS. Korea Social Service. Adoption and General 1965–1966," ISS records.

43. Hwang, "Borderland Intimacies," 127–128; Cherney, "Visit to Korea," 3, 15, ISS records; Gallagher, "Field Trip to Korea," 5, ISS records; Hi Taik Kim and Elaine Reid, "After a Long Journey: A Study on the Process of Initial Adjustment of the Half and Full Korean Children Adopted by American Families, and the Families' Experiences with These Children during the Transitional Period" (MA thesis, University of Minnesota, 1970); "Confucius' Outcasts," *Time*, 10 Dec. 1965; Sue-Je Lee Gage, "Pure Mixed Blood: The Multiple Identities of Amerasians in South Korea" (PhD diss., Indiana University, 2007), 96; J. Anthony Lukas, "A Legacy of the Korean War: Outcast Children," *New York Times*, 6 Feb. 1968; Richard Halloran, "Now-Grown Children of GIs in Korea Are Bitter," *New York Times*, 2 June 1976; Kenneth Paik, "Korean War 'Half-Breeds' Victims of Bias," *Chicago Tribune*, 13 Mar. 1977; John Shade, *America's Forgotten Children: The*

Amerasians (Perkasie, PA: Pearl S. Buck Foundation, 1982), 27; Moen, *Amerasians*, 68; Moon, *Sex Among Allies*, 30; John Lie, "The Transformation of Sexual Work in 20th Century Korea," *Gender and Society* 9, no. 3 (June 1995): 310–327; American Embassy, Seoul to Department of State, Washington, DC, Despatch, 11 July 1959, 7, Box 699, RG 59, Archives II; Susan Zeiger, *Entangling Alliances: Foreign War Brides and American Soldiers in the Twentieth Century* (New York: New York University Press, 2010), 211; Bok-Lim C. Kim, "Asian Wives of U.S. Servicemen: Women in Shadows," *Amerasia Journal* 4, no. 1 (1977): 91–115.

44. James L. Pullman to Advisory Board of Eclair Program, 25 Jan. 1968, Box 35, Folder "Child Placement Service. General 1968–69," ISS records; George P. Whitener to "Dear Friends," 26 Feb. 1964, Box 35, Folder "Korea: Child Placement Service, General. 1964–65," ISS records; Cherney, "Visit to Korea," 9; Youn Taek Tahk to Walter Sherman, 11 Nov. 1966, Box 35, Folder "Korea: General 1966–67," ISS records; Talisman, "Report on Visit to Korea"; Mrs. [Elizabeth] Hayes to Mr. Oliver [no first name given], 17 Feb. 1966, Box 35, Folder "Non-ISS. Korea Social Service. Adoption and General 1965–1966," ISS records; Minutes, KAVA Social Welfare Committee Meeting, 15 Sept. 1965, Box 35, Folder "Non-ISS. Korea Social Service. Adoption and General 1965–1966," ISS records; Minutes, KAVA Social Welfare Committee Meeting, 15 Dec. 1965, Box 35, Folder "Non-ISS. Korea Social Service. Adoption and General 1965–1966," ISS records; Minutes, KAVA Social Welfare Committee Meeting, 19 Jan. 1966, Box 35, Folder "Non-ISS. Korea Social Service. Adoption and General 1965–1966," ISS records; Gage, "Pure Mixed Blood," 92–3; "Magazines: Crumbling Foundation" *Time*, 25 July 1969; "Pearl Buck Aide Quits Under Fire," *New York Times*, 10 July 1969; Kim and Reid, "After a Long Journey," 45; US Command Headquarters, "Amerasian in Korea," 16–17.

45. Hwang, "Borderland Intimacies," 127–128; Susanna McBee, Walter A. Taylor, and Robert Kaylor, "The Amerasians: Tragic Legacy of Our Far East Wars," *US News and World Report*, 7 May 1984, 49; Soon Ho Park, "Spatial Distribution of Korea-Born Adoptees in the United States," *Journal of the Korean Geographic Society* 30, no. 4 (1995): 82.

46. Kim, *Adopted Territory*, 72–73, 277; Miller, "Korea's International Children," 19; Chakerian, *From Rescue to Child Welfare*, 40–41; Kim and Reid, "After a Long Journey," 44–5; Youn Taek Tahk to Charles G. Chakerian [1968], Box 35, Folder "Child Placement Service. General 1968–69," ISS records; Walter R. Sherman to Patricia Nye, 2; ISS Korea to Pettiss ISS AB, 10 July 1964, Case 631324, ISS case files.

47. Hwang, "Borderland Intimacies," 129; Kori Graves, "Domesticating Foreign Affairs: The African-American Family, Korean War Orphans, and Cold War Civil Rights" (PhD diss., University of Wisconsin–Madison, 2011), 224, 229.

48. Halloran, "Now-Grown Children of GIs"; Hurh, "Marginal Children of War," 18; Moen, *Amerasians*; "Confucius' Outcasts"; Paik, "Korean War 'Half-Breeds' Victims of Bias"; Lee, "Mixed Race Peoples," 75; Insook Kwon, "Militarism in My Heart: Militarization of Women's Consciousness and Culture in South Korea" (PhD diss., Clark University, 2000), 264; Margo Okazawa-Rey, "Amerasian Children of GI Town: A Legacy of U.S. Militarism in South Korea," *Asian Journal of Women's Studies* 3 (1997): 86–87. Yuri Doolan notes that although the military law was revised in 2005 to allow mixed-race men to serve, it still excludes those with "prominent mixed-race . . . appearance." Doolan, "Being Amerasian in South Korea: Purebloodedness, Multiculturalism, and Living Alongside the U.S. Military Empire" (Honors thesis, Ohio State University, 2012), 62.

49. In a 1961 survey of "handicapped" children, the complete list of ailments included "paralytic or palsied, deaf and dumb, amputees, deaf only, blind in one eye, hunchback, severe stuttering, totally blind, severe harelip or cleft palate, feeble-minded, epileptic, partially blind, psychotic, club foot, children of mixed racial parentage." Children's Survey Subcommittee, Korea Child Welfare Committee, *Handicapped Children's Survey Report, Korea, 1961*, [Seoul], 98–99.

50. Werner Sollors, *Black-White Intermarriage in American History, Literature, and Law* (New York: Oxford University Press, 2000); Donald Bogle, *Toms, Coons, Mulattoes, Mammies, and Bucks: An Interpretive History of Blacks in American Films* (London: Bloomsbury Academic, 2001); Lee, "Mixed Race Peoples," 60; Paik, "Korean War 'Half-Breeds' Victims of Bias"; Kim and Reid, "After a Long Journey," 37–40; Kim, "From Women to Women," 139, 141; William R. Burkhardt, "Institutional Barriers, Marginality, and Adaptation Among the American-Japanese Mixed Bloods in Japan," *Journal of Asian Studies* 42, no. 3 (May 1983): 519–544; Hurh, "Marginal Children of War"; Moen, *Amerasians*; US Senate, Committee on the Judiciary, *Amerasian Immigration Proposals: Hearing Before the Subcommittee on Immigration and Refugee Policy*, 97th Cong., 2nd sess., 21 June 1982 (Washington, DC: GPO, 1982), 52. For testimony from Korean Amerasians, see pages 47–55. See also testimony on Amerasians in US House Committee on the Judiciary, *Immigration Reform: Hearings Before the Subcommittee on Immigration, Refugees, and International Law*, 97th Cong., 1st sess., 14, 15, 21, 26, 28 Oct. and 12, 17, and 19 Nov. 1981 (Washington, DC: GPO, 1982), 897–934.

51. Hwang, "Borderland Intimacies," 136–138; Whitney Taejin Hwang, "The 'Amerasian' Knot: Transpacific Crossings of 'GI Babies' from Korea to the United States," in *Race and Racism in Modern East Asia: Interactions, Nationalism, Gender and Lineage*, ed. Rotem Kowner and Walter Demel (Leiden, Netherlands: Brill, 2012); "The Amerasian in Korea"; Shade, *America's Forgotten Children*, 1, 15; Jana K. Lipman, "'The Face Is the Road Map': Vietnamese Americans in U.S.

Political and Popular Culture, 1980–1988," *Journal of Asian American Studies* 14, no. 1 (Feb. 2011): 38; Su-Je Le Gage, "The Amerasian Problem: Blood, Duty, and Race," *International Relations* 21, no. 1 (2007): 86–102; Zeiger, *Entangling Alliances*, 233. In 1981 an estimated 170,000 Amerasian children lived in the Philippines, Japan, Korea, Taiwan, Vietnam, Laos, and Thailand. Burkhardt, "Institutional Barriers, Marginality, and Adaptation," 540. Amerasians in the Philippines and Japan (including Okinawa) do not benefit from the Amerasian immigration acts. Marilyn T. Trautfield, "America's Responsibility to Amerasian Children: Too Little, Too Late," *Brooklyn Journal of International Law* 10 (1984): 75; Joseph M. Ahern, "Out of Sight, out of Mind: United States Immigration Law and Policy as Applied to Filipino-Amerasians," *Pacific Rim Law and Policy Association* 1, no. 1 (1992): 105–126.

52. Lipman, "Face Is the Road Map," 42; Hwang, "Borderland Intimacies," 146; Susan Jeffords, *The Remasculinization of America: Gender and the Vietnam War* (Bloomington: Indiana University Press, 1989).

53. Rothschild, "Babies for Sale," 21–22; Nam Soon Huh, "Services for Out-of-Wedlock Children in Korea," *Early Child Development and Care* 85 (1993): 42; "Adoption Agencies Under Fire for Excessive Competition," *Korea Herald*, 29 Sept. 1989.

54. Jane Jeong Trenka, "Adoption Agencies Claim Constitutional 'Right' to Own/Operate Mother Homes," 13 Jan. 2014, *TRACK*, http://www.adoptionjustice.com/adoption-agencies-claim-constitutional-right-ownoperate-unwed-mother-homes/; Korean National Assembly, "Audit of Adoption Agencies" (20 Nov. 2008) [in author's possession]; Office of Audit and Inspection, Ministry of Health and Welfare, "Action Report," June 2014, *TRACK*, http://www.adoptionjustice.com/ministry-health-welfare-audit-holt/.

55. Anne Davison to Samuel Moffett, 27 July 1961, 1–2, Box 2, Folder 1, RG 197, PHS; Byma, "Overseas Adoptions," 9; Bowman, Gjenvick, and Harvey, *Children of Tragedy*, 12; Whang, "Exploratory Descriptive Study," 98; Kim, "From Women to Women," 155.

56. Betty Jean Lifton, "Needed: More Than Love and Patience," *New York Times*, 29 Feb. 1976.

57. Robert Shaplen, "Letter from South Korea," *New Yorker*, 17 Nov. 1980; Howard Sochurek, "South Korea: Success Story in Asia," *National Geographic*, Mar. 1969, 301–345; Emerson Chapin, "Success Story in South Korea," *Foreign Affairs* 47 (1968–1969): 560–574; "South Korea 'Takes Off'—An Asian Success Story," *U.S. News and World Report*, 31 Oct. 1966.

58. Hurh, "Marginal Children of War," 21; Sang Mok Suh, "Effects of the Current World Recession on the Welfare of Children: The Case of Korea," *World Development* 12, no. 3 (1984): 335.

59. Sarri, Baik, and Bombyk, "Goal Displacement," 101, 104; Baik and Chung, "Family Policy in Korea," 104–105; Chang, "Compressed Modernity"; Young Jong Kim, "The Impact of Industrialization and Other Social Changes on the Development of Social Welfare Institution in South Korea" (PhD diss., University of Texas, 1989); Huck-Ju Kwon and Icheong Yi, "Development Strategies, Welfare Regime and Poverty Reduction in the Republic of Korea" (Geneva: UN Research Institute for Social Development, 2008).

60. Tahk, "Intercountry Adoption Program in Korea" 90; Patricia Nye to Audrey Moser, 3 Oct. 1969, 2, Box 35, Folder "Child Placement Service. General 1968–69," ISS records; Ursula Gallagher "Intercountry Adoptions," speech given 25 Mar. 1966 at Eastern Regional Conference of the CWLA, Box 1166, Folder "7-3-1-3 Non-Resident Problems (Include Juvenile Immigration, Transient Boys), Oct. 67," RG 102, Archives II; Ursula Gallagher to Mildred Arnold, 13 Nov. 1967, Box 1166, Folder "7-3-1-3 October '67 Non-Resident Problems (Include Juvenile)," RG 102, Archives II; Chakerian, *From Rescue to Child Welfare*, 50, 70; Graves, "Domesticating Foreign Affairs," 234; Gardner Munro to Edna Weber, 11 Dec. 1965, 2, Box 35, Folder "Korea: Child Placement Service. General. 1964–1965," ISS records; "The Kava Resolution on Children with Racially Mixed Parentage, Adopted on January 22, 1964" [Jan. 1964], Box 35, Folder "Korea: Child Placement Service. General. 1964–1965," ISS records.

61. The Korean government attempted to end its adoption program in Europe in 1974 but resumed it because of high demand. Park, "Forced Child Migration," 52. Korea temporarily suspended adoption to Sweden, Norway, Denmark, the Netherlands, Belgium and Canada several times between 1950 and 1975. Hubinette, "Korean Adoption History," in *Community 2004: Guide to Korea for Overseas Adopted Koreans*, ed. Eleana Kim (Seoul: Overseas Koreans Foundation, 2004), 9; Won, "A Study on Korean Adoption Policy," 31–32.

62. Byma, "Overseas Adoptions," 9; Chun, "Adoption and Korea," 257.

63. Park, "Forced Child Migration," 57; Huh, "Services for Out-of-Wedlock Children," 39.

64. Hosu Kim, "The Biopolitics of Transnational Adoption in South Korea: Preemption and the Governance of Single Birthmothers," *Body and Society* 20, no. 2 (2014): 2, 24n6; Korean Family Preservation Network, "Monitoring South Korean Intercountry and Domestic Adoption from a Human Rights Perspective: Joint Submission to the United Nations Periodical Review, Republic of Korea, Second Cycle, 14th session," Apr. 2012, 15–16.

65. Huh, "Services for Out-of-Wedlock Children," 37, 40, 44; Sang-Hun Choe, "Group Resists Korean Stigma for Unwed Mothers," *New York Times*, 7 Oct. 2009; "Korea's Lost Children" *BBC World Service*, 6 Aug. 2010, http://

www|.bbc.co.uk/worldservice/documentaries/2010/08/100806_koreas_lost_children.shtml; Huh, "Services for Out-of-Wedlock Children," 40–41.

66. "Accuse Korea of Selling Orphans," *Chicago Defender*, 26 Jan. 1959; Korean Central News Agency (KCNA), "Unwanted ROK Citizens Sold Into Slavery," 24 Jan. 1959; KCNA, "ROK Orphan Brokers," 21 June 1960; KCNA, "ROK Sells 100 Orphans to U.S. Slaver," 10 Jan. 1961; Mary Kathleen Benet, *The Politics of Adoption* (New York: Free Press, 1976), 131–132; Park, "Forced Child Migration"; Tobias Hubinette, "Comforting an Orphaned Nation" (PhD diss., Stockholm University, 2005), 70–71; Andrew H. Malcolm, "South Korea Seeks to End Flow of Orphans to Families Abroad," *New York Times*, 10 Aug. 1977; Sarri, Baik, and Bombyk, "Goal Displacement," 95; Tahk, "Intercountry Adoption Program in Korea," 83.

67. Sarri, Baik, and Bombyk, "Goal Displacement," 95; "S. Korea Seeking to Increase Domestic Adoptions," *Asahi Shimbun*, 27 Nov. 2011; Hollee McGinnis, "South Korea and Its Children," *New York Times*, 27 Nov. 2007; Norimitsu Onishi, "Korea Aims to End Stigma of Adoption and Stop 'Exporting' Babies," *New York Times*, 8 Oct. 2008; Tae-jong Kim, "Adoption Quota Causes Backlash," *Korea Times*, 6 May 2011.

68. In 2003, the top five countries sending children to the United States for adoption (and their income per capita in US dollars) were, in order, China (income per capita of $1,100); Russia ($2,610); Guatemala ($1,910); South Korea ($12,030); and Ukraine ($970). Peter Selman, "Trends in Intercountry Adoption: Analysis of Data from 20 Receiving Countries, 1998–2004," *Journal of Population Research* 23, no. 2 (Sept. 2006): 198.

69. OECD, "OECD Economic Surveys: Korea" (Apr. 2012), http://www.oecd.org/eco/50191444.pdf; OECD, "Public and Private Social Expenditure in Percentage of GDP in 2009," OECD Social Expenditure Database (SOCX) via http://www.oecd.org/social/expenditure.htm; "Korea's Spending on Child Welfare Among Lowest in OECD," *Korea Herald*, 24 Sept. 2013, http://www.koreaherald.com/view.php?ud=20130924000605; Dobbs, "Ending South Korea's Child Export Shame"; Hyo-sik Lee, "Korea Next to Last in Social Welfare Spending," *Korea Times*, 12 Feb. 2010.

70. Ben Hancock, "Single Moms: In South Korea, Adoption Remains Priority, but Attitudes Are Shifting," *Christian Science Monitor*, 25 Nov. 2009, http://www.csmonitor.com/World/Asia-Pacific/2009/1125/p09s09-woap.html.

71. International adoption agencies operated seventeen of twenty-five maternity homes in 2007. ShinWoo Kang, trans., "Holt International's Price for Children," *Hankyoreh*, 24 July 2009, http://english.hani.co.kr/arti/english_edition/e_national/367606.html; Kim, "Biopolitics of Transnational Adoption";

Mijeong Lee, "Current Situations of Maternity Facilities for Unwed Mothers," *KUMSN*, 5 Nov. 2012, http://www.kumsn.org/main/22422.

72. "Promoting Adoptions," *Korea Times*, 5 May 2011, http://www.koreatimes.co.kr/www/news/opinon/2011/05/137_86824.html; "Stigma of Baby 'Exporter'" [editorial], *Korea Times*, 24 Nov. 2011, http://www.koreatimes.co.kr/www/news/opinon/2011/11/202_99479.html; KUMSN and KWDI, *Reviewing Issues on Unwed Mothers' Welfare in Korea: Intercountry Adoption, Related Statistics, and Welfare Policies in Developed Countries* (Seoul: 2009), vi.

73. Jane Jeong Trenka, "Abuses in Adoptions from South Korea," *Conducive Chronicle*, 6 Nov. 2009, http://cchronicle.com/2009/11/abuses-in-adoptions-from-s-korea/; Dobbs, "Ending South Korea's Child Export Shame"; "Toby Dawson: Lost and Found," *World of Freesports*, episode 22–23 (Jalbert Productions, 2011), video; Tammy Chu, *Resilience*, 2009, DVD; Deann Borshay Liem, *First Person Plural* (San Francisco: NAATA, 2000), DVD; *Baby Exporting Nation: The Two Faces of Inter-Country Adoption*, prod. Lee Gyun Hup (Seoul: KBS, 2005). The 2012 Special Adoption Law instituted a seven-day deliberation period during which a birth mother can change her mind about relinquishment. The government has found that at least one agency (Holt) has violated this provision. Office of Audit and Inspection, Ministry of Health and Welfare, "Action Report."

74. See, for example, Wilfred Chan, "Raised in America, Activists Lead Fight to End S. Korean Adoptions," *CNN*, 16 Sept. 2013, http://www.cnn.com/2013/09/16/world/international-adoption-korea-adoptee-advocates/. For more on searches and reunions, see Elise Prebin, *Meeting Once More: The Korean Side of Transnational Adoption* (New York: New York University Press, 2013); Leading adoption reform and family preservation organizations include Truth and Reconciliation for the Adoption Community of Korea (TRACK) and Korean Unwed Mothers Families' Association (KUMFA). See Jane Jeong Trenka, "The 2011 Amendment to the Special Adoption Law: A One-Year Evaluation" (MA thesis, Seoul National University, 2014); Shannon Doona Heit, "Diasporic Articulations and the Transformative Power of Haunting: Returning Adoptees' Solidarity Movement with Unwed Mothers in Korea" (MA thesis, Hanyang University, 2013).

75. Trenka, "Abuses in Adoptions from South Korea"; Su-ji Park, "Number of South Korean Children Adopted Drops by Half," *Hankyoreh*, 12 May 2014, http://english.hani.co.kr/arti/english_edition/e_national/636562.html; Claire Lee, "'As Families Evolve, So Should Policies,'" *Korea Herald*, 30 May 2014, http://www.koreaherald.com/view.php?ud=20140530001483.

76. KBS, *Baby Exporting Nation*.

77. Bureau of Consular Affairs, Department of State, "Intercountry Adoption—south Korea" last updated Jan. 2012, http://adoption.state.gov/country

_information/country_specific_info.php?country-select=south_korea; KUMSN and KWDI, *Reviewing Issues on Unwed Mothers' Welfare in Korea*; Park, "Number of South Korean Children Adopted Drops by Half"; Jennifer Ludden and Marisa Penazola, "Would-Be Parents Wait as Foreign Adoptions Plunge," National Public Radio, 7 Aug. 2012, http://www.npr.org/2012/08/07/157844554/would-be-parents-wait-as-foreign-adoptions-plunge.

78. Mary Deborah Lee, "Reading Race: Postcolonial Nationalism in Korea" (PhD diss., University of Hawaii, 2012); Timothy Lim, "Who Is Korean? Migration, Immigration, and the Challenge of Multiculturalism in Homogeneous Societies," *Asia-Pacific Journal* 27 July 2009, http://japanfocus.org/-timothy-lim/3192.

79. The term *Kosian* is controversial but has caught on in popular usage much more than alternate, preferred language. Lee, "Reading Race," 77; Akli Hadid, "South Korea Redefines Multiculturalism," *Diplomat*, 18 July 2014, http://the diplomat.com/2014/07/korea-redefines-multiculturalism/.

CONCLUSION

1. Louise Erdrich, quoted in Leslie Kaufman, "Novel About Racial Injustice Wins National Book Award," *New York Times*, 14 Nov. 2012, http://www.nytimes.com/2012/11/15/us/louise-erdrichs-novel-the-round-house-wins-national-book-award.html.

2. Anne Davison to Samuel Moffett, 27 July 1961, Box 2, Folder 1, RG 197, Presbyterian Historical Society, Philadelphia, PA.

3. Laura Briggs, *Somebody's Children: The Politics of Transracial and Transnational Adoption* (Durham, NC: Duke University Press, 2012), 235.

4. Julie Berebitsky, *Like Our Very Own: Adoption and the Changing Culture of Motherhood, 1851–1950* (Lawrence: University Press of Kansas, 2000), 4–7; David L. Eng, "Transnational Adoption and Queer Diasporas," *Social Text* 21, no. 3 (Autumn 2003): 8, 5; Ann Anagnost, "Scenes of Misrecognition: Maternal Citizenship in the Age of Transnational Adoption," *positions* 8, no. 2 (Fall 2000): 389; Laura Briggs, "Making 'American' Families: Transnational Adoption and U.S. Latin America Policy," in *Haunted by Empire: Geographies of Intimacy in North American History*, ed. Ann Laura Stoler (Durham, NC: Duke University Press, 2006), 619, 638.

5. Megan Twohey, "The Child Exchange: Inside America's Underground Market for Adopted Children" [5-part series], *Reuters Investigates*, 9–11 Sept. 2013, http://www.reuters.com/investigates/adoption/#article/part1.

6. Eng, "Transnational Adoption and Queer Diasporas"; Kim Park Nelson, "Shopping for Children in the International Marketplace," in *Outsiders Within: Writing on Transracial Adoption*, ed. Jane Jeong Trenka, Julia Chinyere Oparah, and Sun Yung Shin (New York: South End Press, 2006); Kristi Brian, *Reframing*

Transracial Adoption: Adopted Koreans, White Parents, and the Politics of Kinship (Philadelphia: Temple University Press, 2012).

7. See, for example, David Smolin, "Intercountry Adoption and Poverty: A Human Rights Analysis," *Capital University Law Review* 36 (2007): 413–453; David Smolin, "Intercountry Adoption as Child Trafficking" *Valparaiso University Law Review* 39, no. 2 (Winter 2004): 281–325; Tobias Hubinette, "A Critique of Intercountry Adoption" *Transracial Abductees*, http://www.transracialabductees.org/politics/samdolcritique.html.

8. Claudia Sadowski-Smith, "Neoliberalism, Global 'Whiteness,' and the Desire for Adoptive Invisibility in US Parental Memoirs of Eastern European Adoption," *Journal of Transnational American Studies* 3, no. 2 (2011): 12.

9. E. J. Graff, "The Lie We Love," *Foreign Policy*, Nov.–Dec. 2008, http://www.foreignpolicy.com/story/cms.php?story_id=4508&print=1.

10. Kathryn Joyce, *The Child Catchers: Rescue, Trafficking, and the New Gospel of Adoption* (New York: PublicAffairs, 2013).

11. Rickie Solinger, *Beggars and Choosers: How the Politics of Choice Shapes Adoption, Abortion, and Welfare in the United States* (New York: Hill and Wang, 2002), 32.

12. Thomas Holt, "Marking: Race, Race-Making and the Writing of History," *American Historical Review* 100, no. 1 (Feb. 1995): 10.

Select Bibliography

ARCHIVAL SOURCES
Center for Migration Studies, Staten Island, NY
    National Catholic Welfare Conference, Department of Immigration Records
    US Catholic Conference, Bureau of Immigration Records
George Drake Personal Collection (in author's possession)
John F. Kennedy Library, Boston
    Pre-presidential Papers
Presbyterian Historical Society, Philadelphia
    National Council of the Churches of Christ in the United States of America—Division of Overseas Ministries Records, Record Group 8
    United Presbyterian Church in the USA Commission on Ecumenical Mission and Relations. Secretaries Files: Korea Mission, 1903–1972, Record Group 140
    Presbyterian Church in the USA Korea Mission. Records, 1940–1982, Record Group 197
    Korea Mission Records, 1896–1986 (formerly housed at Presbyterian Historical Society—Montreat, Montreat, NC)
Social Welfare History Archives, University of Minnesota, Minneapolis
    International Social Service, Administrative Records
    International Social Service, Adoption Case Files
US National Archives and Records Administration
    Dwight D. Eisenhower Library, Abilene, KS
    US Army, Command Reports, Record Group 407, College Park, MD
    US Army, Eighth U.S. Army, Record Group 338, College Park, MD

US Army, Far East Command, Record Group 554, College Park, MD
US Army, Office of the Army Staff, Record Group 319, College Park, MD
US Army, Secretary of the Army, Record Group 335, College Park, MD
US Army, Records of US Army Operational, Tactical and Support Organizations, Record Group 338, College Park, MD
US Children's Bureau, Record Group 102, College Park, MD
US Congress, Senate, Record Group 46, Washington, DC
US Department of Justice, Record Group 85, Washington, DC
US Department of State, Record Group 59, College Park, MD
US Department of State, Foreign Posts, Record Group 84, College Park, MD
US Department of State, Records of US Foreign Assistance Agencies, Record Group 469, College Park, MD

University of Oregon Libraries, Special Collections and University Archives, Eugene
Richard Neuberger Papers

Yonsei University, Seoul
Syngman Rhee Papers

INTERVIEWS AND ORAL HISTORIES

Adult Adoptees: MH, JM, DN, TC, LC, BW, LK, RW, LP. All interviews by the author.

Han, Hyun Sook. Interview by the author, 16 June 2007, Minneapolis.

Holt, Bertha. Interview by Jim Strassmaier, 17 Nov. 1992, Oregon Historical Society, Portland.

Holt, Molly. Interview by the author, 11 Apr. 2007, Seoul.

GOVERNMENT SERIAL PUBLICATIONS

Congressional Record
Department of State Bulletin
I&N Reporter

UNPUBLISHED GOVERNMENT DOCUMENTS

US Congress. Senate. Committee on the Judiciary. "Relating to General Immigration Matters." Hearing before 86th Congress, 1st sess. 20 May 1959.

UNPUBLISHED THESES AND MANUSCRIPTS

"Attitudes of Negro Professional and Business Men Toward Adoption." Vol. 1. Student reports submitted to the School of Social Work in partial fulfillment of the requirements for the degree of master of social service, June 1960, University of Buffalo School of Social Work.

Davis, Michael Gill. "The Cold War, Refugees, and U.S. Immigration Policy." PhD diss., Vanderbilt University, 1996.

Didier, Sydne. "'Just a Drop in the Bucket': An Analysis of Child Rescue Efforts on Behalf of Korean Children, 1951 to 1964." Master's thesis, Portland State University, 1998.

Doolan, Yuri W. "Being Amerasian in South Korea: Purebloodness, Multiculturalism, and Living Alongside the U.S. Military Empire." Honors thesis, Ohio State University, 2012.

Fieldston, Sara Michel. "Bringing Up the World's Boys and Girls: American Child Welfare and Global Politics, 1945–1979." PhD diss., Yale University, 2013.

Fish, Robert A. "The Heiress and the Love Children: Sawada Miki and the Elizabeth Saunders Home for Mixed-Blood Orphans in Postwar Japan." PhD diss., University of Hawaii, 2002.

Forkert, Joshua. "Orphans of Vietnam: A History of Intercountry Adoption Policy and Practice in Australia, 1968–1975." PhD diss., University of Adelaide, 2012.

Gage, Su-Je Lee. "Pure Mixed Blood: The Multiple Identities of Amerasians in South Korea." PhD diss., Indiana University, 2007.

Graves, Kori. "Domesticating Foreign Affairs: The African-American Family, Korean War Orphans, and Cold War Civil Rights." PhD diss., University of Wisconsin–Madison, 2011.

Heit, Shannon Doona. "Diasporic Articulations and the Transformative Power of Haunting: Returning Adoptees' Solidarity Movement with Unwed Mothers in Korea." Master's thesis, Hanyang University, 2013.

Hoover, Nannie C. "Study of Inter-Country Placement of Oriental Children in Indiana from January 1956 to May 1960." Master's thesis, Indiana University, 1961.

Hubinette, Tobias. "Comforting an Orphaned Nation: Representations of International Adoption and Adopted Koreans in Korean Popular Culture." PhD diss., Stockholm University, 2005.

Hwang, Whitney Taejin. "Borderland Intimacies: GIs, Koreans, and American Military Landscapes in Cold War Korea." PhD diss., University of California, Berkeley, 2010.

Kim, Dong Soo. "Intercountry Adoptions." PhD diss., University of Chicago, 1976.

Kim, Hannah. "Ties That Bind: People, Policy, and Perception in US-Korean Relations." PhD diss., University of Delaware, 2011.

Kim, Hi Taik, and Elaine Reid. "After a Long Journey: A Study on the Process of Initial Adjustment of the Half and Full Korean Children Adopted by

American Families, and the Families' Experiences with These Children During the Transitional Period." Master's thesis, University of Minnesota, 1970.

Kim, Young Jong. "The Impact of Industrialization and Other Social Changes on the Development of Social Welfare Institution in South Korea." PhD diss., University of Texas, 1989.

Kwon, Insook. "Militarism in my Heart: Militarization of Women's Consciousness and Culture in South Korea." PhD diss., Clark University, 2000.

Lee, Mary Deborah. "Reading Race: Postcolonial Nationalism in Korea." PhD diss., University of Hawaii, 2012.

Lee, Na Young. "The Construction of U.S. Camptown Prostitution in South Korea: Trans/formation and Resistance." PhD diss., University of Maryland, College Park, 2006.

Matthews, Robert. "The Littlest Immigrants: The Immigration and Adoption of Foreign Orphans." PhD diss., Virginia Polytechnic Institute and State University, 1989.

Myers, Kit. "Love and Violence in Transracial/national Adoption." Master's thesis, University of California, San Diego, 2009.

O'Conner, Louis. "The Adjustment of a Group of Korean and Korean-American Children Adopted by Couples in the United States." Master's thesis, University of Tennessee, 1964.

Oh, Arissa. "Into the Arms of America: The Korean Roots of International Adoption." PhD diss., University of Chicago, 2008.

Park, Bong Soo. "Intimate Encounters, Racial Frontiers: Stateless GI Babies in South Korea and the United States, 1953–1965." PhD diss., University of Minnesota, 2010.

Park, Byung Hyun. "The Development of Social Welfare Institutions in East Asia: Case Studies of Japan, Korea, and the People's Republic of China, 1945–1989." PhD diss., University of Pennsylvania, 1990.

Park, Soon Ho. "Forced Child Migration: Korea-born Intercountry Adoptees in the United States." PhD diss., University of Hawaii, 1994.

Park Nelson, Kim. "Korean Looks, American Eyes: Korean American Adoptees, Race, Culture and Nation." PhD diss., University of Minnesota, 2009.

Pate, Soojin. "Genealogies of Korean Adoption: American Empire, Militarization, and Yellow Desire." PhD diss., University of Minnesota, 2010.

Porter, Steven. "Defining Public Responsibility in a Global Age: Refugees, NGOs, and the American State." PhD diss., University of Chicago, 2009.

Riggs, Lynette. "The Church of Jesus Christ of Latter-day Saints' Indian Student Placement Service: A History." PhD diss., Utah State University, 2008.

Shin, Heisoo. "Women's Sexual Services and Economic Development: The Political Economy of the Entertainment Industry and South Korean Dependent Development." PhD diss., Rutgers University, 1991.

Song, Changzoo. "The Contending Discourses of Nationalism in Post-Colonial Korea and Nationalism as an Oppressive and Anti-Democratic Force." PhD diss., University of Hawaii, 1999.

Trenka, Jane Jeong. "The 2011 Amendment to the Special Adoption Law: A One-Year Evaluation." Master's thesis, Seoul National University, 2014.

Valentine, Janet Graff. "The American Combat Solder in the Korean War." PhD diss., University of Alabama, 2002.

Wagner, Stephen. "The Lingering Death of the National Origins Quota System: A Political History of United States Immigration Policy, 1952–1965." PhD diss., Harvard University, 1986.

Welty, Lily Anne Yumi. "Advantage Through Crisis: Multiracial American Japanese in Post–World War II Japan, Okinawa and America 1945–1972." PhD diss., University of California, Santa Barbara, 2012.

Whang, Minsun Sung. "An Exploratory Descriptive Study of Inter-Country Adoption of Korean Children with Known Parents." PhD diss., University of Hawaii, 1976.

Winslow, Rachel. "Colorblind Empire: International Adoption, Social Policy, and the American Family, 1945–1976." PhD diss., University of California, Santa Barbara, 2012.

Won, Young Hee. "Hanguk ibyang j Ŏngchaeke gwanhan y Ŏngu: Junkaegwaj Ŏng meet munjej Ŏmeul joongshim Ŭlo" [A Study on Korean Adoption Policy: Focusing on Evolution and Problems] [A study on Korean adoption policy]. Master's thesis, Ewha University, 1990.

Woo, Susie. "'A New American Comes Home': Race, Nation, and the Immigration of Korean War Adoptees, 'GI Babies,' and Brides." PhD diss., Yale University, 2010.

Zahra, Tara. *Lost Children: Displaced Children and the Rehabilitation of Postwar Europe.* Draft of working paper (in author's possession).

Index

Page numbers followed by "f" or "t" indicate material in figures or tables.

abandonment due to poverty, 179–180, 182–183, 205
abortion and contraception, 156, 187, 190, 199
acceptance of adoptees by Americans, 137–140
Acheson, Dean, 82
adoptees: age of, 147; memories of "baby lifts," 103, 112; as proud of citizenship, 155–156; working for reform, 199. *See also* full-Korean adoptees; Korean-black adoptees; Korean-white adoptees
adoptees, pictures of: collage, 201f; Diane Shigley (Jung Soon Joo), 122f, 153f; Julie Young, 173f; Kim Hanson, 162f; Kyung Soo Lee (Lee Paladino), 38f; Noel Cross, 134f; Yung Hee Kim, 104f
adopters of Koreans: across-race adoption as "cultural genocide," 157; already rejected for domestic adoption, 65, 109; beliefs about birth mothers, 171–172; blacks as, 6, 74, 133–137; CCF concerns about, 65; Holts on colorblindness of, 105; home study of, 115–116; infertile couples faking pregnancy, 184; of Korean-black children, 132–133; motivations of, 116, 164–165, 244n85; need for speed in screening, 55; preferring girls, 180, 182; preliminary interview of, 115; preparing white adopters for racism, 138; screening for adopter and community racism, 138–139; screening of black adopters, 133–135; screening of for religious beliefs, 96–97, 116; servicemen making decision without wife, 41–42; State Department doubting enough for demand, 63; wanting whiter babies, 127; willing to cross racial/religious lines, 128
agencies, competition among, 185–186, 194–195
airlift of children from war zone, 24–25
AKF (American-Korean Foundation), 42, 56, 64, 66, 83
Amerasian Homecoming Act (US, 1987), 193
Amerasian Immigration Act (US, 1982), 193
"Amerasians," 190–193, 235n67
"American Century, The," 86
American family as social institution, 11
"Americanity," exceptionalism, 85–86
American Mercury, 94
American Relief for Korea, 42
American Service Bureau (ASB), 98
"American" values, 79–80
Anderson family, 134f
Ankara Orphanage, 27
Anthony, Joseph (Korean War mascot), 33
antimiscegenation laws, US, 6, 128
Armed Forces Assistance to Korea, 23
ASB (American Service Bureau), 98

287

Asbury, William, 28, 60
Asians: as exotic and beautiful, 160–161; as intermediate between blacks and whites, 12; as monolithic, 159–160; from "not white" to "not black," 155; as political category, 151; quotas granted to Asians, 154–155; relief efforts to win Cold War allegiance of, 84; stereotypes of women and girls, 160–161
"as if begotten" families, 135, 152
assimilation through dispersion, 73–74
Association for the Aid of Crippled Children (AACC), 64
Australia, 185, 205
Austrian war refugees, adoption of, 148

baby boom, adoption during, 4
"baby drought," 156
"baby hunting," 186
"baby lifts" by HAP, 8, 98–104 (101f, 104f), 112
"baby-rich" and "baby-poor" countries, 165
Baker, Josephine, 107
Battle Cry (film), 25
binary thinking, 13, 209–210
biology and culture, 69
birth certificates, lack of in Korea, 118. *See also* family register (*hojuk*)
birth fathers, Harry Holt on, 124
birth mothers, German, 6
birth mothers, Korean: adopter beliefs about, 171–172; in camptowns (*kijich'on*), 49, 191, 272n41; confused about finality, 125–126; as "heroes," 124–125; poverty as cause for abandonment/removal, 179–180, 182–183, 205; pressured to relinquish children, 119–122, 124–125; social workers' treatment of, 124–125; trying to control process, 126. *See also* prostitutes/prostitution; unwed mothers
birth parents: accompanying "orphans" to airport, 172, 173f; erasure of, 208
birth records, access to, 158
black adoptees: American blacks as "damaged," 157; black-white adoption as "cultural genocide," 157; terminology for black GI babies, 68. *See also* Korean-black adoptees
black adopters, 6, 74, 133–137; as adoptive parents, 74, 133–137; "as if begotten families," 135; black newspaper coverage of baby lifts, 100; complexion matching, 135–137; congressmen enlisted to find adopters, 74; cost a factor, 74; often shut out as adopters, 6
black market adoption, 4, 156, 165–166
black-white binary, preserving, 12
Blaisdell, Russell L., 24
blond, blue-eyed Korean children, 127–128
blood ties, primacy of, 113–114. *See also* patrilineal bloodlines
Bonzo (Korean War mascot), 33, 34
Boston Children's Service Association (BCSA), 132–133, 136, 251n59
Bowha Orphanage, 27
Branham, Ravil B., 36–37
Brazil, 73
Briggs, Laura, 262n69
"brown babies": in African American press, 68; from World War II, 6, 132. *See also* Korean-black adoptees
Brown v. Board of Education, 137–138
Buck, Pearl S., 44; adopting mixed-race children, 88, 107; coining of "Amerasian," 190; concerns about Holt's religion test, 96–97; establishing Welcome House, 241n49; on half-American homeless children, 48; mixed-race adoption as solution to racial conflict, 110; on orphanage conditions, 179; Pearl S. Buck Foundation, 191; on "piteous lonely children," 164; on Rhee's opinion of Korean-white children, 54
Bureau of Indian Affairs, 157–158
Butch (Korean War mascot), 33, 34
buying children, accusations of, 146, 168, 206. *See also* commodities, babies as

"cafeteria approach," 170
Cambodia, 206
camptowns (*kijich'on*), 49, 191, 272n41
Canada, 4, 157, 185, 205
capitalism, 186, 205, 209. *See also* commodities, babies as
CARE, 42
Carp, E. Wayne, 249n44
Catholics: Americans adopting Irish children, 4–5; Catholic Committee for Refugees, 54, 66; Catholic War Relief Services, 42; initially rejected by HAP, 97
CCF (Christian Children's Fund): on absence of child welfare programs, 60; concerns about adopters, 65; employee witnessing homeless children, 25; on GI

generosity to orphanages, 27; as honest business, 61; offering to ship all children to Hawaii, 73; sponsorship program, 19, 43, 180; on state of Korean orphanages, 59
celebrity promotion of Korean adoption, 200f
Chango, Butch (Korean War mascot), 33, 34
charter adoption flights ("babylifts"), 81, 98–104 (100f, 101f, 104f), 112
Cheju Island, 24–25
Chicago Defender newspaper, 132
child-centered approach, 146
childhood, sentimentalization of, 3
child labor: adoption motive before modern era, 3, 146, 165; houseboys as, 32; Koreans acquiring orphans for, 65, 184; parents reclaiming "orphans" for, 180
Child Placement Service (CPS). *See* CPS (Child Placement Service)
child relief services, 43. *See also* sponsorship programs
Children's Aid Society, 262n72
Child Welfare League of America (CWLA), 114, 157–158, 168
China: Chinese American intraethnic adoptions, 5; Chinese exclusion laws, 154; US adoption from, 204, 209, 277n68
Cho, Seihon, 200f
Chong, So Yong (Korean War mascot), 36
Choong Hyun Babies' Home, 58–59, 232n31
Christian Adoption Program of Korea (CAPOK), 183–184
Christian Americanism: adding political and religious meaning to adoption, 10, 80, 87–88, 108–109; adoption of Koreans as anticommunist act, 84; as an "undefined religion," 79; apparent colorblindness of, 80, 104–109; Christian press criticism of, 85; fading in early 1960s, 81; Harry Holt as figurehead of, 8; language of required for HAP adoption, 96, 109; language of used by Sen. Neuberger, 86; nondenominational and nonspecific, 85–86; pushing immigration law amendment (1961), 8; source of most GI baby adoptions, 80
Christian Century, 79, 83–85
Christian Children's Fund (CCF). *See* CCF (Christian Children's Fund)
Christianity and Crisis, 85
Christian Koreans, 45–46
Christian Scientists rejected by HAP, 96

Chun Doo Hwan, 198
Church of Jesus Christ of Latter-day Saints, 96, 259n51
Church World Service, 42–43; food and material aid to institutions, 43; move to nonemergency status, 178; Protestant organization, 42; seeing fewer foreign adoptions in 1960s, 196; token grant to CPS, 56
citizenship for illegitimate children of French fathers, 72
citizenship from father in Korea, 7
Clarke, J. Calvitt, 65, 73, 229n15
cohabitation arrangements transferred between soldiers, 227n7
Cold War: American racism jeopardizing moral leadership, 81–83; Americans learning to distinguish Koreans, 83; and changing ideas about race, 11–12; Christian press criticism of, 85; "Cold War civil rights," 9–10; communist insurgencies a grave concern, 84; suburbia and domesticity during, 88–89
Collier's magazine, 22, 87
Colombia, 166
colonial discourse on Occident and Orient, 236n71
colorblindness, 12, 104–109, 110
commercialism of modern adoption, 11
commodities, babies as, 170–171, 184–186, 189, 203–205, 208. *See also* supply and demand, role of
communism concerns, 72, 84. *See also* Cold War
community opposition to Korean adoptions, 139–140
complexion matching, 135–137
Confucianism, 161, 186–188
consumerism: in baby market, 166, 169–171; in parenthood, 11, 209
contraception and abortion, 156, 187, 190, 199
coolie image, 155
corruption in adoption market: black market, 4, 156, 165–166; fake signs to attract GIs, 61; finders' bonuses for babies, 186; "gray" market, 4, 156; IAC (international adoption complex), 203–206; kidnapping versus rescuing, 169; per-child payments leading to, 60; refusals to release children, 181
cost of adoption: "delivery fees," 195; prohibitive for blacks, 132

CPS (Child Placement Service): and ECLAIR, 191; opening of under Oak Soon Hong, 56; as quasi-governmental adoption agency, 56; on relatives of "orphans," 183; under Tahk, 196
Cuba, 73
"cultural genocide," white adoption of blacks as, 157
culture as biologically rooted, 161
culture camps, 159
CWLA (Child Welfare League of America). *See* Child Welfare League of America (CWLA)

Davison, Anne, 65, 182, 195, 203
DeBolt family, 108
De Hartog, Jan, 159–160
"delivery fees," 195
demand for healthy white infants, 4, 165. *See also* commodities, babies as; supply and demand, role of
Democratic People's Republic of Korea (North Korea), 1, 20, 198
diaspora of Korean adoptees in US, 2, 3f
disabled children, 177
disasters, adoptions in response to, 1
dispersion, assimilation through, 73–74
Displaced Persons Act (US, 1948), 5, 147
divorce by GIs, 50–51
dogs adopted during Vietnam War, 222n48
dojang (official stamp), 119
dormant Frenchness and Americanness, 72
Doss family, 107–108
DP (displaced persons), 147
Drake, George, 26

East Asians, quotas granted to, 154–155
Eastern Child Welfare Services (ECWS), 183
Ebony magazine, 132
Eckardt, A. Roy, 85
ECLAIR (Eurasian Children Living as Indigenous Residents), 191
Eisenhower, Dwight, 84–85, 86, 253n11
"eligible orphan" status, 150, 152
emigration to United States: adoption as, 145–146, 150; to Hawaiian sugar plantations, 45; helping Korean economy, 54; picture brides, 45; students and intellectuals, 45–46
"entertainers," prostitutes as, 124
Ernie Joe (Korean War mascot), 36–37

"escapee" category in RRA, 148
Ethiopian soldiers and Bowha Orphanage, 27
ethnic nationalism, Korean, 6, 53
Eurasian Children Living as Indigenous Residents (ECLAIR), 191
Europe: adopting American black children, 157; adopting Korean children, 185; adoption of Greek war refugees, 5, 147–149; French paternalistic role over Eurasian children, 70–73; Italian war refugees, adoption of, 5, 147–148; Jewish refugees in postwar Europe, 147; US adoption from, 147. *See also* Germany
"exceptional immigrants," Amerasians as, 193
"excess fertility" and oversupply, 165
"expellee" category in RRA, 148
Extraordinary Law of Adoption for the Orphan Child (1961, Korea), 182–183, 268n18

factory girls (*yŏgong*), 187–188
failed adoptions of mascots, 39–41
Fair Share Refugee Act (1960), 150
family as "normalizing institution," 152
family planning under Park, 187
family register (*hojuk*), 51, 118, 184, 192
family reunification process, 150, 152
fertility rates, decreasing, 199
Filipinos: distinguishing from black, 129; intraethnic adoptions, 5; quotas granted to, 154
financial crisis (1997), 196
finders' bonuses for babies, 186
Five-Year Plan for Adoption and Foster Care (1976), 198
foreign exchange from export of children, 177 (177f), 185, 189
foster homes, 114, 185, 197–198
Foster Parents' Plan, 19, 43
foundlings, 118–119
French paternalistic role over Eurasian children, 70–73
Freundlich, Madelyn, 261n65
full-Korean adoptees: accidental placement with black family, 128; distinguishing from mixed-race children, 119–120, 129; Holt initially objecting to placement of, 181; intercountry adoption of, 182; less-adoptable than Korean-white children,

127; number placed abroad, 82t, 151; reasons for relinquishment of, 126, 182; reclassified from refugee to immigrant, 145–146, 150; servicemen adopting, 41; terminology regarding, 15, 22; victimizing mixed-race children, 131

gender and abandonment, 179, 180
gender imbalance as reason for adopting, 116
geneticism, 127
Germany: adoption of war refugees, 5, 147, 148; nationalism hampering exportation, 6; US GI babies, 5–7
GI babies: in 1960s and 1970s, 190; abandonment of, 51–52; adoptions not as separation but return, 69; adoptions of by GIs, 41; as "Amerasians" and repatriates, 190–193; American and Korean agreement on solution to, 48, 67; attempts to hide, disguise, 51; concerns about resentment from, 72; as declining segment of adoptees, 174; in Germany, 5–7; labeled as *t'wigi* or *honhyŏl*, 51; lives of those staying in Korea, 192–193; looking American in Korea, Korean in America, 68; most not orphans, 72; mothers assumed to be prostitutes, 23; mothers living in camptowns, 191, 227n7; number of, 15, 23, 52; problem for country and babies, 52; removal as one-time emergency solution, 48; role of governments towards, 72–73; should live with "their" people, 67; as symbol of Korean dependence, 190; terminology regarding, 15, 23; triple stigma of, 51; in Vietnam, 168; violating "one peopleism," 54; as "Yanks," 67. *See also* illegitimate children
gift language of adoption, 170
GI humanitarianism during Korean War, 23–31 (29f), 164
girls: as dutiful daughters, 187; preferentially abandoned, 179–180; preferred by adopters, 180, 182
"global imaginary," 82
global inequality, 209
"Good Samaritan of Korea," Harry Holt as, 94
"gooks," GIs labeling Koreans as, 30
Gotcha Day, 103
"Grandma's Brag Book," 159
gratitude fees, 195

"gray" market adoption, 4, 156
Greek war refugees, adoption of, 5, 147–149
Green, Edith, 92
Guatemala, 206, 209, 277n68

Hague Convention on the Protection of Children . . . (1993), 206, 208
Haiti, 1, 206
half-breed/half-caste terminology, 15, 68
Han, Hyun Sook, 117–118; on naïveté of birth mothers, 125; pressuring mothers to relinquish babies, 120–121; on trying to identify racial makeup, 129
"handicapped," mixed-race children as, 192–193
"hardship tours," 50
"hard to place" children, 172–174
Hart-Celler Act (US, 1965), 146
Hawaii, 45, 73, 242n68
health of Korean adoptees, 116
"Hermit Kingdom," 20
Hess, Dean, 24–25
hojuk (family register), 51, 118, 184, 192
Holt, Barbara, 122
Holt, Harry and Bertha, 75, 93f; acting as catalyst, 8, 75, 81; adopting eight Korean GI babies, 80, 90; attending World Vision meeting, 90; awarded medal by Korea, 120; Bertha on threats of violence, 105; Bertha's book *Seed from the East*, 90–91; on colorblindness of adopters, 105; criticizing social workers' slowness, race matching, 106–107; denying forcing relinquishment, 122; establishing adoption program (1956), 8, 80; establishing reception centers for mixed-race babies, 92; giving credit to God, 79, 91; Harry not a Christian Americanist, 80; lobbying Congress, 149; as model American family, 94–95; not in civil rights movement, 105; on Oak Soon Hong, 56; Oregon Department of Welfare opposition to, 105–106; placement of Korean-black children, 128, 131–132; as public face of Korean adoption, 89; sponsorship through World Vision, 91; threats against, 105; views on full-Korean adoption, 181. *See also* Holt Adoption Program (HAP)
Holt, Molly, 27, 119

Holt Adoption Program (HAP): aggressive recruitment of relinquishment, 119–123; as "a Negro program," 133; arrival trauma of older children, 103–104; charter adoption flights (baby lifts), 81, 98–104 (100f, 101f, 104f); David Kim and, 69; description of parents' appearance and behavior, 102; establishment of, 8, 46, 80, 95; Korean government support for, 8; lessons learned from Korean experience, 168; merger with CAPOK, 183–184; monetary requirements, 98; not screening for adopter racial views, 138; now Holt International Children's Services, 80; opening Hyochang Park orphanage, 120; parents' ability to pay, 98; preferred by black adopters, 133; as primary agency for adoptees, 123; prompting ISS's participation, 115; race-based criteria, 97; screening for Fundamentalist Christian adopters, 96–97; seeing fewer foreign adoptions in 1960s, 196; streamlining of GI baby adoption, 95; taking babies from orphanages, 119–120; violating deliberation period requirements, 278n73. *See also* Holt, Harry and Bertha

Holt Children's Services, 183. *See also* Holt Adoption Program (HAP)

home study of adopters, 115–116

Hong, Oak Soon, 56, 57f, 65, 97, 121

"hooch" (*uchi*, house) as cohabitation arrangement, 227n7

"hootch girls" in Vietnam, 222n48

"horde of Asiatics," 155

houseboys, 31–35 (32f, 35f)

Hudson, Rock, 25

Hungarian refugees (1956), 149

"hypermasculine authoritarianism," 178, 186–190

ideological battle with North Korea, 87

illegitimate children: assumed for GI babies, 6, 51; foreign adoption as best option for, 124–125; invisible adoptions for, 128; from Ireland, 5; urbanization leading to, 180; of women married but abandoned, 51. *See also* GI babies

ilmin juui (one peopleism), 54

"immediate relative" status, 150, 152

immigrants: as political category, 151; reclassifying Korean orphans as, 145–146, 150

Immigration Act (1924, US), 5, 83

Immigration and Nationality Act of 1952, 147, 150–151, 155, 254n16

Immigration and Naturalization Service (INS), 117, 150

INA–McCarran-Walter Act (Immigration and Nationality Act, US 1952), 147, 150–151, 155, 254n16

India, adoption from, 204

Indian Adoption Project (IAP), 157–158

Indian Child Welfare Act (US, 1978), 158

indigenous agencies, 58–59, 183

industrialization of Korea, 180, 189

infertility as reason for adoption, 116, 184, 249n44

INS (Immigration and Naturalization Service), 117, 150

Insooni, 193

intercountry/international terminology, 15–16

international adoption: formalization of, 4; international adoption complex (IAC), 203–206; as modern concept, 2

internationalism in Cold War, 82

International Migration Service. *See* ISS (International Social Service)

International Monetary Fund bailout (1997), 196

International Social Service (ISS). *See* ISS (International Social Service)

interracial marriage: concerns about mixed-race adoptions and, 137–138; and US antimiscegenation laws, 6, 128, 155

invisible (intraethnic) adoptions, 5, 249n44

Irish children, clandestine adoption of, 4–5

ISS (International Social Service): on adoption encouraging abandonment, 181; approving of foreign adoption, 54; and babylifts, 65–67, 100–101; concerns about adoptions of Asians, 64, 66–67; emphasizing local solutions, 115; emphasizing standards over speed, 123; history of, 115; Korean social workers for, 117–118; lessons learned from Korean experience, 168; losing out to HAP, 123; on mascots, 39; opposing full-Korean adoption, 181; opposition to Holts and proxy adoption, 105–106; professionalization of social workers, 115; retaining temporary legal custody, 117; screening for adopter and community

racism, 138–139; seeing fewer foreign adoptions in 1960s, 196. *See also* Han, Hyun Sook
Italian war refugees, adoption of, 5, 147–148

Japan: under Act of 29 July 1953, 147; Buck adoption of Japanese-Black baby, 88; GI "occupation babies," 5–7, 115
Japanese American internment, 74
Jehovah's Witnesses rejected by HAP, 96
Jet magazine, 132
Jewish refugees in postwar Europe, 147
Jews rejected by HAP, 97
Jim Crow America, 6–7, 133
Johnson-Reed Immigration Act (US, 1924), 45, 147
Joint ROK/KCAC/UNKRA Committee for Child Welfare, 42

Kang Koo Ri (Korean orphan), 89
KATUSA (Korean Augmentation to the US Army), 30
Kennedy, John F., 149
kidnapping versus rescuing, 169
kijich'on (camptowns), 49, 191, 272n41
Kim (Korean War mascot), 33, 37–38
Kim, David, 69, 100–101; positive publicity for HAP, 120
Kim, Dong Soo, 242–243n72, 244n85, 260n60
kisaeng (prostitutes for sex tourists), 189–190, 272n40
Korea (ROK): awarding medal to Harry Holt, 120; baby export as national industry, 165, 170–171, 176; as Christians in face of communism, 83–84; under Chun Doo Hwan, 198; as Cold War partner and responsibility, 83, 86–87; continuing promotion of adoption, 199, 200f; country itself as abandoned, 164; courts establishing legality of intercountry adoption, 55; "economic miracle" and baby export, 177 (177f); GI babies legally stateless, 7, 51, 72; as "Hermit Kingdom," 20; initially unable to assist citizens, 19; law change allowing "stranger adoption" within, 183; no child welfare program, 59–60, 177, 195; no ratification of 1993 Hague Convention, 206; preference for intercountry adoption, 195; remaining battle zone after armistice, 50; soldiers establishing orphanage, 27; traditional adoption in, 117; US direct aid to, 178; withdrawals of American troops from, 193. *See also* Park Chung Hee; Rhee, Syngman
Korea, adoptees' memories of, 103, 112
Korea Association of Voluntary Agencies, 42
Korean adoption, 16, 82t, 177f; assurance of finality, 123, 158–159; as "cheap domestic service," 65; concerns about cultural adjustment, 64–65; disagreement over race matching, 106–107; of "full" Koreans in 1960s, 9; as "going to my daddy in America," 69; as "good-will ambassador" policy, 198; government ban on single parent placement, 97; inter-agency competition, 185; by military couples in Japan, 224n67; of mixed-race occupation children, 5–6; money for better spent in-country, 66; mutually beneficial with United States, 13; numbers on, 202, 211n4; under Park's modernization plan, 178–179; as percentage of US international adoptions, 4f; as pressure valve/racial cleansing mechanism, 13, 64; repeated announcements of end of, 198; solving race problem for country, 52–53; as template for transnational adoptions, 9; US rates of, 2. *See also* orphanages in Korea
Korean Augmentation to the US Army (KATUSA), 30
Korean-black adoptees, 130f; boys harder to place, 131–132; "brown babies," 6, 68, 132; economic barriers to black adopters of, 132–133; facing discrimination in Korea, 131, 191, 192; not placed in white families, 128; passing, 140; physical descriptions of, 129–131
Korean Christian appeals to American Christians, 45
Korean Civil Assistance Command (KCAC), 23, 217n11
Korean Ministry of Foreign Affairs, 117
Korean National Airlines, 99
Korean racial thought: following one-drop rule, 68; following paternity, 69; non-Korean equaling American, 67
Korean Republic (government newspaper), 45–46

Korean social workers: education and training of, 117–118; international adoption spurring need for, 113; pressuring mothers to relinquish babies, 120–121; seeing mothers as "victims of the war," 123–124

Korean Unwed Mothers Families' Association (KUMFA), 278n74

Korean War: armistice, 21; break up of extended families, 42; censorship of US atrocities, 30–31; death toll, 21–22; devastation of, 21; GI child welfare activities, 28–30; GI letters/reports about children, 23–26; GI racism toward "gooks," 30; military actions, 19–21; numbers of orphans, 22–23. *See also* houseboys; mascots, military

Korean-white adoptees: as first nonmilitary adoption, 53; as not-black, therefore white, 12, 68, 127–128; parents not anticipating racism toward, 161; Rhee wanting them removed quickly, 54

Korea Social Service (KSS), 183, 185

Korea Times, 181

"Kosian" (Korean Asian) children, 202

"land of orphans," Korea portrayed as a, 22

language regarding Korean adoption, 15–16

Lazarus, Emma, 86

Lea, Patricia, 53

Leaf, Victor, 25–26

League of Korean Social Workers, 63

Lee, Kyung Soo (Korean War mascot), 37, 38f, 40–41

legacy, babies as: of Korean War, 2–3; of postwar occupation, 6

legal family status for unmarried mother, 192, 197. *See also* patrilineal bloodlines

legislation, Korean: "Basic Policy for Endorcement of Emmigration to the United States," 55; Extraordinary Law of Adoption for the Orphan Child, 182; Five-Year Plan for Adoption and Foster Care (1976), 198

Lemnitzer-Doughty-Clarke Wing, 232n31

letters/reports, American response to, 22

Lieberthal, Joy, 261n65

"lie we love" about so-called orphans, 208

Life magazine, 29f; Christianity issue (Dec. 1955), 84–85; on GIs helping Korean waifs, 30, 87; on Holts' mission, 92, 94; on homeless orphans, 89; influence of, 216–217n6; on Korea rebuilding, 83; on mascots, 36; prompting donations, 22

Lifton, Betty Jean, 195

Look magazine, 22, 94

Luce, Henry, 86

Lyslo, Arnold, 102–103

Madame Rhee, 49

manageable exoticism, 159

Margolies, Marjorie, 160

market for babies. *See* supply and demand, role of

marriageability concerns regarding adoptees, 137–138

marriage between Koreans and GIs, 50–51

mascots, military, 31; Americanization of, 39; animals as, 31–32; drummer boys as, 31; girl as, 223n62; versus houseboys, 32, 35; intercountry adoptions of, 35–38; problems of former mascots, 38–41; relationships with GIs, 32–35; social worker assessments of, 223n56; unconventional adoptions of, 37–38

"maternal instinct" versus professionalization, 115

maternity homes, 188

"maverick mothers," 263n82

May, Elaine Tyler, 249n44

McCarran-Walter Act (US, 1952), 147, 150–151, 155, 254n16

McCune-Reischauer system, 16

media: on "Asian disregard for human life," 27; claims of sales of German children, 6; coverage of Holts, 93–95, 100–102 (101f); coverage of Korean orphans, 22, 86–87; Korean coverage of babylifts, 101; *Look* magazine, 22, 94. *See also Life* magazine

Mennonite Central Committee in Korea, 43

Methodist Committee for Overseas Relief, 43, 181

Mexican, distinguishing from black, 131

Mexican children on "gray" market, 4

MHSA (Ministry of Health and Social Affairs): abandonment statistics from, 179–180; evaluating agencies on revenue not quality, 185; inadequately staffed, 59; letters of support for HAP, 120; mixed-race birth statistics from, 52; on numbers of children in need, 57; on overcharging by adoption agencies, 195; token grant to CPS, 56; working with UNKRA, 55

military couples as adopters, 41–42

Ministry of Health and Social Affairs (MHSA). *See* MHSA (Ministry of Health and Social Affairs)
minjok ("nation," "ethnicity," "race"), 53
"miracle on the Han," 176
missionaries: children as "projects," 170; Christian Americanism and adoption of Korean GI babies, 8, 80–81; as "cultural bridges," 43; presentations to American churches, 44; as two-way "producers of knowledge," 42; widows and orphans as "woman's cause," 44
mixed-race children: classifying, 129–131 (130f); mixed-breed/mixed-blood terminology, 15; pathologizing of, 192–193. *See also* Korean-black adoptees; Korean-white adoptees
model minority, Asians as, 155, 163
modern adoption practices in United States, 3–4
modernization project, Korea's, 13, 15, 178, 186–190
Moon, Katharine, 271n39
"moose" (*musume*, "girl"), 227n7
"moppets," Korean orphans as, 22
Mormon church, 96, 259n51
Morse, Wayne, 88, 92, 94, 108–109, 149
Mosier, Robert, 27–28, 33
motherland tours, 159
multiculturalism, 12

naming conventions in Korea, 118
narratives of "orphan" adoption, 1, 207–210
National Association of Black Social Workers (NABSW), 157, 259n51
"national" category in RRA, 148
National Catholic Welfare Conference, 56, 115
National Council of Churches of Christ, 178
National Geographic, 27–28, 33
nationalism, Korean, 6, 53, 178
national origins quota system, 147
National Urban League, 132
Native Americans: adoption of, 157–158; distinguishing from blacks, 129; and NABSW, 259n51
"natural" mothers, 16
neocolonialism, 13, 166, 209
Neuberger, Maurine, 151
Neuberger, Richard, 86, 92, 94, 149, 240n40, 241n43

New York Times, 30, 37; advice on "shopping around" while adopting, 166
NGOs, 19, 42–46
Nguyen Da Yen v. Kissinger, 264n88
No Gun Ri massacre, 30
non-orphans, misportrayal of, 208; versus financial support for families, 172–174, 180; narratives of "orphan" adoption, 1, 207–210; in Operation Babylift (Vietnam), 264n88; social orphans, 194; in US domestic adoptions, 246n14
non-quota visas for adoptees, 150
North Korea: accusing ROK of slave trade, 198; ideological battle with, 87
North Korean Child Welfare Act (US, 2013), 1
Northwest Airlines, 98

O'Connor, Louis, 242–243n72
OECD (Organisation for Economic Co-operation and Development), 198
one-drop rule, 6, 68, 127
"One-Family UN," 107–108
open adoption, 158
opening of birth records, 16
Operation Babylift (Vietnam), 169, 263n80, 264n88
Operation Kiddy Car, 24–25
Operation Orphan Annie, 25
Operation Santa Claus, 26
orphanages in Korea: conditions in, 59–60; corruption in, 60–61, 181; as de facto child-care facilities, 180–181; increasing oversight by late 1950s, 62; number of, 57–58; only child welfare, 59–60, 177, 195; reciprocal relationships with agencies, 185–186; temporary placement of non-orphans in, 62–63; trust funds from GIs for orphanages, 26; use of mixed blood children for fundraising, 61
orphans, Korean: adopted as domestic help, 65, 184; adoption process becoming permanent, 151; as ambassadors, 189; Americanization of, 39–40; American sense of responsibility for, 87–88; arrival trauma of, 103–104; associated with Americanness, 67; broad category of, 1–2, 63, 118, 126, 164; counternarrative to success story, 163–164; "eligible orphan" status, 150, 152; experiencing racism, 163–164; flown to US for *Battle Cry* filming, 25; houseboys, 31–35 (32f, 35f); as ideal

orphans, Korean (*continued*)
immigrants, 155; in-country placement, 183–184; as little Americans, 36, 152; newborns desired for hiding infertility, 184; not required to be refugees, 148; number of, 57; as political category, 151; receiving one-quarter of orphan visas, 148; studies showing seamless integration, 161–162 (162f); as transformed American, 152, 154; transportation to United States, 65–66, 100–104 (101f, 104f); typhoid and tuberculosis among, 99, 116, 151; as "waifs," 22, 87. *See also* full-Korean adoptees; Korean-black adoptees; Korean-white adoptees; mascots, military; non-orphans, misportrayal of

orphan trains, 165, 262n72

"otherness," white blood easing, 127

Other Sheep documentary, 90

Paladino, Lee James (Korean War mascot), 37, 38f, 40–41

Paladino, Vincent, 37, 38f

paper orphans, 117–127 (122f)

parent as citizen, 152

Park Chung Hee: adoption as only solution, 190; adoption as permanent industry, 176; assassination of, 189; continuing "one peopleism," 54; Extraordinary Law of Adoption for the Orphan Child, 182; Five-Year Plan for Adoption and Foster Care (1976), 198; formalizing rules and procedures, 183; patriarchal nationalism of, 186–190; promoting domestic adoption, 184; social welfare budget under, 179, 196; women as "bodies carrying wombs and labor power," 187

passing as non-Korean, 140

paternalism of American compassion, 28

patriarchal nationalism, 178, 186–190

patrilineal bloodlines: babies belonging with father, not mother, 69, 235n68; family register (*hojuk*), 51, 118, 184, 192; illegitimacy as social death, statelessness, 7, 51, 72; recent legal changes regarding, 192, 197; resistance to adoption of children without, 184

Philippines, 1, 70, 84

picture brides, 45

Pierce, Bob, 90, 94, 240n32

"placing out" in foster homes, 114

Polish war refugees, adoption of, 5, 212n11

poverty as cause for abandonment/removal, 179–180, 182–183, 205

Presbyterian mission, 43, 181

preservation of family as goal, 113–114

Pribbenow, Sambo (Korean War mascot), 35

priceless, children becoming, 165

private agencies, 114. *See also* Holt Adoption Program (HAP)

private and public matters, 10, 73, 152–154

pronatalism, 147

prostitutes/prostitution: in camptowns (*kijich'on*), 49; factory girls resorting to, 188; and long-term relationships, 50–51; "mass-produced," 49–50; social workers' treatment of, 124

proxy adoption, 241n47; elimination of and loophole, 99, 150, 178; in Greek-US adoptions, 149; Holt as promoter of, 8, 81, 106, 165; ISS and, 115, 129; only option in some states, 115; process of, 95; social worker objections to, 95, 98, 106, 149

Puerto Rico, 73, 131

Pusan, 21, 25–26

"put up for adoption," 262n72

quotas, 150–151; abolished by Hart-Celler Act (1965), 146–147; family reunification bypassing, 150; for Filipinos and East Indians, 154–155; Five-Year Plan for Adoption and Foster Care (1976), 198; HAP and CAPOK circumventing, 183–184; in Immigration Act (1924), 5, 147; non-quota visas, 95, 150; RRA orphan visas, 147–148. *See also* INA–McCarran-Walter Act

race: American one-drop rule, 68; biological and cultural, 12; colonial history of race-mixing, 70–73; from culture, not culture from race, 71; and gender stereotypes, 160; Koreans as not black, 12, 155; national origins quota system, 147; race matching in adoption, 106–107, 249n43, 260n59; "racial characteristics" of Asians and Native Americans, 158; racially mixed adoptive families, 9; "racial middle ground," 157; "rainbow families," 107–108; terminology for GI babies, 68

rape, 30, 49–50, 123, 194

rationalization of modern adoption, 113–117

Raynor, Jimmy (Korean War mascot), 37

Reckless (horse mascot), 32

red threads, 207
Refugee Relief Act. *See* RRA (Refugee Relief Act, 1953, US)
Refugee Relief Program Coordinator, 74
refugees as political category, 151
regulation of US adoption. *See* US Congress
"re-homing" children across state lines, 206
"religious fervor" disqualifying adopters, 116
relinquishment: abandonment due to poverty, 179–180, 182–183, 205; abandonment instead of, 181; claims of adoption without, 169; formal and informal, 16; of full-Korean children, 126; ISS and HAP workers pushing, 119–122; letter from a birth mother, 112; little alternative for mothers, 186; "ransom" for mothers seeking to reverse, 199; in response to ostracism, 122; in response to positive publicity, 123; study of reasons for, 266n6; use of physical force in, 121–122; use of term, 16. *See also* unwed mothers
repatriation of adult adoptees, 199
Republic of Korea. *See* Korea (ROK)
rescue narrative, 164, 169, 172–174
responsibilities of Christian Americanism, 86–87
"reunification," adoption as, 152
Rhee, Syngman, 20, 45; "dropping them in the Pacific Ocean" comment, 54; expediting overseas adoption, 48, 55, 182; foreign aid as only social welfare program, 60, 112; on numbers of unwed mothers, 52; on ostracism of GI babies, 51; promoting *ilmin juui* (one peopleism), 54, 64; searching for authority to handle adoptions, 75; special attention to Korean-black children, 74
Robson, Irene, 53
Rocky (Korean War mascot), 38
Romania, 1, 204
RRA (Refugee Relief Act, 1953, US): as "back door" for Asians, 148; and INA, 151; intended for European refugees, 148; passing of, 48; providing 4000 visas, 53; Rhee administration support for, 64; State Department interpretation of, 55; time limit on, 73, 112–113, 253n11; two-orphan limit requiring Holt exception, 92
Rue, George and Grace, 53
Rusk, Howard, 59, 83
Russia, adoption from, 204, 209, 277n68

Said, Edward, 236n71
"Sammy Hop-a-long" (Korean War mascot), 221n36
Save the Children Federation, 43
screening: by ASB, 98; of black adopters, 102, 133–135; by HAP, 96–98, 102; by ISS, 133; social workers' approach to, 115–116
secular religion, 79
Seed from the East, The (Holt), 90
segregation and Cold War, 81
sending countries for US adoption, 167t
sentimentalization of childhood, 3
Seoul: during and after Korean War, 21, 24; Olympics in, 176, 189, 198; Sanitarium and Hospital Orphanage, 53
Sergeant Yo-Yo, 32
servicemen, US: camptowns (*kijich'on*), 49, 191, 272n41; GI humanitarianism during Korean War, 23–31 (29f), 164; houseboys for, 31–35 (32f, 35f); laying foundation for Korean adoption, 8; marriage and divorce in Korea, 50–51; mascot and "split home" adoptions, 38–42; separated from wives by commanding officers, 6. *See also* GI babies; mascots, military
Seventh-Day Adventists, 42, 53
Severance Hospital, Seoul, 56
sexualization of Asian girls and women, 160
Shin, Paull H. (Korean War mascot), 35
shopping around for best adoption deal, 170–171
Short Round (fictional mascot), 34
single motherhood in Korea, 178, 197
"slickyboys," 222n48
social death under patriarchal order, 72
social orphans, 194
social welfare, Korean: cost savings of exporting, 189; orphanages as child welfare, 59–60, 177, 195; rank in OECD countries, 198; reliance on foreign adoption as, 60, 112, 205–206
Social Welfare Service, 183. *See also* CPS (Child Placement Service)
social workers, 13; actions seen as intrusive, invasive, 11, 113; assessing adopter motivations, 116; attempting invisible adoptions, 128; avoiding camptowns, 191; concerns about ASB screening, 98; concerns about HAP, 95, 97; discouraging mascot and "split home" adoptions, 38–42; emergence of in Korea, 13; HAP's

social workers (*continued*)
staff portrayed as, 97; initially opposing permanent adoptions, 113–114; interview and home study procedures, 115–116; from ISS to match children with adopters, 55; laying groundwork for adoption, 45; moving adoption into public sphere, 114; NABSW (National Association of Black Social Workers), 157; not understanding GI babies circumstances, 107; objections to proxy adoption, 95; professionalization of, 4, 114–115; "religious fervor" disqualifying adopters, 116; role of "negotiated power," 114; screening of black adopters, 133–134; on supply and demand of orphans, 63–64. *See also* Korean social workers

SOS Children's Villages, 197
Southeast Asian refugees, 74
South Vietnam ban on mass child emigration, 168
Special Adoption Law (US, 2012), 278n73
Special Orphan Adoption Act (Korea, proposed), 55
Spence-Chapin agency, 250n57
"split home" adoptions, 41
sponsorship programs: allowing children to remain in home country, 65; origin of, 43; sometimes leading to adoption, 45
Stars and Stripes: 1918 "adoption" program in France, 217n10; on donations from troops, 26; on GI humanitarianism, 29–30; on homeless children, 24; on mascots, 34–37; suppressing stories of GI atrocities, 30
stateless nonpersons, Korean GI babies as, 7, 51, 72
Steel Helmet, The (film), 34
storytelling in adoption, 206–210
stranger adoption: in early 1900s, 3, 113–114; within Korea, 183
supervisory period for adoptions, 117
supply and demand, role of, 199, 205; adopters' impatience with process, 171; "baby hunting," 186; "baby-rich" and "baby-poor" countries, 165; "cafeteria approach" of adopters, 170; commodities, babies as, 170–171, 184–186, 189, 203–205, 208; "gray" and "black" markets for white babies, 4; social orphans, 208; supply driven by demand, 183

Swedish National Board of Health and Welfare, 185
Swing, Joseph, 150

Tahk, Youn Taek, 196
Time magazine: on Holts' mission, 92; on homeless orphans, 89
TRACK (Truth and Reconciliation for the Adoption Community of Korea), 278n74
"tragic mulatto," 192–193
transportation of orphans to United States, 65–66
triangulation, racial, 12–13, 128
Truman, Harry, 147
tuberculosis among adoptees, 99, 116, 151, 179
Turkish soldiers and Ankara Orphanage, 27

Ukraine, adoption from, 277n68
"unadoptable" babies, 127–128, 156–157
"UN Aunties," 49
UN babies/UN orphans, 15, 66, 67. *See also* GI babies
United Nations, 42; Orderly Departure Program, 193; statements by Korean ambassador to, 54; UNCRIK (Civil Relief in Korea), 178; UNKRA (Korea Reconstruction Agency), 55, 57, 64–66, 178
United Presbyterian Mission of Korea, 51
United States: anti-Asian immigration laws, 6; antimiscegenation laws, 6; Army investigation into orphanages, 62; as Cold War standard-bearer, 84, 86; Fifties religious revival, 85; image concerns during Cold War, 28, 46, 111; one-drop rule, 6, 68, 127; overseas children of Americans not addressed until 1980s, 70; as postwar imperial power, 13, 70, 84, 86; President Eisenhower, 84–85, 86, 253n11; presidential directive, 147; receiving Koreans, sending blacks, 157. *See also* GI babies; servicemen, US; US Congress; US State Department
unwed mothers: adoption agencies running maternity homes, 188; choice of abortion or adoption, 188, 199; hiding, disguising, abandoning babies, 51–52; increase in keeping babies, 199–200; living in woods, 52; recent laws awarding some rights

to, 192, 197; use of term, 16. *See also* patrilineal bloodlines
urbanization of Korea, 180
"urchins," Korean orphans as, 22
US Children's Bureau, 114
US Congress: Act of 11 September 1957, 149, 254nn16–17; Act of 26 September 1961, 150; Act of 29 July 1953, 147; Amerasian Homecoming Act (1987), 193; Amerasian Immigration Act (1982), 193; changes to laws in 1950s, 114, 122; disallowing Japanese wives, 6; ending proxy adoptions, 99, 106, 178–179; Immigration Act (1924), 5, 83; INA–McCarran-Walter Act (1952), 147, 150–151, 155, 254n16; making orphan statutes permanent, 145–146; refugees and immigrants under US law, 146–151; responding to pressure from Holts, 92, 94; setting race-based quotas, 146; temporary extensions, 149–150. *See also* RRA (Refugee Relief Act, 1953, US)
US State Department: doubting enough adopters for demand, 63; Far East Refugee Relief Program, 55; involvement in adoption screening, 117

Valk, Margaret, 54; on conditions in orphanages, 59; objecting to temporary fix, 56; preparing white adopters for racism, 138
Vietnam: adoption from, 166–169, 204; communist insurgency in, 84; French Eurasian children in, 70–71
virtual "adoption" programs, 19
"visual iconography of rescue," 1

"waifs," Korean orphans as, 22
Walter, Francis, 155
war bride image, 155
wartime civilian donations for children, 25–26
Welcome House, 53
White, Link S. (Korean War mascot), 33, 35, 38
"white baby famine," 156
"white French," 70
white man's burden, 84
White Mother, 110
Whitener, George, 191
"Why Negroes Don't Adopt Children" (*Ebony*), 132
widows: forced into prostitution, 49; remarriage culturally prohibited, 62
Wild Bill (Korean War mascot), 36
women, Korean: as "bodies carrying wombs and labor power," 187; factory girls (*yŏgong*), 187–188; widows, 49, 62; working girl (*kongsuni*), 187–188; working women, 186–188. *See also* birth mothers, Korean; patrilineal bloodlines; unwed mothers
working girl (*kongsuni*), 187–188
World Vision, 19, 43; Child Center as reception center, 120; founding of, 240n32; Holts attending meeting of, 90; as honest business, 61; opposing full-Korean adoption, 181; trying to keep GI babies in Korea, 65

"yellow niggers," GIs labeling Koreans as, 30
Yellow Peril, 155
Yonsei university, 118
Youn, Laurent, 63–64

The authorized representative in the EU for product safety and compliance is:
Mare Nostrum Group
B.V Doelen 72
4831 GR Breda
The Netherlands

www.ingramcontent.com/pod-product-compliance
Lightning Source LLC
Chambersburg PA
CBHW031758220426
43662CB00007B/445